TOWARDS CYBERPSYCHOLOGY

Emerging Communication

Studies in New Technologies and Practices in Communication

Emerging Communication is publishing state-of-the-art papers that examine a broad range of issues in communication technology, theories, research, practices and applications.
It presents the latest development in the field of traditional and computer-mediated communication with emphasis on novel technologies and theoretical work in this multidisciplinary area of pure and applied research.
Since *Emerging Communication* seeks to be a general forum for advanced communication scholarship, it is especially interested in research whose significance crosses disciplinary and sub-field boundaries.

Editors-in-Chief
Giuseppe Riva, *Applied Technology for Neuro-Psychology Lab., Istituto Auxologico Italiano, Verbania, Italy*
Fabrizio Davide, *Headquarters, Learning Services, TELECOM ITALIA S.p.A., Rome, Italy*

Editorial Board
Luigi Anolli, *Università Cattolica del Sacro Cuore, Milan, Italy*
Cristina Botella, *Universitat Jaume I, Castellon, Spain*
Martin Holmberg, *Linköping University, Linköping, Sweden*
Ingemar Lundström, *Linköping University, Linköping, Sweden*
Salvatore Nicosia, *University of Tor Vergata, Rome, Italy*
Brenda K. Wiederhold, *CSPP Research and Service Foundation, San Diego, CA, USA*

Volume 2

Earlier published in this series

Vol. 1. G. Riva and F. Davide (Eds.), Communications Through Virtual Technologies: Identity, Community and Technology in the Communication Age

Towards CyberPsychology

Mind, Cognition and Society
in the Internet Age

Edited by

Giuseppe Riva
Istituto Auxologico Italiano, Milan, Italy

and

Carlo Galimberti
Università Cattolica, Milan, Italy

IOS
P r e s s

Ohmsha

Amsterdam • Berlin • Oxford • Tokyo • Washington, DC

ISBN 1 58603 197 X (IOS Press)
ISBN 4 274 90466 0 C3055 (Ohmsha)
Library of Congress Control Number: 2001094315

Publisher
IOS Press
Nieuwe Hemweg 6B
1013 BG Amsterdam
The Netherlands
fax: +31 20 620 3419
e-mail: order@iospress.nl

Distributor in the UK and Ireland
IOS Press/Lavis Marketing
73 Lime Walk
Headington
Oxford OX3 7AD
England
fax: +44 1865 75 0079

Distributor in the USA and Canada
IOS Press, Inc.
5795-G Burke Centre Parkway
Burke, VA 22015
USA
fax: +1 703 323 3668
e-mail: iosbooks@iospress.com

Distributor in Germany, Austria and Switzerland
IOS Press/LSL.de
Gerichtsweg 28
D-04103 Leipzig
Germany
fax: +49 341 995 4255

Distributor in Japan
Ohmsha, Ltd.
3-1 Kanda Nishiki-cho
Chiyoda-ku, Tokyo 101
Japan
fax: +81 3 3233 2426

Cover illustration: Third generation mobile systems from Ericsson. © 2001, Ericsson Corporate Communication.

LEGAL NOTICE
The publisher is not responsible for the use which might be made of the following information.

PRINTED IN THE NETHERLANDS

PREFACE

Beyond the development of networked technologies, the most striking trend in contemporary telecommunications is the tendency to convergence among the various media, a convergence that involves the computer as well. The convergence of the computer with telephone and television technologies is, in fact, producing new communication environment — from distance learning to cybermalls — that are shaping our experience.

Riccio, 2001

The diffusion of new communication devices and experiences will soon change our interaction experience.

Suppose our cellular telephone could connect to the Internet at speeds *faster* than many DSL or cable modems or even corporate local area networks. How would that change things? That's a question we may find out the answer to much sooner than we expected, now that third-generation (3G) cellular devices are going to appear.

New forms of content will probably emerge, representing complex or real life objects, perhaps designed to be shared between collaborative user groups. How do we can face this new challenge? Researchers in this area must actively promote cross-disciplinary and federating research into content management, multimedia content processing, visualization and language technologies, to make the whole larger than the sum of the parts. Today these areas exist with too little interaction.

The functional driver of future works will be the *user perspective* and the way in which content gains new value in new communication systems by improving its usability. The challenge is not just a question of more technology. In fact, the research effort would be missing the point if it did not facilitate increased enrichment and satisfaction for users as a result of using advanced services, or joining in network interaction of any sort.

To be successful, we have to provide new contents and services, not just new technologies. For instance, 3G portals will be intelligent and knowledge-based. They will filter unwanted content as well as enable knowledge acquisition and retrieval. They will have advanced visualization features and will support information transformation and integration models e.g. for e-business.

In order to sustain this vision it is necessary to model the process of knowledge discovery as well and to apply new findings about user behavior to the whole knowledge lifecycle. And if the ultimate goal is human-to-human interaction in a networked context, the knowledge process in a device-to-device environment is vitally important as well.

Key questions the researchers have to answer are: how can heterogeneous objects be handled in virtual knowledge and information environments? How can knowledge content be valued and translated? How would meta-knowledge be handled? How are such environments evaluated or benchmarked? How can their performance be enhanced?

This book provides some answers to these questions. By defining a new research area, the "CyberPsychology", the Editors tries to provide some guidelines for understanding the processes by which we manage our experience - construct identities, create communities and make meanings — through the most advanced communication media. The topics discussed directly involve critical issues for designers and users, and are presented with scientific competence and suggestions for actual use.

Assessing the meaning and impact of new communication technologies is always a challenge. In fact it is very difficult to separate "social" from "technical" issues. This book wants to help researchers and user of these exciting new technologies in identifying some key paths for reaching this goal.

Fabrizio Davide, Ph.D
Telecom Italia, S.p.A.
Rome, Italy

POSTFACE

Until recently, the application of VR technology in mental health was severely limited by the lack of inexpensive, easy-to-maintain and easy-to-use personal computers (PC) based system... The development of PC-based VR platforms with more user-friendly programming software is helping to launch this great second wave of applications... The second wave is expanding rapidly, and the international community has already provided the basis upon which continued growth and development will occur.

Wiederhold, M., 1998

It has been nearly ten years since virtual reality was first used to treat acrophobia or fear of heights. Since that first study demonstrated that the concept itself was workable--that a computer-simulated world delivered through a pair of goggles (head-mounted display) could be systematically applied to an individual in such a way as to illicit fear and anxiety and then used to alleviate those symptoms, a variety of additional applications have been introduced for the evaluation and treatment of mental health disorders. New applications include controlled trials for the treatment of eating disorders, phobias and other anxiety disorders, neuropsychological diagnosis, assessment, and testing, male erectile disorders, and as a distraction technique during painful procedures. The use of virtual environments for mental health applications appears to be limited only by the imagination of its users. Other areas being explored include drug and alcohol rehabilitation, assessment and treatment of schizophrenia, and treatment of depression, to name a few.

As our clinic has discovered over the past five years in using virtual environments during the therapy session, it is important to go slowly and assess the interaction and response of the patient with the world. Care should always be taken to ensure that the patient does not experience side effects that are serious or long lasting, and that the patient is ready for the exposure to begin. For instance, rapport must certainly be established before having a patient wear a head-mounted display and explore a new environment containing elements known to invoke anxiety in those with his/her phobia. In anxiety disorders we know that many patients do not seek treatment, either because of their inability to imagine well (hence the lack of a response to visualization of the phobic stimuli) or their refusal to confront the phobic stimuli in real life (*in vivo*) in the beginning stages of therapy. Therefore, an intuitive fit in the form of virtual therapy, offers a reasonable initial experience in which the patient could begin treatment. The goal remains the same — to have the phobic patient confront their fears in real life — but many see the means to the end as more palatable. In numerous controlled studies worldwide, virtual therapy for phobias has demonstrated success rates varying between 80 and 92%.

Using virtual worlds in eating disorders treatment similarly has provided an exciting new approach. Prior to virtual reality, the patient was either confronted with two-dimensional photographs of himself/herself, which for many were not realistic enough to allow them to recognize the body image distortion. Or, the patient was placed in a mirrored room to confront their distortion. This, as with *in vivo* therapy for phobias, was too overwhelming for many patients, who would "shut down", close their eyes, and refuse to deal with the distortion. Controlled trials held in both Italy and Spain have shown that eating disorders treatment can be enhanced through the use of virtual reality in anorexia, bulimia, binge-eating disorder, and obesity.

Studies have shown, beginning over 25 years ago, that distraction can be a successful non-pharmacological technique during painful procedures. However, for many, meditation, deep breathing, or even playing engaging videogames has not been enough of a distraction to alleviate the discomfort. With the advent of virtual reality, however, recent controlled trials have shown that immersive and interactive virtual reality environments are more effective than Nintendo for children during their wound care and physical therapy following severe burns. Trials have also shown virtual reality to be effective for alleviating the nausea that often accompanies chemotherapy and for reducing pain perception during dental procedures and bone marrow transplants.

Neuropsychological testing to determine the extent of a patient's brain damage following stroke or other traumatic brain injury has long relied on two-dimensional testing procedures to decide if someone is able to perform tasks in a three-dimensional world. Virtual reality provides a three-dimensional platform in which to administer these tests — and in some cases proves a more realistic determinant of actual abilities (or inabilities). Virtual reality is also being explored as a means of diagnosing disorders such as attention-deficit hyperactivity disorder and Alzheimer's disease.

Clinicians and researchers who use virtual reality must continue to ensure that this new tool is not used inappropriately, and that the application being investigated provides added benefit over existing approaches. This book wants to support this approach by presenting the selected work of a distinguished group of researchers working in this area.

Virtual reality does not replace standard therapeutic paradigms, but can be a useful adjunct when used correctly. Many have sought to objectify concepts such as "presence" and "immersion", as well as to determine when the patient's anxiety is elicited and when desensitization occurs. This is necessary and helps to further the maturation of the field, proving the tool actually works and is not being swayed by social desirability or reporting bias.

As the 2000's continue and as technology decreases in price, and as virtual worlds are made available through the Internet, we feel more and more clinicians and researchers will continue to embrace this ever-changing technology to benefit their patients and society as a whole. Subsets of mental health specialization such as industrial-organizational psychology, social psychology, clinical psychology, neuropsychology, rehabilitation psychology, and health psychology are but a few of the areas benefiting from these new technologies. This book tries to provide to the researchers working in these areas some insights about the "CyberPsychology", an exciting new scientific area that studies the strict link between advanced communication technology and psychology.

Brenda K. Wiederhold, MBA, Ph.D.
The Virtual Reality Medical Center
San Diego, CA, USA

Mark D. Wiederhold, M.D., Ph.D.
CyberPsychology & Behavior Journal
San Diego, CA, USA

INTRODUCTION

The emergence of information technology is changing the way people interact with computers. Technological advances have gradually shifted the focus from computers which have become less of an end in themselves, and more of a means in terms of what people actually do with them. The most evident sign of this change has been the diffusion of the Internet.

Riva and Galimberti, 2001

The technological evolution of the media leads us to believe that Internet could become in the very near future, the predominant *medium*, or rather, it is possible that will become a general communication interface: an interface used for interpersonal relationship and for the creation and management of information. Its success is creating a new psycho-social space that is the fertile ground for social relationships, roles, and a new sense of self. As recently noted in a recent interview by Sherry Turkle, a Massachusetts Institute of Technology researcher, "The Internet is the identity technology — much of what people do online, is self-explanation and presentation, from searching and e-mailing, to chatting or creating a home page" (Murray, B., 2000, A mirror on the self. *Monitor on Psychology, 31*(4), 2000, p. 17).

"The Web is a safe place to try out different roles, voices and identities" confirms John Suler, psychologist and Web researcher for the Rider University. "It's a sort of like training wheels for the self you want to bring out in real life" (Murray, B., A mirror on the self. *Monitor on Psychology, 31*(4), 2000, p. 17).

The result of these new selves is a new sense of presence that fills the space with a fluid form of network/community that is usually called *cyberspace*. Cyberspace is a universe made up of things that can be seen and heard, but they are neither physical objects nor necessarily a representation of physical objects. They are built of information coming partly from operations of the physical world, but largely from the accumulation and exchange of knowledge arising from human initiatives in the fields of culture, science and art. In this sense, a key goal for psychology is doing more thinking and theorizing about how to get people to make better connections between the cyberspace and the rest of their lives.

If we accept the definition of the Internet as a general communication interface, questions arise spontaneously on what form the Internet is taking, how it is possible to give it a form and, most important, how it will affect us. This inevitably leads us to ask ourselves what type of reality is the Internet.

In this sense psychologists have a double task. First, Internet research calls for careful longitudinal study of technology-related social routines in the groups and organizations in which they happen. But, it also calls for the analysis of the relationship between objectives, technology and actors to explain why similar groups, though working to fulfill the same objectives, perceive and use this technology in different ways.

Even if psychologists are already hard at work studying the Internet's effects, research in this area is still sparse and limited in both the number and scope of studies: actual research, especially studies with strict methodologies, is only just beginning. This is why their findings have been mixed so far. For instance, Kraut and colleagues recently examined the Internet's impact on emotional well-being (Kraut, R., Patterson, M., Lundmark, V., Kiesler, S., Mukopadhyay, T., & Scherlis, W., Internet paradox: A social technology that reduces social involvement and psychological well-being? *American Psychologist, 53*(9), 1017-1031, 1998). The results, showed that greater use of the Internet resulted in small but statistically significant increase in depression and loneliness and decreases in social engagement. Even if these data are usually used by the press to support the risk of the Internet experience, according to different critics these results are biased by a weak methodology (Clay, R. A., Linking up on line. *Monitor on Psychology, 31*(4), 20-23, 2000). The study lacks of random selection and a control group, which the researchers say they couldn't afford.

In general Web-based experiments present specific problems:

- it is difficult to control the study environment because Web users use different types of hardware, software and Internet connection. There is no way to ensure that everyone who participates in the experiment will receive exactly the same stimuli in terms of sound, color or timing;
- study participants are usually unmonitored, so the researcher cannot be sure about the information collected. Members of electronic communities very often adopt false 'nickname' identities or gender switches, and openly accept them in others;
- people who participate in online experiments are self-selected and by no means random representative of the general population. In particular they are usually skewed toward the high end of the socio-economic and educational spectrum.

However, when Web-related research technology will mature, the opportunity for more creative and interactive experiments will grow. It is also true that the benefits of larger and different study samples and the reduced costs far outweigh the disadvantages for most types of psychological research.

Apart from studying the Internet, psychology is also discovering the great opportunities inherent in this medium. Psychological applications using the Internet, especially the World Wide Web, have recently appeared. Specifically, according to Barak (Barak, A., Psychological application on the Internet: A discipline on the threshold of a new millenium. *Applied and Preventive Psychology, 8*, 231-246, 1999) it is possible to identify ten types of psychological Internet applications: information resources on psychological concepts and issues; self-help guides; psychological testing and assessment; help in deciding to undergo therapy; information about specific psychological services; single-session psychological advice through e-mail or e-bulletin boards; ongoing personal counseling and therapy through e-mail; real-time counseling through chat, web telephony, and videoconferencing; synchronous and asynchronous support groups, discussion groups, and group counseling; and psychological and social research.

Drawing on research in the social sciences, communications, and other fields, this book wants to analyze how the online environment is influencing the experience of psychology. To help the reader in finding a coherent reading path, we have put a great deal of thought and effort in the structure of this book and in the sequence of the contributions. To this end we have divided the book in four main Sections comprising 15 chapters overall:

1 *Towards CyberPsychology: Theory and Methods*
2 *CyberPsychology in practice: The Internet*
3 *CyberPsychology in practice: Virtual Reality*
4 *CyberPsychology in practice: Telemedicine and e-Health*

In every Section the chapters begins with a brief abstract and a table of contents that help the reader to identify the relationships among the section's chapters.

In the first Section the chapters by Galimberti and Riva outlines the theory and methods behind CyberPsychology. Starting from this theoretical background the next Sections present how CyberPsychology can be applied for the study and exploitation of different communication technologies: Internet (Section 2) and Virtual Reality (Section 3). Given the importance of counseling and therapy for the future of CyberPsychology, in the final Section of the book we presented and discussed the rationale and some possible applications of Telemedicine and e-Health.

The contributions selected are among the first scientific attempts to take a serious look at various aspects of Internet-related psychology. However, we need not start from scratch. Psychology has a broad knowledge about the factors that affect human behavior in other setting. So, the chapters collected for this book are descriptive and practical-oriented in nature. The wide array of research areas represented here strengthens the idea of a CyberPsychology as a new area. As the field continues to grow, we eagerly expect larger on-the-field trials as well as outcome comparisons to existing methods of practice, supporting continued growth of new applications.

The editors want to thank all the people and institutions that have supported this book. We have benefited from Brenda Wiederhold and Cristina Botella friendship and from our many discussions of conceptual issues and clinical cases. We were also inspired by Mark Wiederhold, editor-in-Chief of the *CyberPsychology and Behavior* journal. In particular Mark has not only provided detailed comments on the topics discussed, but has discussed the content of this project with us over many months.

Moreover, Riva wants to thank his bosses and colleagues al Istituto Auxologico Italiano, one of the leading research and health care center in Italy, for believing in the possibility of CyberPsychology for counseling and therapy. In particular, his thanks go to the President of the Institute, Prof. Giovanni Ancarani, to the General Manager, Dr. Mario Colombo, to the Scientific Director, Prof. Alberto Zanchetti, and to the Director of the Laboratorio di Ricerche Psicologiche, Prof. Eugenia Scabini. A final thank goes to Prof. Luigi Anolli, Head of the Centro Studi e Ricerche di Psicologia della Comunicazione at the Università Cattolica del Sacro Cuore, Milan, Italy.

In the end, we hope that the contents of this book will stimulate more research on technical, cognitive and human factors connected to the virtual experience and on how best use new communication technologies in education, research, design and telemedicine.

Giuseppe Riva, Ph.D.
Istituto Auxologico Italiano,
Milan, Italy

Carlo Galimberti, Ph.D.
Università Cattolica,
Milan, Italy

CONTRIBUTORS

Jill ARNOLD
Department of Social Sciences, The Nottingham Trent University,
Nottingham, United Kingdom

Monica BACCHETTA
Applied Technology for Neuro-Psychology, Istituto Auxologico Italiano,
Milan, Italy

Irene CABRAL
Department of Biomedical Engineering, College of Medicine, Hanyang University,
Seoul, Korea

Gianluca CASTELNUOVO
Applied Technology for Neuro-Psychology, Istituto Auxologico Italiano,
Milan, Italy

Gianluca CESA
Applied Technology for Neuro-Psychology, Istituto Auxologico Italiano,
Milan, Italy

Sara CONTI
Applied Technology for Neuro-Psychology, Istituto Auxologico Italiano,
Milan, Italy

Andrea GAGGIOLI
Applied Technology for Neuro-Psychology, Istituto Auxologico Italiano,
Milan, Italy

Carlo GALIMBERTI
LICENT, Dipartimento di Psicologia, Università Cattolica,
Milan, Italy

Luciano GAMBERINI
Department of General Psychology, University of Padova,
Padova, Italy

Richard N. GEVIRTZ
California School of Professional Psychology,
San Diego, CA, USA

Sabrina IGNAZI
LICENT, Department of Psychology, Universita Cattolica del Sacro Cuore,
Milan, Italy

Dong P. JANG
Center for Advanced Multimedia Psychotherapy,
San Diego, CA, USA

Mayumi KANEDA
Department of Biomedical Engineering, College of Medicine, Hanyang University,
Seoul, Korea

In Y. KIM
Center for Advanced Multimedia Psychotherapy,
San Diego, CA, USA

Sun I. KIM
Center for Advanced Multimedia Psychotherapy,
San Diego, CA, USA

Maria Beatrice LIGORIO
University of Salerno,
Salerno, Italy

University of Nijmegen,
Nijmegen, the Netherlands

Yair LURIE
Department of Biomedical Engineering, College of Medicine, Hanyang University,
Seoul, Korea

Fabrizia MANTOVANI
Applied Technology for Neuro-Psychology, Istituto Auxologico Italiano,
Milan, Italy

Centro Studi e Ricerche di Psicologia della Comunicazione, Università Cattolica,
Milan, Italy

Giuseppe MANTOVANI
Department of General Psychology, University of Padova,
Padova, Italy

Todd MAY
Department of Biomedical Engineering, College of Medicine, Hanyang University,
Seoul, Korea

Hugh MILLER
Department of Social Sciences, The Nottingham Trent University,
Nottingham, United Kingdom

Enrico MOLINARI
Laboratorio Sperimentale di Ricerche Psicologiche, Istituto Auxologico Italiano,
Milan, Italy

Dipartimento di Psicologia, Università Cattolica,
Milan, Italy

Giuseppe RIVA
Applied Technology for Neuro-Psychology, Istituto Auxologico Italiano,
Milan, Italy

Centro Studi e Ricerche di Psicologia della Comunicazione, Università Cattolica,
Milan, Italy

Richard C. SHERMAN
Department of Psychology, Miami University,
Oxford, OH, USA

James L. SPIRA
Navy Medical Center,
San Diego, CA, USA

Steven STANLEY
Discourse and Rhetoric Group, Department of Social Sciences, Loughborough University,
Leicestershire, United Kingdom

Alessandra TALAMO
Department of Social and Developmental Psychology, University of Rome,
Rome, Italy

Elisabetta VALENTINI
Department of General Psychology University of Padova,
Padova, Italy

Pietro VERCESI
LICENT, Department of Psychology, Universita Cattolica del Sacro Cuore,
Milan, Italy

Brenda K. WIEDERHOLD
The Virtual Reality Medical Center,
San Diego, CA, USA

Center for Advanced Multimedia Psychotherapy,
San Diego, CA, USA

Mark D. WIEDERHOLD
Department of Internal Medicine, Scripps Clinic Medical Group,
San Diego, CA, USA

Cristina ZUCCHERMAGLIO
Department of Social and Developmental Psychology, University of Rome,
Rome, Italy

Contents

SECTION I

TOWARDS CYBERPSYCHOLOGY: THEORY AND METHODS

With the advance of computers and online networks - especially the Internet - a new dimension of human experience is rapidly opening up. The term "cyberspace" has been mentioned so often that it may at this point seem trite and overly commercialized. However, the experience created by computers and computer networks can in many ways be understood as a psychological "space." When they power up their computers, launch a program, write e-mail, or log on to their online service, users often feel - consciously or subconsciously - that they are entering a "place" or "space" that is filled with a wide array of meanings and purposes.

Suler, 1999
(http://www.rider.edu/users/suler/psycyber/psycyber.html)

Towards CyberPsychology
G. Riva and C. Galimberti (Eds.)
IOS Press, 2001

1   Actors, Artifacts and Inter-Actions. Outline for a Social Psychology of Cyberspace

Carlo GALIMBERTI, Giuseppe RIVA

Abstract. Cyberspace is standing out there waiting for us to study it from a psychosocial perspective. A lot of work has been done by researchers in these past years but what is still missing is a discussion over the structure of a *genuine* psychosocial point of view.

The authors in this work discuss the opportunity to found this point of view on a three pillars: a theory of subjects, a theory of objects and a theory of processes relevant to the features of artifacts and services actives in Cyberspace.

The issues raised here constitute just the first essential step towards a definitive study of communication technology and the culture that has grown up around it: its goal is to open a conceptual and dialogical space to settle theoretical, methodological and operational standards to study cyber-interaction.

Contents

1.1   Introduction

Even if social researchers are already hard at work studying the Internet's effects [1] research in this area is still scarce and limited in terms of both the number and scope of studies: actual research, and especially studies with relevant methodologies, is only just beginning. This is why their findings have been mixed so far. For instance, Kraut et al recently examined the Internet's impact on emotional well-being [2]. The results, discussed in the American Psychologist, showed that greater use of the Internet resulted in a small but statistically significant increase in depression and loneliness, and a decrease in social engagement. Even if these data are usually used by the press to support the risk of the Internet experience, according to a number of critics these results are biased by weak methodology [3]. The study lacks random selection and a control group, which the researchers say they couldn't afford.

However, when Web-related research technology matures, the opportunity for more creative, more interactive experiments will grow [4]. It is also true that the benefits of larger and different study samples and the reduced costs far outweigh the disadvantages for most types of psychological research [5]. We feel that the above considerations give rise to two different kinds of problem for the psychosocial study of Cyberspace.

First, it is by no means easy to arrive at an accurate definition of the subject under study – namely, that universe of objects which can be referred back to the concept of Cyberspace. Cyberspace is a universe made up of things that can be seen and heard, but they are neither physical objects nor necessarily a representation of physical objects. They are built up of information coming partly from operations within the physical world, but largely from the accumulation and exchange of knowledge arising from human initiatives in the fields of culture, science, and art [6]. In this sense, if a key goal for psychology is doing more thinking about how to get people to make better connections between Cyberspace and the rest of their lives [7] social psychology is facing the challenge of theorizing about how people live and move in the Cyberspace and how they master the net's services and contents to develop a culture of how to use what Cyberspace offers them. The main reason for this is that the artifacts that populate this universe are not only multifaceted in nature, but are also used in a wide range of different ways.

The second kind of problem - which is intimately linked to the first – has to deal with methodology. This lack of knowledge about the universe of objects which we would like to deal with is, at one and the same time, the cause and the consequence of methodological uncertainties. If we cannot yet give an exhaustive answer to the questions that surround the awareness of this situation, we cannot, however, help recognizing that a strictly experimental approach to the psychosocial phenomena of Cyberspace is hardly suitable at all. Generally speaking, Web-based experiments present specific problems [5, 8]:

- it is difficult to control the study environment because Web users use different types of hardware, software, and Internet connections. There is no way to ensure that everyone who participates in the experiment will receive exactly the same stimuli in terms of sound, colour, or timing;
- study participants are usually unmonitored, so the researcher cannot be sure about the information collected. Members of electronic communities very often adopt false "nickname" identities or gender switches, and openly accept them in others; and
- people who participate in online experiments are self-selected and by no means randomly representative of the general population. In particular they are usually skewed toward the high end of the socioeconomic and educational spectrum.

In this chapter, however, we will not be dealing with methodology. An explanation of why the methods of data analysis and production may be the best methodological approach will be dealt with in the second Chapter. Rather, in the pages that follow we would like to develop some ideas about how to set about defining a point of view from which to observe the information-based artifacts and forms of interaction that are present in Cyberspace, so that they can become valid objects for psychosocial investigation.

1.2 Definition of a point-of-view (I). Cyberspace as a universe of relevant psychosocial objects

The first step in defining a psychosocial point of view, we feel, is to identify the characteristics of the objects that are to be found on the Net, using as a starting point the way that subjects who interact within Cyberspace actually use those objects. Recently, Wallace [9] has identified six different Internet environments. Their basic features differ, and these basic features affect the way we behave when we experience them:

- the World Wide Web (web pages; web sites; portals; vortals; hubs)
- electronic mail (E-mail);
- asynchronous discussion forums (news-groups);
- synchronous chat (Internet Relay Chat)
- multi-user dungeons (MUD): text based virtual environments:
- metaworlds (3D MUDs): 3D virtual environments; and
- interactive video and voice (Web cam).

These artifacts can be considered:

- complex cultural objects [10-12];
- used by aware actors for their own ends [13, 14];
- which are active and used in contexts which are, in part, pre-built and in part the outcome of local subject-artefact interaction [15, 16];
- and which, in communicative terms, have their own specific identity – thoroughgoing, independent *enunciative mechanisms* capable of actively determining the communicative modes produced through those who use them [17-20].

In order to judge how important the artefacts on the Web are from a psychosocial point of view, we will now elaborate upon these four "initial intuitive ideas" in order to understand how the interrelations between them in the context of the ways in which they are used help us to arrive at a psychosocial definition of Cyberspace.

Recent developments in communication studies have revealed profound changes in how the relationship between interaction and communication is defined [17-20]. CMC studies are particularly affected by new stances emerging from this re-orientation in communication research. Communication was once seen as a process which can be switched on and off at will, an alternation of action and reaction or a series of actions performed in an inter-subjective vacuum; now it is seen as the outcome of a complex, coordinated activity, an event which generates conversational space within intertwined personal and social relationships. Thus, communication is not only – or not so much – a question of the transfer of information, but rather the activation of a psychosocial relationship, the process by which interlocutors co-construct an area of reality. As

Heidegger puts it, "Man speaks. We speak when we are awake and in our sleep. We are always speaking, even when we do not use words" [21]

Bakhtin, on the other hand, reminds us that "the effective reality of language, discourse, is not an abstract system of linguistic forms...or even the psycho/physiological act of using it, but the social event of verbal interaction using one or more speech acts" [22]. Two concepts have now become reference points for psychosocial research: the belief that language is the inescapable horizon of human experience and the recognition of language as a social act that goes beyond the individual himself. Awareness of the fact that a speech act is used during interaction, something that is shared and something that becomes the subject of a dialogue even when it comes in the form of a monologue, and even when it is guided by the intention on the part of the speaker to hide something from his listener, is now an integral part of the psychosocial researcher's own awareness. What is more, the desire to investigate this *act of sharing* is leading research more and more in the direction of an examination of *conversation*, for this is the *natural* context in which it occurs. The aim here is to uncover the reasons that make it a *form* of social action. The most recent discoveries in this area would seem to suggest that, if this is to happen, we need to work on a number of different levels of analysis and inspect the phenomena involved from different points of view if we are to see them in *psychosocial, pragmatic,* and *cognitive* terms, as well as in terms of the *logic of the everyday*. This is the reason why conversation has become such an interesting object for psychosocial researchers [23, 24].

As human communication gives rise to high levels of ambiguity which are resolved by the 'inference-validation' and 'ambiguity-dispersal' device known as conversation, researchers' attention has come to be focused on this [25]. Now conversation - including *virtual conversation* - is studied as both the theatre, the physical and symbolic location for this exchange, and the set of control conditions which ensure that it happens, with a probability of success that makes it the favourite communication tool in the ongoing process of human evolution. People involved in the process of communication are no longer seen as 'senders' and 'receivers', 'locutors' and 'locutees', but as co-utterers, i.e., interlocutors engaged in a coordinated communicative activity for which they are jointly responsible.

On the one hand, the psychosocial dimension of interlocutor individuation has become increasingly important. 'Sender' and 'receiver', both of which are abstract, monofunctional entities, have been replaced by interlocutors endowed with thoughts, emotions, affects, and a psychosocial identity which expresses their positioning within families, groups, organisations and institutions. This shift in emphasis has influenced the development of research models, concepts of communicative interaction, and CMC itself.

In parallel with this, researchers have started to study the dematerialisation of interlocutors, or rather, the increasing marginalisation of their physical presence, an effect of the use of the new media's communication devices. The increasing irrelevance of the face-to-face mode in interaction has enabled communication researchers to mediate/represent the subjectivity of interlocutors using simulacra of various kinds. The anthropomorphism of the machines they have devised ranges from the telephone (minimum) to virtual reality (maximum), but this has never obscured the presence of the interlocutors who use them. In this perspective, we can say that to study communicative interaction the physical co-presence of interlocutors is not required, but the "co-presence of utterance, meaning the outcome of a communicative exchange in which two interlocutors mutually influences each other's actions ... and regulate the meaning of their communication through some form of feedback" [17, 26] is. This is a far cry from the mechanical abstraction of 'sender' and 'receiver': the machines which determine the mode and degree of 'co-presence of utterance' do not obscure, still less eliminate the subjective presence of the interlocutors who use them. In communication, the identities of interlocutors cannot be regarded as wholly physical, or of only secondary importance: they result from the interweaving of many reality-levels which are symbolic and cultural as well as psychological and social.

As Mantovani [13] says, contexts are not only physical but also conceptual in the sense that the actors perceive the situations through the models introduced by the cultural context and they act according to those; contexts are unstable because continually re-built in the interaction and constantly transformed by actions and choices of the subjects itself. The social context becomes "the symbolic system of a given culture, continually altered by practical human intervention." [27]. Thanks to the writings of Norman [10-12]and the contributions of cultural psychology, researchers have pointed out the impossibility of studying environment and people as separate from the consideration of artifacts and their role. These are no longer considered mere 'things', but rather as 'things for', good for making other things, invented for purposes that are 'graven' into their statute [13, 14].

It is not, therefore, possible to consider participants in a communication act mediated by the computer as consumers of a technology, but "as social actors, with purposes and autonomy of orientation in the situations" [14]. To understand how social actors move in virtual environments, it is useful to construct a three-level model of the social context [13] through situations, social norms and the use of artifacts: the first level is in general that of the social context, the second is that of the situations of daily life, the third is that of local interaction with the environment through artifacts.

As regards the status of language in psychosocial research into communication, the most important outcome of the shift towards conversational models has been the realisation that language is crucial to the way human beings attribute meaning to reality. Now verbal language is seen as fundamental to the construction of intra-subjective experience, inter-subjective relationships and the transformation of physical and social reality.

Thus, the linguistic and social dimensions of communication are inextricably intertwined, and this is true even of cybercommunication, in the sense that language generates the conventions we need to regulate social interaction. To say this implies an interactional and interlocutory concept of communication which attributes greater importance to the pragmatic rather than the representational features of language. As a result, discourse strategies and practices are seen not as epiphenomena of other less visible behaviour patterns or of latent non-verbal psychosocial structures – attitudes, representations, cognitive categorisations, personality traits – but as genuine instances of autonomous behaviour. We are now seeing the emergence of a pragmatics of conversation which is shifting the emphasis "from subjectivity to inter-subjectivity, from illocution to inter-illocution" [25].

1.3 Definition of a point-of-view (II). Three theories to explain how artifacts in Cyberspace are experienced

In the preceding paragraph we began to construct a psychosocial point of view from which to observe Cyberspace, identifying the reasons why the artifacts present within it are important for the researcher, shedding light on possible interconnections between them and developing theoretical and methodological ideas in psycho-social disciplines.

Now we shall attempt to define this point of view still further by turning our attention to the way the researcher can look at these objects in an attempt to understand the structure and thereby identify the logical co-ordinates that can be used as a basis for "theorising" about virtual interaction. This will be done by looking in particular at the way communicative action takes place in virtual contexts and the consequences of substituting *physical co-presence* with *enunciative co-presence*, seen as the result of a communicative exchange in which the interlocutors are able to influence each other's actions and imbue the exchange with value [17, 26].

In order to be investigated correctly, a process such as this requires a model capable of describing how interaction between human beings in contexts whose level of virtuality varies actually works. This model must also be capable of integrating, from a psychosocial point of view, a *theory of subjects,* a *theory of objects,* and a *theory of processes* [28].

In the following paragraphs, we will identify a number of ideas which can be used as a basis for these theories and for their integration, which is indispensable.

1.3.1 Theory of subjects

We have shown elsewhere how the ways subjectivity is built up within digital communicative interaction are essentially based on three *psycho-social "roots"* [18, 20, 29]: cognition, communication and identity. We also outlined a "path" for each of these "roots". By following these "paths" we feel it is possible to identify suitable conceptual tools for "fine-tuning" a more mature approach to the study of subjectivity in Cyberspace, moving:

- from an intra-subjective interpretation of the cognitive processes to the idea that cognition is an activity which is the result of combined effort; furthermore, its products do not reside *within* the minds of the participants, but *between* their minds [30, 31]
- from communication seen as a linear process to the adoption of a "dialogic/conversational" model as a paradigm for communicative interaction [17, 26];
- from the passivity of an individual who simply uses a certain type of communication technology to the active participation of a subject and a mechanism which, while it is at work, actually influences the user's definition of himself, as it does those who interact with him [27].

We are now going to "dismantle" the conceptual framework which has guided us in the past. We feel, in fact, that it is the paths relating to the first two "roots" described above – cognition and communication – which contribute most usefully to the construction of a *theory of subjects.* We will deal with the third path when we turn our attention to problems relating to the *theory of processes.* More and more, in fact, identity, when related to the ways information technology artifacts are used, seems to be the result of a 'process' rather than a starting point in itself. There are ever more complex links and interconnections between the construction of a subject's identity and the context or contexts in which artifacts are used. They are less and less "stable" and increasingly sensitive to variations between themselves. This is why we need to deal with them together. They need to be seen as the basis of what we are going to say about the processes through which subjects and objects dynamically intertwine.

Given the above, let us now try to analyse the two "roots" which are most important for the way subjectivity is built up, in an attempt to understand how cognitions and communication are used in Cyberspace in such a way as to become co-determinate to a decisive degree.

1.3.1.1   Networked reality and cognition as a coordinated activity

"Cognitions emerge [...] from the conversational interactions in which children participate from a very early age [...]. Far from being circumscribed by experimental laboratory settings, cognitive activities are routine daily activities. In other words, *it is in everyday life, and in conversational interaction especially, that we put our cognitive skills to practical use"* (Trognon [32], p.117. Our italics).

"The higher mental functions are dialogic processes derived from interpersonal activity. (They) develop through the progressive internalization of semiotically manifested perspectives on reality [...]. The emergence of these functions in the context of social activity constitutes the cultural line of development". (Fernyhough, [33], p. 47)

These two quotations illustrate well the so called "dialogic approach" [33, 34] which is trying to assess how cognition relates to interaction, and especially to conversational interaction. Although methodological problems still have to be solved, cognitive studies are increasingly concerned with defining and exploring the relationship between cognition and interaction. As Perret-Clermont and Brossard [35] and Fernyhough [33] have shown, the essential groundwork for this new approach, in psychological terms at least, is provided by Bakhtin [36, 37], Bartlett [38], Gergen [39], Piaget [40], and of course, Vygotsky [41].

Though they differ in detail on many points, all of them agree that the social system should be seen as a network of relationships providing the *space* in which cognitions are elaborated. They would agree, for instance, on the fact that cognition has a dual social connotation. On the one hand, it is both "action, to the extent that those who take part in it have to organise a flow of shared activities by coordinating and concatenating their actions ... [and] communication, to the extent that the interlocutors make themselves mutually accessible, or make explicit the elements that enable them to understand each other and act together" [42, p. 19]. On the other hand, cognition is always a function of social action and is always action-oriented, never an end in itself [32, 34, 43].

Most researchers, or at least those who adopt a psychosocial approach to cognition, would find little to disagree with here. What is new, however, is that cognitive activities are increasingly being performed in networked contexts which, to varying degrees, are undeniably virtual. The network model is therefore essential to how the matrices of cognitive functions - De Kerckhove's brainframes [30, 44] - are constructed, and to the overall configuration of the knowledge system, which Pierre Lévy's [31] recent concept of *collective intelligence* describes particularly well. Thus, cognition is now seen as something that happens 'between' rather than 'inside' subjects, a media-structured loop that begins and ends with the subjects themselves, a continuous exchange which generates a shared construction of reality at the interface between individual and collective, cognition and interaction, mental activity and social activity [33, 34, 45]. Cognition has lost its traditional connotation as a private event, and is now regarded as both a coordinated activity (in terms of process) and as a networked reality (in terms of how the products of the process are distributed).

The concepts of brainframe and collective intelligence are especially useful because they enable us to describe this type of cognition [18-20]. in terms of two levels - micro and macro, depending on 'closeness' to subject - interconnected by a self/other-oriented process of self-definition which resembles the auto-poietic phenomena described by Varela [46].

1.3.1.2 Virtual conversation

Another important change in psychosocial terms taken by CMC is in the concept of communication: the model of communication as the passage of information from one person to another is becoming obsolete. This model, usually called the "parcel-post model" [47, 48], is now in a state of crisis, partly because of some of the peculiar features of electronic environments, such as the asymmetry between message sender and message receiver.

The model of communication as information transfer does not take into account the cooperative component, which stimulates reciprocal responsibility for successful interaction and a series of subtle adaptations among interlocutors. As Dohény-Farina [49] notes: "The theory of communication as information transfer separates knowledge from communication; it treats knowledge as an object that exists independently of the participants in the innovation venture. With this independent existence, information becomes an object that can be carried through channels" (p.8). However, it is possible to communicate only to the extent that participants have some common ground for shared beliefs, recognize reciprocal expectations and accept rules for interaction which serve as necessary anchors in the development of conversation [50]. So, with CMC is emerging a new, alternative concept: communication is a common construction of meanings [23, 24].

The shift towards the interactive nature of communication is the key characteristic of the *interlocutory* (conversational) models [26]. The importance attributed to *interlocution* in these models results from efforts to combine pragmatic linguistics with social psychology on the part of researchers in France such as Charaudeau [51], Ghiglione [23] and Trognon [32, 43], as well as American and British researchers like Potter and Wetherell [52].

Interlocutory models are based more or less explicitly on the concept of communicative interactionism and place much stress on the crucial importance of interaction and conversation in communication. Major features of the interlocutory approach include a new conceptual definition of communication [53, 54], clarification of the contractual (negotiable) nature of some aspects of communication [23] and a radical revision of the concept of the interlocutor [51].

As an "irreducible relational fact" [54, p.115] communication is seen as a primary form of human recognition, and as the foundation of the intersubjectivity through which the reciprocity of all human relationships is expressed. *Verbal cooperation*, which accounts for most of communicative phenomenology, is thus a genuinely *coordinated activity* in which the utterances of one interlocutor are interwoven with those of another.

At the beginning of the 90s, Stasser gave a definition of computer mediated communication – CMC - which is particularly interesting for the discussion that is to follow. In his words, CMC may be defined as *a process by which a group of social actors in a given situation negotiates the meaning of the various situations which arise between them* [55].

This definition can be applied both to synchronous and asynchronous CMC [56]. As we know, synchronous CMC - video-conferencing, Internet Relay Chat, or IRC, MUD (also MOO, MUSH and VEE), etc. - is produced when communication occurs simultaneously between two or more users, as in any normal telephone or face-to-face conversation.

Asynchronous CMC – E-mail, newsgroups and so on - is produced when communication is not simultaneous. Hence the essential difference between the two is a temporal one: for CMC to be synchronous, the computers involved must be linked in real time.

Despite the predominance of the textual mode, it has been shown that asynchronous CMC differs in psychosocial terms from non-electronic written communication as well as from other existing means of communication. Experimental studies have revealed significant differences between CMC and non-electronic written communication [57, 58] relating to degree of *social presence* and *media richness*. Social presence is the user's perception of the ability of the means of communication to marshal and focus the presence of communicating subjects [59], while media richness is the ability of the means of communication to interlink a variety of topics, render them less ambiguous, and enable users to learn about them within a given time-span [60]. Studies by Rice [58, 61] have shown that there are significant differences in user perceptions of the degree of social presence/media richness in E-mail and video-conferencing compared with other means of communication, such as the telephone and written texts.

In addition to the fact that synchronous CMC does provide a real-time link between users' computers, it also has special features which distinguish it from other forms of communication. According to Newhagen [62] these include (especially in synchronous CMC via Internet) multimediality, hypertextuality, packet switching, synchronicity and interactivity.

There is a technical reason for these differences between synchronous and asynchronous CMC. Communication with a keyboard and computer screen takes longer than normal face-to-face communication, and the absence of metacommunicative features like facial expression, posture and tone of voice encourages users to find other ways of making communication as complete as possible. These limitations make CMC interaction more *rarefied* than the kind of interaction that happens in normal conversation, in the sense that CMC uses mainly textual devices - abbreviations and smiles [56] as well as MUD metacommands - to reproduce the metacommunicative features (emotions, illocutionary force) of face-to-face conversation.

However, the differences between CMC and face-to-face conversation are important from a psychosocial point of view. While face-to-face conversation occurs in a cooperative environment constantly regulated by mutual adjustment and correction [26, 63], CMC occurs in a much less cooperative environment because of the special conditions imposed by the medium itself [64]. In most CMC environments, and in asynchronous CMC environments especially, two typical features of face-to-face conversation are missing [13]:

- the collaborative commitment of participants and co-formulation of the message;
- the feedback which allows the social meaning of the message to be processed immediately.

In addition, CMC in no way guarantees that a user's declared identity is the real one, but this topic has much to do with theory of processes and will find its place in next paragraph. At this point, however, it is worth bearing in mind that the use of false identities, often of a different sex, is widespread in electronic communities and in MUDs especially [27, 65].

In this sense, CMC may be regarded as an example of virtual conversation, i.e., a necessarily 'pared-down' or, perhaps, more accurately, *rarefied* form of conversation which lacks the rules on which effective interaction depends [18, 20, 29]. Computer mediation creates an asymmetrical imbalance in the sender-receiver relationship: the sender can transmit information and get cooperation under way, but has no guarantee that the receiver receives the transmission, while the receiver has no guarantee that the sender's declared identity is the real one.

Ghiglione's definition [23] of communication as the co-construction of a reality using systems of signs and rules applies equally well to CMC as an instance of virtual *conversation*, with the important difference that in CMC a reality is asymmetrically co-constructed because the receiver can decide at will to terminate interaction, or continue it by turning himself into a sender. This decision is far from casual: it depends on how the receiver interprets the situation, what his aims are, and the social rules that govern his behaviour. Some researchers have even used the term "electronic opportunism" to describe this feature of CMC [66].

The characteristics of CMC which we have been dealing with here, taken as a whole, form an out-and-out "virtual conversation". They make it an essential component of Cyberspace, allowing us to see how it works, because they form an enunciative mechanism, well expressed by the words of Stasser presented before, but which bear repeating because, after this analysis, they now seem much clearer than before: CMC may be defined as *a process by which a group of social actors in a given situation negotiates the meaning of the various situations which arise between them* [55].

1.3.2   Theory of objects (artifacts)

In recent years, the belief that if we want to understand the meaning of people's actions we have to pay attention to the environments in which they live has become widespread in the psychosocial sciences. In more concrete terms, this means that, in order to sustain the operations that take place within our minds - operations that represent the process of planning the actions that we then carry out - we inevitably need some awareness of the environment within which those operations take place. As we know, a large part of the environment in which we work is made up of objects. Most of these can be considered as *artifacts,* or objects made to make other objects and "things used to do or make other things" [27, p.23]. They have been invented with an aim in mind and are used to fulfil certain functions which are, as it were, "programmed" into them.

This is as true for a pencil as it is for a typewriter or a computer. Moreover, it is true for the non-material objects that populate Cyberspace which we listed above, elaborating upon Wallace's list [9]: the World Wide Web (web pages; web sites; portals; vortals; hubs); electronic mail (E-mail); asynchronous discussion forums (news-groups); synchronous chat rooms (IRC); multi-user dungeons (MUD): text based virtual environments; metaworlds (3D MUDs); 3D virtual environments and interactive video and voice (Web cams).

As these are artifacts or "things made to do other things", it is not possible to discuss them without making some reference to the subjects who use them. As noted by Gibson [67] the relation between actors and their environment is circular: "actions of the organism have consequences for the environment, and the nature of environment has consequences for the organism" [68, p. 81].

So, the process of knowledge does not mean people contemplating "external" objects without touching them, but means also moving in the environment, using it for their goals [69, 70]. Zahoric and Jenison clearly explain this point: "Gibson's unique insight rests with the notion that the perceiving organism and the environment are intimately related - namely, that the environment has provided conditions commensurate with the organism's evolution.

As a result, perception for the organism is the pickup of information that supports action, and ultimately evolution" [68, p. 83]. Perceiving is an activity by means of which the organism identifies the resources it needs in the environment and attempts to capture them in order to achieve its own evolutionary aim – sustenance and transmission of its own genetic pool [69].

If artifacts are social objects, the result of ideas or physical structures, then every time that one is planned or constructed, the needs of the people who are to use it must be borne in mind. As Norman [12] and Zhang have demonstrated on more than one occasion, [71] the way we approach a problem is influenced by the way data is presented to us. Using a blackboard or a computer means producing different kinds of representations and setting off different types of processes. For example, if we want to "automate a working environment through the introduction of computer technologies", considerations such as these naturally carry a certain weight. Even more so, given the fact that information technology artifacts – be they software or hardware – go to make up "the essential interface between actors and their environment" [27, p.105]. As Suchman has already pointed out, "their meaning is given to them by the social world at the moment in which they act as mediators of the way we interact with it" [72]. It is also worth adding at this point that, as Flores says, "technology consists not in planning physical objects, but in planning practice and the possibility of realisation through artifacts", in planning "modes of being" [73].

In this sense the Internet does not provide undifferentiated information, ready-made objects equal for everyone. It offers different opportunities according to the actors and their needs: "Affordances are not 'things which are outside' simply waiting for someone to come and take a view of them. They are resources, which are revealed to those who seek them. If 'a nipple is for sucking', then this affordance is taken up by a hungry calf which perceives the nipple precisely because it needs it, but this is not the case of an eagle circling high in the sky which does not need milk for its survival. The tree in the middle of a field on a summer's day is an affordance only to those who seek its cool shade" [69, p. 544].

One or two other points to give an even clearer idea of the importance of a suitable *theory of objects*. Let us bear in mind Gregory Bateson's line of reasoning [74]: "Imagine that I'm blind and use a stick. While I walk along, I touch things as I go: tap, tap, tap. Where do I actually begin? Does my mental system finish at the grip of the stick? Or does it finish with my skin? Does it start halfway up the stick? Or at the end of the stick?" [74].

One thing we can say, in order to give a brief answer to Bateson's questions, is that the stick is the means through which information flows – the information the blind man needs if he is to walk along the road. The stick is, in fact, neither "inside" nor "outside" the blind man's system of cognition/action. It is simply the "end point", limit or "frontier", and like all frontiers it belongs neither to one nor to the other of the two territories that communicate through it, even though it is a part of them both. What can be said is that as soon as the blind man starts to walk along the street, the stick becomes an offshoot of his mind. Just like any information technology artifact, be it a research engine or a simple pop-up menu. A suitable *theory of objects* must be capable of telling us something about the points at which the blind man's hand meets the stick, the stick touches the pavement, and so on. In other words, to leave the metaphor behind, it needs to tell us something about the characteristics of the artifacts – be they cognitive, material or "natural" – that go to make up the system as a whole. What is clear from the above is just how delicate the place of a *theory of objects* is in terms of the overall dynamics of a suitable psychosocial point of view for observing Cyberspace. It acts like a hinge, so to speak, between the *theory of subjects* and the *theory of processes,* whose job it is – as we shall see shortly – to generate data and hypotheses about what happens in the interaction between user, information system and the surrounding working environment.

1.3.3   Theory of processes

Lastly, as far as the theory of processes is concerned, it seems to us that one of the most interesting ideas in the context of this chapter is the Theory of Activity [75]. As we know, this theory focuses on "practice", on the activity of subjects. The aim here is to show how activity is united with knowledge. Here, knowledge is not meant as a series of discrete, disembodied cognitive acts, such as acts of decision-making, classification, or memory.

Nor does it refer directly to the brain as such. As Nardi says, knowledge can be summed up in everyday activity – "we are what we do; and what we do is closely and inextricably linked to the social matrix of which every person is a part. This social matrix is made up of people and artifacts" [75].

The mechanism which structures the organic whole that is this social matrix is mediation, and mediation is a function of artefacts, as we noticed when discussing the theory of objects. Artifacts, in fact, connect us closely and organically with the physical environment that surrounds us and help develop knowledge and the functions of knowledge.

As noted by Gergen [76] "all that is meaningful grows from relationships" (p. ix). In fact, according to this author the human experience is constructed through relationships between social actors and their social and physical environments: "Discourse is not the possession of a single individual. Meaningful language is the product of social interdependence. It requires the coordinated actions of at least two persons, and until there is mutual agreement on the meaningful character of words, they fail to constitute language.

If we follow this line of argument to its ineluctable conclusion, we find that it is not the mind of the single individual that provides whatever certitude we possess, but relationships of interdependency'' [76, p. ix].

In this sense, knowledge is no longer to be seen as a "mental" entity. Instead, it takes on the characteristics of a "situated" phenomenon, where the material and social contexts have a fundamental role to play. So the subject – artifact – action triangle of Cyberspace assumes those forms and modes of interaction which are specially suited to the setting up and development of knowledge, skills and learning and training control loops which are rather rare in the settings traditionally used for processes such as these. The utility of this theoretical standpoint for observing the phenomenology of subject-artifact interaction on the net becomes even clearer when we bear in mind the fact that, alongside the idea of the unity of action and knowledge, it is also orientated towards the objects of human action, their organisation into hierarchies, the central importance of mechanisms governing interiorisation/exteriorisation in managing relationships with the environment, the way that artifacts act as mediators, and the central importance of the idea of development.

The Theory of Activity is further bolstered when related to Situated Action Theory - SAT - developed within the field of socio-cognitive research known as 'cognition in practice', which gives it a broader hermeneutical base useful if we want to understand how subject-object interaction can be seen as a part of a dynamic process involving the immediate context. Though based on traditional cognitivist analyses of information processing and symbolisation, SAT introduces a change of perspective in that it sees action not as the execution of a ready-conceived plan, but as adaptation to context As Suchman [72] notes, "instead of separating action from the circumstances in which it occurs as the execution of a carefully thought out plan ... [SAT] tries to study how people use circumstances to develop an intelligent course of action" (p.167).

This necessitates profound changes in how 'social context' has previously been defined. In SAT, social context is not something physical and highly stable like an organisation or the power structure within it. As Mantovani [13] stresses, contexts are not given, but made, so that:

- context is conceptual as well as physical: actors perceive situations using cultural models, and act accordingly in cultural ways;
- context is unstable: cultural models are constantly modified by subjects' actions and choices.

In this sense, social context may be regarded as the symbolic system of a given culture which is continually being altered by practical human intervention [77].

So, as we have seen, social context may be defined as the symbolic system of a given culture which is continually being altered by practical human intervention and it cannot be explained exclusively in terms of interpersonal relationships or the physical environment in which information exchanges take place. It is a prerequisite of communication, "a shared symbolic order in which action becomes meaningful, and so generates meaning" [13, p.106].

Thus, SAT implies a radical redefinition of the meaning of communication. Context may be co-constructed by social actors, but they use communication to exchange meanings, not pieces of information. More precisely, the content of communication is interpretations of the situations which actors are involved in. In this sense, the most effective way of clarifying the meaning of messages is to relate them to a shared context of meaning.

The last trend in cultural psychology [78] was the analysis of distribution of knowledge in the social world: "Within each local setting, such 'cognitive actions' as remembering and decision making are distributed not only among the artifacts but among the rules and among people according to the division of labor" [79, pp. 17-18]. Following this vision, action can be described as part of a strategic game [80] in which certain goals, both individual and collective, are aimed at, through the joint efforts of several actors. In order to be achieved, many human activities, including the shared experience of new communication media, require that knowledge relevant to the goal be distributed and that actions be coordinated among the various actors by means of cultural modes which pre-exist those interactions (between actors, and between them and the environment) and make them possible [69, 70].

1.4   Conclusions

As the reader will already have realised, the *raison d'etre* of this chapter is not so much the novelty of the material we have dealt, which is for the most part already well-known or has already been used elsewhere. Rather, it is the way in which we have attempted to make these concepts interact in an attempt to build up a useful approach to the psychosocial investigation of interaction occurring in Cyberspace. Obviously, there are now two final steps to make.

Firstly, we need to develop a methodology for the application of this theoretical approach. The following chapter is a first step in this direction, but more work will of course need to be done to create a working model for applying the techniques of data analysis and production referred to above.

Second, we need to analyse the literature relating to interaction in Internet and in virtual environments in the light of the theoretical approach we have developed above. A start has already been made in this sense. The aim of an analysis of this kind would be to catalogue works that have already been published or are to be published with reference to the three theories of subjects, objects and processes. As we have already pointed out, work has already begun on this, but it will require some time before we have an instrument which can be used for the debate taking place at present.

To conclude, it is clear that this is only the beginning of a task which will require much more work and, most important of all, active participation in the debate on themes relating to the study of virtual interaction that has been going on within the scientific community for some time now.

In this sense, we know that the issues raised here constitute just the first essential step towards a definitive study of communication technology and the culture that has grown up around it. However, we are also just as aware that for some time now communication technologies have no longer been seen by researchers as 'rigid prostheses', external tools marking the limits and limitations of users who are slaves rather than masters, but as 'transparent interfaces', ways of genuinely enhancing the communication of interlocutors who use them, whether singly or in networks. And this should create room for new theories which, until some time ago, were crushed on the one hand by the weight of the technologies and on the other by sociologising.

Our approach supports the research directed to build usable and socially plausible communication tools which can account for communication, co-operation, and conflict among different actors and not only for the characteristics of graphic design. Animated and 3D web sites can stand as a superb piece of computer graphics but they cannot substitute for the social dimension of the interaction process as culturally constructed human activity. Attention for the social distribution of knowledge and action between communicative subjects, objects and processes, the rules governing them, the cultural grid providing the common reference ground for their joint activity is what our chapter wishes to introduce in research on Internet and new communication media.

This new forum for thought and debate will – at a theoretical and methodological level and in terms of the techniques of intervention - be the central issue in our approach to the study of cyberinteraction.

1.5   Acknowledgments

This work was supported by the Commission of the European Communities (CEC), and in particular by the IST programme (Project VEPSY UPDATED, IST-2000-25323 - http://www.psicologia.net; http://www.vepsy.com) and by a Murst (Italian Ministero dell'Università e della Ricerca Scientifica) fund "Modalità di costruzione della fiducia nelle interazioni in rete. Il caso business-to-consumer" (D1 – 2001).

1.6   References

[1]   L. W. Jerome, P. H. DeLeon, L. C. James, R. Folen, J. Earles, and J. J. Gedney, The coming of age of telecommunications in psychological research and practice, *American Psychologist* 55 (2000) 407-21.
[2]   R. Kraut, M. Patterson, V. Lundmark, S. Kiesler, T. Mukopadhyay, and W. Scherlis, Internet paradox: A social technology that reduces social involvement and psychological well-being?, *American Psychologist* 53 (1998) 1017-1031.
[3]   R. A. Clay, Linking up on line, *Monitor on Psychology* 31 (2000) 20-23.
[4]   G. Riva and C. Galimberti, The mind in the Web: Psychology in the Internet age, *CyberPsychology and Behavior* 4 (2001) 1-5.
[5]   B. Azar, A Web of research, *Monitor on Psychology* 31 (2000) 42-44.
[6]   S. Tagliagambe, *Epistemologia del Cyberspazio [Episthemology of Cyberspace]*. Cagliari, Italy: Demos, 1997.
[7]   S. Turkle, Constructions and reconstructions of self in virtual reality: Playing in the MUDs, in *Culture of the Internet*, K. Sara, Ed.: Lawrence Erlbaum Associates, Inc., Publishers, Mahwah, NJ, US, 1997, pp. 143-155.
[8]   M. H. Birnbaum, Psychological experiments on the Internet. San Diego: Academic Press, 2000.
[9]   P. Wallace, *The psychology of the Internet*. New York: Cambridge University Press, 1999.
[10]   D. A. Norman, *Things that make us smart*. Reading, MA: Addison-Wesley, 1993.
[11]   D. A. Norman, *The psychology of ordinary things*. New York: Basic Books, 1988.
[12]   D. A. Norman, *Turn signal are the facial expression of automobiles*. Reading, MA: Addison-Wesley, 1992.
[13]   G. Mantovani, *New communication environments: from everyday to virtual*. London: Taylor & Francis, 1996.
[14]   G. Mantovani, Social context in HCI: A new framework for mental models, cooperation and communication, *Cognitive Science* 20 (1996) 237-296.
[15]   G. Riva, Design of clinically oriented virtual environments: A communicative approach, *CyberPsychology & Behavior* 3 (2000) 351-358.
[16]   G. Riva, The mind in the Web: Psychology in the Internet age, *CyberPsychology and Behavior* 4 (2001) 1-6.
[17]   C. Galimberti, *La conversazione [Conversation]*. Milan: Guerini e Associati, 1992.
[18]   G. Riva and C. Galimberti, Computer-mediated communication: identity and social interaction in an electronic environment, *Genetic, Social and General Psychology Monographs* 124 (1998) 434-464.
[19]   G. Riva and C. Galimberti, Interbrain frame: interaction and cognition in computer-mediated communication, *CyberPsychology & Behavior* 1 (1998) 295-310.
[20]   G. Riva and C. Galimberti, The psychology of cyberspace: a socio-cognitive framework to computer mediated communication, *New Ideas in Psychology* 15 (1997) 141-158.
[21]   M. Heidegger, *Unterwegs zur Sprache*. Neske: Pfullingen, 1959.
[22]   V. N. Volosinov, *Marxismo e filosofia del linguaggio [Marxism and language philosophy]*. Bari: Dedalo, 1976.
[23]   R. Ghiglione, *L'homme communiquant*. Paris: A. Colin, 1986.

[24] R. E. Kraut and L. A. Streeter, Coordination in software development, *Communication of the ACM* 38 (1995) 69-81.
[25] C. Kerbrat-Orecchioni, *Les interactions verbales*. Paris: Armand Colin, 1990.
[26] C. Galimberti, Dalla comunicazione alla conversazione [From communication to conversation]. *Ricerche di Psicologia* 18 (1994) 113-152.
[27] G. Mantovani, Virtual reality as a communication environment: Consensual hallucination, fiction, and possible selves, *Human Relations* 48 (1995) 669-683.
[28] W. Doise, *Levels of explanation in social psychology*. Cambridge: Cambridge University Press, 1986.
[29] C. Galimberti and G. Riva, *La comunicazione virtuale [Virtual communication]*. Milan, Italy: Guerini e Associati, 1997.
[30] D. De Kerckhove, *Planetary Mind: Collective intelligence in the digital age*. New York: HardWired, 1997.
[31] P. Lévy, *L'intelligence collectif [Collective intelligence]*. Paris: La Découverte., 1994.
[32] A. Trognon, Psicologia cognitiva e analisi delle conversazioni [Cognitive psychology and conversation analysis], in *La conversazione. Prospettive sull'interazione psicosociale [Conversation: perspectives in psycho-social interaction]*, C. Galimberti, Ed. Milan: Guerini e Associati, 1992, pp. 110-122.
[33] C. Fernyhough, The dialogic mind: A dialogic approach to the higher mental functions, *New Ideas in Psychology* 14 (1996) 47-62.
[34] A. Saito, Social origins of cognition: Bartlett, evolutionary perspective and embodied mind approach, *Journal of the Theory of Social Behaviour* 26 (1996) 399-422.
[35] A. N. Perret-Clermont and A. Brossard, L'intrication des processus cognitifs et sociaux dans les interactions [The network of cognitive and social processes during interaction], in *Relations interpersonnelles et développement des savoirs [Interpersonal relationships and knowledge development]*, I. R. Hinde, A. N. Perret-Clermont, and J. Stevenson-Hinde, Eds. Berne: Delval, 1988, pp. 441-465.
[36] M. M. Bakhtin, Discover in the novel, in *Dialogic Imagination: Four Essays by M.M. Bakhtin*, M. Holquist, Ed. Austin, TX: University of Texas Press, 1981, pp. 259-422.
[37] M. M. Bakhtin, *Speech genres and other late essays*. Austin, TX: University of Texas Press, 1986.
[38] F. C. Bartlett, *Remembering: A study in experimental and social psychology*. Cambridge, MA: Cambridge University Press, 1932.
[39] K. J. Gergen, *Toward transformation in social knowledge*. New York: Springer, 1982.
[40] J. Piaget, *Sociological Studies*. London: Routledge, 1995.
[41] L. S. Vygotsky, *Mind in society: The development of higher psychological processes*, vol. Harvard University Press: Cambridge, MA, 1978.
[42] B. Conein, M. De Fornel, and L. Quere, *Les formes de la conversation*, vol. Vol. 1. Paris: CNET, 1990.
[43] A. Trognon, Fonctions de la conversation [Functions of conversation], in *Le dialogue [Dialog]*, G. Maurand, Ed. Albi: L'Union, 1990.
[44] D. De Kerckhove and C. J. Lumsden, The alphabet and the brain. New York: Springer Verlag, 1988.
[45] R. Ghiglione and A. Trognon, *Où va la pragmatique*. Grenoble: PUG, 1993.
[46] F. Varela, *Autonomie et connassaince*. Paris: Seuil, 1989.
[47] C. E. Shannon and W. Weaver, *The mathematical theory of communication*. Urbana: University of Illinois Press, 1949.
[48] D. G. Tatar, G. Foster, and D. G. Bobrow, Design for conversation: Lessons from Cognoter, *International Journal of Man-Machine Studies* 34 (1991) 185-209.
[49] S. Dohény-Farina, *Rhetoric, innovation, technology: case studies of technical communication in technology transfers*. Cambridge, MA: MIT Press, 1991.
[50] H. H. Clark and E. F. Schaefer, Contributing to discourse, *Cognitive Science* 13 (1989) 259-294.
[51] P. Charaudeau, *Langage et discours*. Paris: Hachette, 1983.
[52] J. Potter and M. Wetherell, *Discourse and social psychology*. London: Sage, 1987.
[53] F. Jacques, *L'espace logique de l'interlocution*. Paris: PUF, 1985.
[54] F. Jacques, La réciprocité interpersonnelle, *Connexions* 47 (1986) 110-136.
[55] G. Stasser, Pooling of unshared information during group discussion, in *Group processes and productivity*, S. Worchell, W. Wood, and J. A. Simpson, Eds. Newbury Park, CA: Sage, 1992, pp. 48-67.
[56] A. Dix, J. Finlay, G. Abowd, and R. Beale, *Human-computer interaction*. New York: Prentice Hall, 1993.
[57] M. Lea, Rationalist assumptions in cross media comparisons of computer mediated communication, *Behavior and Information Technology* 10 (1991) 153-172.
[58] R. R. Rice, Media appropriateness - Using social presence theory to compare raditional and new organizationa media, *Human Communication Research* 19 (1993) 451-458.

[59]   J. Short, E. Williams, and B. Christie, *The social psychology of telecommunications*. London: Wiley, 1976.

[60]   R. L. Daft and R. H. Lengel, Organisational information requirements, media richness and structural design, *Management Science* 32 (1986) 554-571.

[61]   R. R. Rice, Contexts of research on organizational computer-mediated communication: A recursive review., in *Context of computer-mediated communication*, M. Lea, Ed. Hemel Hempstead: Harvester-Wheatsheaf, 1992, pp. 113-143.

[62]   J. E. Newhagen, Why communication researchers should study the Internet: A dialogue., *Journal of Communication* 46 (1996) 4-13.

[63]   C. Goodwin and J. Heritage, Conversation analysis, *Annual Review of Anthropology* 19 (1990) 283-307.

[64]   S. E. Brennan, Conversation with and through computers, *User modelling and user-adapted interaction* 1 (1991) 67-86.

[65]   P. Curtis, Mudding: Social phenomena in text-based virtual realities, in *Culture of the Internet*, K. Sara, Ed.: Lawrence Erlbaum Associates, 1997, pp. 121-142.

[66]   E. Rocco and M. Warglien, La comunicazione mediata da computer e l'emergere dell'opportunismo elettronico [The growth of electronic opportunism in computer-mediated communication], *Sistemi Intelligenti* 7 (1995) 393-420.

[67]   J. J. Gibson, *The ecological approach to visual perception*. Hillsdale, NJ: Erlbaum, 1979.

[68]   P. Zahoric and R. L. Jenison, Presence as being-in-the-world, *Presence, Teleoperators, and Virtual Environments* 7 (1998) 78-89.

[69]   G. Mantovani and G. Riva, "Real" presence: How different ontologies generate different criteria for presence, telepresence, and virtual presence, *Presence, Teleoperators, and Virtual Environments* 8 (1999) 538-548.

[70]   G. Riva and G. Mantovani, The need for a socio-cultural perspective in the implementation of virtual environments, *Virtual Reality* (2000) 32-38.

[71]   J. Zhang and D. A. Norman, Representations in distributed cognitive task, *Cognitive Science* (1994) 87-122.

[72]   L. Suchman, *Plans and situated action*. Cambridge, UK: Cambridge University Press, 1987.

[73]   F. Flores, M. Graves, B. Hartfield, and T. Winograd, Computer systems and the design of organizationale interaction, *ACM Transaction on Office Information Systems* 6 (1988) 153-172.

[74]   G. Bateson, *Steps to an ecology of mind*. London: Paladin, 1973.

[75]   B. Nardi, Context and consciousness: Activity theory and Human-Computer Interaction. Cambridge, MA: MIT Press, 1996.

[76]   K. J. Gergen, *Realities and relationships: Soundings in social contruction*. Cambridge, MA: Harvard University Press, 1994.

[77]   G. Mantovani and A. Spagnolli, Imagination and culture: What is it like being in the cyberspace?, *Mind, Culture, & Activity* 7 (2000) 217-226.

[78]   M. Cole, *Cultural psychology: A once and future discipline*. Cambridge, MA: Harvard University Press, 1996.

[79]   M. Cole and J. Engestrom, A cultural-historical approach to distributed cognition, in *Distributed cognitions*, G. Salomon, Ed. Cambridge: Cambridge University Press, 1993, pp. 1-46.

[80]   J. G. March, How decision happen in organizations, *Human-Computer Interaction* 6 (1991) 95-117.

Towards CyberPsychology
G. Riva and C. Galimberti (Eds.)
IOS Press, 2001

2   Complementary Explorative Multilevel Data Analysis – CEMDA: A Socio-Cognitive Model of Data Analysis for Internet Research

Giuseppe RIVA, Carlo GALIMBERTI

Abstract. The Internet can be considered a strategic research site in which to study fundamental social and psychological processes. In fact, online communication systems structure interaction in new ways with dramatic effect on the types of social organizations that emerge from people using them.

Many methods that have been traditionally, and successfully, used in communication research are now being used to study the Internet. Other methods come from anthropology, cultural studies, linguistic, psychology and sociology. How is it possible to choose from and/or integrate all these different approaches?

Starting from a general three-level model of interpersonal interaction in the Web, this chapter tries to define a model of data analysis (Complementary Explorative Multilevel Data Analysis - CEMDA) suited to the constraints of Internet research. Main characteristics of the model are: its roots in the distributed cognition perspective; the focus on different frames and objects for each considered unit of research; the mixed use of quantitative and qualitative tools; the final integration of results in a general framework.

Contents

2.1   Introduction

The Internet can be considered a strategic research site in which to study fundamental social and psychological processes. In fact, online communication systems structure interaction in new ways with dramatic effect on the types of social organizations that emerge from people using them [1]. As recently noted by Jones [2], "The Internet is not only a technology but an engine of social change, one that has modified work habits, educations, social relations generally, and, maybe most important, our hopes and dreams. .... The Internet is a social space, a milieu, made up of and made possible by communication" (p. 2).

As underlined by Mantovani and Spagnolli [3], this can be seen as a general effect of the introduction of new artifacts that disrupt preexisting routines and interactions. In fact, new computer artifacts alter not only the social fabric of communities, but also the kind of relations that tools once had with human minds. These authors also suggest [3] that making sense of new communication environments means "making them part of the sociocultural network that maintains communities and reconfiguring in imaginative ways the existing sociocultural networks" (p. 217).

To describe this new sociocultural network that is the result of communication in the electronic environment researchers and writers are using the term "cyberspace" [4, 5]. In this sense, a key goal for psychology is doing more thinking and theorizing about how to get people to make better connections between the cyberspace and the rest of their lives [6]. However, studying the Internet is not a simple task.

First, the Internet is a medium which can be experienced in many different ways [7]. Though a computer and keyboard are usually the mediator of our Internet experience, there are different ways in which the users can explore the Internet, present themselves and communicate using it.

Second, the Internet is a social and cognitive space [5]. The handling of information is linked to the activation of psychosocial relationships in which cognitions are elaborated. As recently noted by Garton and colleagues [8], "when a computer network connects people or organizations, it is a social network. Just as a computer network is a set of machines connected by a set of cables, a social network is a set of people (or organizations or other social entities) connected by a set of social relations, such as friendship, co-working, or information exchange" (p. 75). Within this network we create relationships but also elaborate cognition. As underlined by Trognon [9], "far from being circumscribed by experimental laboratory settings, cognitive activities are routine daily activities. In other words, it is in everyday life, and in conversational interaction especially, that we put our cognitive skills to practical use" (p.117).

Third, the Internet experience is always situated in a specific context, even when we are chatting alone in a room. In this sense interaction can only be fully understood through detailed analysis of the social context in which it happens [10]: "... at this point we should no longer see people simply as 'users' of given systems, but as social 'actors'. In other words, whether expert computer users or not, people act independently and have their own reasons for what they do, and it is computers and systems that have to adapt to people, not vice versa" (p. 63).

These points clearly underline the situated nature of the Internet experience. More in detail, we can define it as a process by which a group of social actors in a given situation negotiate the meaning of the various situations which arise between them within an electronic environment.

How can we study this complex process? Many methods that have been traditionally, and successfully, used in communication research are now being used to study the Internet. Other methods come from anthropology, cultural studies, linguistic, psychology and sociology.

For instance, McKenna & Bargh [11] suggest that research on the social psychology of the Internet should be organized around three different time phases (before, during, and after extensive social interactions and group participation) and two distinct types of motivations that drive Internet social behavior (self-related and socially related).

According to Tuten & Bosnjak [12] the relationship between personality and Web usage can be studied Using the Five-Factor Model of Personality and Need for Cognition.

Using a sociolinguistic approach, in which social network relations are recognized as the principal vehicle of language change, Paolillo [13] analyzed logfiles of Internet Relay Chat interaction to investigate if and how online interaction have a long-term effect on the evolution of language.

How is it possible to choose from and/or integrate all these different approaches? This is the main goal of this paper. Starting from a general three-level model of interpersonal interaction in the Web, the paper will try to define a complementary model of data analysis suited to the Internet research. Main characteristics of the model are:

- A different focus (general frame and objects included in it) for each of the level considered;
- The mixed use of quantitative and qualitative tools;
- The final integration of results in a general framework.

2.2   Units of analysis for Internet research

The first step in our quest for a new method is to more precisely define what levels/features of the negotiation process need an examination. It's important to note that the definition of the units of analysis doesn't imply that only these units can be profitably used to define a research setting, in isolation of other factors. Indeed, as I noted above, an Internet research study will involve a wide range of considerations, such as social setting and context, user characteristics, or the purpose of the negotiation. But by defining the units of analysis, a researcher can clearly identify what types of processes and settings are under study.

In the previous paragraph, we considered Internet users as social actors with their own aims and autonomy in situations. Particularly the Internet users adapt themselves to the specific situation to achieve their aims. In this sense, social context may regarded as the symbolic system of a given culture which is continually being altered by practical human intervention. Thus:

- *context is conceptual as well as physical:* actors perceive situations using cultural models, and act accordingly in cultural ways;
- *context is unstable:* cultural models are constantly changed by subjects' actions and choices.
- *social context is a prerequisite of communication:* "a shared symbolic order in which action becomes meaningful, and so generates meaning" [10], p.106.

This idea poses serious problems, however [14]. If social actors actively respond to their environment and end up changing it, how can context ever be analysed properly? Mantovani [10, 15] meets the difficulty with a three-level (domain) model of social context which links *the situation* and *social norms* to the *use of computer technology*. The first level is social context in general, the second, ordinary situations of everyday life, and the third, local interaction with the artifact.

The links among the three levels can be studied in either direction, starting from use of computers or from social context. Thus, the use of computers may be regarded as part of everyday life, which is in turn part of the broader social context. By interacting with each other, the physical environment and the social context, subjects activate a *spiral* of actor-environment exchanges. The First-level person-computer interaction leads to interaction in everyday situations, and thence to cultural changes.

Working in the opposite direction, social context supplies the elements needed to interpret situations correctly, and situations generate the aims which determine a local interaction with the other actors via computer.

Mantovani's model doesn't directly address the mediated communication between different actors. However, it can be easily adapted to arrange all the aspects of the Internet experience. We propose here a revised three-level model - composed by *context, situation* and *interaction* - that mutually define the social context in which the Internet experience is situated (see Figure 2.1). These three levels can be considered the basic units of analysis for Internet research.

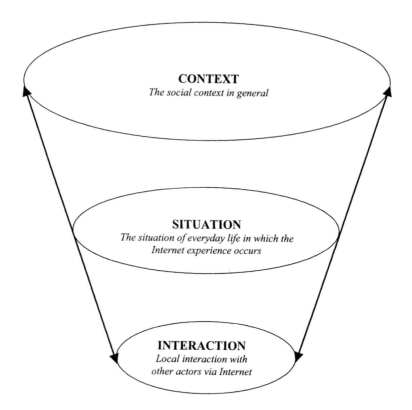

Figure 2.1 A three-level model of the Internet experience

The first level remains social context in general (the context); the second, is the situation of everyday life (the situation) in which the Internet experience happens; and the third, the local interaction with the other actors via Internet (the interaction). This interaction is direct during computer mediated communication (actors are directly experienced), and indirect in other Internet experiences such as browsing a Web site. However, also during Internet surfing, the artifacts experienced reflect the characteristics and goals of the actors who created them.

2.3 Complementary Explorative Multilevel Data Analysis

Identifying the units of analysis is just the first step in our quest for a method. The next one is to define how to study them. At this point, when the methodology needs to be chosen, the qualitative versus quantitative debate begins. As noted by Sudweeks and Simoff [16], "Quantitative and qualitative methods are quite distinct in the emphasis they place on each.

In quantitative analyses, argumentation is based on a representation of the phenomenon as a finite set of variables. There, we seek systematic statistical or other functional relations between these variables. In qualitative analyses, argumentation is based on a description of the research objects or observation units instead of on approximation of a limited number of variables. In other words, in qualitative analyses, references to excerpts or cases in the data are used as clues." (p. 39).

To overcome this opposition many attempts at integrating the two methods appeared over the past two decades. The final aim is to define a combination of research methods so that the weakness of any single method - qualitative or quantitative - is balanced by the strengths of other methods. In reality, however, the qualitative and quantitative analyses are usually distinct, mutually exclusive components of the research. A possible sample of this approach is reported by Sudweeks and Simoff [16]: "One component is unstructured textual data of a phenomenon being investigated (e.g., transcripts of interviews or verbal reports from protocol studies), analyzed with an interpretative or hermeneutic method. The other component is numerical data of the same phenomenon (e.g., from a content analysis or a survey questionnaire), analyzed with some statistical procedure. The result is an integrated view that narrowly focuses on a particular social phenomenon" (p. 40).

A further improvement over this integrated approach is the appearance of the Complementary Explorative Data Analysis (CEDA) framework [16]. CEDA incorporates complementary use of both methods, depending on the particular research stage or the initial assumptions that need to be taken into consideration. More in detail, the first stage is devoted to the identification of domain specifics, the applicable research methods and the possible research aims. Once the scope is specified, CEDA follows the following processes: after the data mining and the qualitative reasoning, qualitative and quantitative methods are used to collect data; the results obtained are tuned using a qualitative refinement.

Note that the data collected in any of the research domains are a combination of quantitative measurements and qualitative observations. Specifically, CEDA uses quantitative methods to extract reliable patterns, whereas qualitative methods are incorporated to ensure capturing of the essence of phenomena. In this approach the use of different data sets in the same research is allowed.

In this paper we propose a Complementary Explorative Multilevel Data Analysis (CEMDA) framework that applies the CEDA approach to the three-level model used for the analysis of the Internet experience. CEMDA has the potential to conduct parallel and interconnected research on the same domain. In particular, CEMDA allows the researcher to focus on the different levels of the Internet experience. As we have seen before, the proposed model for the analysis of the Internet experience is structured on three different levels:

- *the context*: social context in general;
- *the situation*: ordinary situations of everyday life in which the Internet experience occurs;
- *the interaction*: local interaction with the other actors using a technological artifact (Internet).

How can CEMDA approach each of them? The first step is the definition of domain specifics. Particularly, for each of the three levels the researcher has to identify the general frame of analysis and the objects included in it (see Figure 2.2). Let's use an example to explain this point.

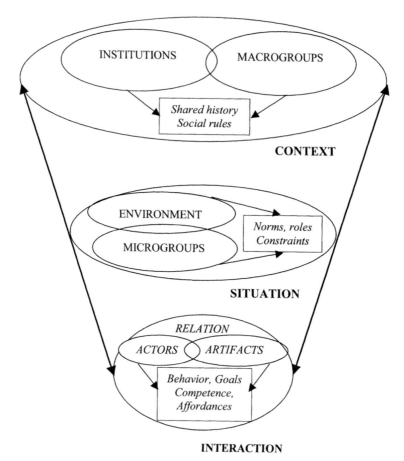

Figure 2.2 Frames and objects in the three-level model

A researcher is interested in studying how the doctors in different hospitals use e-mail for preparing and sharing clinical diagnoses. The starting point of the analysis will be the identification of the different frames and objects of analysis. If we start from the context, the frames analyzed are both the institutions that shape the social context - in this case the hospital - and the macrogroups which interact in them: the different departments/institutes.

Specifically, the objects included are the history of the hospitals - their backgrounds, how their collaboration started, etc. - and the social rules structuring the general interaction processes: how departments decide, when, how it is possible to obtain resources, etc.

The second level of analysis is the situation in which the Internet experience is located. In the example presented the frame includes all the doctors (microgroup) directly involved in the definition of the clinical diagnosis and the social/physical environment in which the process happens. Objects analyzed by the researcher are the roles within the microgroup -

how is structured the diagnosis process, the roles of the different actors, etc. - and more in particular the norms that regulate the interpersonal interaction in it: who starts the diagnosis process, who takes the final decision, etc.

Also, relevant objects are the environmental constraints (social and physical) that can limit the Internet experience. We can find communities of practices or the availability of the tools (e.g., I can use them only when the head of the department is present), on the social side. Bandwidth or a limited connection time is typical constraints on the physical side.

The final level of analysis is the interaction. The general frame of the analysis is the relation process. Specifically, how the actors interact between them using the artifacts. The first object explored by the researchers is the reciprocal goals of the actors - integrating in a coherent diagnosis the information received, doing it in the less possible time, etc. After understanding them, the analysis moves on the affordances perceived in the situation and the availability of the competencies needed to exploit them: e.g., opening the image it is possible to identify possible disturbances; but is the doctor able to open the images received? Final objects are all the behaviors, including the communicative ones, produced by the actors in their interaction with the artifacts: switching on the computer, opening the e-mail software, the production of text, etc.

2.4   Applying CEMDA to Internet research: choosing and mixing the methods

2.4.1   The choice of the overall approach to the research

For each of the frames and objects identified, the researcher has to identify the more suitable methods for the analysis [16]. What is the starting point?

The first step is the choice of the overall approach to the research. Most researches are based on two approaches: studies aimed at discovering causal relationship, and descriptive studies that use collected data to describe a phenomenon [17].

Table 2.1 The possible approaches to the research

Experimental approach
- can truly test hypotheses concerning cause-and-effect relationships;
- requires *randomized* groups (not required in quasi-experiments);
- requires the control of many variables and the possibility of manipulating at least one of them (independent variable/s);
- requires the control of *internal validity* (the changes observed in the dependent variable are due to the effect of the independent variable) and *external validity* (the extent to which findings in one study can be applied to a different context) by means of *research designs* (i.e. pretest-posttest control group design).
- requires a specific statistic method: t-test, ANOVA, MANOVA, non-parametric tests.

Causal Comparative approach
- the results cannot be used as a proof of a cause-and-effect relationship;
- requires at least two different groups (defined group and comparison group);
- requires a clear basis for categorization (i.e. gender, or age);
- requires a specific statistic method: t-test, ANOVA, MANOVA, non-parametric tests.

Correlational approach
- the results cannot be used as a proof of a cause-and-effect relationship;
- several variables can be easily included in one study;
- requires the identification of *exploratory/predictor* variables and *outcome/criterion* variables;
- requires a specific statistic method: simple correlation, regression analysis, multiple regression analysis, discriminant function analysis, canonical correlation, path analysis, and factor analysis.

In general causal studies require experimental (subjects randomly assigned to the groups) or quasi-experimental (subjects are not randomly assigned to the groups) designs in which the researcher can manipulate the independent variable/s (see Table 2.1). However, given the peculiar characteristics of the Internet, in many situations this is impossible for the researcher. In these settings the researcher can use a causal comparative or a correlational approach (see Table 2.1).

There is a significant difference between these two approaches. If correlational approach is used when the goal of the researcher is to investigate the magnitude of the relationship between two or more variables (i.e the dimension of a banner and the click-through rate), the causal comparative approach allows the comparison of individuals/groups who differ on a specific variable (i.e. how genders differ in the click-through rate). However, given their characteristics neither the correlational nor the causal comparative results can be used as a proof of a cause-and-effect relationship.

2.4.2   The choice between quantitative and qualitative methods

The second step is the choice between quantitative and qualitative methods: the researcher can use just one or both of them. The general guideline for this choice is the final goal of the analysis. Generally, qualitative methods are used to understand an observed phenomenon, while quantitative methods aim at explaining it.

Another important point to discriminate between the two approaches is the starting point of the analysis. Qualitative analysis usually begins with a theory formulated as a set of hypotheses, and the purpose of a study is to find support for or to disprove the theory. Quantitative research is instead used to provide the ability to predict, and control examined concepts. To reach this goal, the researcher needs to start from the design of an experiment. This calls for the knowledge of the form, type, and range of the content of the data before the start of the analysis.

A third point to identify the right method is the role played by the researcher. In qualitative analysis the role of the researcher is participatory and personal. This is usually needed when the final goal of the study is to improve or tune a specific Internet experience - i.e. improve the characteristics of a Web site. On the opposite, quantitative methods require that the researcher acts just as an observer with a limited control of the setting. If in a passive experiment, the researcher just records the observations, in an active experiment the researcher may need to set up and control some of the independent variables.

As noted by Sudweeks and Simoff [16], the issue which these approaches differ most is the priority placed on the role of interpretation. In every research some form of interpretation is required. But, whereas quantitative research calls for the suspension of interpretation during the experiment, qualitative research actively interprets phenomena during the observation phase.

When does the researcher mix quantitative and qualitative methods? Mixed methods are usually found in two situations:

-   lack of a clear starting point for the analysis: no theory to confirm or experiment to design. In this situation, typical of explorative analysis, the merging of methods can offer to the researcher a broader data set;
-   multi-step analyses: after testing a hypothesis using qualitative methods, the researcher tries to control examined objects in an experimental settings. This approach is usually used when the final goal of the researcher is to modify/improve the original Internet experience.

After identifying the right approach, the next step is the definition of the methods to be used. In fact, each approach has to be targeted to the level considered. In Table 2.2 specific qualitative and quantitative methods are reported for the different levels: context, situation and interaction. A more detailed description of the methods reported can be found in the next paragraphs.

Table 2.2 Units of analysis and methods used within the Complementary Explorative Multilevel Data Analysis (CEMDA) Framework

Levels	Frames	Objects	Quantitative analysis	Qualitative analysis
Context	Institutions, Macrogroups	Shared history, social rules	Survey questionnaires	Social network analysis, Interviews, Document and records review
Situation	Microgroups, Social and physical environment	Norms, Roles, Environmental constraints, Practices	Survey questionnaires	Social network analysis, Interviews, Focus groups, Document and records review
Interaction	Relations, Actors, Artifacts	Goals, Competence, Affordances, Behaviors (including the communicative ones)	Individual questionnaires, Quantitative interaction analysis (duration and structure, computer monitoring, eye tracking, etc.)	Qualitative interaction analysis (Speech acts analysis, discourse analysis, analysis of conversations, etc.) Participant observation, Interviews, Diaries

2.4.2.1 Survey and questionnaires

A typical quantitative tool used in CEMDA is the questionnaire. Usually the researcher has three different possibilities [17]:

- to use a measurement instrument that is commercially available or that has been developed by other researchers;
- to adapt an existing instrument;
- create a new one to meet the needs of the proposed research.

Given the limited number of questionnaires targeted to the Internet experience, it is possible that the researcher will be forced to develop his/her own data collection instrument. The steps outlined here give a rough guide to this complex process [18].

The first step is the *definition the objective of the instrument*. To reach this goal the researcher has to answer to these general questions: what is the specific purpose of the proposed measurement instrument? What information do you want on what attribute?

After the identification of the overall goal of the instrument the next step is the *review of existing measures*. The previous work conducted by other researchers can help in finding methods for formatting and administering the measure as well as for determining its reliability and validity.

The third step is the *identification of the possible respondents*. The choice of the possible respondents allows the definition of key factors related to the administration of the instrument: the amount of time required to complete it, reading level, format for items, response option formats, and test setting. Format options usually include true-false, matching, multiple-choice, sentence completion, ranking items, Likert-type scales (1:

strongly agree; 2: moderately agree; 3: neutral; 4: moderately disagree; 5: strongly disagree), and open-ended, essay-type questions [17].

The fourth step is the *definition of an appropriate title for the questionnaire*. This is the first thing that the respondent will read, so it has to be motivating and conceptually consistent with the content of the instrument. Following the title, is usually included a short, introductory paragraph explaining the purpose of the instrument and its intended use.

The fifth step is the *definition of pool of possible items*. Usually some items are adopted or adapted from similar questionnaires. Others might be developed using experts or program staff responsible for the program being studied.

After the identification of the items the next step is the *pilot test of the questionnaire*. To develop a good instrument, different pilot tests are required. At first, it is recommended that the developer ask other professionals expert in the field to review the prototype. After a first revision, the prototype can be tried out on a small sample of the intended respondents. Typically, this is done by the researcher under expected administration procedures to get a general idea of the quality of the information as well as any problems in administration and scoring. The final pilot test should be conducted with a larger sample. The goal of this test is to enable the researcher to gather reliability and validity information.

The last step is the *final revision of the instrument using an item analysis*. The answers to each item should be reviewed to verify if a pattern suggests ambiguity or bias in the item.

2.4.2.2   Observation

Observation is a qualitative method occurring in naturalistic settings without the use of predetermined categories of measurement or response [19]. Adler and Adler [19] distinguish between observation and participant observation: in participant observation the researcher usually   interacts with the participants while collecting data from them. According to Spradley [20] it is possible to identifies five levels of participation:

- *Non-participation*: The lowest level of involvement is usually obtained by watching a through a unidirectional mirror or by examining a videotape.
- *Passive participation*: The researcher is present but does not interact with the participants.
- *Moderate participation*: The researcher attempts to balance the insider and outsider roles by observing and by participating in some but not all of the activities.
- *Active participation*: The researcher does what the others do, generally, but does not try to blend in completely.
- *Complete participation*: The researcher becomes a natural participant, which has the disadvantage of trying to collect data and maintain a questioning and reflective stance.

What has to be observed during a session? According to Patton [21], key features are:

- *the physical environment*: the amount of space available, how the space is used, the nature of the lighting, how people are organized in the space, and the interpretive reactions of participants to the physical setting.
- *the social environment*: the focus is the way in which participants organize themselves into groups and subgroups. In particular have to be examined the patterns of interaction, frequency of interaction, direction of communication and decision-making patterns.
- *nonverbal communication:* dress, expression of affection, physical spacing, and arrangements are typical nonverbal cues. Other important cues are the patterns established for the participants to get the attention of or approach another person.

Finally, also fidgeting, moving about, or trying to get comfortable can provide information about attention to and concentration on group processes.
- *observing what does not happen*: If the session has a specific goal suggesting that certain things are expected to happen, it is appropriate for the observer to note what things did not happen.

2.4.2.3 Interview

As we have just seen, observation allows collection of data through the researcher's direct contact with the setting of the research. However, it is not always possible to have intimate, repeated, and prolonged involvement in the setting of the research [22]. To solve this problem, usually researchers plan interviews with key subjects.

Interviews can be structured or unstructured, group or individual. Typically, interviews in a qualitative study are done with an unstructured or minimally structured format. Interviewing can be conducted as a part of participant observation or even as a casual conversation. As the study evolves, interviewing can become more structured and formal.

It is also possible to use questionnaires in interviewing. As noted by McCracken [22] "The questionnaire has several functions. Its first responsibility is to ensure that the investigator covers all the terrain in the same order for each respondent. .... The second function is the care and scheduling of the prompts necessary to manufacture distance .... The third function of the questionnaire is that it establishes channels for the direction and scope of discourse. .... The fourth function of the questionnaire is that it allows the investigator to give all his or her attention to the informant's testimony" (pp. 24-25).

2.4.2.4 Focus group

Focus groups, can be seen as group interviews that rely, not on a question-and-answer format of interview but on the interaction within the group [17]. The key role of the interaction between participants is designed to elicit more of the participants' points of view. In fact, the main advantage of focus group research is the additional insight gained from the interaction of ideas among the group participants.

The use of focus groups is appropriate when the researcher is interested in how individuals form a schema or perspective of a problem. In this sense the focus group can be considered a "guided" discussion, in which the facilitator usually has a list of five to seven questions to ask during a 1.5- to 2-hour session. The questions are used in a semi-structured way to ensure coverage of important issues allowing for flexibility in responding to group-initiated concerns.

A key variable for the researcher is the number of groups to be included in the study. According to Morgan [23] only three or four groups are necessary when the research is highly structured and exploratory. However, he recommends the use of six to eight groups if the goal is a detailed content analysis with relatively unstructured groups.

2.4.2.5 On-line focus group

Usually focus groups occur in a face-to-face setting. However, the latest and most interesting forms of synchronous computer mediated communication – *shared hypermedia* – now allow the set up of web-based focus groups.

Shared Hypermedia are new Internet tools attaching computer mediated communication to Web browsing (see Table 2.3 for a list of available shared hypermedia). In shared hypermedia, different users, who are simultaneously browsing the same Web site, can communicate with each other and share files or web addresses.

Table 2.3 Shared hypermedia tools

Tool	Developer	Website
Cahoots	Cahoots	http://www.cahoots.com
Instant Rendezvous	Multimate	http://www.multimate.net
Odigo	NovaWiz	http://www.odigo.com
ICQSurf	ICQ	http://www.icq.com/icqsurf

Using a simple interface, usually resembling a little remote control, shared hypermedia users can get a constantly updated list of all the other online users who are visiting the same Web site. All they have to do is click on any person icon, open a message window, and start the communication.

Usually a shared hypermedia lets the user conduct group and private chats, exchange information or files, and share the same web pages (for a more detailed characteristics of a typical shared hypermedia see Table 2.4).

Table 2.4 Features of shared hypermedia tools

One-on-one or multi-user chat (text, audio and video)	*Users can make calls to multiple people up to 100/1000 users. In multi-user chat one ore more moderators can control group participation by sharing the microphone. It is also possible to broadcast a radio-style Internet talk show where the host maintains control and invites listeners to participate to the event.*
Email (text and voice)	*User can send text and voice messages to users who are not online.*
Web tour	*Users can create their own Web Tour and escort other users through a list favourite web sites.*
Search engine	*Users can find other users with a specific sex, age and/or similar interests.*
Transfer of files	*Users can upload and download from other users documents and files.*

On any Web site, shared hypermedia users can see a list of other users and talk with them on group and private levels. Shared hypermedia further enhances the user experience by consolidating different form of computer mediated communication (e-mail, Internet Relay Chat, etc.) into one fully integrated interface. Many shared hypermedia also have a search engine that can be used to find users with a specific age and/or similar interests. In this way it is really easy to set up a group with a common interest, like medical oriented web sites.

The most advanced shared hypermedia (i.e., Cahoots) have an option - the *web tour* - very interesting for its possible use in Internet oriented focus groups. During a web tour a facilitator can guide the browsing of a small group of users (usually up to 20), who can discuss and interact between them in real time.

2.4.2.6   Documents and record review

Usually every organization has huge amounts of documents and records that describe its history and current status. In general, it is possible to define a *record* any output of the organization prepared for official reasons (i.e.: bank statements, file records, etc.). A document is any output of the organization prepared for personal reasons (i.e.: letters, memos, etc.). Documents and records include not only the typical paper products, such as memos, reports, and plans, but also computer files, tapes (audio and video), and other artifacts [24].

The Internet researcher must analyse these documents and records to get the necessary background of the general context and insights into the dynamics of everyday functioning.

In particular the researcher has to be sensitive to the types of records and documents that might be associated with a particular context or situation. Must be noted that the use of these materials has to be tempered with an understanding of the time, context, and intended use for which the materials were created. In many situations it may not be possible to interact with the people who produced the materials. The researcher then faces the challenge of how to interpret the meaning of such materials.

2.4.2.7 Social network analysis

Social network analysis focuses on the relations among actors, and not individual actors and their attributes [25]. This means that the subjects are usually not sampled independently, as in many other kinds of studies (most typically, questionnaires). In particular, network analysts study the patterning of the social connections that link sets of actors. For the most part they seek to uncover either or both of two kinds of patterns. They often look for *social groups* -- collections of actors who are closely linked to one another. Or, alternatively, they look for *social positions* -- sets of actors who are linked into the total social system in similar ways [26].

So, if the nodes or actors included in non-network studies tend to be the result of independent probability sampling, network studies are much more likely to include all of the actors who occur within some boundary. Suppose we are studying friendship ties developed in a chat, for example. John has been selected to be in our sample. When we ask him, John identifies three friends he knew in the chat. Network analysis requires to track down each of those three friends and ask them about their friendship ties, as well. The three friends are in the sample because John is (and vice-versa), so the "sample elements" are no longer "independent." In this sense, within social network analysis, a group is an empirically discovered structure: it emerges by the pattern of relations among members of a population [8].

Given a set of actors, there are several strategies for deciding how to go about collecting measurements on the relations among them [25]. The broadest but more demanding approaches are "full network" methods. Full network methods require that the researcher collects information about each actor's ties with all other actors. In essence, this approach is taking a census of ties in a population of actors -- rather than a sample.

At the other end of the spectrum there are "ego-centric networks". In this approach the researcher begins with a selection of focal nodes (egos), and identify the nodes to which they are connected. Then, he determines which of the nodes identified in the first stage are connected to one another.

Information about the ties is usually gathered by a combination of methods including questionnaires, interviews, diaries, observations and more recently through computer monitoring. People are also asked to identify the frequency of communication with others as well as the medium of interaction.

To analyze these data researchers usually used specific designed software: *Multinet, Negopy, Krackplot,* and *Gradap (see Table 2.5)*, with the combination of *UCINET* and *Krackplot* being the mostly widely used [8]. To use these applications, data often must be transformed into a matrix with rows and columns representing the units of analysis (people, events, groups or other entities that are related to one another).

Table 2.5 Software for Social Network Analysis

Tool	Developer	Website
Multinet	Vancouver Network Analysis Team	http://www.sfu.ca/~richards/Multinet/Pages/multinet.htm
KrackPlot	Analytic Technologies	http://www.contrib.andrew.cmu.edu/~krack/
Negopy	Vancouver Network Analysis Team	http://www.sfu.ca/~richards/Pages/negopy.htm
Gradap	ProGAMMA	http://www.gamma.rug.nl/files/p315.html
UCINET	Analytic Technologies	http://eclectic.ss.uci.edu/~lin/ucinet.html

2.5   Applying CEMDA to Internet research: the linking of results

This complementary analysis is based on the linking of the results obtained by each of its components. Specifically, the main advantage of CEMDA is the possibility of using the data collected on one of the level to tune/define the characteristics of the analysis in the other levels. How can this be done?

As underlined by Mantovani [10] the links among the three levels can be studied in either direction, starting from the mediated interaction between the actors or from the general social context. Usually, the researcher identifies the starting level according to the general aims and hypotheses of the study. For instance, if the goal of the research is to identify how to improve the diagnosis process using the Internet, the starting point can be the interaction between the actors during the actual diagnostic tasks.

On the opposite, if the researcher wants to explore the effect of the Internet-based diagnostic process on the organization of the hospital, the general social context could be the starting point.

However, in both cases, the main characteristic of CEMDA is to analyze a level without forgetting the possible influences of the remaining ones. In the first example the diagnosis process has to be considered as part of everyday life of the department considered, which is in turn part of the broader social context of the hospital. More in detail, this can be done using the following approach (see Table 2.6 for a detailed breakdown):

- definition of the starting level. For example, the interaction between the actors during the actual diagnostic tasks.
- identification of the links between the starting level and the previous or next one. In particular, *if* and *how* a specific frame in the starting level is connected to the objects of the next one (e.g., the relation between the actors is related to the constraints of the environment).
- when a direct link is identified, the researcher has to understand its *direction* (cause and effect). For instance at the *situation* level, the physical constraints of the environment (e.g., the location of the networked computer) may influence the characteristics of the relation between the actors (e.g., too much time is needed to reach the computer, so the interaction time is limited) in the *interaction* level.
- if a frame is causally influenced by an object found in a different level, the data coming from the other level will be used in the definition of methods (e.g., use of survey and interviews to explore the constraints of the environment) and in the final discussion (e.g., actual interaction time is limited, but this can be explained by the wrong location of the networked computer).
- the final results may lead to revision of the identified domain (e.g, we can decide to investigate why the networked computer is in the actual location) and changes in the combination of analysis methods. Specifically, the results can be used to produce

new hypotheses (e.g., if we move the computer to a better position, the interaction time will be longer) or to define new experiments (e.g., we can measure interaction time using computers in different positions).

Table 2.6 Stages of Complementary Explorative Multilevel Data Analysis

- Scope of research
- Levels identification
- Definition of a starting level
- Definition of frames and objects (starting level)
- Definition of frames and objects (other levels)
- Identifications of links between the starting level and other levels
- Analysis of the links (direction)
- Definition of hypotheses or experiments (starting level and causally connected levels)
- Definition of methods (starting level and causally connected levels)
- Data Collection and Selection of the Data Sets (starting level and causally connected levels)
- Eventual integration of quantitative and qualitative results (starting level and causally connected levels)
- Integration of data from different levels
- Interpretation and presentation
- Eventual production of new hypotheses or formulation of a new experiments

2.6   Conclusions

As we have seen in the Introduction, studying the Internet is not a simple task. First, the Internet is a medium which can be experienced in many different ways. Second, the Internet is a social and cognitive space. Third, the Internet experience is always situated in a specific context, even when we are chatting alone in a room. In this sense it can only be fully understood through detailed analysis of the social context in which it happens. These points clearly underlined the situated nature of the Internet experience, defined as a process by which a group of social actors in a given situation negotiate the meaning of the various situations which arise between them within an electronic environment.

In this paper we tried to address a very simple problem: how can we study this process? The starting point in our quest for a method was the identification of the units of analysis. Using a three-level model of the Internet experience we identified three macro units (levels): the social context (the context); the situation of everyday life (the situation) in which the Internet experience happens; and the local interaction with the other actors via Internet (the interaction).

To explore these units we proposed a new approach, the Complementary Explorative Multilevel Data Analysis (CEMDA) framework, allowing the conduction of parallel and interconnected research on the same domain. This complementary analysis is based on the linking of the results obtained by each of its components.

As with all research methods, however, the CEMDA framework is only a tool for simplifying and understanding rather complex data, and are not a substitute for insight, clear thinking, and intimate knowledge of the subject matter. Properly used this approach will provide researchers interested in the area of with powerful and more efficient analytic tools for examining the characteristics of the Internet experience. Specifically, the main advantage of CEMDA is the possibility of using the data collected on one of the level to tune/define the characteristics of the analysis in the other levels.

2.7   Acknowledgments

A preliminary version of this chapter was originally published with the title "The mind over the Web: The quest for the definition of a method for Internet research" by the journal "CyberPsychology & Behavior", 4 (1), 7-16, 2001. Copyright Mary Ann Liebert, Inc., 2001.

The present work was supported by the Commission of the European Communities (CEC), in particular by the IST programme (Project VEPSY UPDATED, IST-2000-25323 - http://www.psicologia.net; http://www.vepsy.com).

2.8   References

[1]   P. Kollock and M. A. Smith, Communities in cyberspace, in *Communities in cyberspace*, M. A. Smith and P. Kollock, Eds. London: Routledge, 1999, pp. 3-25.
[2]   S. Jones, Studying the Net: Intricacies and issues, in *Doing Internet research: Critical issues and methods for examining the Net*, S. Jones, Ed. Thousand Oaks, CA: Sage Publications, Inc., 1999, pp. 1-27.
[3]   G. Mantovani and A. Spagnolli, Imagination and culture: What is it like being in the cyberspace?, *Mind, Culture, & Activity* 7 (2000) 217-226.
[4]   L. Strate, R. Jacobson, and S. B. Gibson, Communication and Cyberspace: Social interaction in an electronic environment. Cresskill, NY: Hampton Press, 1996.
[5]   S. Kiesler, Culture of the Internet. Mahwah, NJ, US: Lawrence Erlbaum Associates, Inc., Publishers, 1997, pp. xvi, 463.
[6]   S. Turkle, Parallel lives: Working on identity in virtual space, in *Constructing the self in a mediated world. Inquiries in social construction*, T. R. L. Debra Grodin, Ed.: Sage Publications, Inc, Thousand Oaks, CA, US, 1996, pp. 156-175.
[7]   P. Wallace, *The psychology of the Internet*. New York: Cambridge University Press, 1999.
[8]   L. Garton, C. Haythornthwaite, and B. Wellman, Studying on-line social networks, in *Doing Internet research: Critical issues and methods for examining the Net*, S. Jones, Ed. Thousand Oaks, CA: Sage Publications, Inc., 1999, pp. 75-105.
[9]   A. Trognon, Psicologia cognitiva e analisi delle conversazioni [Cognitive psychology and conversation analysis], in *La conversazione. Prospettive sull'interazione psicosociale [Conversation: perspectives in psycho-social interaction]*, C. Galimberti, Ed. Milan: Guerini e Associati, 1992, pp. 110-122.
[10]   G. Mantovani, *New communication environments: from everyday to virtual*. London: Taylor & Francis, 1996.
[11]   K. McKenna, Y.,A. and J. Bargh, A., Causes and consequences of social interaction on the Internet: A conceptual framework, *Media Psychology* 1 (1999) 249-269.
[12]   T. Tuten, L. and M. Bosnjak, Understanding differences in web usage: The role of need for cognition and the five factor model of personality, *Social Behavior & Personality* 29 (2001) 391-398.
[13]   J. Paolillo, The virtual speech community: Social network and language variation on IRC, *Journal of Computer-Mediated Communication* 4 (1999) online: www.ascusc.org/jcmc/vol4/issue4/paolillo.html.
[14]   G. Riva and C. Galimberti, Interbrain frame: interaction and cognition in computer-mediated communication, *CyberPsychology & Behavior* 1 (1998) 295-310.
[15]   G. Mantovani, Social context in HCI: A new framework for mental models, cooperation and communication, *Cognitive Science* 20 (1996) 237-296.
[16]   F. Sudweeks and S. J. Simoff, Complementary Explorative Data Analysis: The reconciliation of quantitative and qualitative principles, in *Doing Internet research: Critical issues and methods for examining the Net*, S. Jones, Ed. Thousand Oaks, CA: Sage Publications, Inc., 1999, pp. 29-56.
[17]   D. M. Mertens, *Research methods in education and psychology*. Thousand Oaks, CA: SAGE Publications, 1998.
[18]   R. F. DeVellis, *Scale development: Theory and applications*. Newbury Park, CA: Sage Publishing, 1991.
[19]   P. A. Adler and P. Adler, Observational techniques, in *Handbook of qualitative research*, N. K. Denzin and Y. S. Lincoln, Eds. Thousand Oaks, CA: Sage Publishing, 1994, pp. 377-392.
[20]   J. P. Spradley, *Participant observation*. New York: Holt, Rinehart & Winston, 1980.
[21]   M. Q. Patton, *Qualitative evaluation and research methods*. Newbury Park, CA: Sage Publishing, 1990.
[22]   G. McCracken, *The long interview*. Newbury Park, CA: Sage Publishing, 1988.

[23]   D. L. Morgan, *Focus group as qualitative research.* Newbury Park, CA: Sage Publishing, 1988.
[24]   Y. S. Lincoln and E. G. Guba, *Naturalistic inquiry.* Newbury Park, CA: Sage Publishing, 1985.
[25]   S. Wasserman and K. Faust, *Social Network Analysis: Methods and Applications.* Cambridge: Cambridge University Press, 1994.
[26]   L. C. Freeman, Visualizing Social Networks, *Journal of Social Structure* 1 (2000) online: http://www.heinz.cmu.edu/project/INSNA/joss/vsn.html.

SECTION II

CYBERPSYCHOLOGY IN PRACTICE: THE INTERNET

Whether you like it or not, cyberspace has become the new frontier in social relationships. People are making friends, colleagues, lovers, and enemies on the internet. The fervor with which many people have pursued this new social realm is matched by a backlash reaction from the skeptics. Relationships on the internet aren't really real, some people say - not like relationships in the real world. Socializing in cyberspace is just a cultural fad, a novelty, a phase that people go through. The critics say it can't compare to real relationships - and if some people prefer communicating with others via wires and circuits, there must be something wrong with them. They must be addicted. They must fear the challenging intimacy of real relationships.

Suler, 1999
(http://www.rider.edu/users/suler/psycyber/psycyber.html)

Towards CyberPsychology
G. Riva and C. Galimberti (Eds.)
IOS Press, 2001

3   Beyond the "Impact" Metaphor: The Mutual Shaping of Psychological Theory and Internet Development

Giuseppe MANTOVANI

Abstract. Studies aiming at identifying the social effects of the Internet usually assume that technology exerts a causal, unidirectional and deterministic action on individuals, groups, and organizations. This conception, embodied in the metaphor of the "impact" of technology on society, is rejected by research on Science, Technology, and Society (STS) and by cultural psychology, which see in the Internet an artifact that shapes social processes and at the same time is shaped by them. The Internet is constructed through its current use which is shaped by current psychological theories and - vice versa - the spread of the Internet creates new environments which call for development of new psychological theories of both cognition and communication. From a cognitive perspective the Internet is above all a huge reservoir of data for *information foraging*. From a social perspective it is an environment for the setting up of online societies, a space for *social gathering*. Lastly, the Internet is, within the cultural psychology perspective, a *new artifact*, a communication medium still being built. The cultural conception does not expect that the Internet may produce uniformed and generalized *effects* in the various social contexts, but rather it maintains that the Internet carries out its mediation function in differentiated ways, according to the interests of the communities using it, to the different ongoing situations, and to the different visions of the social function of the Web. Artifacts are embodied social projects: important political choices about the Internet may be embedded in apparently esoteric technical matters such as the design of search engines. At present the original vision of the Internet as a public space, a popular medium granting equal access to all people, is challenged by current practice which builds the Internet as a market in which top visibility is conquered by powerful individuals, groups and organizations.

Contents

3.1 The "impact" of the Internet: a misleading metaphor

Psychological research studies on the social *effects* of the Internet are very topical. This is quite understandable if we consider the diffusion rate of the Internet and the economic and cultural importance it has come to have in advanced societies. Unfortunately, research results are often discrepant and puzzling both to researchers and the public at large who would like to know whether the Internet is "good" or "bad" for them, and in what sense.

Result discrepancy is not in itself a bad thing: it may be due to the fact that different research studies highlight in turn different aspects of a change process which is multifaceted both from the technical and social perspective. If this were the case, we would now be witnessing a first, and necessarily tentative, mapping of the *effects* of the current technological innovation which would have to give way to a unitary view as the single pieces of the puzzle fall into place. Actually, the problem we are facing has originated from the fact that the research on the social effects of the Internet starts from a wrong premise, i.e. the assumption that technology is detached from the social reality that produces it and that it can generate social changes by itself.

The idea that "technology" changes "society" is advocated by computer firms' advertising initiatives, by several technical-scientific works, and by publications of well known scientists [1] supporting technological utopianism [2, 3]. In favor of this hypothesis – incorporated in the ubiquitous metaphor of the "impact" technologies have on social reality – are its seeming simplicity, the huge persuasion power of the political and economic forces that want to identify technological innovation with social progress *tout court*, and the fact that it "echoes the naive technological determinism which is a standard pattern of American discourse" [4]. Research on Science, Technology, and Society (STS) has shown the falseness of the assumption according to which technologies would be separated from social processes and cause social changes per se. A number of field research studies have rejected as unfounded the society-technology dualism, showing how technological innovation originates within the social context which guides its invention and shapes its use [5-10]. Notwithstanding its groundlessness, the ides that computer technologies produce social *effects* is so widespread that we, too, had to use the term social *effects* of the Internet to get our purpose across.

The "impact" metaphor originates a problem space where a separate entity, be it the Internet or "technology" in general, hits an external entity, "society" in its various parts. It is worth noting that the "impact" metaphor has a strongly aggressive connotation as it indicates the action of a missile coming into contact with its target. It conveys the idea that the Internet changes social processes at various levels: micro (individuals), meso (groups) and macro (organizations and institutions). With reference to the debate on the *slums* within the USA social policy of the Seventies, Schön [11] has shown that metaphors generate a problem-setting which strongly affects the ensuing problem-solving. If slums are infected *bubos* that might contaminate the whole city, then they must be removed and rebuilt; if, on the contrary, they are *poor communities*, then the most plausible solutions will be those oriented toward offering residents social support to improve their conditions.

The first metaphor, the plague, calls for bulldozers; the second, the community in distress, calls for social workers. The former sees the problem in terms of surgical interventions to defeat the infection and relocate the residents, the latter sees a problem made up of disadvantaged individuals and communities in distress. The impact metaphor assumes a causality, both unidirectional, i.e. technology would influence society without the converse taking place, and deterministic, i.e. a given technology would produce specific social *effects*.

This conception of the relationships between technology and society, which we have called "technological determinism" [12, 13], is – with few exceptions [14-18] – accepted as the undisputed framework in the studies on the *social effects* of the Internet. Sproull & Kiesler [19] find that the Internet has the *effect* of promoting democracy in organizations because it makes information available to everyone and speaks up for those who cannot. Rice's [20] research study highlights an opposite *effect*: the Internet increases status and power differences within organizations. Stoll [21] claims that the Internet favors social isolation by moving people from their "real" communities. Turkle [22-24], albeit with some reservation, maintains the opposite: in Mult-user Dungeons (MUDs; they are textual virtual environments shared by many participants at the same time), people experience new forms of communication and identity, even if anonymity and the possibility of concealing the participants' "real" identity can have bewildering effects. The extensive literature on the supposed *social effects* of the Internet shows that while the nature of the *effects* is controversial, the idea that the Internet has per se *social effects* is almost universally accepted.

A recent case is represented by Kraut at al.'s [25] paper devoted to the paradox of a "social technology that reduces social involvement". Although the authors make it clear that "arguments based on the attributes of the technology alone do not resolve this debate" because "people can use home computers and the Internet in many different ways and for many purposes, including entertainment, education, information retrieval, and communication" (p. 1017), the aim is to identify the *consequences* of the use of the Internet. "The findings of this research provide a surprisingly consistent picture of the consequences of using the Internet" (p. 1028). The consequences highlighted by the research study – decline in social involvement, increase in loneliness, increase in depression – allow the authors to conclude that "using the Internet adversely affects social involvement and psychological well-being" (p. 1028). The conclusions of Kraut et al.'s study had ample national media coverage and triggered off lively discussions. However, the idea that the Internet as such had specific social effects was not generally questioned.

3.2   The Internet: an artifact under construction

A recent exception to the general acceptance of the "impact" metaphor is McKenna and Bargh's [26] study in which they maintain that "*the Internet by itself is not a main effect cause of anything*, and that psychology must move beyond this notion to an informed analysis of how social identity, social interaction, and relationship formation may be different on the Internet than in real life" (p. 57; the italic is ours). Their study, however, has the limitation of ignoring the cultural dimension of artifacts, as is apparent by the fact that McKenna and Bargh distinguish the processes that take place on the Internet from those that take place in the "real" world, as if the Internet did not belong to the "real" world in the same way the telephone, the radio and the car belong to it. Human environments are always interwoven with artifacts and it is not possible to separate, within the human experience, "natural" and "artificial" contexts: even natural parks are social products, the result of shared sets of values, political decisions, and legislative measures.

In our everyday experience we do not deal with separate worlds – one of face-to-face relationships, another of telephone relationships, another of Internet relationships and so on – but with a single world in which our is always mediated by cultural artifacts [27, 28]. Culture enables the members of a given community to successfully interact with the environment and with the other community members by means of physical and conceptual artifacts – among which language has a privileged place – that allow to attribute a shared meaning to actions and situations [29, 30]. The artifacts present in the environment can be either physical instruments, such as the Internet or the telephone, or conceptual instruments, such as the categories that organize face-to-face interactions. Also in the latter case the relationship is mediated by artifacts, only in this instance it goes through immaterial artifacts, such as the preference systems and the values typical of a given culture, which make the interlocutor in turn attractive or unpleasant, interesting or boring, reliable or unreliable.

McKenna and Bargh basically ignore the role of cultural mediation: they think that "key situation variables that make the Internet a unique and special social domain: anonymity, the mitigation of physical proximity, and physical attractiveness as gating features to relationship formation, and the enhanced personal control over the time and pacing of interpersonal interactions" (p. 72) interact without mediation with individuals' interests and goals. The direct interaction between the Internet and the people who use it would be, according to McKenna and Bargh, the actual object of the social studies on the Internet which "will be most profitably directed toward identifying the critical individual differences that will mediate and moderate the Internet's powerful situational forces to determine whether the effect on the self, social identity, relationship formation and maintenance, social interactions, organizational functioning, and mental health will be positive and fulfilling or negative and destructive" (p. 72). In their paper McKenna and Bargh conclude that the Internet is a medium like others that have been developed before, and that, as already occurred in the past, it will be individuals who will decide its destiny: "Like the communication advances before it, the Internet will always and only be what individuals make of it" (p. 72).

McKenna and Bargh's neglect of the historical-cultural dimension is the reason why they fail to grasp the two main issues that the development of the Internet presents to the psychologist: on the one hand that of understanding the specific characteristics, and specific potential, of the Internet as the product of history and of a peculiar scientific and technological community [31]; on the other, that of understanding individuals' behaviors within the functioning of the communities (business, school, family, etc.) to which they belong. Unlike McKenna and Bragh, in the Internet we see a new artifact, originated by a particular moment of history and full of potentialities which will be implemented and revealed in time by the different "communities of practices" that will use it [32, 33, 34]. It is these communities – who supply individuals with the reference frames necessary to communicate and collaborate, frames which individuals will continually change through their situated and inevitably creative activity [35] – who will teach people how to properly utilize a medium like the Internet which is already in all offices and in over 40% of American homes, but whose social meaning is still under construction.

Instead of asking only what effects the Internet has on social actors (individuals, groups, and organizations), we may ask what social actors are making of the Internet. People interact with the Internet not in an "immediate" way, but going through several instruments of mediation, both physical and conceptual. In particular, people perceive the characteristics of an artifact on the basis of social processes such as the shared experience acquired in using it, the building up of expectations, the definition of the proper and desirable ways to utilize the artifact [36]. The meaning of an artifact is built through its socially recognized use, stabilized across time: in the history of inventions a technological innovation has often come about not in a research laboratory but in the everyday context of its use, as Bijker [37] shows when studying the invention of fluorescent lighting. The outline of an artifact is defined in its actual use; the Internet is at present simply one of the names (together with others, such as "Cyberspace", "World Wide Web", "Advanced Information Technology", "Information Superhighways" etc.) which we use to designate that particular constellation of metaphors which define the many potentialities and the several current uses of an artifact still *under construction*.

What metaphors are we using to construct the Internet through its use? We use three types of metaphors, each of which reflects a particular way of interpreting the human experience developed by recent psychological research. First of all there are metaphors that see the Internet as a space in which to gather information; these metaphors include within them the approach of the early cognitive psychology, which saw cognition as individual information processing (Human Information Processing, HIP; [38, 39]). Then there are metaphors that consider the Internet as a space for communication and social gathering; these metaphors develop a vision which is no longer only cognitive, but also "social" (in the limited sense of "interpersonal") of human experience [40-45]. Lastly, there are metaphors that consider the Internet as a new artifact, an environment in which existing "communities of practices" can meet overcoming physical distances and new communities can form online; these metaphors use concepts coming from anthropological research, communication studies, and cultural psychology [46-50].

3.3 The Internet as a space for information seeking: the cognitive approach

The Internet is constructed – by the media, by those who take up web pages, by providers, by users – especially as a huge store of information. Bharat and Broder [51] estimate the development of the Internet in 400 million pages, with a growth rate of 7.5 pages a second. Since 1998 estimates have been revised several times to keep up with the enormous increase in the amount of information available on the Internet. The use of the Internet is mostly devoted to the exploitation of these huge mines of information: Bikson & Panis [52], basing their study on research carried out on a national scale in the USA, estimate that in accessing the Internet from their homes, 21% of the adults intend to consult databases (at work the percentage reaches 34%) to which is added another 15% of adults and 39% of young people who access the Internet to use educational programs. The tremendous growth of the information available has changed the way we consider information. While previously information was a scarce resource difficult to obtain, on the Internet we risk information overload. Critical human activities such as information seeking, gathering and consumption have changed deeply in the Internet era: "Providing people with access to more information is not the problem. Rather, the problem is one of maximizing the allocation of human attention to information that will be useful" [53], p. 643. The resource which is now becoming scarce is attention, not information. This paradox of the Internet seems unquestionable: a technology centered on information overturns the relationship between information and attention in favor of the latter.

To cope with the current situation, characterized by the overload of information with respect to human attention resources, an evolutionary ecological model has recently been presented – *the information foraging theory* [54] – which considers people's adaptation to the ongoing flux of information present in information-rich environments in the same way in which biologists study the adaptation of organisms to their physical environments. The merits and the faults of the *information foraging theory* are the same as those of the Internet in its cognitive-informational version. On the one hand, it has the merit to go beyond the old cognitive paradigm included in the Human Information Processing (HIP), both because it places information in the environment (understood in the evolutionary and adaptive sense) and because it attributes to the social actors capabilities of strategic initiative (*foraging* is a highly planned and at the same time highly situated activity) in which knowledge and action are closely interwoven. Information is no longer "supplied" but it is built by the actors through their activities of environment exploration. On the other hand, the *information foraging theory* inherits the more serious limitation of the HIP model, the neglect of communication, collaboration and culture. It does not see individual human beings as members of communities interacting with the environment through the mediation of artifacts. And yet, curiously enough, it is indeed an artifact – the Internet – which has produced the situation of information over-abundance the theory intends to cope with.

Is the information available on the Internet truly available? Actually, human beings often cannot keep up with the exponential growth of the "available" information stored within the Internet. And so they resort to other artifacts. The problems which the Internet, as an artifact planned to hold exceptionally huge amount of information, gives human beings are partly solved by constructing other artifacts. A solution to exploit the deposits of data stored in the Internet – the metaphor used is *data mining* – goes through the construction of learning algorithms for discovering regularities in those databases which are intractable for human experts because of their hugeness, like, for example, the gigabytes of functional magnetic resonance imaging data describing brain activity in humans [55]. In this way -in general resorting to knowledge discovery techniques like those used for semiautomatic scientific discovery in Inductive Logic Programming (ILP) algorithms [56] - it becomes possible to explore masses of information that would otherwise be unmanageable by unassisted human beings.

3.4   The Internet as a space for social gathering: the interpersonal approach

The Internet is also constructed as a space for the coming together of people. "People on the net are not only solitary information processors but also social beings. They are not only looking for information; they are also looking for affiliation, support, and affirmation.

Thinking of people on the net as social actors evokes a metaphor of gathering. Behaviors appropriate at a gathering include chatting, discussing, arguing, and confiding" [57], p. 38. This approach captures much of what is currently happening in the net: according to Kling [58], 30% of home Internet use is spent in chat room discussions; USENET – a network of bilateral agreements among administrators of Bulletin Board Systems (BBS) – is supported by 16,000 organizations and has more than 2 million subscribers; in 1997 America Online had more than 350 organized clubs and forums and countless spontaneous interest groups; thousands of MUDs (Multi-user Dungeons) and MOOs (Muds Object-Oriented) allow people real time interaction in textual – and often also 3D – virtual spaces [59].

The social gathering metaphor shifts the focus of the Internet from individual information processing to social processes such as communication, discussion, and mutual narratives on the self. Communication is understood by this metaphor basically as an interaction between individuals: "If we view people as social actors, then we should view the net as a social technology. Any technology combines artifacts and procedures to apply knowledge for practical ends. A social technology does so to allow people with common interests to find each other, talk and listen, and sustain connections over time. Dinner parties, bowling teams, college reunions, coffeehouses, 12-step programs, neighborhood pubs - all are examples of social technologies" [60]. Interpersonal interaction in the Internet can stimulate personal reflection, disclosure, and investigation into personal and social identities: "Engagement with computational technologies facilitates a series of 'second chances' for adults to work and rework unresolved personal issues and, more generally, to think through questions about the nature of self, including questions about definitions of life, intentionality, and intelligence" [61].

One characteristic of communication in electronic environments is the possibility to experiment new forms of self presentations as happens in *gender swapping* (men presenting themselves as women and vice versa, and various combinations and shifts in using *handles*, as these provisional *personae* are sometimes called) widely used in MUDs and MOOs. What sort of communication environment is the Internet? Does it have special characteristics, or it is just a new medium joining other existing communication media such as the telephone, fax, radio and TV? The sense that Computer-Mediated Communication (CMC) can change people's ways of thinking about communication emerged at the very beginning of the development of the Internet. Some characteristics of CMC are undisputable: it cancels physical distance among participants, makes physical location no longer important, removes indication of physical appearance making body presentation not focal. It also reduces costs, in terms of money and time, of sending mail, thus favoring information diffusion (and information overload). Other characteristics are open to debate, as we saw in the previous discussion of the studies of Kraut et al. [62] and McKenna and Bargh [63] on the social "effects" of the Internet.

CMC has been credited with encouraging people to express themselves more freely than in face-to-face social situations; the other side of the coin is the likelihood of rude and offensive behavior (*flaming*). The factors which stimulate the uninhibited style of communication sometimes surfacing in electronic environments are unclear. Sproull and Kiesler [64] think that lack of social context in electronic environments drives people to act more freely and even in impulsive and anti-normative ways: "People interacting on a computer are isolated from social cues and feel safe from surveillance and criticism" (pp. 48-49). This view was questioned on the basis of both field studies and theoretical concepts drawn from social psychology research, namely social identity theory [65], [66]: people sitting in front of a computer screen are not isolated from social context, claim Spears and Lea [67]. A person, even if physically removed from other people's presence, is not separated from the normative influence of her social group or groups (the group or groups with which she identifies). "Empirically, the assumption that CMC is characterized by a weakening of social norms seems to have little direct or independent support. In fact, it could be argued that an absence of social cues from other interacting individuals, together with the resulting uncertainty, forces people to resort to default social norms to guide their behaviour" [68], p. 286. Although default social norms shaping CMC may be even stronger and more inflexible than face-to-face negotiated norms, the idea that the Internet favors people's freedom of expressing themselves survives as it has deep roots in the history of the Internet [69].

3.5   The Internet as a new artifact: the cultural approach

A most suitable framework for understanding the relationships existing between the ongoing development of the Internet and the unfolding of human experience is offered by cultural psychology which sees the Internet as a new artifact, a new medium, a new communication environment. According to cultural psychology, all artifacts mediate between social actors (who are considered not as separate entities but as members of peculiar communities) and their environment. All artifacts, the Internet included, are *embodied social projects*: the dualism between technology and society does not have any space in the cultural model. "Cultural artifacts are simultaneously ideal (conceptual) and material. They are ideal in that they contain in coded form the interactions of which they were previously a part and which they mediate in the present. They are material in that they exist only insofar as they are embodied in material artifacts" [70]. Considering the Internet as an artifact means closing the gap between technology and agency.

An example of this approach can be found in Lemke's study [71] about the way in which an academic library redesignes its website and at the same time reorganizes its structure: "Our usual view of organizational communication and discourse places face-to-face encounters at the center of attention: people in meeting, agreeing and disagreeing. The corresponding analytical focus is generally on speakers and the thematic content of their utterances. We do not usually foreground the *medium* of communication" (p. 21). New artifacts introduce new social games: in the library "a particular, novel discourse medium, the organization's website, seems to be playing a catalytic role in on-going processes of institutional change" (*ibidem*, p. 21). The question that cultural psychology deals with when it studies the Internet is this: which social processes is the Internet mediating in this particular situation? In which way are the replanning of the library and the redesign of its website connected? The cultural conception puts technology fully into the social and organizational games from which it originates and of which it is an important part.

Unlike previous artifacts, the Internet may bewilder us by challenging our current way of acknowledging reality and making necessary for us to invent new conceptual frameworks to make sense of the experiences we do in cyberspace [72-75]. We may be confused when having to make a decision about the meaning of experiences such as "playing doctor" in virtual reality: would we accept this experience as equal to that of being a doctor in "real" reality [76]? Artifacts always redesign the boundaries of what is or is not "real" [77], but new communication environments do it to a new extent. We are beginning to realize that the separation between "natural" and "artificial" environments is groundless. We understand now clearly that we inhabit a world which has always been both "natural" and "artificial": "Virtual reality is not 'real', but it has a relationship to the real. By being betwixt and between, it becomes a play space for thinking about the real world. It is an exemplary evocative object" [78]. Human experience is always mediated by artifacts and the Internet is only the latest step in the long history of human inventions. The problem of electronic communication is that it is still not smoothly integrated into our everyday routines: the domestication of the Internet is in progress and will require time.

In cyberspace situation ambiguity can grow to unprecedented heights: "Individuals find friends and groups find shared identities on-line, through the aggregated networks of relationships and commitments that make any community possible. But are relationships and commitments as we know them even possible in a place where identities are fluid? The physical world is a place where the identity and position of the people you communicate with are well known, fixed, and highly visual. In cyberspace, everything is in the dark. We can only exchange words with each other – no glances or shrugs or ironic smiles. Even the nuances of voice and intonation are stripped away" [79]. The Internet expands and at the same time ruptures the fine texture of people's everyday experience. The *darkness* of cyberspace seems to be due mainly to the physical absence of the other participants to the interaction. Yet, separation of experience from physical presence is not new for human beings. If we think of the situation in which language was first used to refer to someone (or something) not physically present, we see that a good measure of *darkness* entered human discourse at that point, but human experience was able to make sense of the newly opened space and to expand its domain through language. Think of when human beings started using written language to talk of absent people, or of strange entities such as gods and demons, totemic animals and dead heroes.

The *darkness* produced by artifacts grew thicker and thicker with every stage of human cultural development, yet human control over the environment increased with the invention and use of artifacts mediating between human actors and their physical, social, and ideal worlds. Human beings invented artifacts such as language and writing, but they learned to control them so to enhance their experience, not to be lost in the darkness they had created.

Human beings persist in creating fictitious, artificial, "unreal" worlds which bewilder them until they find ways of assimilating them within their ordinary lives. It is often said that our understanding of situations depends on the mass of information available; the current situation of the Internet use gives evidence of the contrary. We know a lot about the Internet and its current use, yet we are still confused about its nature as a social artifact. Especially, we may be mislead by metaphors like that of the "impact" of technology on society. While the Internet has achieved very good standards in the physical presentation of "reality", much work still remains to be done to develop an equally robust conceptual framework capable of supporting its ongoing social construction as a mediating environment for human experience.

Artifacts are *embodied social projects* and as such they have politics [80]. The Internet is no exception to this norm; in fact, it is the space in which two different visions of communication and society are clashing. The original project of the Internet as a totally accessible communication space was produced by a small community of scientists and technologists which was formed since the early 1960s by the Advanced Research Projects Agency (ARPA) of the US Department of Defense. This community of scientists, which prospered for almost three decades in splendid isolation protected by the "great divide" provided by ARPA and separating it from the broader social world, nurtured "deeply engrained institutional values of intellectual curiosity, informal meritocratic reward structures, and egalitarian presumptions enabled a highly disaggregated and distributed population to work together to create an artifact quite unlike any seen before" [81]. This state of affairs changed abruptly in the early 1990s when the creation of cyberspace was accomplished and the Web made available to the outside world: commercial firms, non-profit organizations, and the media. With the achievement of its task, this unique scientific, social, and moral community began to dissolve and the net was invaded by a host of newcomers. The ethos of the original community which created the Internet is still present in the Web but it is at present challenged by many of the new inhabitants of Netville.

A different ethos is currently pervading the Internet: that of profit for "private investment", ranked first among the five "values" which should direct the development of the Global Internet Infrastructure (GII) by the U.S. Vice-President Gore (Office of the Vice-President, [82]). Many analysts think that the Internet is prone to become prey of "unrestrained corporate ambition and private design" [83], following in that the fate of the other American media: "The American media system is spinning out of control in a hyper-commercialized frenzy. Fewer than ten transnational media conglomerates dominate much of our media; fewer than two dozen account for the overwhelming majority of our newspapers, magazines, films, television, radio, and books" [84]. Although more optimistic experts believe that the Internet can escape the dire fate of the previous media thanks to its decentralized structure [85], there are good reasons to consider the survival of the Internet as a "public good" - open to communications of all kinds coming from associations of all kinds - seriously endangered.

There is strong evidence of the fact that search engines "systematically exclude (in some cases by design and in some, accidentally) certain sites and certain types of sites in favor of others, systematically giving prominence to some at the expenses of others" [86] p. 169. Information seekers, whose navigation depends heavily on search engines, are guided to sites whose owners are able to pay to be indexed quickly and ranked high [87]. Software agents - also called softbots, spiders, crawlers, or robots - which explore the Web to retrieve documents to be indexed tend to favor the rich and powerful over the less fortunate site owners: "of the 100 top sites - based on traffic - just 6 are not .com commercial sites. If we exclude universities, NASA, and the U.S. government, this number drops to two" [88]. If we think that, according to Lawrence & Giles [89], none of the search engines considered in their study is able to index (individually) more than 16% of the total information indexable we realize how little coverage is granted by current search engines and of how scarce visibility is given to social actors who are not rich and powerful and can hardly be found in the immense space of the Web. If this bias will not be corrected soon it will jeopardize the values which have gained vast social support to the development of the Internet. Artifacts have politics, and politics may mean social conflict for access to the net. Equal access is not always granted, although it is somehow written in the DNA of the Web.

3.6   Conclusions

The current use of the Web is not homogeneous, but much diversified: from e-commerce to gambling and pornography, from psychotherapy in the cyberspace to electronic mail in corporations. The Internet is also pervading various different environments, moving toward a less U.S.-centric international Internet [90] in which situations of Western Europe, India [91], China [92] and the developing countries [93], present different landscapes. The ubiquitous presence of the Internet does not suppress but rather enhances the particularities of the different professional, linguistic, organizational, cultural communities that use it; the ways in which global and local interweave in the Internet finds a fitting explanation in Bakhtin's [94] conception of culture as a realm made only of boundaries, a space in which differences can be acknowledged.

The spread of the Internet is changing the way people use information and communicates among themselves. Cultural psychology provides researchers on new media with suitable conceptual tools to understand the relationship between technological innovation and social change. They focus our attention on mediation processes, on the subtle shifts in human agency which accompany the diffusion of new technological tools, on the emergence of new landscapes for human cognition and communication.

3.7   References

[1]   Negroponte, N., *Being digital*. London: Hodder & Stoughton, 1995.
[2]   Kling, R., Reading "All about" computerization: How genre conventions shape nonfiction social analysis. *The Information Society*, 10 (3), 1994, 147-172.
[3]   Kling, R., *Computerization and controversy*. San Diego, CA: Academic., 1995
[4]   Hakken, D., Cyborgs @ Cyberspace - An Ethnographer looks to the future. New York & London: Routledge, 1999.
[5]   Bijker, W. E. & Law, J. (Eds.), *Shaping technology, building society: Studies in sociotechnical change*. Cambridge, MA: The MIT Press, 1992.
[6]   Bowker, G., & Star, S. L., Social science, technical systems and cooperative work: Beyond the great divide. Hillsdale, NJ: Erlbaum, 1997.
[7]   Latour, B., Aramis or the love of technology. Cambridge, MA: Harvard University Press, 1996.
[8]   Law, J., Organizing modernity, Oxford: Blackwell, 1994.
[9]   Law, J., & Callon, M., Engineering and sociology in a military aircraft project: A network analysis of technological change. In S. L. Star (Ed.), Ecologies of knowledge: Work and politics in science and technology. New York: State University of New York Press, 1995.
[10]   McKenzie, D., How do we know the properties of the artifacts? In R. Fox (Ed.), Technological change. Reading: Harwood, 1998.
[11]   Schön, D. A. Generative metaphor: A perspective on problem setting in social policy. In A. Orthony (Ed.), Metaphor and thought. Cambridge, England: Cambridge University Press, 1979.
[12]   Mantovani, G. Is computer-mediated communication intrinsically apt to enhance democracy in organizations? Human Relations, 47 (1), 45-62., 1994.
[13]   Mantovani, G., New communication environments: From everyday to virtual. London: Taylor & Francis, 1996a
[14]   Bikson. T. K. & Eveland, J. D., The interplay of work group structures and computer support. In J. Galegher, R. E. Kraut, & C. Egido (Eds.), Intellectual teamwork: Social and technological foundations of cooperative work. Hillsdale, NJ: Erlbaum, 1990.
[15]   Hakken, D., Cyborgs @ Cyberspace - An Ethnographer looks to the future. New York & London: Routledge. 1999.
[16]   Kling, R. Reading "All about" computerization: How genre conventions shape nonfiction social analysis. The Information Society, 10 (3), 147-172, 1994.
[17]   Kling, R., Computerization and controversy. San Diego, CA: Academic, 1995.

[18]   Spears, R., & Lea, M., Social influence and the influence of the "social" in computer-mediated communication. In L. Lea (Ed.), Contexts of computer-mediated communication. Hemel Hempstead: Harvester Wheatsheaf, 1992.

[19]   Sproull, L., & Kiesler, S., Connections: New ways of working in the networked organizations. Cambridge, MA: The MIT Press, 1991.

[20]   Rice, R. R., Computer-mediated communication system network data: Theoretical concerns and empirical examples. International Journal of Man-Machine Studies, 32 1990, 627-647.

[21]   Stoll, C., Silicon snake oil: Second thoughts on the information highway. New York: Anchor Books, 1995.

[22]   Turkle, S., Life on the screen. Identity in the age of the Internet. New York: Simon and Schuster, 1995.

[23]   Turkle, S., Virtuality and its discontents: Searching for community in the cyberspace. The American Prospect, 24 (4), 1996, 50-57.

[24]   Turkle, S., Construction and reconstruction of self in virtual reality: Playing in the MUDs. In S. Kiesler (Ed.), Culture of the Internet, pp. 143-153. Mahwah, NJ: Erlbaum, 1997.

[26]   McKenna, K. Y. A., & Bargh, J. A., Plan 9 from cyberspace: The implications of the Internet for personality and social psychology. Personality and Social Psychology Review, 4 (1), 2000, 57-75.

[27]   Mantovani, G., Exploring borders. Understanding culture and psychology. London: Routledge, 2000.

[28]   Tomasello, M., The cultural origins of human cognition. Cambridge, MA: Harvard University Press, 1999.

[29]   Cole, M., Cultural psychology - A once and future discipline. Cambridge, MA: Harvard University Press,1996.

[30]   Duranti, A., Linguistic anthropology. Cambridge, England: Cambridge University Press, 1997.

[31]   King, J. L., Grinter, R., & Pickering, J. M., The rise and fall of Netville: The saga of a cyberspace boomtown in the great divide. In S. Kiesler (Ed.), Culture of the Internet. Mahwah, NJ: Erlbaum, 1997.

[32]   Brown, J. S., & Duguid, P., Organizational learning and communities of practice: Towards a unified view of working, learning, and innovation. Organizational Science, 2 (1), 1991, 40-57.

[33]   Brown, J. S., & Duguid, P., Organizing knowledge. California Management Review, 40 (3), 1998, 90-111.

[34]   Wenger, E., Communities of practice. Learning, meaning, and identity. Cambridge, England: Cambridge University Press, 1998.

[35]   Clancey, W. J., Situated cognition. On human knowledge and computer representations. Cambridge: Cambridge University Press, 1997.

[36]   McKenzie, D., How do we know the properties of the artifacts? In R. Fox (Ed.), Technological change. Reading: Harwood, 1998.

[37]   Bijker, W. E. & Law, J. (Eds.), Shaping technology, building society: Studies in sociotechnical change. Cambridge, MA: The MIT Press, 1992

[38]   Simon, H. A., The sciences of the artificial. Cambridge, MA: The MIT Press, 1981.

[39]   Newell, A., Unified theories of cognition. Cambridge, MA: Harvard University Press, 1990.

[40]   Sproull, L., & Kiesler, S:, Connections: New ways of working in the networked organizations. Cambridge, MA: The MIT Press, 1991.

[41]   Turkle, S., Life on the screen. Identity in the age of the Internet. New York: Simon and Schuster, 1995.

[42]   Turkle, S., Virtuality and its discontents: Searching for community in the cyberspace. The American Prospect, 24 (4), 1996, 50-57.

[43]   Turkle, S., Construction and reconstruction of self in virtual reality: Playing in the MUDs. In S. Kiesler (Ed.), Culture of the Internet, pp. 143-153. Mahwah, NJ: Erlbaum, 1997.

[44]   Schuler, D., New community networks: Wired for change. Reading, MA: Addison-Wesley, 1996.

[45]   Van Dijk, J., The network society. London: Sage, 1999.

[46]   Cole, M., Cultural psychology - A once and future discipline. Cambridge, MA: Harvard University Press, 1996.

[47]   Hakken, D., Cyborgs @ Cyberspace - An Ethnographer looks to the future. New York & London: Routledge, 1999.

[48]   Mantovani, G., New communication environments: From everyday to virtual. London: Taylor & Francis. 1996a.

[49]   Mantovani, G., Social context in human-computer interaction: A new framework for mental models, cooperation, and communication. Cognitive Science, 20 (4), 1996b, 237-269.

[50]   A. R. Stone, The war of desire and technology at the close of the Mechanical Age. Cambridge, MA: MIT Press, 1996.

[51]   Bharat, K., & Broder, A., Estimating the size and overlap of public web search engines. Proceedings of the 7th International WWW Conference. Brisbane, Australia: WWW Organization, 1998.

[52]   Bikson, T. K.. & Panis, C. W. A., Computers and connectivity: Current trends. In S. Kiesler (Ed.),
        Culture of the Internet. Mahwah, NJ: Erlbaum, 1997.
[53]   Pirolli, P., & Card, S., Information foraging. Psychological Review, 106 (4), 1999, 643-675.
[54]   Ibid, 643.
[55]   Mitchell, T. M., Machine learning and data mining. Communications of the ACM, 42 (11), 1999, 31-
        36.
[56]   Muggleton, S., Scientific knowledge discovery using inductive logic programming. Communications
        of the ACM, 42 (11), 1999, 42-46.
[57]   Sproull, L., & Faraj, S., Atheism, sex, and databases: The Net as a social technology. In S. Kiesler
        (Ed.), Culture of the Internet. Mahwah, NJ: Erlbaum, 1997.
[58]   Kling, R., Can the 'next generation' Internet effectively support 'ordinary citizens'? The Information
        Society, 15 (1), 57-64. 1999.
[59]   Curtis, P., Mudding: Social phenomena in text-based virtual realities in S. Kiesler (Ed.), Culture of the
        Internet. Mahwah, NJ: Erlbaum, 1997.
[60]   Sproull, L., & Faraj, S., Atheism, sex, and databases: The Net as a social technology. In S. Kiesler
        (Ed.), Culture of the Internet. Mahwah, NJ: Erlbaum, 1997.
[61]   Turkle, S., Construction and reconstruction of self in virtual reality: Playing in the MUDs. In S.
        Kiesler (Ed.), Culture of the Internet, pp. 143-153. Mahwah, NJ: Erlbaum, 1997.
[62]   Kraut, R. E., Patterson, M., Lundmark, W., Kiesler, S., Mukhopadhyay, T., & Scherlis, W., Internet
        paradox: A social technology that reduces social involvement and psychological well-being?
        American Psychologist, 53, 1998, 1017-1031.
[63]   McKenna, K. Y. A., & Bargh, J. A., Plan 9 from cyberspace: The implications of the Internet for
        personality and social psychology. Personality and Social Psychology Review, 4 (1), 2000, 57-75.
[64]   Sproull, L., & Kiesler, S, Connections: New ways of working in the networked organizations.
        Cambridge, MA: The MIT Press, 1991.
[65]   H. Tajfel and J. C. Turner, The social identity theory of intergroup behaviour, in Psychology of
        intergroup relations, S. Worchell and W. G. Austin, Eds. Chicago: Nelson-Hall, 1986, pp. 7-24.
[66]   M. A. Hogg and D. Abrams, Social identifications: a social psychology of intergroup relations and
        group processes. London: Routledge, 1988.
[67]   Spears, R., & Lea, M., Social influence and the influence of the "social" in computer-mediated
        communication. In L. Lea (Ed.), Contexts of computer-mediated communication. Hemel Hempstead:
        Harvester Wheatsheaf, 1992.
[68]   Lea, M., & Spears, R., Computer-mediated communication, de-individuation and group decision-
        making. International Journal of Man-Machine Studies, 34, 1991, 283-301.
[69]   King, J. L., Grinter, R., & Pickering, J. M., The rise and fall of Netville: The saga of a cyberspace
        boomtown in the great divide. In S. Kiesler (Ed.), Culture of the Internet. Mahwah, NJ: Erlbaum,
        1997.
[70]   Cole, M., Culture and cognitive development: From cross-cultural research to creating systems of
        cultural mediation. Culture and Psychology, 1 (1), 1995, 25-54.
[71]   Lemke, J. L., Discourse and organizational dynamics: Website communication and institutional
        change. Discourse and Society, 10 (1), 1999, 21-47.
[72]   Mantovani, G., & Riva, G., "Real" presence: How different ontologies generate different criteria for
        presence, telepresence, and virtual presence. Presence - Teleoperators and Virtual Environments, 8 (5),
        1999, 540-550.
[73]   Sheridan, T. B., Further musing on the psychophysics of presence. Presence - Teleoperators and
        Virtual Environments, 5 (3), 1996, 241-246.
[74]   Sheridan, T.B., Descartes, Heidegger, Gibson, and God: Toward an eclectic ontology of presence.
        Presence - Teleoperators and Virtual Environments, 8 (5), 1999, 551-559.
[75]   Zahoric, P., & Jenison, R., Presence as being-in-the-world. Presence - Teleoperators and Virtual
        Environments, 7 (2), 1998, 78-89.
[76]   Shapiro, M. A., & McDonald, D. G., I am not a real doctor but I play one in virtual reality:
        Implications of virtual reality for judgments about reality. Journal of Communication, 42 (4), 1992,
        94-114.
[77]   Mantovani, G., & Spagnolli, A., Imagination and culture. What is like being in the Cyberspace? Mind,
        Culture, and Activity, 7 (3), 2000, 217-228.
[78]   Turkle, S., Construction and reconstruction of self in virtual reality: Playing in the MUDs. In S.
        Kiesler (Ed.), Culture of the Internet, Mahwah, NJ: Erlbaum, 1997, pp. 143-153.
[79]   Rheingold, H.R., A slice of life in my virtual community. In L.M. Harasim (ed), Global networks.
        Cambridge, MA: The MIT Press, 1993.
[80]   Winner, L., Do artifacts have politics? Daedalus, 109, 1980, 191-197.

[81] King, J. L., Grinter, R., & Pickering, J. M., The rise and fall of Netville: The saga of a cyberspace boomtown in the great divide. In S. Kiesler (Ed.), Culture of the Internet, Mahwah, NJ: Erlbaum, 1997.

[82] Office of the Vice-President, Remarks as delivered by Vice-President Gore to the Networked Economy Conference, 12 September, 1995.

[83] Schiller, D., Ambush on the I-way: Information commoditization on the electronic frontier. BCLA Information Policy Conference, Vancoluver, 27-28 October, 1995.

[84] McChesney, R.W, Making media democratic. Boston Review: New Democracy Forum http://polisci.mit.edu/BostonReview/BR23.3/mccesney.html, 1999.

[85] Poster, M., Cyberdemocracy. In D. Porter (ed), Internet culture. New York, NY: Routledge, 1995.

[86] Introna, L.D. & Nissenbaum, H., Shaping the web: Why the politics of search engines matters. The Information Society, 16 (3), 2000, 169-185.

[87] Hansell, S., AltaVista invites advertisers to pay for top ranking. New York Times, 15 April, 1999.

[88] Introna, L.D. & Nissenbaum, H., Shaping the web: Why the politics of search engines matters. The Information Society, 16 (3), 2000, 169-185.

[89] Lawrence, S. & Giles, C.L., Accessibility and distribution of information on the Web. Nature, 400, 1999, 107-109.

[90] Cohen, R. B., Moving toward a non-U.S.-centric international Internet. Communications of the ACM, 42, 6, 37-43, 1999.

[91] Agarwal, P. K., Building India's national Internet backbone. Communications of the ACM, 42 (6), 1999, 53-58.

[92] Zixiang, T., Foster, W., & Goodman, S., China's state-coordinated Internet Infrastructure. Communications of the ACM, 42 (6), 1999, 44-52.

[93] Petrazzini, B., & Kibati, M., The Internet in developing countries. Communications of the ACM, 42 (6), 1999, 31-36.

[94] Bakhtin, M.M., The dialogical imagination. Austin, TX: The University of Texas Press, 1981.

4   The Mind's Eye in Cyberspace: Online Perceptions of Self and Others

Richard C. SHERMAN

Abstract. The Internet has greatly expanded the ways in which we communicate and interact with others. This chapter explores how are our perceptions of others and of ourselves effected by these new ways of communicating. The first section examines the nature of computer-mediated communication (CMC) as viewed by several prominent theoretical models, exploring how these models assess possible sources of accurate and inaccurate perceptions online and the impact of perceptions in cyberspace on everyday face-to-face social relationships. Next, the chapter explores the role of relevant cognitive processes in the development of online perceptions, including the activation of stereotypes, self-confirmation of attributions, and the instantiation of social identity. The final section examines the problem of accurately knowing how others perceive oneself in cyberspace versus in face-to-face interactions. Current literature supports the general idea that perceptions are indeed influenced by the medium, but not always in straightforward ways. First, despite the apparently impoverished text-based nature of most forms of CMC, people do form impressions of each other and they do develop strong interpersonal relationships online. Second, CMC may foster perceptions that are more extreme than in face-to-face situations, but the positive or negative direction of the effect may depend on factors external to the medium itself. Finally, meta-perceptions are distorted by at least some forms of the medium such that people may be less accurate in judging how others view them than they are in face-to-face interactions.

Contents

4.1   Overview

In our daily lives we depend heavily on our perceptions of other people to determine how we should behave toward them. Our interactions and relationships with others are strongly influenced by our assessments of their intentions, motives, personality traits, skills and abilities. Likewise, we are concerned with how others perceive us because we believe their assessments and impressions will shape their behavior towards us. In recent years the Internet has greatly expanded the ways in which we communicate and interact with others. Email, instant messaging, chat rooms, newsgroups, listservs, world wide web home pages, and online interactive games are becoming important venues for developing and maintaining social relationships, and our perceptions in these contexts have increasing importance to our daily lives. It is currently estimated that over 400 million people worldwide are online [1], and one of the main uses of the Internet in the home is for social communication [2]. Yet, as Wallace [3] has observed, "The Internet explosion happened so rapidly that we have not had much time to step back from the medium and look at it more systematically, as a new environment that can have potent effects on our behavior…it is an environment that we, as Internet users, can affect and mold – provided we have some inkling of how, and why, it can change our perceptions and behavior" (p. 1).

How are our perceptions of others and of ourselves effected by these new ways of communicating? Are we as accurate in our assessments of others when we interact with them in cyberspace, as opposed to face-to-face situations? Aside from the accuracy question, do our online and offline perceptions differ in content and tone? Do we communicate more openly and honestly in cyberspace, or are we more apt to hide our true feelings and personalities? How accurate are our beliefs about how others see us – can we effectively view ourselves through other people's eyes?

This chapter will explore ways that social perception in cyberspace can be better understood by applying psychological principles, research, and theory. There are three major sections. The first is an examination of the nature of computer-mediated communication CMC as viewed by several prominent theoretical models, outlining how these models assess possible sources of accurate and inaccurate perceptions online and the impact of perceptions in cyberspace on everyday face-to-face social relationships. Next, the chapter explores the role of relevant cognitive processes in the development of online perceptions, including the activation of stereotypes, self-confirmation of attributions, and the instantiation of social identity. The final section examines the problem of accurately knowing how others perceive oneself in cyberspace versus in face-to-face interactions.

4.2   The Nature of Computer-Mediated Communication

Communication in cyberspace is primarily text-based and therefore does not provide visual and auditory cues that are available in face-to face interaction. This limitation would seem to make it very difficult to develop complete and accurate perceptions of the personalities and characters of other people. Early research tended to support this view, showing that users rated computer mediated communication (CMC) as cold, impersonal, and unsociable [4].

More recent work, however, has revealed that under certain conditions CMC is nevertheless capable of fostering well-developed impressions among people who interact online and of supporting strong, positive relationships among some users [5, 6, 7, 8]. As Walther [6] has noted, "Although novice users and the uninitiated still seem to suspect that

CMC may be impersonal, growing numbers of reports are appearing that reflect more personal CMC interaction, sometimes *just* as personal as face-to-face (FtF) interaction, or even describing interaction that surpasses FtF in some interpersonal aspects. It is these dynamics that undergird phenomena such as 'on-line friendships' and 'virtual communities'" (p. 4). In short, the nature of CMC is complex and its effects on interpersonal perception are not as straightforward as one might initially think.

4.2.1   Models of Computer-Mediated Communication

The complexities of CMC are reflected in the diversity of theoretical models that attempt to explain the implications of electronic communication (for excellent reviews of these models, see papers by Walther [6] and Lea & Spears [9]). The different approaches are not necessarily contradictory, but rather emphasize different qualities of CMC. Four of the most prominent models will be briefly reviewed here: Social Presence, Reduced Social Cues, Social Information Processing, and Hyperpersonal Communication.

According to *Social Presence Theory*, communication media differ in the number of channels through which interpersonal information can be conveyed – more channels give the medium greater "social presence" [4]. For example, in a telephone conference call only auditory information is available, whereas a video conference transmits both auditory and visual information, giving it higher social presence. An online chat session or an exchange of email messages, in which communication is restricted to text, would have the lowest social presence of all. According to the theory, one implication of low social presence is that communication will necessarily be very task-oriented and impersonal, leading to less positive perceptions among those who are interacting. As noted above, early research did tend to show that users of CMC rated it as impersonal [4], but other studies have contradicted the notion that media lower in social presence lead to less positive social perceptions. For example, Chiacoan and Define [10] compared perceptions of social attractiveness, credibility, and attitude similarity among people interacting face to face, in video-conferences, or in audio-conferences. The results showed that the most positive perceptions occurred in the audio-conferencing contexts – the situations that were lowest in social presence, according to the model.

A related approach is the *Media Richness Model* developed by Daft & Engel [11]. According to this analysis, media vary in their ability to reduce ambiguity in communications – rich media facilitate feedback, communicate multiple cues, permit individually tailored and highly specific messages, etc., and thereby allow non-ambiguous communication. Face-to-face communication is the richest possible medium, whereas various forms of CMC are much lower. The model predicts that people should prefer a medium that is most suitable to a given communication context, which is not always the richest medium. For example, in some contexts a letter or an email message may be seen as a more appropriate way to communicate than the telephone or in person, even though text-based media are not as rich or personal. Research on media selection has shown that people do indeed vary their preference for different forms of communication under different circumstances, though the basis for the selection seems to have to do with factors other than the objective characteristics of the media, such as socially constructed views of richness and usefulness [12], and with a communicator's assessment of the "social utility" of the medium [13, 14].

The *Reduced Social Cues Model* focuses on a specific type of information that it proposes is filtered out in text-based CMC – social context information [15]. Social context cues define the nature of the social situation, indicate normatively appropriate boundaries for behavior, and convey the social status and identities of those in the interaction. In face-to-face communication these cues might include visible features of the environment itself (a bar versus a seminar meeting room), gestures and facial expressions, symbols of authority and status (clothing, jewelry, etc.), physical appearance, and spatial behavior (seating choices, interpersonal distance). According to the model, when these cues are absent, as in CMC, people become more self-oriented and less concerned with the feelings, opinions, and evaluations of others. This, in turn, is thought to lead to uninhibited and even hostile behavior, with accompanying negative perceptions of others [16, 17]. Another predicted outcome is that the general lack of visible status cues, along with reduced evaluation anxiety on the part of low status and shy individuals, may lead to more equal participation in CMC contexts [18], presumably with a change in how shy individuals are perceived by other group members. Support for the Reduced Social Cues model has been found in some contexts, particularly those involving short-term interacting groups with no previous histories, but evidence in other contexts has been contradictory [6, 19, 20], suggesting that there are likely additional mediating factors in CMC effects than those proposed by the model.

A third prominent model of CMC is *Social Information Processing Theory*. The basic notion of this approach is that people are motivated to develop social relationships in any communication context, including CMC, and in the service of this motivation they form impressions of each other on the basis of whatever information is available [21]. They subsequently test the assumptions associated with their perceptions using a variety of strategies. Text-based CMC slows down this process but does not prevent it from occurring.

Thus, according to the Social Information Processing (SIP) model, impressions may take longer to form than in face-to-face communications, but they are not essentially different in CMC than face-to-face contexts. The model recognizes that certain kinds of social cues are missing in CMC, but it maintains that people are motivated to obtain social information in other ways (for example, by learning to communicate emotion through textual devices such as emoticons and linguistic modifiers) and thus overcome these limitations, given enough time. There is considerable support for the model's claim that CMC and face-to-face communication produce impressions that have comparable levels of structure if enough time is available for CMC interaction [5, 20, 22]. Perhaps the two main shortcomings of the SIP model are that does not specify what differences, if any, there might be in the content or tone of CMC versus face-to-face perceptions, and it doesn't recognize important individual and situational differences in people's social motivations to overcome the challenges posed by CMC [5].

A fourth approach to understanding the nature of CMC is the *Hyperpersonal Communication Model*. The model was proposed by Walther [6] to account for the phenomenon that CMC is sometimes "...more socially desirable than we tend to experience in parallel FtF [face-to-face] interaction " (p. 17). Specifically, Walther suggests that "Combinations of media attributes, social phenomena, and social psychological processes may lead CMC to become 'hyperpersonal,' that is, to exceed FtF interpersonal communication" in terms of "...heightened levels of intimacy, solidarity, and liking" (p. 4-5).

According to the model, interpersonal perceptions in hyperpersonal communication are not accurate assessments, but rather positive exaggerations based on selective self-presentation by the target person and faulty inferences by the perceiver. The gist of the model's assumptions are succinctly described by Utz [5]:

"In CMC, users have the opportunity for selective self-presentation. They have time to think about how to present themselves and can choose the positive aspects. On the other hand, the reduced social cues in CMC lead to an idealized perception by the perceiver. S/he has only the positive information, and inflates the impression of the partner by generalizing these positive cues on other unknown personality aspects. CMC can, therefore, be more social and intimate, or "hyperpersonal" relative to FTF communication."

There is considerable evidence that strong friendships and even romantic relationships often develop through online interactions [5, 8, 23], and that people can achieve a sense of community and solidarity with others in cyberspace [24, 25, 26, 27]. It is also the case, as suggested by the Hyperpersonal model, that when individuals meet in person they frequently find their online impressions were overly positive [28]. Furthermore, the heightened sense of community and solidarity experienced by group members may lead to greater vulnerability to disruption, such that violations of community standards and trust may have particularly severe consequences for online communities [29, 30, 31].

Though these findings are in line with the Hyperpersonal Communication theory, there have been only a few direct tests of the underlying mechanisms proposed by the model. Utz [5] has found that self-presentation of positive sentiment through the use of using paralinguistic cues does indeed correlate with developing positive relationships online. However, Utz also showed that the correlation is mediated by individual differences in skepticism about the medium: "Individuals who believe it possible to build up relationships in virtual worlds learn how to use smileys, feelings, and emotes and thus make friends...but those who are more skeptical of CMC do not." In a recent series of experimental studies by Joinson [7], self-disclosure of personal and intimate information was higher in CMC than in face-to-face interactions, as predicted by the Hyperpersonal model. But independent manipulations of the participants'' anonymity and the degree to which their attention was self-focused revealed that self-disclosure was highest when they were anonymous. Anonymity would seem to remove strategic self-presentation as a motivation for disclosure, and thus Joinson's findings are a challenge to the model as originally proposed.

In summary, the Hyperpersonal Communication model is a valuable attempt to explain the positive effects of CMC, though more research is needed to test and to refine its assumptions.

4.2.2   Assessment of CMC Models

The approaches reviewed above give the flavor of ways researchers have tried to characterize the nature of CMC and its implications for social perception. All the models recognize that the information available for forming impressions and making judgments of other people is restricted in CMC relative to face-to-face communication. They differ, however, in their views of how severe the consequences of such restrictions are likely to be. Social Presence theory and the Reduced Social Cues model are perhaps the most negative in this respect, viewing interpersonal perceptions that arise in CMC as likely to be poorly developed, impersonal, and largely negative. The Social Information Processing and Hyperpersonal Communication theories are much more positive, proposing that social impressions arising from CMC can be just as well-developed and positive in tone as those generated from face-to-face interactions, and under certain circumstances may even exceed them in intimacy and positivity.

4.3   Cognitive Processes in Cyberspace

Everyday social perceptions are influenced by a number of cognitive processes that determine the kind of information that is attended to and the way it is interpreted. Several of these processes are particularly relevant to social perception in cyberspace because they influence the nature and quality of online impressions. These processes are "snowballing," social identification, and the activation of social categories.

4.3.1   Snowballing

Our initial impression of someone often leads us to behave toward that person in certain ways. For example, if we perceive the person to be warm and friendly, we are apt to be open and responsive to them. The other person, in turn, may respond to our treatment by being even more friendly and jovial than they would normally. We then infer that the person's behavior is confirming evidence that s/he is indeed a very warm and friendly person, unaware that their actions might be due to our own behavior, not the manifestation of a central feature of the person's personality.

Social psychologist Daniel Gilbert refers to this phenomenon as the "snowball effect," in which an initial perception can start a process that gathers momentum and becomes harder and harder to alter over time [32]. Gilbert's analysis was originally developed to apply to face-to-face interaction but it is also relevant to CMC. Gilbert proposes that the snowball effect is particularly robust because it leads to a mistaken inference that the target person's behavior is the result of a disposition or trait that the person possesses, rather than the result of the perceiver's own behavior which produces what Gilbert terms "perceiver-induced constraints" on the target's actions: "Snowball effects occur when perceivers make dispositional attributions about those who are operating under the influence of perceiver-induced constraints – in other words, when I cause you to act in certain ways and then conclude that you are predisposed to those actions" (p. 137).

How might this operate in text-based CMC? Gilbert proposes three factors that contribute to the snowball effect, each of which is relevant to CMC.

- *Response matching:* Much of our behavior in face-to-face situations is simply a matched reaction to the behavior of another person. According to Gilbert, "In social life, behaviors play 'call and answer,' and everyone knows just which kinds of offers warrant just which kinds of responses. *If* a person is cold and hostile toward us, then we will probably act coolly in return; if a person is lively and interested, we will feel flattered and repay their warmth with our own" (p. 128).

Response matching is also characteristic of online interactions. Wallace [3] suggests that people who are new to CMC are not yet facile with ways to overcome the medium's limitations for expressing emotion and social responsiveness, such as adding emoticons and linguistic modifiers to their messages. The result is a perception-behavior cycle that is an online version of the snowball effect:

"We don't just appear a little cooler, testier, and disagreeable because of the limitations of the medium. Online, we appear to be less inclined to perform those little civilities common to social interactions. Predictably, people react to our cooler, more task-oriented impression and respond in kind [italics added]. Unless we realize what is happening, an escalating cycle begins. The online group members could have typed simple phrases to express more agreement and to release tension if they had realized the importance of such utterances to the impression they were making and to the group's functioning." (p.17)

- *Providing opportunities:* People test the assumptions associated with their impressions of others using a variety of strategies that provide opportunities for confirming or disconfirming their initial perceptions [6, 33]. As Gilbert describes the process, "...our beliefs about people, right or wrong, determine our behavior toward them – specifically, they determine the sorts of opportunities we provide for others to corroborate or rectify our first impressions." (p.133). It is well documented, however, that in face-to-face interaction this process is biased toward confirming one's initial impressions [33]. In Gilbert's words, " ... not only do we fail to provide opportunities for others to repudiate our suspicions, but we also *create* special opportunities for them to confirm what we suspect" (p. 133). Creating opportunities in CMC can include starting a specific thread, or line of discussion that invites responses from others, or posing questions and challenges to a target person to see how s/he responds. The text-based nature of CMC provides an archive that can play a role in these confirmation strategies. Wallace [3] suggests that:

"As cognitive misers, we are reluctant to rethink the impressions we form of others ... That first impression is so critical because of this human resistance to admit mistakes, and the desire to leave the label in place leads to confirmation bias . Not only do we ignore evidence that might contradict our original impressions; we actively search for information to confirm them...Once we form some impression we selectively pick up confirming evidence. In long Internet messages, it is usually not difficult to find snippets to support our first impression and to ignore the rest." (p. 26)

- Setting norms: If we interpret a situation as calling for a certain kind of behavior, our actions will set the norms for others to behave in a similar way. Note that the other people are responding to what they perceive to be the norm governing the situation, not in their mind to our behavior. In the snowball phenomenon, a person's initial impression of another will lead to certain behaviors that the other interprets as indicative of the norm to be followed, which nevertheless will be observed by a perceiver as behavior arising from the target person's personality or character. Balm [26] has identified the presence of both implicit and implicit norms in online interactions. These norms govern the use of paralinguistic elements, expression of negative statements, disclosure of personal information, and reciprocation of positive, supportive messages. Thus, people may adapt their behavior to what they perceive as the normative standards of the online community, just as they would in face-to-face situations, with the result that they will be perceived as having personality characteristics consistent with the normative behavior they exhibit. Their actual personality might be quite different, however.

- Barriers to being aware of perceiver-induced behavior: An important element of the snowball effect is that the perceiver is unaware that s/he is actually producing the behavior of the target person. Gilbert proposes two reasons why it is difficult to overcome this problem.

First, if we are the cause of the other person's behavior, it is quite likely that they behave differently when we are not around. However, we have no opportunity to see the other person behave in a manner that might contradict our impression because we only encounter the person when we are present. Second, during social interactions we devote considerable effort and attention to monitoring our own behavior and the impression we are giving to others.

This distracts us from thinking deeply about the causes of other people's behavior. Both of these conditions are present in many forms of CMC. For example, our knowledge of someone might be restricted to a single USENET forum so that all our inferences about their character are based on behavior that occurs in our presence. Another illustration might be the inferences that take place in chat sessions, where the interactions are often rapid fire and require careful attention to one's own activity, giving little opportunity for analyzing alternative reasons for someone's behavior.

4.3.2   Social Identity

A second important process that shapes the nature of social perceptions in cyberspace is the activation of social identities. Social identities are linked to memberships in social categories, such as those based on gender, age, or culture, and also to memberships in work groups and organizations. Personal identity, on the other hand, is tied to a person's unique qualities and characteristics, including physical features and appearance, character traits, attitudes, and values. Social identity has an important psychological function. It can contribute to our self-esteem by allowing us to assume we possess the positively evaluated characteristics that are stereotypically attributed to the groups with which we are associated [34, 35, 36, 37]. Social identity can also have an important influence on how we behave in social situations. Under conditions where social identity is more salient than personal identity, behavior will likely follow the group's norms for appropriate actions rather than being idiosyncratic [36], [37].

Social Identity De-individuation (SIDE) theory, developed by Spears & Lea [36, 37], offers a useful framework for examining the relevance of social identity to online interactions and the social perceptions that develop during CMC. According to the theory, a major factor that moderates the effects of salience is *de-individuation*. De-individuation is a cognitive state produced by visual anonymity and physical isolation, two qualities that characterize much of CMC. Spears & Lea propose that de-individuation accentuates the effects of whichever type of identity is salient [38]:

"The effects of group identity will be accentuated when subjects are de-individuated, as visual anonymity and physical isolation will reduce perceptions of individual (intragroup) differences. However, if individual identity is already salient, physical isolation from the group is predicted to further undermine any sense of group belonging, and further accentuate individualistic norms and tendencies. (p. 331-332)."

The theory is not only able to resolve contradictions between studies that have found both positive and negative social behavior to be enhanced in CMC, it also makes some interesting predictions concerning the impressions people develop of each other during CMC. One prediction is that the same cues can lead to both positive and negative social perceptions, depending upon certain conditions in which social identity is more or less salient relative to personal identity. Paralinguistic cues, for example, might be either positively or negatively evaluated, depending upon the salience of the perceivers' social identities. According to Lea & Spears [38]:

"...when group identity is salient, paralinguistic cues will tend to be seen as a prototypical feature of the group (the inductive aspect of stereotyping), whereas when individual identity is salient, they will tend to be seen more in terms of the idiosyncratic style of the individual users. As a result, such cues will tend to be evaluated differently in the two conditions, being evaluated more positively when group identity is salient, and increasingly less so as a more individualistic context becomes salient." (p.331)

In a test of this prediction, Lea & Spears [38] assessed the relation in online discussions between use of paralanguage (ellipses, inverted commas, quotation marks, and exclamation marks) and perceptions of warmth, dominance, uninhibitedness, responsibility, liking, and competence. Half of the discussions took place under conditions of high group salience, in which instructions to participants emphasized their common group membership. In the remaining discussions instructions stressed the individuality of each person and the unique contributions of each to the discussion, thus making personal identity more salient. Within each salience condition Lea & Spears manipulated de-individuation by physically and visually isolating participants in half the online discussions (de-individuation condition) or by having participants use the computer conferencing system while seated in the same room and in view of each other, but without allowing them to talk to one another (individuation condition).

The results of Lea & Spears' study were in line with the SIDE theory. When participants were de-individuated, paralanguage use was positively associated with perceptions of likeableness, warmth, competence, uninhibitedness, and responsibility if group salience was high, but *negatively* associated with these qualities when personal salience was high. These relationships were weaker when participants were individuated, as expected by the theory. In summary, the qualities of CMC as a medium cannot by themselves account for the perceptions of these participants. Rather, the de-individuated nature of CMC appears to exaggerate the different effects of social and personal identities. When group membership is salient, paralinguistic cues are seen as positive contributions to group solidarity and commonality. When individual identity is salient, "a more individualistic and competitive context will be perceived for the communication task," and the same cues may be interpreted as negative manifestations of "competitive individualism."

4.3.3   Activation of Social Categories, Schemas, and Stereotypes

We like to think that our assessments of other people are based only on careful and thorough considerations of hard evidence regarding each person's unique personality. In truth, however, the process of forming an impression is more often characterized by rapid processing of incomplete information and making inferences on the basis of mental shortcuts and generalizations [3, 39, 40]. Particularly in the initial stages of social perception, we rely on social categories, schemas, and stereotypes to help make sense of another person's behavior. Cues about a person's occupation, for example, may lead us to assume a number of interrelated things about his or her attitudes, values, interests, abilities, etc. A farmer is likely to value practical, down-to-earth approaches to life, and not enjoy the opera or ballet. A college professor is likely to value abstract and theoretical thinking, and not enjoy a rock concert. There may be some statistical truth in these assumptions, but they are apt to miss the mark if applied to every farmer or college professor.

Social categories, schemas, and stereotypes help us process information about others quickly and efficiently even if not accurately. As Wallace [3] describes it (p. 19-20):

"Barraged by sensory information and rushed for time, we take shortcuts and rely on just a few cues. Once we have those, we think we have that person nailed and can move onto other matters...It would be too time-consuming to collect comprehensive information to form unique impressions of everyone we meet, so we overuse certain cues that serve as rules of thumb. The impression of a person's warmth or coldness is one example. It dominates the picture as soon as we know anything at all about it and our conclusions about other personal characteristics flow from it."

Wallace gives a person's email address or choice of online nickname as examples of an initial cue that can stimulate initial impressions on the basis of social categories, schemas, and stereotypes [3, 41]. For instance, consider the difference in impressions generated by "tufdude888@aol.com" versus "jtravis@vs2.harvard.edu". We would perhaps expect that "tufdude" holds traditional attitudes about the role of women and takes a dim view of women's rights, and that "jtravis" has an intellectual orientation, is probably liberal in social attitudes, and appreciates art and literature. These impressions may be incorrect, of course, but they nevertheless would influence our initial online interactions with the two individuals, perhaps in ways that would lead to snowball effects as described earlier. Other cues that may stimulate online impressions based on categorization include explicit evidence of age, gender, or cultural background through a person's responses to direct queries [3], as well as more subtle information contained in a person's language use, such as word choice and diversity of vocabulary, sentence structure, and spelling errors [22, 28, 38, 42]. For example, a person who mentions "dons," "lorries," and "roundabouts" may be categorized as English, with additional inferences associated with the category, such as the person preferring warm beer [28].

4.3.4   Prototype Effects

A useful analysis of categorization processes in online impression formation is offered by Jacobson [28]. Jacobson's analysis draws on concepts from cognitive and social psychology, particularly Prototype theory [42, 43, 44]. A "prototype" is the clearest case of membership in a particular category, with individuals varying in how good an example of the category they are. These variations among individuals in how well they fit a category, as well as differences among perceivers in their judgements of how well the same individuals fit the category, are termed "prototype effects."

Understanding prototype effects entails explaining their source – why are some individuals perceived as fitting a category better than others, and why do some perceivers regard a particular individual as fitting a category better than other perceivers do? One source is the lack of fit between a category and its background assumptions. For example, "bachelor" is a category that assumes men in society marry at a typical age – an unmarried man of that age may therefore be initially considered a good fit to the category. Yet there are a number of circumstances where the assumption doesn't apply and a specific unmarried man may fit the category less well – for instance a priest or a homosexual [28, 43]. In CMC contexts, gender and marital status might be among the first qualities that are perceived, with the attendant potential for error in assuming an unmarried male encountered online is a good fit to the category of "bachelor."

A second source of prototype effects is the nature of the cognitive model a perceiver applies to a given situation. Two such models that Jacobson proposes are prevalent in cyberspace are *stereotypes* and *exemplars*. A stereotype is model in which an individual is taken to represent the entire category, the characteristics of which are culturally recognized.

Thus, an impression based on a stereotype will contain inferences based on the belief that all individuals in the same category possesses the same characteristics. Exemplars are "specific individuals whom people have encountered and who are taken as representative of others who are thought to be members of the same category" [28]. For instance, a new acquaintance may remind us of someone else we already know and on that basis we infer they share many characteristics. Prototype effects in this case may arise either because other perceivers are reminded of different exemplars, leading to different impressions, or because through experience we come to regard different people as exemplars of the same category, leading us to generate different inferences about the target person.

Two additional models are *typical examples* and *ideal types*. "A model of 'typical examples' is based on knowledge about features common to a number of individuals that distinguish them as an identifiable class" [28, p. 5]. Thus, it might be "typical" of computer programmers to be socially withdrawn, but prototype effects would occur if this inference is applied to an atypical case. Ideal types, in contrast to typical examples, are not necessarily either typical or stereotypical. For example, qualities associated with the ideal husband may overlap very little with those of the stereotypical husband, and neither may overlap with those of the typical husband. Prototype effects in the case of ideal types take the form of impressions that lead to inferences of ideal qualities, whereas the non-ideal case better reflects reality. Some forms of CMC may encourage this idealization effect, as Walther has outlined in his Hyperpersonal Communication Theory discussed earlier [6].

Jacobson [28] examined the role of various prototype effects among participants in several virtual communities, known as MOOs (Mud, Objected Oriented – see Curtis [45] for an informative explanation of MOO's and Muds). He interviewed one group of individuals who had interacted with other community members in both online and face-to-face contexts, asking them to describe the fit (or lack thereof) between their expectations based on their interactions online and their experiences face-to-face. Questions included, "Are people what you expected them to be?" and "In what ways do their online and offline characteristics differ?" A second group of participants wrote down their impressions of individuals based on their online interactions with them. They were asked to describe the individuals "...including their physical features, their mannerisms, and any other personal attributes that come to mind" and to analyze how they had arrived at their interpretations. Jacobson was able to obtain photographs of some of the target individuals, allowing a comparison of the descriptions to actual physical features.

The results showed that impressions were frequently formed on the basis of stereotypes and exemplars, with typical examples and ideal types being somewhat less prevalent. An example of a stereotype-based impression, apparently stimulated by the target's online nickname was the following:

"JoshSamBob's name sounds like a white southerner. He fits my idea of a stereotypical frat boy. He's just under 6 feet tall, medium build, blonde hair, blue eyes, his lips are thin. He's particular about what he wears and is in general very neat. He tends to fidget a lot and would much rather be out playing sports than sitting in a lecture hall or library. He enjoys horseplay and being where the action is."

Another impression illustrates the exemplar-based approach, in this case based on linguistic style:

"Whenever I think I know enough about a MOOer's mannerisms to form an image, I tend to map em into someone I already know IRL [in real life or offline]. Perhaps a mixture of several people that I know. When I first got on here, [one] MOOer's writing style – specifically, his debating style – WAS extremely similar to a coworker's, so much so that when I read the MOOer's words I imagined my coworker sitting in his chair, staring at his screen, typing and squinting and whatever."

The use of typical examples and ideal types are illustrated by a woman who reported to Jacobson that she supposed, in the absence of disconfirming evidence, that her fellow participants' were white, a statistically typical characteristic of the online population, and that they would tend to be slender, a culturally ideal characteristic in her view: "I think we all like to assume the people we like are attractive, which usually means thinner in this culture."

For most of Jacobson's participants their face-to-face experiences did not match online expectations, particularly in the areas of physical appearance and talkativeness. In many cases the online impressions were more positive than the perceptions from face-to-face interaction, in line with Walther's notion of hyperpersonal communication effects. One of Jacobson's participants commented (p. 14):

"On Moo everything can seem larger than life – it can be quite a surprise to realize the people are ordinary. People here can seem more witty and amusing and clever and sexy than the people one knows irl [in real life]. People project a persona here sometimes, and when you meet them they are shyer or whatever. A friend of mine was disappointed when he first started meeting people from the Moo. He had the impression they were demi-gods."

Prototype effects characterized many of the discrepancies between online expectations and face-to-face experiences. Jacobson found that these arose from applications of stereotypes, typical examples, and exemplars, either singularly or in combination. One description that combines all three is of a woman in her late teens who was actually a petite brunette with long hair:

"I imagined that Malaika was high-school to early college age. This I inferred from something she said about her parents "letting" her go to Canada (no one keeps their 24-year-old home at gunpoint, at least no one I know of). [typical] Another thing she said made me think she was a lesbian and I have an image of short blond hair and a lot of leather clothing for that image. This is based on the fact that of the two gay people I've known well, they've both been blond. [exemplar] In addition, the media stereotypes influenced the length portion; after seeing multiple "stereotypical" lesbian characters, the word always conjures in my mind an image of shorter hair. [stereotype] Having no information to support these images, I assumed her to be fairly "average" looking – a typical person one might encounter while walking down the street. In other words, I did not imagine her to be exceptionally thin or obese, exceptionally tall or short... [typical]"

4.3.5   Priming of Social Categories

A well-studied aspect of how people process social information in everyday life concerns the accessibility of categories and concepts. At any given moment some categories are more available than others and are therefore more likely to be used to form an impression of a new person [40]. Availability is often influenced by a process called "priming". For example, if I have just viewed a movie in which the main character is motivated throughout by greed, the concept of greed may remain very active for some time afterward. If I encounter a new acquaintance during that period, I may be more likely to interpret his or her behavior as indicative of greed than some other motivation, providing the behavior is ambiguous enough to allow this. The category of "greedy-person" is momentarily more accessible than other social categories, having been "primed" by the movie.

In CMC contexts behavior is frequently ambiguous enough to be open to interpretation as to its exact meaning for the character of the person performing it, and therefore CMC-based impressions might be particularly prone to priming effects. Wallace [3] offers the following fictitious illustration of how this might operate. Assume that you have just logged on to a chat room using the nickname "solo" and encounter Trajyk, and newcomer to the room. You exchange the following remarks:

> *<Trajyk> I've had some tough times in my life*
> *<solo> heh, heh, what difficult times were those Traj?*
> *<Trajyk> much sadness, much disappointment*

<solo> are you happy now?
<Trajyk> I've found real, true friends :)
<solo> here?
<Trajyk> No, in our little community of friends
<Trajyk> Are you lonely, solo?

By themselves, Trajyk's comments are not very informative about his or her personality, other than possibly displaying a certain resilience and willingness to look to others for emotional support. Imagine now, though, that just before logging on to the chat room you had read a newspaper account of how a number of religious cults are using the Internet to recruit new members, particularly those who are depressed and lonely. Trajyk's comments would have seemed more sinister because you would be momentarily more inclined to interpret them as consistent with a social category of "fanatic" or "treacherous enticer" [3].

Priming of social categories can occur offline and then carry over to perceptions in online situations, as the above example illustrates. It can also occur as a result of the way online interactions are structured. For example, USENET discussion forums are designated with a label that indicates their topical focus, such as alt.paranormal, or alt.philosophy.greek. These labels activate social categories that are associated with people who believe in paranormal phenomena or who are familiar with ancient Greek philosophers, and we may be more likely to interpret ambiguous postings we find in those forums in terms of the primed categories.

Other examples of structural priming include the "neighborhoods" on the popular home page hosting service, Geocities. Users of the service choose to locate their page in themed communities of people with similar interests, such as "Vienna" for those who like classical music, or "Hollywood" for movie buffs. Visitors to Geocities arrive with social categories associated with the neighborhood labels primed, and thus may interpret ambiguous information as being consistent with primed categories. On Ebay, the online auction house, visitors can interact in discussion forums focused on specific interests, such as Beanie Babies, antiques, or rare recordings. Wallace [3] suggests that "...when you start reading the posts in your favorite forum the category you associate with people who hang out there is already primed ... you will be the miser, conserving your cognitive energy, by relying on your person-type for stamp collectors or rare book lovers to get some impression of new posters" (p. 26).

4.4   Self-Perception and Impression Management in Cyberspace

Thus far the discussion has focused on perceptions of *other people* in various computer-mediated contexts. An equally important topic, though one that has received much less attention in the literature, is how we perceive *ourselves* in cyberspace. As we interact with others, either online or face-to-face, we monitor the impression we are creating by attempting to view ourselves as others might see us. If necessary, we engage in various "impression management" tactics to alter the perceptions others have of us, selectively presenting information that is self-relevant. Erving Goffman's classic work *The Presentation of Self in Everyday Life* [46] details many of these strategies as they occur in face-to-face situations.

CMC offers some unique challenges to both managing our impressions and to assessing how others are perceiving us. As discussed earlier, reliance on text-based communication means that visual and auditory tools for self-presentation are not available and therefore require adjustment in strategy. "Managing your own impression on the Internet is like navigating white water with two-by-fours for oars. Your impression management toolkit is strangely devoid of the tools most familiar to you, and news ones appear that you may not know how to use...nevertheless, the drive to manage our impressions in any social setting is strong, and Internet users are extraordinarily creative" [3, p.28].

Some of the ways people can shape their online persona include strategic use of paralinguistic elements and linguistic modifiers in textual messages, such as emoticons and acronyms. As discussed earlier, there is evidence that such features do modify social perceptions. However, the newness of these devices makes it likely that achieving the desired impact requires experience and feedback. For example, from the work of Lea & Spears [38] we know that in order for authors of messages to correctly gauge the impact of paralinguistic cues, they have to be sensitive to the salience of group identity from the perceiver's point of view. Another tool can be one's choice of nickname for e-mail or for interactions in online forums. Bechar-Israeli [41] queried regular participants in several chat forums as to the nature and meaning of their online nicknames, and found strong indications that many used this as an impression management device. People rarely changed their nicknames, evidence that they regarded consistency in their online persona to be important. Nearly half (45%) reported that they chose a name that related in some way to their personalities, indicating that they were aware of the name's significance for impression management.

Wallace [3] notes that when people join an online mailing list or discussion forum, they are often invited to provide self-descriptions that will introduce them to the other forum members. These self-descriptions are clear opportunities for impression management, in that the person can choose what information to include and how to present it to project a desired persona. However, Wallace [3] suggests that there is also a challenge to using this tool effectively (p. 30):

"...many people are new at this self-presentation mode and in this context they have no model to follow. They just joined and have not yet seen anyone else's introductions, or even had much chance to see what others are discussing. The result is a bizarre mixture of first impressions that range from the brief and highly professional to the heart-rending personal confessional."

4.4.1   Home Page Meta-Accuracy

With the advent of the World Wide Web (WWW) in the early 1990's, the home page has become a widespread instance of self-presentation, and researchers have recently begun to assess the psychological and social implications of this new form of expression. [3, 47, 48, 49, 50, 51, 52, 53, 57]. As a number of authors have noted, the ease with which a person can create a home page has made it possible to convey a sense of self on an unprecedented scale. The basic nature of the home page as a self-presentation venue is described succinctly by Chan (pp. 272-273):

"Much like the way personal belongings, trophies, and souvenirs show off our accomplishments and tell the story of our lives, home pages bring together a collection of text, graphics, photographs, and links to create a distinctive online presence. Indeed, we can draw further parallels between the home page and physical space...Home pages, like rooms, are spaces where we can project our personalities, hopes, dreams, and fears. They are symbolic representations of our selves..."

At first glance, the graphical and hypertextual nature of home pages would seem to make it easier for individuals to manage their self-presentation and project a desired image [3, 57].

The creator of a home page has a high degree of control over the selection and arrangement of photographs and other graphical elements, as well as in the number and type of external links that can be chosen to convey interests, attitudes, and other personal qualities [52]. These features seem in line with Walther's notion of Hyperpersonal Communication [6] discussed earlier, and suggest that the home page creator might produce a more positive impression than through other media, perhaps even more positive than through face-to-face interaction.

However, there may also be a number of limitations to impression management through home pages. For one thing, the home page is largely a one-way presentation medium, whereas text-based CMC and face-to-face contexts are more interactive. This means that projecting a desired image in one's home page requires what social psychologists call "generalized meta-accuracy"[53] – the home page creator must accurately know how he or she is generally viewed by others in a particular audience. The problem is that neither the size nor the makeup of the audience for a home page is usually known. As Wynn & Katz [47] have observed:

"By contrast to the random nature of the home page audience, in traditional self-presentation formats, professional or political, the nature and numbers of the audiences are explicit. In home page 'advertisements for one's self,' audience is a self-selected unknown. There may be a presumption that the home page in and of itself will be an audience definer, but presenters have little knowledge of the range and size of potential audiences. It is thus possible to construct a presentation of self for an imagined audience while the actual audiences vary."

A home page creator's meta-accuracy would also seem to require accurate assumptions about the characteristics of who is viewing one's page. In face-to-face situations this is far easier than in cyberspace. As Wynn and Katz put it, "At any given time and place in physical life, we can look around and see who else is there. Based on that assessment, we can adjust our presentation of self." For home page creators this is not possible, and may lead them to rely on assumptions that do not hold:

"Some home page creators appear to perceive a more private world of readers than is in fact the case. Frequently the pages are not so much personally private but are located at an intermediate level of privacy, the sheltered environment of a peer group or work group. The problem is that anyone can access these pages. That is a fact of their existence. Yet how much social understanding do the creators of pages have, and how accordingly do they mediate their self-expression to account for possibilities of a limitless audience?"

Sherman et al. [52] recently explored these issues by having authors of home pages judge how positive they thought the impressions generated by their home page were and how likeable other people might find them based on information in the home page. The home page authors also estimated how accurate and complete others would regard the impression they had from the home page. These judgments constitute *meta-perceptions* – assumptions about the perceptions of others. Sherman et al. compared home page authors' meta-perceptions to actual first-hand impressions of the home pages obtained from a separate group of participants. This allowed an assessment of *meta-accuracy* – the degree to which home page authors were accurate in their assumptions about how others viewed them. Judgments were also obtained from groups of people who recorded their perceptions and meta-perceptions following face-to-face interactions. Thus, Sherman et al. were able to compare the meta-accuracy of home page authors to the accuracy of people in face-to-face encounters.

The results showed a strong tendency for the home page creators to believe they were perceived more positively than they actually were. On all the impression scales used in the study the authors of home pages thought viewers would rate them higher than was actually the case. They also overestimated how confident viewers of the page would be in the completeness and accuracy of their impressions. In comparing this pattern to the face-to-face results, Sherman et al. found that the degree of meta-accuracy was higher in the face-to-face condition. In addition, impressions formed from face-to-face interaction were more positive than in the WWW context, yet people who were the focus of the impressions thought others would view them in much the same way. This implies that "...the source of online inaccuracy seems to lie in people's beliefs that others develop the same impression of them in both online and offline contexts" [52].

Sherman et al. suggest two possible reasons for low meta-accuracy of home page creators: (1) faulty assumptions concerning interactivity and (2) the medium's exaggeration of egocentric biases [52]. In line with the first possibility, Wynn & Katz [47] have observed:

"The home page seems to bend over backward to pretend to be interactive by being preemptively disclosive about the self. Without the preliminaries of two people 'feeling each other out' to sense what would be appropriate to disclose, the home page jumps to state 'this is who I am.' Who-I-am tends to be expressed in a photograph, a list of interests which are active by being clickable, and a list of friends which is also active. The one is invited unilaterally to engage in an exploration that normally would occur at least dyadically. Indeed the dyadic nature of it would be the purpose for finding out about the person in the first place."

Creators of home pages seldom receive feedback about the reactions of others to their self-disclosure, and therefore they have no corrective mechanism for adjusting the impression they may be giving. This limitation is less characteristic of email exchanges, news group postings, and text-based chat interactions, leading to the prediction that meta-accuracy would be greater in those contexts than with WWW home pages, though still probably less than in face-to-face interactions.

A second reason for low meta-accuracy might be that the "billboard" nature of the home page may exaggerate egocentric biases, or tendencies to assume others view the world the same way we do, including our positive self-evaluations [54]. For example, in face-to-face interactions research has shown a tendency to assume others take more notice of us than they actually do, and to believe that our emotions, values, and attitudes are more apparent to others than they actually are [54]. Sherman et al. [52] suggest that these biases may operate in the case of home pages to the extent that people are assuming others will base their impressions on information that may actually be ignored, including information contained in photographs and other graphical elements. Again, the lack of interaction in the home page context prevents feedback that might allow the person to detect the discrepancy and correct the meta-perception.

4.5   Conclusions

This chapter has explored some of the ways that computer-mediated communication influences how we view others and ourselves. Based on our examination of available theory and research, there are three overall conclusions that seem to be warranted regarding the characteristics of social perceptions in cyberspace. All three are related to the general idea that perceptions are indeed influenced by the medium, but not always in ways that are straightforward.

First, despite the apparently impoverished text-based nature of most forms of CMC, people do form impressions of each other and they do develop strong interpersonal relationships online. The cues that influence perceptions may differ from those present in face-to-face interaction, but it seems people can learn to attend to them and to use them, given enough time and motivation to do so.

Second, the medium can produce negative perceptions of others as cold, uncaring, hostile, etc., but it can also exaggerate positive aspects of impressions as well. In general, CMC may make certain interpersonal processes more extreme than they are in face-to-face situations, with the direction of the effect dependent on factors external to the medium itself. For example, the same cues can produce impressions that are opposite in affective tone, depending on the salience of perceiver's group identity or the cognitive categories that are most accessible to the perceiver.

A third conclusion is that meta-perceptions are distorted by at least some forms of the medium such that people may be less accurate in judging how others view them than they are in face-to-face interactions. This may be because people have not yet developed a clear idea of how much others attend to certain cues and how they interpret them in CMC. It is also likely that reduced feedback from others when interaction is limited makes assessing the impact of an impression on others difficult.

The impact of CMC on society is still evolving and our understanding of its social, psychological, political, and economic implications is far from complete. It is useful to keep in mind that although the impact of this technology is dramatic, it is not unprecedented and there may be some lessons to be gleaned from the past. As Gackenbach [55] has pointed out, there are parallels that have occurred with past technologies. For example, in the early development of radio, some of the questions we now ask regarding computers, the Internet, and CMC were salient at that time regarding the impact of a "revolutionary" form of communication (p. 14):

"..the uncritical enthusiasm with which society first greeted radio soon gave way to grave doubts about its negative effects. After the rise of private radio in the United States, dozens of scholarly books were written from the late 1920's into the 1940's studying the ways in which the new technology was reshaping personal relationships, the structure of the family, the literacy of children, and the ability of people to think critically and express themselves clearly. We have only to pass by the shelves of any bookstore to see this whole process repeating itself with respect to the Internet."

Gackenbach's analysis emphasizes that approaches to studying the impact of CMC will benefit by placing it in a broader context. One lesson that derives from doing so is an appreciation of the nature and extent of a technology's impact, as in the distinction that Kiesler [56] makes between *amplifying* and *transformative* effects (pp. xii-xiii):

"Some technological change is primarily amplifying, making it possible for people to do what they have done before, but more accurately, quickly, or cheaply. In other cases, technology is truly transformative: It leads to qualitative change in how people think about the world, in their social roles and institutions, in the ways they work, and in the political and economic challenges they face...Sometimes the amplifying effect is what we see first, never realizing there is a later transformative effect to come, or that the amplifying technology is part of a larger social change."

According to Kiesler, it is people's behavior, not just the attributes of the technology, that determine whether a technology is amplifying or transformative. This certainly seems to be true in the case of CMC. As this review has documented, a deterministic view that focuses only on the technical qualities of the medium is insufficient to account for the impact of CMC on social perceptions. Whether the impact is amplifying or transformative is not yet clearly established, and an assessment would be premature. As history has illustrated, it is wise to remain open to all possibilities.

4.6   References

[1]   Nua Internet Surveys, How many online? Retrieved Friday, December 29, 2000 from the World Wide Web: http://www.nua.ie/surveys/how_many_online/index.html .

[2]   Kraut, R., Mukhopadhyay, T., Szczpula, J., Kiesler, S., & Scherlis, B., Information and communication: Alternative uses of the Internet in households. *Information Systems Research, 10,* 2000, 287-303.

[3]   Wallace., P., *The Psychology of the Internet.* Cambridge, U.K.: Cambridge University Press, 1999.

[4]   Short, J., Williams, E., & Christie, B., *The Social Psychology of Telecommunications.* London: Wiley, 1976.

[5]   Utz, S., Social information processing in MUDs: The development of friendships in virtual worlds. *Journal of Online Behavior, 1*(1), 2000. Retrieved Friday, December 29, 2000 from the World Wide Web: http://www.behavior.net/JOB/v1n1/utz.html .

[6]   Walther, J.B. Computer-mediated communication: Impersonal, interpersonal, and hyperpersonal interaction. *Communication Research, 23,* 1996, 3-43.

[7]   Joinson, A. Self-disclosure in computer-mediated communication: The role of self-awareness and visual anonymity. *European Journal of Social Psychology,* 2000, in press.

[8]   Parks, M., & Floyd, K. Making friends in Cyberspace. *Journal of Computer-Mediated Communication,* 1(4) 1996. Retrieved Friday, December 29, 2000 from the World Wide Web: http://www.ascusc.org/jcmc/vol1/issue4/vol1no4.html .

[9]   Lea, M. & Spears, R., Paralanguage and social perception in computer-mediated communication. *Journal of Organizational Computing, 2,* 1992, 321-341.

[10]   Chilcoat, Y., & DeWine, S., Teleconferencing and interpersonal communication perception. *Journal of Applied Communication Research, 18,* 1985, 14-32.

[11]   Daft, R. & Lengel, R. Information richness: A new approach to managerial behavior and organization design. In B.M. Shaw & L.L. Cummings (Eds.), *Research in Organizational Behavior,* 1984, pp. 191-233.

[12]   Fulk, J., Schmitz, J., & Ryu, D., Cognitive elements in the social construction of technology. *Management Communication Quarterly, 8,* 1995, 259-288.

[13]   Soe, L., & Markus, L., Technological or social utility? Unraveling explanations of email, vmail, and fax use. *The Information Society, 9(3),* 1993, 223-236.

[14]   Johnson, J., Chang, H., Pobocik, S., Ethington, C., Ruesch, D., & Wooldridge, J., Functional work groups and evaluations of communication channels: Comparisons of six competing theoretical perspectives. *Journal of Computer-Mediated Communication, 6(1),* 2000. Retrieved Friday, December 29, 2000 from the World Wide Web: http://www.ascusc.org/jcmc/vol6/issue1/johnson.html .

[15]   Sproull, L., & Kiesler, S., Reducing social context cues: Electronic mail in organizational communication. *Management Science, 32,* 1986, 1492-1512.

[16]   Kiesler, S., Siegel, J., & McGuire, T., Social psychological aspects of computer-mediated communication. *American Psychologist, 39,* 1984, 1123-1134.

[17]   Siegel, J., Dubrovsky, V., Kiesler, S., & McGuire, T., Group processes in computer-mediated communication. *Organizational Behavior and Human Decision Processes, 37,* 1986, 157-187.

[18]   Dubrovsky, V., Kiesler, S., & Sethna, B., The equalization phenomenon: Status effects in computer-mediated and face-to-face decision-making groups. *Human Computer Interaction, 6,* 1991, 119-146.

[19]   Lea, M., O'Shea, T., Fung, P., & Spears, R., 'Flaming' in computer-mediated communication: Observations, explanations, implication. In M. Lea (Ed.), *Contexts of Computer-Mediated Communication* (pp. 89-112). London: Harvester-Wheatsheaf, 1992.

[20]   Walther, J., Anderson, J., & Park, D., Interpersonal effects in computer-mediated communication: A meta-analysis of social and anti-social communication. *Communication Research, 21,* 1994, 460-487.

[21] Walther, J., Interpersonal effects in computer-mediated interaction: A relational perspective. *Communication Research, 19*, 1992, 52-90.

[22] Walther, J. Impression development in computer-mediated interaction. *Western Journal of Communication, 57*, 1993, 381-398.

[23] Turkle, S. *Life on the screen: Identity in the Age of the Internet.* New York: Simon & Shuster, 1995.

[24] Rheingold, H. Real-time tribes. In *The Virtual Community: Homesteading on the Electronic Frontier* (pp. 176-196). New York: Addison-Wesley, 1993.

[25] Jones S.G. Understanding community in the information age. In S.G. Jones (Ed.), *CyberSociety:Computer-Mediated Communication and Community* (pp.10-35). Thousand Oaks, CA: Sage, 1995.

[26] Baym, N. K. The emergence of community in computer-mediated communication. In S.G. Jones (Ed.), *CyberSociety: Computer-Mediated Communication and Community* (pp. 138-163). Thousand Oaks, CA: Sage, 1995.

[27] Haythornthwaite, C., Wellman, B., & Garton, L., Work and community via computer-mediated communication. In J. Gackenbach (Ed.), *Psychology and the Internet: Intrapersonal, Interpersonal, and Transpersonal Implications* (pp. 199-226), San Diego: Academic Press, 1998.

[28] Jacobson, D. Impression formation in Cyberspace: Online expectations and offline experiences in text-base virtual communities. *Journal of Computer-Mediated Communication, 5(1) 1999.* Retrieved Friday, December 29, 2000 from the World Wide Web: http://www.ascusc.org/jcmc/vol5/issue1/jacobson.html

[29] Van Gelder, L., The strange case of the electronic lover. In Kling, R (Ed.) *Computerization and Controversy: Value Conflicts and Social Choices* (2nd Edition, pp. 533-546). New York: Academic Press, 1996.

[30] Dibbell, J., Taboo, consensus, and the challenge of democracy in an electronic forum. In Kling, R (Ed.) *Computerization and Controversy: Value Conflicts and Social Choices* (2nd Edition, pp. 552-568). New York: Academic Press, 1996.

[31] Reid, E. The self and the Internet: Variations on the illusion of one self. In J. Gackenbach (Ed.), *Psychology and the Internet: Intrapersonal, Interpersonal, and Transpersonal Implications* (pp. 29-42). San Diego: Academic Press, 1998.

[32] Gilbert, D., Attribution and interpersonal perception. In A. Tesser (Ed.) *Advanced Social Psychology* (pp. 99-148). Boston: McGraw-Hill, 1995.

[33] Snyder, M., & Swann, W. Hypothesis testing processes in social interaction. *Journal of Personality and Social Psychology, 10*, 1978, 1202-1212.

[34] Hogg, M., Social identity and group cohesiveness. In J.C. Turner, M.A. Hogg, P.J. Oakes. S.D. Reicher, & M.S. Wetherell (Eds.), *Rediscovering the social group: A self-categorization theory* (pp. 89-116). Oxford: Blackwell, 1987.

[35] Hogg, M., & Abrams, D., *Social Identification.* London: Routledge, 1988.

[36] Lea, M., & Spears, R. Computer-mediated communication, de-individuation, and group decision making. *International Journal of Man-Machine Studies, 39*, 1991, 283-301.

[37] Spears, R. & Lea, M. Panacea or panopticon? The hidden power in computer-mediated communication. *Communication Research, 21*, 1994, 427-459.

[38] Lea, M. & Spears, R., Paralanguage and social perception in computer-mediated communication. *Journal of Organizational Computing, 2*, 1992, 321-341.

[39] Fiske, S. & Taylor, S., *Social Cognition.* New York: McGraw-Hill, 1991.

[40] Fiske, S., Social cognition. In A. Tesser (Ed.) *Advanced Social Psychology* (pp. 149-194). Boston: McGraw-Hill, 1995.

[41] Bechar-Israeli, H., From <Bonehead> to <cLoNehEAd>: Nicknames, play, and identity on Internet relay chat. *Journal of Computer-Mediated Communication, 1(2) 1996.* Retrieved Friday, December 29, 2000 from the World Wide Web: http://www.ascusc.org/jcmc/vol1/issue2/bechar.html .

[42] Rosch, E., Principles of categorization. In E. Rosch & B. Loyd (Eds.), *Cognition and Categorization,* (pp.27-48). Hillsdale, N.J.: Erlbaum, 1978.

[43] Lakoff, G., Cognitive models and prototype theory. In U. Neisser (Ed.), *Concepts and Conceptual Development: Ecological and Intellectual Factors in Categorization* (pp. 63-100). Cambridge: Cambridge University Press, 1987.

[44] Cantor, N., & Mischel, W., Prototypes in person perception. *Advances in Experimental Social Psychology, 12*, 1979, 3-52.

[45] Curtis, P., Mudding: Social phenomena in text-based virtual realities. In S. Kiesler (Ed.), *Culture of the Internet* (pp. 121-142). Hillsdale, N.J.: Erlbaum, 1997.

[46] Goffman. E. *The Presentation of Self in Everyday Life.* Garden City, New York: Doubleday, 1959.

[47]   Wynn, E., & Katz, J.E. Hyperbole over cyberspace: Self-presentation & social boundaries in Internet home pages and discourse. *The Information Society, 13(4)*, 1997, 297-328. Also available as online document: http://www-slis.lib.indiana.edu/TIS/articles/hyperbole.html .

[48]   Miller, H., The presentation of self in electronic life: Goffman on the Internet. Paper presented at Embodied Knowledge and Virtual Space Conference, Goldsmith's College, University of London, June. Retrieved   Friday,   December   29,   2000   from   the   World   Wide   Web: http://www.ntu.ac.uk/soc/psych/miller/goffman.htm .

[49]   Miller, H. & Mather, R. The presentation of self in WWW home pages. Paper presented at IRISS Conference, Bristol U.K., 1998, March. Retrieved Friday, December 29, 2000 from the World Wide Web: http://www.sosig.ac.uk/iriss/papers/paper21.htm

[50]   Miller, H., The hypertext home: Images and metaphors of home of World Wide Web home pages. Paper presented at the Design History Home and Away Conference, Nottingham Trent University, September. Retrieved   Friday,   December   29,   2000   from   the   World   Wide   Web: http://www.ntu.ac.uk/soc/psych/miller/homeweb.htm.

[51]   Arnold, J., & Miller, H. Gender and Web home pages. Paper presented at CAL99 Virtuality in Education Conference, Institute of Education, London, 1999, March. Retrieved Friday, December 29, 2000 from the World Wide Web: http://www.ntu.ac.uk/soc/psych/miller/cal99.htm

[52]   Sherman, R., End, C., Kraan, E., Cole, A., Campbell, J., Klausner, J., & Birchmeier, Z., Meta-perception in Cyberspace. *CyberPsychology & Behavior, 2001*, in press.

[53]   Kenny, D.A., & DePaulo, B.M., Do people know how others view them? An empirical and theoretical account. *Psychological Bulletin, 114*, 1993, 145-161.

[54]   Gilovich, T., & Savitsky, K., The spotlight effect and the illusion of transparency: Egocentric assessments of how we are seen by others. *Current Directions in Psychological Science, 8*, 1999, 165-168.

[55]   Gackenbach, J., & Ellerman, E., Introduction to psychological aspects of Internet use. In J. Gackenbach (Ed.), *Psychology and the Internet: Intrapersonal, Interpersonal, and Transpersonal Implications* (pp. 1-28), San Diego: Academic Press, 1998.

[56]   Kiesler, S. Preface. In S. Kiesler (Ed.), *Culture of the Internet* (pp.*ix-xvi*). Hillsdale, N.J.: Erlbaum, 1997.

[57]   Chan, S. Wired_Selves: From artifact to performance. *CybersPyschology & Behavior, 3(2)*, 271-285.

Towards CyberPsychology
G. Riva and C. Galimberti (Eds.)
IOS Press, 2001

5   Self in Web Home Pages: Gender, Identity and Power in Cyberspace

Hugh MILLER, Jill ARNOLD

Abstract. World Wide Web home pages have provided new ways for people to present and establish their identity and to find out about others. This chapter discusses the presentation of self in personal home pages in terms of Goffman's ideas as well as more recent social constructionist and feminist perspectives and approaches. Studies of personal home pages, comparing men's and women's pages, are reported. This is followed by a study in which women academics gave accounts of their experiences of the problems and opportunities that arose for them in creating and managing a public presentation of self and the proactive ways they were exploiting the opportunities of the Web.

It is assumed here that the Web is not different from the 'real world' and so our psychological perspectives therefore are critical reflections and commentaries on activities that take place in the context of real world and everyday activities. Oppression and difficulties which exclusion and prejudice can exert on any activity undertaken in (particular institutional) places, will inform our social constructs of identity and be part of the process of a predominantly male and patriarchal discourse. The discussion presented here reflects a growing interest in issues that surround challenges to the professional and private boundaries of the academic web user, and how the frame which institutions give to the establishment of a public identity often conflicts with an individual's need to have a personal presence on the Web.

There are grounds for being optimistic that the Web provides useful possibilities for encouraging links between academics, especially for those with less formal status.

The real space of cyberspace is on the bodily side of the screen, and the Web page presence may be a means by which people can increasingly find ways (in their own voice) to tell their stories.

Contents

5.1 Introduction

Over the last ten years, in the light of increased and diverse use of information technology, necessary and re-invigorated discussions of psychological conceptions of self and identity have begun to take place - especially once it was realised that some of the psychological issues we face in real-life social interactions do not necessarily disappear in cyberspace.

In the late modern or post-modern view, the self is a flexible, varied, sometimes fleeting construction, which must be established and maintained by effort and involvement from one who would lay claim to it [1, 2, 3]. Indeed, as Gergen points out, as the consequence of technological and social change:

"With this confluence of changing conditions, it becomes increasingly difficult to determine precisely what the contents of the psychological self may be, what actions constitute their expressions, where and when they occur, and what social purposes may be served by one's continued belief in such occurrences." [2].

New technologies and changing patterns of communication provide new boundaries and opportunities for self, and new routes through which the self can be established. The personal home page on the World Wide Web is one of those routes.

Many approaches to the study of the relationship between psychology and information technology develop the idea that the new technology will give rise to new ways of being: that life in cyberspace is, or can be, different from what is called, by comparison, 'real' life. It is noticeable however, that these accounts are based mainly on information which is *delivered to* the person by all the newly-available channels, and do not say much about how the self is expressed in the ways that are provided by new technology. Those who have studied the expression of self in Computer Mediated Communication (CMC) have either concentrated on how CMC allows the presentation of markedly 'different' aspects of the self, sometimes a disguised or other self [4, 5], or on how patterns of communication are different between genders [6]. Although a number of people have commented on the personal homepage as a rather different site for identity construction, making comments like "The medium where people tend to ostensibly be more their 'true' selves is the World Wide Web" [7], there are not many detailed studies of what people actually do with personal Web pages. Some accounts of WWW homepages and self can be found in work by Chandler and his associates [8, 9], Karlsson [10], Cheung [11], Kibby [12], Erikson [13], Shedroff [14], and our own [15-19].

5.2 Self presentation on the web

The World Wide Web gives anyone with a computer and an Internet account the opportunity of publishing whatever she or he wishes to an enormous public around the world. The personal home page provides the possibility of presenting one (or several) views of the self to that audience. We will examine the use of various kinds of personal home pages in establishing and presenting versions of the self from several theoretical perspectives, beginning with Goffman's Dramaturgical approach and including earlier Symbolic Interactionism and more recent work by Gergen, and other social constructionist and feminist perspectives.

Goffman [20, 21] has described how people negotiate and validate identities in face-to-face encounters and how people establish 'frames' within which to evaluate the meaning of encounters. These ideas have been influential in how sociologists and psychologists see person-to-person encounters. Branaman [22] gives a useful summary of Goffman's theory of self.

According to Goffman, one of the things that people need to do in their interactions with others is to present themselves as an acceptable person: one who is entitled to certain kinds of consideration, who has certain kinds of expertise, who is morally relatively unblemished, and so on. People have techniques and resources available to allow them to do this. There are 'back regions' in which backstage preparation can help in presenting an effective performance in 'front regions'; 'expressive resources' can be mobilised; and cooperation from others present in the interaction can often be relied upon to smooth over jagged places and provide opportunities for redeeming gaffes. Information about the self is displayed, but also needs to be managed, so that irrelevant or disconfirming information doesn't detract from the impression being maintained.

In face-to-face encounters, much information about the self is communicated in ways incidental to the 'main business' of the encounter, and some is communicated involuntarily: Goffman distinguishes between information 'given', that is, intended and managed in some way, and that 'given off' which 'leaks through' without any intention. He also points out a difference between the 'main' or 'attended track' of the interaction and other 'unattended tracks' which are at that moment less salient. For instance, if a colleague calls round, I may discuss a work problem and prepare a cup of coffee simultaneously, both of these going on cooperatively and interactively with the other person, but it is generally clear that the 'point' of the interaction is the discussion, not the coffee making.

Much of Goffman's interest lies in his analysis of the depth and richness of everyday interaction. This depth and richness is not immediately apparent in electronic interaction (though we will argue later that there is the possibility of depth and richness in the information provided by a personal home page), but the problem of establishing and maintaining an acceptable self remains, and there is a range of expressive resources available for this end. As the technology develops, more expressive resources become available. Also, as the culture of electronic communication has developed, people will construct expressive resources out of whatever facilities are available, as with the development of emoticons for email (and their adaptation to phone text messages, where they're even better suited). 'Electronic' communication has become more and more 'human' communication to the extent that there is more to it than just efficiently passing information to each other.

Goffman sees embarrassment as an important indicator of where people fail to present an acceptable self, and also an important motivator. A person wishes to present themself effectively to minimise the embarrassment of a failing presentation, but other participants are also motivated to help the performance by their wish to avoid the embarrassment they feel at its failure. So, most of the time, we interact in a cosy conspiracy in which it appears as if everyone knows what they are talking about, can remember the names of those who they're talking to, and has an appearance and presence which is pleasant and unexceptionable, even though it often happens that this is not the case. In this sense, our 'selves' are presented for the purpose of interacting with others, and are developed and maintained with the cooperation of others through the interaction.

Before looking at how the resources electronically available are deployed to produce impressions of self, it is necessary to establish how Web pages differ from face-to-face interaction and to work out what expressive resources are available.

Most Web pages are to some extent interactive. There is usually an email address where the author can be contacted, and homepage authors often solicit comment, or ask readers to 'sign my guestbook'. Pages may change and develop in response to this feedback. However, the pages aren't initially constructed interactively and authors cannot be sure who will access them. Structuring devices like Webrings and the 'themed neighbourhoods' of free site providers like Geocities do make it more likely that certain kinds of people (or at least people with certain kinds of expectations) will arrive at your site, and perhaps the popularity of these structuring devices shows our desire not to be completely promiscuous in our home page contacts.

However, this promiscuity of the Web goes deep. To talk to you face-to-face, we would have to travel to your town, walk up your street, knock on your door, and maybe get invited into your kitchen. Alternatively we might visit you at work. Even on the phone, one needs to know the appropriate area code and may have to go through various gatekeepers to talk to you. So when we finally interact, we both know to some extent where we both are (geographically) and probably where the other is coming from (socially or organisationally). We also know what kind of interaction this is: whether it's a customer order, a chance encounter in the street, or a bedroom conversation. This enables us to 'frame' the interaction appropriately [21], so that we both know how to interpret what goes on in the context of what is really going on. When you call up our individual University home pages, by comparison, you may get there through an orderly route via our institution, department, speciality, and so on, but you might have found one of the pages because it is 'nerdy homepage of the month' on the home page of someone in Mexico. If I knew that that was the way people were going to get to me, I might have arranged my public face differently.

Worse still, your communications (to the supposed audience of your pages) may be repeated by people you don't know to audiences you never intended.

So what is the communication involved in putting up a homepage? It *is* putting yourself up for interaction in some way, even if only a limited way. That limitation can be liberating. Goffman points out that one of the difficulties of interaction lies in establishing contact, because an offer to interact always leaves one open to rebuff. Conversely, starting an interaction always involves a risk about what the interaction might lead to, and possible difficulty in ending it. On the Web you can put yourself up for interaction without being aware of a rebuff, and others can try you out without risking being involved further than they would wish.

There is another liberation that can be negative, too. As discussed above, one of the regulating and controlling forces in face-to-face interaction is embarrassment. That is less likely to work on the Web. Others may find your Web page ridiculous, but you probably won't be aware of it. Those others who might be prompted to find ways to mend your presentation to reduce their own embarrassment in a face-to-face encounter are unlikely to feel pressure to smooth over the interaction between themselves and a Web page. So, in two senses, it is easy to make a fool of yourself on the Web: there is little to stop you doing it, but doing it will cause you little pain.

There are plenty of resources for presenting the self that can be mobilised. On Web pages, people can present photos of themselves (and their children), favourite graphics, snatches of speech and music, and access to a labyrinth of their interests and contacts. The homepage provides a locus for electronic self. These resources can be managed in the 'back area' provided by the web authoring package. There is plenty of possibility for misrepresentation because 'front area' Web pages are carefully set up before presentation to the world, and are only slightly interactive, though Buten [23] reports that most people he surveyed felt that they presented themselves 'accurately' on their home pages.

Now that people are becoming familiar with the Web, and know the 'usual' structure and content of homepages, it is possible to use this 'frame' more or less ironically to convey more subtle information.

The 'more or less' of the last sentence is an introduction to further consideration of the given/given off distinction suggested by Goffman. In many ways, this distinction would seem not to apply in electronic communication. Information about the self is explicitly stated and can be managed by the person making the communication. On the Internet, you can't smell my breath, catch the tremor in my voice, or realise that I'm watching the rest of the party over your shoulder. The implicit information that does leak through is paralinguistic, rather than non-verbal - a matter of style, structure and vocabulary - or paracommunicational - a matter of how I deal with a Web page compared with customary ways of doing it. Try calling up a succession of homepages and see if they give you hints about the nature of the people who composed them, even without reading any of the information given. Beware of taking these impressions too seriously. Someone may chose to include a picture of their partner on their page: that picture may be incorporated innocently and seriously, ironically, or in irony-transcending seriousness.

Other information may be given, or given off: as Mark Twain might have said: "show me what your links are, and I'll tell you what kind of person you are". The style and skill of the pages' presentation may be a major part of what's being presented, incidental to the main message, or a regrettable lapse that casts doubt on other aspects of the presentation. Even the domain name can be part of the show nowadays.

5.3   Towards the electronic self

Where does this lead to in a discussion of 'electronic self'? One of the things that has been a background worry in this discussion is the idea that Web pages are not interpersonal interaction of the kind that Goffman was describing. An interpretation of Goffman's work, and that of the Symbolic Interactionist school in sociology [24, 25] is that self is developed and maintained, as well as presented, in interaction. Perhaps the electronic self of the homepage can not be developed and maintained on the Web, but has to derive from face-to-face interaction, or at least email interaction. Or are there kinds and categories of electronic selves which can be presented and maintained in cyberspace, apart from our corporeal selves? That is one of the fantasies of cyberspace, but the selves presented in Web pages have not seemed to us to be qualitatively different from selves presented in other ways, and their styles of presentation can easily be likened to non-electronic presentations of self. This might mean that this aspect of electronic communication, at least, is not rich enough to support the interactive development and definition of distinctive 'electronic selves', or it might mean that we should wait to see what happens when people have actually grown up with the Web.

Another view, though, is that we shouldn't be concerning ourselves with 'fantasies of cyberspace': what people are doing on the Web is primarily what *people* are *doing* - just as is what they are doing at work, in the pub - and although the new medium offers new opportunities, those opportunities will be taken up in a way which is be continuous and coherent with the rest of life. As Daniel Miller and Don Slater [26] point out in their study of Internet use in Trinidad, people use the system to accomplish things - keeping in touch with relatives, proclaiming their faith, looking cool, promoting Trinidad - which are not at all 'electronic' projects, but social, personal, religious or cultural activities which are routinely carried on in many other ways as well as on the Internet. So, by and large, the things that people do on the Web, and the selves presented there, should not be expected to be distinct and separated from actions and self in other areas of life. As Lawley [27] says "The Web is not a new world, but an electronic reflection of the world we currently inhabit." People are likely to construct Web pages for some 'real world' purpose, and the content of those pages will reflect the aims, pressures and difficulties of the rest of their lives. This is the point from which begin a wider analysis of the implications for self and identity and the nature of the interactions people have with the Web and in the production and use of home pages.

The development over the last twenty years of approaches in psychology which emphasise the cultural and social *context* in which to understand such 'real world purposes', has also enabled a significant shift in approach to the study of self, identity and personhood.

Feminist and other post-structuralist psychologists, for example [28-31] have challenged those methodologies which claimed objectivity and dealt with abstractions of identity without acknowledging the importance of the actuality (and voices) of "somatic bodies weighed down by race, gender, sexuality, ethnicity, age etc prompted by desires, memories and love" [32]. As we have argued, in many ways, the Web *is not* different from the real world as a site for identity - it is part of it and "like other seemingly private/public spaces into which we construct an identity" [18]. The body that lives the life 'outside' of the presence on the Web remains a core issue, and we need to explore psychological perspectives that enable us to at understand what it is that might make it "easier for people to find a way of connecting to others [and acceptance of]...the self as other" [18].

The psychology of identity in traditional forms suffers from bias towards providing accounts which make the object of their studies seem exotic or rarefied (especially when dealing with a relatively new phenomenon such as the Web) and compared to an assumed 'everyday' or 'real world' from a (usually male) western scientistic view. A useful psychology will be one which allows analysis of our ways of knowing and doing (even in this technologically extended circumstances) in terms of everyday rhetoric [33], (Stanley, this volume). In our research and in the development of a psychological account of Web interactions, we assume we are involved in 'real life' concerns, not just with 'observations' of texts of identity, or with some new way of behaving and being. One aim of our analysis as it developed, therefore, was to understand what Gergen calls the "conventions of warrant" [34] that make ourselves intelligible, "hammered out on the forge of daily relationships" [35]. The perspectives that will enable us to take such a wide, yet grounded, view of what can be said about what people are *doing* at the interface with the Web's self-altering technology, and that can adequately deal with what happens when people cross the so called 'cyborg' boundaries, [36], are those which take account of the narratives and the interpretations we *usually use* to construct our social identity. Furthermore, whether individuals' 'presentations of self' are relatively confident and consistent in terms of their self-narratives [28], or are 'acts' created out of institutional hierarchical hegemony or text based identity constructs from dominant patriarch cal discourse [37-41], our experiences of creating a Web identity need to be treated as phenomena to be explained "in [terms of] a dialectical relationship between them and the social context" [42].

The Symbolic Interactionist approach offers a way of discussing the problem of embodiment with respect to the nature of Web identity presence. We don't want to 'abstract' the body - either as an 'organism' of the behaviourist school, or a 'system' of the information theorists [43], but try to understand how the psycho-social context and the discursively moral issues affect 'real' bodies. So, in our attempts to consider what is happening when people *do* their interacting with the Web, we don't want to talk of 'anybody' and so impose boundaries and specific discourses. We would rather find a way of talking about how experiences are in relation to contexts which are social, gendered, racial, or historical [44]. "What is at stake in the struggle for control of the body... is control of the social relations of personal production" [43].

Individuals are predominantly *self*-reflexive as well as in a subject-object relationship to society. So, one way we could consider the Web, is as functioning as an act of communication [45], technologically saturated as these communicative selves might be.

The claim is that in the post-modern era, the 'virtually real self' is as real as the 'real', because in the virtual space of the Web, multiple identities can be 'communicated' simultaneously. In this approach, there is no contradiction between fluidity of identity and accepting the virtual real as 'real' [4], where identity is both the 'thing' and 'not the thing' and not transcendent [46]. However, this is not to reject those that treat [e.g. gender] coherence and consistency [21] as qualities that men or women use performatively (maybe narratively). Similarly, we still need to develop a critical framework which challenges the inequality of power differences in the 'doing ' of identity in cyberspace.

In our work we have explored a number aspects of what happens when 'selves' include 'selves as hypertext'. The notions of embodiment which Goffman's approach elucidates, in terms of the 'display' of our bodies, need to elaborated if we wish to discuss bodily 'boundaries' to include 'the text' of the Web home page. When we are 'in cyberspace' are we 'there' as extensions of ourselves or as versions of our selves? Mead in his approach identifies how the symbolisms of the social discourse of everyday life describes the self as only existing in relationship to other selves [24] and in this sense we would view people as self productive (or identity productive). To do this we must include reference to subjective experiences and ideas of the 'self in relation to others', as more than the merely performative aspects of identity [47]. We are dealing with the sense in which we *own* our identities without implying an essentialist idea of 'one singular identity'. As researchers therefore, we do not attempt to 'interpret' the multiplicity of presentations and contradictory feelings associated with the diversity of situations and symbolic 'requirements' or 'restricted meanings' and absence of co-equivalences of many 'dichotomised' concepts (e.g. masculine/feminine; internal/external; real/virtual) on our performances of self at any one time or in any one place: "We do not conduct ourselves as 'one continuing thing.'... nor 'characteristics along a continuum' nor as 'having a multiple, fractured identity" [1, 48, 18]. We experience ourselves holistically and act discretely .

We realise that Goffman's theory too retains something of what the social-cognitivist would traditionally call 'schemas' or 'understandings' and though this could be misconstrued as being limited to notions of individual socially skilled performances in role, derived from the norms and conventions of group characteristics, we would not wish to obscure what might be taking place in web home pages as the completion of an idea [49-50] in a performative way. Much of traditional social psychology from the 1960's onwards attempted to objectively describe [51] the fulfilment of social roles and interactions in terms of encoded (and as far as we are concerned oppressive) social categorisations, whether as personality characteristics, group norms of behaviour (e.g. gender-roles), or as psychological truth which interpreted role boundary changes as abnormal or even clinical deviance [39].

5.4 A framework for understanding web page identity

In attempting to provide a framework for understanding web page identity and the personal decisions and action required to make a public web home page, we argue that people take active decisions about the ways we organise and classify our and others' *actions*. This is what Shotter calls 'joint action' [52], which denotes the combination of thought and meaningfulness in our behaviour(s). In this way we hope to present ideas in terms of *practical* effectiveness for people who are not puppets of predetermined character or stereotypical role behaviour. "The idea of the relatively autonomous, self-contained and distinctive person ....reflect [s] the sham and illusion that is the bourgeois individual, not its reality" [53]. From a Critical Theory point of view [54], the myth of the integrated individual with power to shape events, and the impact of ideological notions about the active/reactive agent of deterministic forces, still needs to be challenged.

If we adopt a range of ideas that bring together Goffman and symbolic interactionist perspectives with wider feminist social constructionist views, then we can also take account of how personal identity is created in the context of a mass market of individualistic consumption and awareness of collective identities. We will presume that our interactions with others take place in *negotiation* of social meanings. Therefore the use of the Web is a negotiation that is flexible and a continuously interpretive process. Part of the difficulty, however, of moving towards such a social construction and 'psychologising' of the body into a language of discourse style and performativity, is that we risk losing our assertion that we are discussing a practical and embodied phenomenon. The web self is both part of and contingent upon society, "constructed by the symbolic not its point of origin" [55].

Although we do feel that the most useful approach to the influence of new technology on personal psychology is to consider how people continue to do 'being people' with the technology, not how technology forms new psychologies, it would be a mistake to deny the possible effects of new media on the psychological message. If we believe that the self is constructed out of the doing of things, then the new thing to be done, for instance constructing a personal Website, will give the possibility of new aspects of the self. The opportunity to make a complex, multi-layered, but controlled presentation - the hypertext self - does raise new possibilities for how people can think about themselves, and get others to think about them.

5.4.1 Gender differences in personal home pages on the WWW

Our research on presentation of self on the Web started in 1995 with a fairly impressionistic survey of an unstructured sample of the then mainly male personal home pages [15]. This lead to the conclusion that home pages at that time reflected established print-based self-presentations.

We then went on to look at gender differences in personal home pages on the WWW [16], to see whether there were differences between the kinds of identity presented by men and women, or in the ways that identity is presented. Gender has been a significant topic in writings about electronic communication [4, 5, 56, 57], but this has mainly been about the negotiation of gender or gendered styles of communication in interactive communication. There are criticisms of focusing on gender differences, of course. Looking for differences between the genders has long been criticised as being sexist in itself. Why establish differences, unless it's for the sake of validating discrimination [58]? On the other hand, in a psychology where masculine is 'normal', it seems important to give equal attention to other ways of being, especially in male-dominated areas like electronic communication. We looked at a fairly random sampling of 35 each of men's and women's Yahoo! homepages, printed out the first page that loaded on each site (unless it was an almost content-free 'Welcome' page, in which case we took the second page), and did a quite simple analysis of main features of the page. The word 'fairly' in the last sentence reflects our continuing uncertainty about our sampling methods. To have an effective strategy for obtaining a representative sample of a population, one needs some idea of what the population might be, or where it could be found. We don't have any idea of what the total population of personal home pages are, or of how to go about finding them all. The most we can say of the pages we have looked at over the years is that we have mainly been concerned with 'ordinary' ones, although we have also picked out a few that seemed 'interesting'.

A traditionally-identified gender difference has been between 'expressive' and 'instrumental' orientation. We examined this by looking at what was mentioned and linked to on the page. A more expressive style would focus on feelings, people, and relationships, while the instrumental style might show itself in reference to abilities and achievements, material goods, and organisations and products rather than people. Mary Gergen has pointed out similar biases in popular autobiographies [59], and Csikszentmihalyi [60] and

Belk [61] both found male-female differences along these lines in people's reactions to material objects and accounts of how those objects related to their idea of self. Various measures might relate to this dimension. We counted links to other people, compared with links to non-personal sites. Women did put up more links to other people (mean of 1.8 compared with 1.2 for men), but they also had more links to non-personal sites (12.0 vs 9.4). Women also show more awareness of, and engagement with, the visitor to the site.

Women's pages had a mean of 4.5 references to the reader (using words like 'you', 'yours', or expressions of awareness of the reader), whereas men's pages had 2.6. Guestbooks were more common on women's pages (10 to 6) as were counters (21 to 13).

Many home pages show pictures of the author. This is so common that it has become a norm, that can be satirised, opposed, or apologised for ('sorry no picture - I'll get one up just as soon as I can get my scanner working'). We thought there might be gender differences here. Aspects of objectification and male gaze [62], the way the dominant culture problematises self-portraits for women [63], and abuse by men (as in the 'Babes on the Web' page, on which women who put their photo on their Web pages were rated by a distant observer for their attractiveness), all make the posting of a photo more problematic for women than for men.

We identified four categories for self-image on the page:

- straight: an image which purports to be a straightforward likeness;
- joke: a distorted or caricatured or unrepresentative image: cartoon, baby photo, author just after falling off bike into mudhole, author caricatured as frog, etc;
- symbolic: an image which represents a human being, but not the actual person who posted the page. This is often a piece of clip art, like a cherub or a generic silhouette;
- none: no images of humans.

We counted blurred or pixellated photos which might be of the author, but were so unclear that they didn't really represent an individual, in the 'symbolic' category. We were a bit surprised to find that there were several (15 out of 35 for both groups) pages with no images at all. Men's pages had more 'real' images (10 compared with 6), as we expected.

The big difference was in the other two categories. Joke images only featured on men's pages (on 4), and symbolic images only on women's (on 10 pages; the most common form of image on women's pages). The issue of what kind of picture of the self is presented on the page has seemed relevant in all our studies of personal Web pages. In the first study, in 1995, when pictures on Web pages were less common, only one woman's homepage looked at had a photo, and that was of the grainy, blurred, non-individualised type. This issue will be discussed further when we report on interviews with women academics.

It's interesting that these pages often use buildings as metaphors for the structure being presented. The use of spatial metaphors for data is very common - it is cyber*space* after all - ever since William Gibson's Neuromancer [64]. Perhaps pure non-spatial hypertext is too difficult to navigate - or perhaps the authors themselves need a structure within which to conceptualise their extended selves. A house or home does seem to be the ideal metaphor for the structure of the data of the self. One of Chandler's [8] home page categories is 'entire living spaces and homes, with their furnishings, posters, bookshelves, music collections, photos and so on'. Auerbach [65] suggests that the real-house home is a useful analogy to help people evolve an acceptable etiquette in the undefined social setting of the Web.

In the context of the rather informal home pages on Yahoo!, issues like status, authority and credibility, one of Goffman's areas of focus in 'The Presentation of Self', were not very noticeable. In a later paper [18], we looked at home pages produced by people in institutional or commercial settings, where the impression given of these aspects of the self can be important. Given that it is often suggested that in such settings women find it difficult to have their status, authority and credibility recognised, it seemed worthwhile to see how the 'official' personal Web pages of women and men might differ in these aspects.

In the home pages of women academics, the awareness of the reader shown in the Miller and Mather [16] study seemed to be modified by their need to establish their credibility and authority, prior to communication about their 'work' presentation of self.

Our impression was, also, that women's pages were likely to refer to safe, established genres like 'academic CV', 'author's profile', or 'institutional factfile', whereas some academic men's pages subverted or sidestepped these models. This brought us back to Goffman's idea of presenting an 'acceptable' self. In terms of academic identity, to be 'acceptable' is to be adequately qualified, to have appropriate experience, peer-recognised publications and to present all that information in an appropriately academic structure. But (as Goffman would have agreed, and discussed to some extent in 'Stigma' [66]) what it takes to be 'acceptable' depends on power relations and on the extent to which one's 'basic' nature fits with others' ideas of an acceptable person for that place or role. Perhaps men just don't have to try so hard to be acceptable in the academic role, and don't feel the need to reassure others that they are appropriately qualified and competent. The real life sources of potential discrimination are not left behind at the computer screen and it seems that women may not wish to risk experimenting with the freedoms implicit in the new medium.

The men on the other hand are able to be confident about the way they present themselves and their work (which they can assume is the reason for the visit to their page) and discovery of their credentials is possible, but is not the most important presenting feature of their page. For men what they do is who they are.

Questions about the difficulties that might have to be addressed (especially by women) when they contemplated creating a web home page (or more usually modifying or 'customizing' the standard format given by the institution or department's Web wizard) led us on to the last study discussed here [19]. We also wanted to investigate further the idea raised previously, that women see themselves as 'interactional' and claim part of their identity (academic or otherwise) as part of a web-of-relationships [67]. Another aspect of this work was to explore the idea that the gendered self for women is constructed out of some constraint or even potential 'threat' [18], even in the privileged cultural environment of academia. We looked, for example, for ambivalence and caution in the use of the web by academic women who may have a less secure professional status than men.

In our analyses, therefore, we began to move away from the dramaturgical framework and take on board more recent discussions of self and identity [68, 41]. Also, the way these presentations have to appear within an institutional context, and are perhaps controlled by institutional guidelines, provide other interesting constraints for the negotiation of the self. The blurry distinctions between person, worker, and professional have to be dealt with.

This led on to a series of interviews with Women academics about their personal home pages. The main focus of our conversations were on current and potential interactions with the Web which the women interviewed perceived as significantly affecting their working academic practices. Initial contact was made with 10 academic women who were interviewed by one of the researchers on the phone and in person. In the interviews with this small sample of women academics, we asked what they 'did' with information from the web and about its status for providing information at a personal as well as an academic level. We also wanted to get some immediate responses to something which would provide us with ongoing ideas and exchanges with women that would extend into a wider project to discover how the use of the web impacts on concepts of professional self and identity in academia.

5.4.2   Women academics' views of the Web and their self-presentation

The second stage of the research was to construct a questionnaire about women academics' views of the Web and their self-presentation on it, and post it as a Web page. We emailed about 20 women academics: people we knew, and women academics whose pages we had found in a fairly unsystematic sampling of faculty pages, mainly in Britain, Europe and the USA, asking them to complete the questionnaire, and inviting them to pass the URL on to any other women who they thought would be interested. The questionnaire itself was anonymous, but we provided an opportunity for those who were prepared to be interviewed further to give us contact details. We contacted these people by email or phone (occasionally face-to-face, if convenient), for a semi-structured interview, based on elaborating their responses to the questionnaire.

To understand more about the personal and subjective experiences of dealing with virtual academia and its people, we asked our respondents to reflect upon how their sense of identity was affected in the decisions they made about their own academic Web pages and in responding to those of others. We wanted to know whether there were any gender issues arising, either out of having to make specific decisions about the presentation of both personal and professional details, or when they were more generally engaged with interactions on the Web.

Some commented that this was the first time that they had considered this explicitly with regard to their Web pages. If, as we assumed, the self is 'fluid and multifaceted and dynamic' [48] then we could look not just for shifts in the ways roles and relationships are conducted, but also for changes in the ways that women viewed their 'constructed' identities [69]. All unattributed quotes that follow are from the respondents to this stage of the research, either from the on-line questionnaire, or from the follow-up interviews we conducted. The basis for seeking to discuss these matters further and in depth was to explore how far the new technology provides opportunities for new 'forms' of identity in contrast to the extent to which we remain grounded in physical and institutional existence.

Our enquiry was practical rather than theoretical. We assumed that we all have to make some effort to achieve a 'face' that is acceptable, because "in whatever media ... most people need to have interactions with each other to present themselves as acceptable people" [15]. The frustration experienced with the Web, as well as the feelings of recognition it affords, are because as yet the narratives and constructions which give us a sense of self on the Web are not yet part of a developed culture which has all the resonances and subtleties of taste, style, obvious political framework, etc. which we rely on in everyday life to position ourselves, know ourselves, or play our part.

Both men and women vary in the extent to which the technology is welcomed, and there are those who find personal home pages unnecessary, embarrassing or even frightening. Others don't really think of them as public documents. We were surprised at how often people we contacted about their pages were themselves surprised - "How did you find my page?" - as though it wasn't freely there for absolutely anyone who visited their institutional Website, or who did a search on their research topic. For the last fifty years or so, feminist concerns have been to promote non-discriminatory opportunities actively at the legal and macro levels of social interaction for women.

There has also been a considerable amount of effort to find ways that allow well-being in all areas of life at an inter-personal and intra-personal psycho-social level. The idea that the type of language used in communication was significant [70], and the pervasiveness of political in-correctness within the dominant (media) discourse out of which our identities are constructed, led women to learn how to claim equality through assertively developing a 'voice' that was their own [67, 71, 72], and which had influence and power without threatening the institutions upon which they relied for their livelihood and personal security.

Ideas of cyber self-identity cannot leave behind real world gender matters, and women recognise the implications:

"We want our work to be taken seriously - the men have far more space to be able to be 'playful' cos they don't have to think about not being taken seriously - but of course women do."

We also came across not just expression of the difficulties but also the intrinsic nature of the problem, but without much idea of how to get round it:

"I think men know how to make it easier for people to get to know what they are about - I want to do in a way that isn't too revealing."

The need to do the same thing only not in a revealing way indicates the depth of the trouble - gender trouble [73]. Women cannot afford to show too much about themselves.

The mixed feelings about this reflect a deep seated ambivalence by women about pushing the boundaries too far too quickly, even in cyberspace, where there are opportunities to bypass conventional routes to success and recognition. The safety found in remaining part of a group or acting collectively is both salient and possibly contrasts with the confidence that men can show about individuality:

"I don't want to present myself as so individualistic and about my career and so on: It breaks the rule to step out as an individual - women are used to the culture of the collective and the group."

There are contradictions that arise in the psychological struggle to present oneself as the person fulfilling the role of the academic rather than as a gendered person. Frequent academic Web users are as aware of the gender of the owners of the sites that they visit as they are in real life, but there may well be a lack of particular interest in gender when viewing a site. We argue, though, that gender interacts with many key issues raised in our considerations of identity on the Web. We assume that gender will apply to constructions or interpretations of identity on the Web just as in other domains: "especially prejudice on the part of people [...] to weigh masculine opinion more heavily than feminine."

On the other hand the impact of the new technology is recognisable in traditional ways but with some optimism too:

"There is such a risk of being a woman stepping out: it's a psychological shift - men don't question themselves so much: they don't have to worry about what they're doing. The interface challenges the essences of Women's lives, but we need to model our voice so that other women will recognise."

These are issues which are understood by all women, not just academics and not just on the Web:

"Women have different concerns and issues - an awareness of discriminations and substantive issues - learning to say 'I am legitimate' - 'I am an authority' - using the Websites for real academic acceptability."

"We can be honest about (crossing) lines and boundaries ...[having] someone to 'talk' to -

it can be so isolating for women in real life."

"One of my concerns is that we don't get behind in the tech race and that women learn to use the Internet ...women should learn to just play with the medium."

"The point of establishing who we are is for discovering like-minded people: we are always reinventing ourselves."

Or the comment:

"There is something positive about the web being a gateway and we can get access to appropriate subjects and documentation for conferences. etc. Women still don't always have much confidence."

Old fears can of course reassert themselves, and we found that negative self-deprecating factors are also part of the initial problem, and women don't value themselves enough and lack confidence about what they have done:

"I suppose I react on the web no differently from any other seemingly private/public space in which we construct some identity - but we get concerned not to be pushing ourselves forward - not to be separated off by being too prominent - if I've gone beyond a whole paragraph I think 'Oops, I've said too much'."

"I don't want to become a Babe on the Web - hah ha - I don't think so!"

Our respondents had clear ideas about what kind of a Web presence was appropriate for women:

"I think by having a Web page, I have a more 'techie' persona, which counters my frumpy, middle-aged woman persona."

"I wanted to include an element of fun, but I was also conscious of wanting them to look professional. Professional and fun were difficult enough, but I also wanted to avoid having the pages viewed as being either cutesy, or too feminine."

"I don't want to have too fancy software full of fancy stuff that can't be opened - surely the whole feminist critique of the technology would be that you think 'Hey, let's make this accessible'."

Establishing an identity on the Web involves the problem of underrating the significance of representation while at the same time acknowledging that as an 'intervention' activity establishing control without conflict is important for the maintenance of one's 'objective' self worth: safely maintaining 'face' in Goffman's terms.

"Assertiveness is keeping our mind to the path - e.g. we [need to be aware] of both traditional and future aspects of our work - it is a risk to be visible, and women are not used to having too much force."

Assertive communication skills can be what some women have already learnt: there's the point of establishing 'who we are', and an understanding that:

"It's very important to keep a profile even though blokes are trying to dominate the Web."
and recognising that credibility relies on active participation in educational technology:

"I find I'm talking more and more about the technology (and to my students) and using the Internet and needing to use it to find information."

"Women are often single-minded and at the cutting edge of use of technology - not in a nerdy way but practical."

What means do we have to make something which speaks in ways that do not offend but at the same time indicates a political or personal statement?

"We can use the Website design - floral patterns and flashy flags - it's very subjective - but how to make a feminist Website?"

"The Web is one of the more woman-friendly environments on the Internet. Usenet news, chat, and other sorts of environment are much less woman-friendly than the Web. Having said that, I think that whatever I am doing online I am always in some sense guarded because I am female. This is not necessarily different to when I am walking along an empty street though."

Experiences in face-to-face interactions of gendered stereotyping would not have lead women to expect Web interactions or reactions to their own presentations of their identity on their home page to be any different from the rest of their academic life. So the possibility that the Web could provide women with a sense of freedom - unrestricted by the usual limitations of hierarchical academic structures and associated notions of identity - meant that they were able to engage in discussions and to present their work and their views, and as a result - in terms of professional claims - who they were.

When we looked for examples of whether the establishment of credibility or authority and the difficulties of presenting a credible Web 'status' were issues, both for young academics as well as those with tenure and very well established positions within the academy, we found that:

"For young researchers there's no prestige to lose and it's easier to try new things, and established people get the 'professionals' to make a home page so they keep status - but they notice there's a race to 'be there' and be 'visible'... my presence is there all the time" (young researcher) though with the rider (from a senior academic) that so long as: *"presenting a 'gendered' identity [..] did not undermine my academic credibility."* (No man would ever say this.)

Many women felt that titles and qualifications were neutrally acceptable for a Web presence to maintain status, in a way no different from real life, conservatively fulfilling academic requirements.

The younger women academics in particular (postgraduate research students or women in research assistant posts or junior lecturers) were aware that the Web was providing them with some new freedoms. They found that they had access to people, and they were not restricted by the usual limitations of power which normally arose from age and status. In fact, one respondent suggested that the increased readiness of junior staff and research students to put up Web pages might trouble the academic hierarchy:

"For the person visiting the web page of my department, I am more visible than the professors (who don't have pages). This might have interesting implications for academic hierarchy. The page listing the staff also indicates who has personal pages - and these are mostly PhD students. In addition, some of the pages are rather place-taking - both visually and when it comes to the amount of information. Interestingly enough, one of the professors (a woman, if that is important) wants to organise a centralised creation of web pages for all employees at the department, where someone (the system operator, for example) would make standardised pages for all. An attempt to bring things back to order perhaps?"

There was a difficult balance between the formal requirements of an academic website and revealing some non-pompous aspect of the self (and women seemed very aware of the dangers of the medium to allow self indulgence and pomposity and the opportunity to 'show off', instead of modestly hoping to share ideas with others of like mind). At the same time women are aware of the opportunities of self-promotion not to be missed and considered carefully the amount of personal or political information it was wise to put in.

At another level there was an awareness that the academy itself is not 'about' individual personality, and in an area where for women the 'wrong' impression could so easily be given (sexuality and youthfulness or even blondeness being in antithesis to serious research), women seemed concerned to represent their research, not themselves:

"It's my programme that's important... not what I look like."

"I tried to give both myself and my research as much credibility as possible by making us both appear professional."

They try to strike a balance by appearing capable, approachable and friendly in order not to let the worthiness of their work become adversely associated with the personal. The Web home page is a public arena. Calling attention to themselves: 'look here I am', 'this is me: this is what I do' is potentially in conflict with what they are showing off, what they can 'do'.

5.4.2.1   Women on the web: Internet as opportunity
It is difficult to create the text content of the web page to be something which could be recognised as being an electronic version or extension of a person's (professional) persona.

However, for some the machine is a tool: "My Website is currently a teaching tool, focusing on my courses and students' work, rather than my own." This aspect of professionalism as providing a service rather than as a means of enabling an experience blocks the possibility that this new medium could be the means for accessibility and a directness of exchange reminiscent of the old fashioned academy where there was time to think and engage in dialogue.

The challenge may well be that new ways of communication mean that the nature of the relationship in such interactions focuses on how the gendered roles are played out and become visible, but the idea persists that there also might be an opportunity for an extension of existing ways of being, doing, sharing:

"It starts off with a conversation and three years later we can be running a conference together."

Even if information about the author available on Web pages is limited, the freedoms might outweigh the difficulties. The opportunity to 'meet' people, usually outside individuals' limited spheres (real time, real space, real status, real officially tenured credibility or place in the hierarchy, or fast-tracking mentoring) does allow real life preferences and judgements of personal likes and tolerances (e.g. "If they seemed friendly and not pompous") to be made, through 'content' and 'layout of web site' and the good links provided. Ease of accessibility and the apparent willingness to share work is inspirational, if the contact is with people who have something to offer and who can be participated with on their own terms and in their own time. Perhaps the Web is a place where women can achieve credibility and possible equal status too:

"I feel strongly that collectively we need to be supportive - it's a great way of networking - mostly women in academia are trying just to keep things together - it's important that feminists organise and have a good profile"

"We could see the Web as something useful. Women in academia can be so isolated... It can mean that women become more powerful outside the system. Women could be using Websites for real academic acceptability."

"Like getting a bicycle must have been for the freedom of movement and liberation of women."

In all our investigations into how women academics interacted with the Web, the omnipresence of the institution and struggles to have some control in the decision-making about institutional sites emerged as a reminder of the context in which the drama of cyberspace presence was being enacted. The idea that women (and men) could, in whichever part of cyberspace, become other than who they were, or do other than what they do, is confounded by the notion that how we perform our self-identities cannot entirely escape into another realm.

The idea that we are "only ourselves in relation to other selves" [24], and we are always in some sense negotiating our position through our interactions, raises questions about the relative power of hierarchical demands and constraints that are placed upon us. This is clearly shown in some of the ways many have to literally negotiate [45] an identity whilst using the 'corporate pro-forma' provided by the institution. This is the professional approach - the uniformity implied by the role and the requirements of conformity. The extent to which this is adhered to or broken free from might well be an indicator of a quality of 'independence' of the home page designer, or merely pose yet another set of dilemmas about how much one can be 'who you really are' in a professional role, where the presentation of individuality is subsumed under the closely guarded image of the institution. Problems of what can be placed on the web and the restrictions produced by institutional control, especially when mediated by technical staff, leave the dissatisfaction of wishing for "a more hands-on procedure which allowed me to construct and edit my own Website."

How could it be said that the site is even an 'extension of me', let alone a version of me, if it was entirely a 'ready-made', a thing off the shelf, and so constrained that individuality could not find its way through? People make attempts (e.g. use of different type faces, pictures in non-academic settings, informality, as we have already mentioned), just as at school we constantly tried to prevent the uniform overwhelming the differences between us and we each developed a 'signature' mark of rebellion that did not go so far as to infringe the rules of authority and bring censure. So when the women try to seem professional and individual while using a formal or standard format they could follow departmental guidelines and discuss the content with the Web manager, but could quite subtly "resist going more formal, though - I think it's a mistake to take oneself too seriously. Pomposity is to be avoided!"

In academic personal home pages, in contrast to individual personal home pages, it might be seen as more appropriate to be 'professional' than 'personal'. For those whose status can be questioned, it may be important to play down the personal content of one's page:

"I was particularly careful not to include personal information, as that only makes it easier for visitors to discount my professional persona."

"I have felt sad that I did not feel that I wanted to be up front about who I am on my Web pages, preferring instead to remove all traces of myself in order to present a credible research project to the world."

Also, even where self-presentation on the Web is an individual choice, not an institutional one, then people may choose not to include any personal details: "only when I know who I'm talking to" or to see the value such details (pets, gardens, partners, music we like, hobbies and past relevant experience etc) may give, but still feel uneasy:

"People do want to relate to you as a whole person, not just as a lecturer - but it seems very invasive."

Women do attempt to address this difficulty by making very clear distinctions between the private and the way that personal (and therefore accessible) aspects of themselves are presented as style of communication:

"I guess that's why I have put photos on my site - the style and the way I've put it up and written an accessible style (not holiday snaps) and I guess it's not about me personally but it's about my personal mode of communication and getting things across."

Also, just as in real life, people will make choices in what is and is not disclosed, so academics are aware of the dangers of exposing private matters in an interaction that would provoke negative discrimination:

"Yes, I realised that if I hadn't just been chosen director of [a program], I would probably do something to identify myself as lesbian [...] I don't want my identity to hurt our program."

"As a lesbian I have had to think about whether or not to present my 'private self' (in much the same way as I must deal with these issues in RL I'd say!"

Perhaps the real issues of identity seem to be that both men and women struggle to maintain a balance between the personal and the professional. Although people's professional sites are not always highly personalised, in some ways having any 'off-topic' personal information on an academic site needs some explanation: people don't attach photos of their pets to their CVs, or on the covers of their books. In the interviews, a comparison with the office was made: a web page is a personal space as well as a publication, and it seems right and comfortable to allow it to be furnished with a few personal touches. Daniel Chandler and Dilwyn Roberts-Young made the same point in their study of adolescent home pages:

"While it seems useful in some ways to compare the genre of the personal home page with conventional written genres, the nearest real-world analogy for the personal home pages of teenagers is probably the environmental space of teenagers' own bedrooms in their real-life homes." [9]

As in our previous research, an important aspect was the presence or use of the photograph - the decisions that have to be made about actual body 'image' and how it is represented. The difficulties ("it was expected - though I don't really like it") were resolved in a number of ways:

"I don't have my photo immediately visible on the page - but you have to click on a link to get it"

"There is an issue about the distance between personal boundary and the public. I don't want to present [...] my personal self alongside my professional self."

"OK, it's relevant to see what a person looks like - but it is not the first thing you should promote - it has a place but not so dominant."

"I happen to have a holiday photo and I like the symbolism of it ...that is 'this could be one of the things I am in certain circumstances'."

However, there is an awareness by women that there is a dilemma whether to have a photograph or not. It is difficult to make decisions over the management of a style of image which would at least do no harm:

"I hesitated over choosing the picture, because I realised that whatever image I portrayed to the Web, people would make assumptions about me. Eventually I went for the one that I show to the world the rest of the time - the one on my travelcard!"

So what do we make of this level of ambivalence over the photo? To be so very cagey about whether or not to have a photograph, or what kind to use, recognises its potential to be revealing, capable of deceit, and at worst to create unwarranted stereotypical and negative impressions:

"We are never going to change anything if we let personal appearance affect what people want to make of what I do or about my work."

Some of the self-deprecation and throwaway embarrassment we found about photos shows, we think, that some of the difficulties which women faced with the issue of the photograph were whether or not they could get away with being ironic in some way, or just had to go for the friendly but normal, or serious and academic.

We can go further with this idea of overcoming fears of violation of boundaries implied in the photograph dilemma - and reflected in the expression of more deep-seated qualms about being 'misunderstood'. Firstly, the fear that what we look like might affect our status, credibility and the authority of our work is very real, and second, some interpretations by the viewer of the 'absence' of a photo might result in some threat to 'real-life identity':

"...eventually decided to include one on the grounds that I didn't want to be a faceless person ....to emphasise that there was a real person behind the bits."

As Marj Kibby says in a review of non-academic women's pages:

"...many women in creating their personal home pages seem reluctant to abandon the body as a marker of their identity, representing themselves through images of a sexualised body." [12]

Women seemed to appreciate attempts to make their site part of a friendly 'community' and that enabled some to overcome their reticence enough to be able to reveal personal characteristics (so long as they were photogenic) as well formal ones. This was especially true if seeing others' friendly photos made them think it was OK to make contact - send an email, join a chat line, because there was a 'real person' out there. The fact that the work did not just sit there as if produced by a faceless academic as in journals or books, made a real difference to how they felt about who they were too:

"At first it was a small, black and white passport photo (the most dull photo I could find). Recently I changed it into a holiday photo where I looked a bit happier (partly, again, because that is what I like to meet on other people's pages - men's and women's)"

The fact that both of us are practising academics means that we test our own interpretive insights on our own experiences. The continuing difficulties of working in academia mean that if we have to have a presence 'out there' as well as at our desk and in the classroom there will be challenges for our praxis and we anticipate that the dominance of male discourse will prevail (to the furtherance of male/female discriminations) unless we can voice some of our concerns. It is a space that has possibilities: "I'm allowed to dawdle."

The Web is a medium where women could be in control, in the timing and pacing of their activities at least. It is an opportunity for women to take time to be 'explorers' too (though not too much time and they can be impatient with some of it: "I haven't got time to get by some of the personal things - I just want the nitty-gritty").

This getting to the 'nitty-gritty' is a positive attitude, but is also a reflection of the way the women we talked to never forgot that who they are is part of a community of others; that it is the 'professional' that legitimises and gives intelligibility to what they do. We have used examples from our conversations with these respondents, to illustrate identity in process, as reflections on praxis, governed of course by the parameters of available discourse. It is this discourse that contains all the richness of contradiction and change of people struggling to live in this increasingly complex 'stage'. The extension of the 'workplace' into cyberspace may be as much another 'place' as it is another 'self': a place to be, which can extend the range of what can be communicated about your place in the scheme of things. What we have established through our discussions with users of Web pages (and even though the context is the rarefied sphere of academia) is that what people can present in home pages is not just a matter of limitations of the medium, the constraints of hypertext or problems of communicating about 'selves'.

5.5   Conclusions

Our concerns with the psychology of 'doing' does not contradict the fact that corporeal selves have found ways to 'represent' something of who they are in a different medium - and we resist the particularly western opposing of personal/social, private/public. Across a range of situations it is possible to suggest the "'common ground' for electronic communicative acts and non-electronic ones (e.g. [10]).

The people we talked to did not think of themselves as becoming 'cyborg'. The extent to which their Web presence was part of themselves varied widely, from those who had a page only because the institution required it, to those who felt that it was an integral part of their academic (and personal) life. For some, the internet had developed aspects of the self and extended personal powers - but so can the camera and the mobile phone. Losing any of these can lead to a sense of personal loss and diminishment. It seems that what the Web and the

Internet provide are new ways of being in the World, but not in a way which is intrinsically mysterious or different from other aspects of being. We claim and construct identities in order to authenticate our experience as we did in infancy when we first discovered our separateness and along with it our identity [52]. The frames for action in cyberspace are not necessarily less (or more) problematical than in real life - because they are part of real life.

In looking forward we realise that there will continue to be as many different feminist preoccupations as there are voices to be heard in the cyberspace [74]. Opportunities may arise from the sheer presence of this diversity as women link into this new Web, who will by their 'representations' challenge the power of stories currently told in many other places.

Women across the world are discovering that whatever the cultural or political regime, it is possible to dream of 'new worlds' using the Web to 'tell the story' differently. There are likely to be changes in ways we understand the idea and use of 'autobiography' [75, 76, 59] from all of those creatively making individual or collective Web pages, and these will influence how we then make psychology narratives as well [77]. There is much work to be done to raise awareness that story telling is doing something positive. People will always tell stories. As psychologists we are ready to listen and to make up our own too. The stories might start to be different.

5.6   References

[1]   Gergen, K.J., The Saturated Self: Dilemmas of Identity in Contemporary Life, New York: Basic Books, 1991.
[2]   Gergen, K., Technology and the self: From the Essential to the Sublime, 1996.
[3]   Giddens, A., Modernity and Self-Identity, Cambridge: Polity, 1991.
[4]   Turkle, S., Life on the Screen: Identity in the Age of the Internet, New York: Simon & Schuster, 1996.
[5]   Stone, A.R., Will the Real Body Please Stand Up?, in Cyberspace: First steps, M. Benedikt, Editor, Cambridge, MA, 1992.
[6]   Herring, S., ed. Computer-mediated Communication: Linguistic, social and cross-cultural perspectives, John Benjamins: Philadelphia, Pa, 1996.
[7]   Kelly, P., Human Identity Part 1: Who Are You?, 1997.
[8]   Chandler, D., Personal Home Pages and the Construction of Identities on the Web, 1998.
[9]   Chandler, D. and D. Roberts-Young, The Construction of Identity in the Personal Homepages of Adolescents, 1998.
[10]   Karlsson, A.-M., Selves, Frames, and Functions of Two Swedish Teenagers' Personal Homepages, in Paper presented at 6th International Pragmatics Conference: Reims, 1998.
[11]   Cheung, C., A Home on the Web: Presentations of self in Personal Homepages, in web.studies, D. Gauntlett, Editor, Arnold: London, 2000, p. 43-51.
[12]   Kibby, M., Babes on the Web: Sex, Identity and the Home page, 1997.
[13]   Erikson, T., The World Wide Web as Social Hypertext, 1996.
[14]   Shedroff, N., Personal Websites, 2000.
[15]   Miller, H., The Presentation of Self in Electronic Life: Goffman on the Internet, 1995.
[16]   Miller, H. and R. Mather, The Presentation of Self in WWW Home Pages, 1998.
[17]   Arnold, J. and H. Miller. Women Academics on the Web: the same old Gender plot in a New Theatre? in Identities in Action! University of Wales, UK, 1999.
[18]   Miller, H. and J. Arnold, Gender and Web Home Pages. Computers & Education, 34, p. 335-339 2000.

[19]   Miller, H. and J. Arnold, breaking Away Form Grounded Ientity? Women academics on the Web. Cyberpsychology and Behaviour, in press.
[20]   Goffman, E., The Presentation of Self in Everyday Life, New York: Doubleday Anchor, 1959.
[21]   Goffman, E., Frame Analysis: An essay on the organisation of experience, Cambridge, Ma: Harvard, 1974.
[22]   Branaman, A., Goffman's Social Theory, in The Goffman Reader, A. Branaman and C. Lemert, Editors, Blackwell: Oxford. p. xlv-lxxxii, 1997.
[23]   Buten, Personal Home Page Survey, 1996.
[24]   Mead, G., Mind Self and Society, Chicago: University of Chicago Press, 1934.
[25]   Reymers, K., A Symbolic Interactionist perspective on Computer-Mediated Social Networks, 1998.
[26]   Miller, D. and D. Slater, The Internet, London: Berg, 2000.
[27]   Lawley, E.L., Computers and the Communication of Gender, 1993.
[28]   Harré, R., Language Games and the Texts of Identity, in Texts of Identity, J. Shotter and K. Gergen, Editors, Sage: London, 1989.
[29]   Harré, R., Social Being: A Theory for Social Psychology, Oxford: Blackwell, 1979.
[30]   Ibáñez, T. and L. Iñiguez, eds. Critical Social Psychology, Sage: London, 1997.
[31]   Butler, J., Gender as Perfomance, in A Critical Sense: Interviews with intellectuals, P. Osborne, Editor, Routledge: London, 1996.
[32]   Pizanias, C., Habitus: from the Inside Out and the Outside In, in The Body and Psychology, H.J.Stam, Editor, Sage: London, 1998.
[33]   Billig, M., Arguing and Thinking: a Rhetorical approach to Social Psychology, Cambridge: Cambridge U P, 1987.
[34]   Shotter, J. and K. Gergen, Texts of Identity, London: Sage, 1989.
[35]   Gergen, K.J. and G.M. M, Narratives and the Self as Relationship. Advances in Experimental Social Psychology, 21: 1988, p. 17-56.
[36]   Haraway, D.J., Simians, Cyborgs and Women: The Re-invention of Nature, London: Free Association Books, 1991.
[37]   Stokoe, E., Toward a Conversation Analytic Approach to Gender and Discourse. Feminism & Psychology, 01(4): 2000, p. 552-563.
[38]   Hepburn, A., On the Alleged Incompatibility between Relativism and Feminist Psychology. Feminism & Psychology, 10(1): 2000, p. 91-106.
[39]   Burman, E., Feminists and Psychological Practice, London: Sage, 1990.
[40]   Burman, E., Deconstructing Feminist Psychology, London: Sage, 1991.
[41]   Gergen, K.J., Toward Self as Relationship, in Self and Identity: Psychosocial Relationships, K. Yardley and T. Honess, Editors, Wiley: London, 1987.
[42]   Breakwell, G.M., Threatened Identities, London: Wiley, 1983.
[43]   Stam, H., ed. The Body and Psychology, Sage: London, 1998.
[44]   Radley, A., Social Relationships, 1991, Milton Keynes: OUP.
[45]   Gergen, K., The Self in the Age of Information. The Washington Quarterly, 23(1), 1999, p. 210-214.
[46]   Derrida, J., Of Grammatology, 1976, Baltimore, MD: John Hopkins University Press.
[47]   Holzman, l., ed. Performing Psychology: A Postmodern Culture of the Mind, Routledge: New York, 1999.
[48]   Markus, H. and E. Wurf, The Dynamic Self Concept: A Social Psychological Perspective. Annual Review of Psychology, 38: 1987, p. 299-33.
[49]   Newman, F. and L. Holzman, Beyond Narrative to Performed Conversation, in Performing Psychology: A Postmodern Culture of the Mind, L. Holzman, Editor, Routledge: New York, 1999.
[50]   Vygotsky, L.S., Mind in Society, Cambridge, MA: Harvard University Press, 1978.
[51]   Turner, J., Rediscovering the Social Group, Oxford: Blackwell, 1987.
[52]   Shotter, J., Conversational Realities: Construction of Life Through Language, London: Sage, 1993.
[53]   Adorno, T., Minima Moralia, London: New Left Books, 1974.
[54]   Fox, D. and I. Prilleltensky, Critical Psychology: An Introduction, London: Sage, 1997.
[55]   Spivak, G., Translator's Preface, in Of Grammatology, J. Derrida, Editor, John Hopkins University Press: Baltimore, 1974.
[56]   Herring, S., Gender Differences in Computer Mediated Communication: Bringing familiar baggage to the new frontier, 1994.
[57]   Donath, J., Identity and Deception in the Virtual Community, in Communities in Cyberspace, P. Kollack and M. Smith, Editors, University of California, 1988.
[58]   Wilkinson, S. and C. Kitzinger, eds. Feminism and Discourse: Psychological Perspectives, Sage: Thousand Oaks, CA, 1995.
[59]   Gergen, M.M., The Social Construction of Personal Histories: Gendered lives in popular autobiographies, in Constructing the Social, T.R. Sarbin and J.I. Kituse, Editors, Sage: London, 1994.
[60]   Csikszentmihalyi, M., Design & Order in Everyday Life. Design Issues, 8: 1991 p. 26-34.

[61] Belk, R., Identity and the Relevance of Market, Personal, and Community Objects, in Marketing and Semiotics, D. Umiker-Sebeok, Editor, Mouton de Gruyter: New York, 1987, p. 151-164.
[62] Berger, J., Ways of Seeing, Harmonsworth: Penguin, 1972.
[63] Edholm, F., Beyond the Mirror: Women's Self Portraits, in Imagining Women, Bonner, et al., Editors, Polity Press: London, 1992, p. 154-172.
[64] Gibson, W., Neuromancer, London: Gollancz, 1984.
[65] Auerbach, S., Meditations on the Metaphysics of Home Pages, 1995.
[66] Goffman, E., Stigma: Notes on the management of spoiled identity, Englewood Cliffs, NJ: Prentice Hall, 1963.
[67] Gilligan, C., The Relational Self, Boston: Harvard University Press, 1982.
[68] Braidotti, R., Cyberfeminism With a Difference, 1996.
[69] Gergen, K.J., Realities and Relationships: Soundings in Social Construction, Cambridge MA: Harvard University Press, 1994.
[70] Gergen, K., Beyond the Self-Society Antimony. Journal of Constructivist Psychology, 12(173-178), 1999.
[71] Gilligan, C., In a Different Voice: Psychological Theory and Women's Development, Boston: Harvard University Press, 1982.
[72] Kitzinger, C., The Spoken Word: Listening to a Different Voice: Celia Kitzinger Interviews Carol Gilligan. Feminism and Psychology, 4, 1995, 408-419.
[73] Butler, J., Gender Trouble: Feminism and the Subversion of Identity, New York: Routledge, 1990.
[74] Kramarae, C., Feminist Fictions of Future Technology, in Cybersociety 2.0: Revisiting Computer Mediated Communication and Community, S. Jones, Editor, Sage: London, 1998.
[75] Smith, S., Subjectivity, Identity and the Body: Women's autobiographical practices in the twentieth century, Bloomngton, IN: Indiana University Press, 1993.
[76] Griffiths, M., Feminisms and the Self: The Web of Identity, London: Sage, 1995.
[77] Larkin, M. and S. Watts. The Thing and the Oher Thing: a brief narrative analysis of the limits of theoretical imagination in social psychology, in BPS Social Psychology Conference: Nottingham, 2000.

Towards CyberPsychology
G. Riva and C. Galimberti (Eds.)
IOS Press, 2001

6 Discursive Cyberpsychology: Rhetoric, Repression and the Loneliness of Talking the Internet

Steven STANLEY

Abstract. A discursive cyberpsychological approach to the study of the internet is pioneered in this chapter. The internet is conceptualised as a discursively constituted phenomena: a collection of talk and texts as social practices. Furthermore, were it not for conversation, the internet would not exist. Consequently the present study reports upon data from a face to face interview with one internet user. The detailed analysis begins with what was expressed, and then moves on to what might have been repressed, by a French international student, as he spoke about his internet experiences. It is suggested that "Jean-Paul" rhetorically designed his utterances so as to avoid presenting himself as a stereotypical male computer user. It is possible that he did this by repressing an admission of his loneliness. In conclusion, it is asserted that the internet does not exist outside of social practices. As such, the author recommends that any theory of the internet must be grounded in detailed, systematic, empirical analyses of these practices.

Contents

6.1 Introduction

6.1.1 Arguing for detailed, systematic, empirical analysis of internet social practices

In the introduction to the recent book *Cyberpsychology* [1], Angel J. Gordo-Lopez and Ian Parker stake out their claims as to what 'cyberpsychology' is. They argue that it "exists in a field of tense relationships between classic and alternative cybernetics, and between the histories of art, science and technology" [2]. The word 'histories' is important, because the authors of this edited volume are interested in how technologies have been theorised about, in works which have been published previously. A case in point is the work of Donna Haraway [3] and her development of the term 'cyborg.' This word is used by one author as a metaphor to convey the experience of the human using the machine. The person is part human and part machine, or cyborg. *Cyberpsychology* "traces the development, history and contradictory understandings of cyberpsychology" [4]. These authors are concerned with the 'understandings' of academicians and professionals as expressed in their written accounts rather than through the study of ordinary people's practices when they use technology. We are being offered something of a potted intellectual history of the ways in which cyberpsychological terminology has been used by authors across the disciplines. Furthermore, this kind of cyberpsychology is a reflexive enterprise. According to the editors, it might 'self-destruct' because of the paralysing self-reflexivity that they employ.

A second author which this edited book draws upon is the cyber feminist Sadie Plant. In her book *Zeros + Ones* [5] she also gives an historical account, but of the computing age itself and recent developments in network technologies. In summary she claims that the role of women in the creation of these technologies has heretofore been neglected. Plant argues that rather then being the victims of male-dominated technologies women are in fact automatically emancipated by them. She uses the example of Ada Lovelace, the first computer programmer, and emphasises the importance of women in the processes of computer manufacturing in order to make this argument.

The books *Cyberpsychology* and *Zeros + Ones* are not about the internet per se, although the internet is variously alluded to, often implicitly. They are nevertheless good examples of the new trend of 'cyber' writings. This is partly because of the kind of rhetoric the authors use. As versions of what it is like to use the internet, they are particularly vague; they variously use the word 'cyberspace.' Actually, the kinds of experiences that these authors describe might be unrecognisable to the uninitiated reader. For example, Plant argues how an individual becomes a "population explosion" on the internet, with "many sexes, many species" [6]. Now, the internet is only being described in this way because Plant has not empirically studied in detail any individual internet users, what they do, and what they say about what they do. In fact both of these works are good examples of the 'fashionably critical' writings which Michael Billig mentions in his development of the term depopulation [7]. Their pages are rhetorically depopulated because they provide accounts of internet social life wherein there are no traces of individuals. Cyberpsychology has come to resemble this because the authors have not grounded their theories in the study of social practices. Actually most social scientific writing about the internet is theoretical [8], and when empirical analyses have been carried out they have generally been cursory and unsystematic [9]. To continue along the same path as the majority of these cyber researchers would be a mistake. The internet does not exist outside of social practices and so any theory of the internet must be grounded in the detailed, systematic, empirical analysis of these practices.

6.1.2 The importance of the off-line

Most detailed, systematic, empirical studies of the internet concern internet interaction itself [10]. One example of this kind of work is Nancy K. Baym's study of internet fan culture [11]. She ethnographically studied the on-line practices of a discussion group of female television soap opera fans. In her analysis of their postings Baym suggested that the fans were creating an internet 'community.' In other studies, distinctions have been made between the on-line and the off-line. Notably the dilemmas internet users face when meeting face to face are discussed by Barnes [12]. In this study, the interactants of an on-line discussion group meet after relating with one another on the internet. Barnes showed how their email activities changed as a result of their off-line encounter.

The internet researcher Lori Kendall [13] is cautious of making a hard separation between the on-line and the off-line. It is her argument that people are never entirely 'on' or 'off.' Rather, it is the case that people intersperse both kinds of activities. A simple example of this would be if an internet user conversed with a person who is physically in the room with them. Kendall therefore recommends that internet researchers analyse both on-line and off-line practices. This kind of approach is rare but one exception is Clark [14], who has studied teen dating. Texts taken from an internet dating chat room, together with off-line interviews with the dating teens, were analysed. Clark claimed that a re-theorisation of post-modern relationship practices is called for, and used the (off-line) social theory of Anthony Giddens in order to make this argument. So in conclusion, although activities occurring on the internet have been variously analysed, activities occurring *off* the internet have been largely neglected. It is the view of the present chapter that the on-line actually relies upon the off-line. In this sense it is a mistake for internet researchers to disregard the importance of the off-line.

6.1.3 A discursive cyberpsychology

The main argument of the present chapter is that cyberpsychology should be rooted in the study of discursive interaction. The inception of such an approach can be seen in an earlier paper which demonstrated how both face to face talk about the internet and email texts are discursively embodied. When one looks at the detail of what people say and what people type when they use or talk about the internet one can appreciate that 'cyberspace' is not a disembodied form of reality [15]. In the present approach, the internet is conceptualised as a discursively constituted phenomenon. To borrow from Potter and Wetherell's [16] classic definition of discourse, the internet is a collection of talk and texts as social practices. Now, it might seem something of a truism to say that when a person types they are partly constructing the internet. For it is the case that 'the internet' is almost entirely textual. The internet would not exist without the typing practices of people. So, we can see that this is one of the ways in which the internet is constructed. However, the present chapter argues that 'talking the internet' is as important as 'typing the internet.' This is for two reasons. Firstly, conversation is a fundamental reality of social life [17], and the internet would not exist were it not for conversation. Secondly, when they talk, people are partly constructing the reality of the internet.

The present chapter draws upon the tradition of discursive psychology [18]. It is the view of discursive psychologists that language use is an activity in itself, rather than a mirroring device for the representation of reality or perception. When people speak about the internet they are not merely 'reflecting the reality' of the internet. Rather, when a person tells a story, gives an account or offers a description, they are participating in a social life. In life, people can be held morally accountable for what they say. So speakers argue, explain, and justify when they interact. Furthermore, it is argued that psychological concepts are used by speakers for particular social purposes. For example, the discourse of emotions can be used to make criticisms.

When one treats language use as an activity, one must come to an understanding of the variability of spoken discourse. Why do people give different versions of their experiences at different times and in different contexts? This is partly because thinking itself is dilemmatic; it contains contrary themes [19]. People draw upon the disparate themes of common sense, in order to argue with themselves, and with others. As such, thinking and speaking are rhetorically designed [20].

According to recent theories of conversational repression, what is said is intimately tied to what is not said [21]. Simply, by giving one particular view one is concomitantly not giving a counter view. In this sense speaking is both expressive and repressive. So again the morality of social life is emphasised. To express a thought is to negotiate the ideological dilemmas of the time; what is normal is in tension with what is taboo. There are likely to be social pressures guarding against the expression of ideologically taboo topics. These 'unmentionables' might be repressed in the course of a conversation. People sometimes avoid discussing particular topics, and an analysis of conversational repression involves tracing the possible avoidances, so as to chart the realm of what is unspeakable for a particular topic.

6.2 Methodology

Steve Jones calls for reflexivity in academic internet research when he writes that "the Internet is both embedded in academic life and owes much of its existence and conceptualization to academia" [22]. In the same edited book, Sterne uses an anecdote to argue that university students routinely use the internet in their everyday lives [23]. The present chapter takes a more in-depth look at how students understand their use of the internet. The study began with the ethnographic investigation of *Arkwright*, the twenty-four hour computer room of a UK university, where internet access and word processing facilities are available to students all year around. So as to decide the best method of finding people who would be willing to talk about their internet usage, the author became a part of the late night culture of this room. This involved working, emailing, and browsing the web between the hours of 22:00 and 02:00, several times a week.

The individualistic nature of the room as a social space meant that flyers were deemed to be the most appropriate method of finding people who 'used the internet a lot.' These were then variously posted over a four month period. Thirteen people responded via email and face to face contact. All but one of these were male and the majority were international students. A heretofore neglected area of interest is how necessary the internet has come to be for international students. They regularly use the internet to relate with family and friends in their home countries. The author followed up three of the male undergraduate students, and carried out both email and face to face interviews with them. The present chapter analyses parts of a face to face interview with one of these volunteers.

Jean-Paul described himself as a 22 year old "French guy." He had previously studied Law and Politics in France, and at the time of the interview was studying Philosophy and Politics. He had been resident in the UK for around seven months. He was guaranteed anonymity and confidentiality. As is appropriate for the discourse approach, the interviews with Jean-Paul took the form of semi-structured conversations. The author asked him questions about his experiences of using the internet, but he spoke freely and often changed the topic on his own accord. The 90 minutes of dialogue was digitally recorded and listened to repeatedly. The sequences that follow are taken from the second interview with Jean-Paul, as it was during this session that he spoke most personally about his internet experiences. The transcripts are given as Appendices: A, B and C. The selected sequences are referenced in the body of the text, first by letter and then by line number. For example, A/14-18 refers to Appendix A, lines 14 to 18.

6.3 Analysis

The analysis begins with what was expressed, and then moves on to what might have been repressed, by Jean-Paul in his talk about the internet.

6.3.1 Criticising the French people

Jean-Paul first mentions the email relationship after a brief exchange about Arkwright, and the computer room inside. He contrasts the computer room and the email relationship when he says "it's strange the contrast you can have between the relationship you can have in email with person and the ugly aspect of the room" (A/14-18). This statement is not qualified in any more detail; it is a general assertion, wherein the email relationship is presumably beautiful. By praising the email relationship in this way so early on in the interview, Jean-Paul does some identity work. He implicitly presents himself as someone who is generally positive about email relationships. Jean-Paul then goes on to describe the "ugly aspect" of the computer room more specifically. He strongly argues against what he refers to as the "agitation" of the room. This agitation is embodied in the French students, who are there in the room when he is using the internet. Jean-Paul says that "you have a lot of French people I no want to meet a lot of French people I am not here for that" (A/29-32). Although Jean-Paul is actually French, he accomplishes a rhetorical distancing from his compatriots. He does this by referring to them as "French people." Furthermore, his justification for not meeting them is formulated as his own choice: he does not want to meet them. He then gives a general rule to support his choice: he is not here to meet with French people.

Jean-Paul criticises the French people when he says that "they think I can't understand what they say and I can understand it often it's stupid thing stupid stuff" (A/34-37). Here Jean-Paul is constructing the inner mental lives of the French people. This particular utterance involves two subjectivity constructions. The first is marked by "they think," which is a claim about the French people's minds. The second is marked by "I can't understand;" Jean-Paul is constructing what he thinks the French people are assuming about his own subjectivity. We can suggest that Jean-Paul is implying that they think he is English. Potter and Edwards [24] have argued that constructing subjectivity gets particular conversational business done. Rhetorically, Jean-Paul is using this utterance to justify his decision not to talk with them; they are assuming something incorrect. He *can* understand what they say and what is more he claims that what they say is often stupid. Why would anyone want to talk with people who are by implication, stupid?

What is left implicit in what Jean-Paul says here is a presentation of a situation wherein Jean-Paul is on his own in the computer room, overhearing a group of French people talking to one another. An implicit solitariness is being established; the people who Jean-Paul should normally be talking to are being avoided, or at least so he says. For, it is commonly assumed that a lonely person has not chosen to be alone. It is generally the other people themselves who have chosen to keep their distance. Jean-Paul counters any assumptions that he might be lonely, by how he talks of his relationship with the French people. It is his choice not to meet, because they say "stupid stuff." Of course, it is not their choice.

Jean-Paul moves on and gives a fascinating account of his "strange relationship with the machine" (A/39-40) and tells me that he is with his "friend in France" (A/45). This particular sequence is analysed in detail below. It suffices to say here that by making this claim about being with his friend Jean-Paul is doing two things. Firstly, he is dealing with the solitariness he has been implicitly working up. Secondly, he is countering the possible judgement that he is lonely, and without friends.

6.3.2 Criticising the machine

I will now analyse a short sequence - which takes place five minutes into the interview - in which Jean-Paul describes the machine. The descriptions are given in the context of a "little story" about the first email Jean-Paul received from his mother. Note that the sequence is given in full in Appendix B. Jean-Paul complains that he can only react to the machine; he constructs the machine problematically, questioning its status mediating his relationship with his mother. He then goes on to give several descriptions of the machine. He talks of trying to convince himself that it is "only a machine" (B/9) and then parallels it with books, which he claims are not beautiful but nevertheless allow a person to imagine so much "behind" them. The machine is then upgraded to a "powerful machine" (B/17-18), which rhetorically works as a factual description. The utterance "just because it's connected at internet" (B/18-19) is designed to chart the machine's power: the machine is merely a gatekeeper to the internet. In each of these descriptions the machine is the problematic mediator. Soon after however, Jean-Paul's assessments become more abrasive. The machine is "ugly" (B/22) and then "horrible" (B/26). Jean-Paul's relationship with the machine is indeed strange, because although he is using the machine routinely in his everyday life, he criticises the machine in his interview talk. Why would someone who uses computers describe them in such negative ways? The present sequence might help us to answer this question. If one is using a computer routinely one is not using that time to relate with people face to face. So when he is criticising computers Jean-Paul is not arguing against them *per se*. Rather, he is arguing against the negative stereotypical *identity* of the male computer user. One facet of this identity is that the person prefers machines to people. Giving descriptions of the machine in such ways gets this kind of rhetorical business done.

Jean-Paul talks about relating with a person through the machine. He refers to this as "this kind of relationship" (B/26-27). What kind of relationship this is, is not absolutely clear although it is being mediated by a "horrible machine." Seven minutes later however he elaborates upon what it is like relating with people through the machine. Jean-Paul gives an account of suffering from having email relationships with his friends (put into context in Appendix C):

65.		authenticity . because definitely . I suffer . this
66.		year . to have a lot of relationship-only
67.		relationship with email with some friend
68.	Steven	Um
69.	Jean-Paul	. you know some- something uh miss me

These utterances are given in the context of speaking about the authenticity of relationships, a theme which is picked up again later in the telling of the love story. Lines 111 to 115 are the most explicit denouncements of the email relationship in any of Jean-Paul's accounts. But there is some suggestion that Jean-Paul is not telling me something about his use of the internet. Just as Jean-Paul is claiming that he is missing "something," so there is something missing from his talk. Something is being left unsaid.

6.3.3 Trying to forget

The first sign that Jean-Paul might be forgetting something comes after his account of spurning the French people. He himself raises the question of what it means to forget, when he says "in my mind I try and I forgot it I I forget" (A/73). Jean-Paul is expressing the dilemma of repression. As Michael Billig has asked, "How can one intentionally forget something? The moment one concentrates on accomplishing the forgetting, one is surely remembering the very thing which is to be forgotten" [25]. However, as Billig goes on to argue this dilemma is predicated upon the common sense notion that remembering and forgetting are polar opposites of one another. This is not necessarily the case. What is not said, or forgotten, is bound up with what is said, or remembered. Let us analyse the sequence immediately prior to Jean-Paul's forgetting claim, in order to see how this might work (Two minutes into interview; put into context in Appendix A).

65.		but but but I have uh strange relationship
66.		with the machine
67.	Steven	Yeah
68.	Jean-Paul	and uh you know sometime I'm not in the
69.		Arkwright building
70.	Steven	Um
71.	Jean-Paul	I'm with my friend uh in France sometime
72.	Steven	Right
73.	Jean-Paul	in my mind I try and I forgot it I I forget and
74.		um it's very easy to to to to forget all the all what you
75.		have uh around and I can put music and uh music
76.		it's perfect to to to change the atmosphere

After accounting for not meeting with the French students Jean-Paul introduces his "strange relationship with the machine." He then makes two contestable claims. The first is that sometimes he is not in the Arkwright building, and the second is that sometimes he is with his friend in France. Then he says that he tries to forget "it." But what? Jean-Paul does not actually tell me what he is trying to forget. He just gives a general rule, that "it's very easy to forget all what you have around." He does not explain what was personally forgetting in the previous line. It might be that Jean-Paul is repressing particular thoughts or feelings in this very interview. A clue about what this might be can be found before the forgetting claim. Jean-Paul does not follow "I am not in the Arkwright building" with "I am in France." What he actually says is "I am *with my friend* in France" (emphasis added.) By claiming that he is with his friend, Jean-Paul might be avoiding expressing the feelings of loneliness that he is experiencing in his everyday life.

It might seem unusual that one can talk of repressing feelings, in this case feelings of loneliness. But as Billig has also argued: "Talk about emotions generally concerns more than a description of an internal subjective state. It is essentially talk about social relations" [26]. Loneliness is a perfect example of this; it is an emotion which connotes social isolation. I will now go on to argue that similar avoidances are practised in two further sequences of talk.

6.3.4 Saying no to the machine

Around twelve minutes into the interview Jean-Paul tells me something more about his strange relationship with the machine. He at first makes some claims about him being a robot when he is using the machine; he claims that he does not feel himself because he is only reacting to the "little screen." Jean-Paul then goes on to say that "sometime ... I cannot say no to the machine but I can say no to a person" (C/99-103). It might be helpful to use Freud's concept of *negation* to analyse this utterance about saying no. The idea is that a repressed thought "can make its way into consciousness on condition that it is negated" [27]. If we negate Jean-Paul's utterance we can suggest that a person can say no to him but that a machine cannot.

The lonely person is in a dilemma. Is it possible to break out of loneliness and meet people? It might be that people will just reject you. Thinking back to the situation with the French people, it might be the case that Jean-Paul is repressing the possibility that they would not want to meet him anyway, even if he did choose to meet with them. Them saying no to him is avoided by him claiming to say no to them. Jean-Paul 'chooses' the distance offered by the machine, which will implicitly never say no to him. I will now look at what happens in a fascinating sequence in which a person actually says yes to Jean-Paul. This will be the final analysis of conversational repression.

6.3.5 The love story

Soon after the sequence about saying no to the machine Jean-Paul talks about an email message which he has received (put into context in Appendix C).

127		know that and . the the this ye- uh this week
128		I receive an email from uh a girl . and she
129		says she fall in love uh of me . but . by internet
130		just by my message . and uh I feel very bad
131		when I receive that
132	Steven	yeah
133	Jean-Paul	. and uh what is strange is this girl is romantic
134		girl
135	Steven	um
136	Jean-Paul	and she fall in love of me just by internet

The story is introduced with little preamble; there is no prior accounting for how they met. This kind of telling reinforces Jean-Paul's subsequent characterisation of the girl. She is someone who falls in love too quickly and easily. Jean-Paul reports how the girl "says" she has fallen in love with him. Note how he does not say "she has fallen in love with me." By making the girl's statement a claim Jean-Paul shows that he is doubting her love. He then retrospectively constructs his subjectivity, saying how he felt "very bad" when he received the message. Jean-Paul then continues to undermine the "girl," dismissing her supposed love when he says "but by internet just by my message," "what is strange is this girl is romantic girl" and "she fall in love of me just by internet." These accountings undermine both the technologies of email and the internet as well as the subjectivity of the girl. He is questioning whether she really is romantic. Each utterance conjures up phenomena outside of Jean-Paul. Things 'out there' are the problem whether it be the technology, or the girl on the other side of the screen.

When you tell someone that you love them their response is very important. There is the expectation that they will reciprocate your feelings. However in this sequence Jean-Paul does not tell me how he replied to this girl. The only account of what happened afterwards is that he felt very bad. Furthermore he does not say *why* he felt very bad upon receiving this email. He could have felt   flattered for example? Jean-Paul might be avoiding particular kinds of talk about himself. Could it be that Jean-Paul is feeling inadequate because no one really falls in love with him? By dismissing the girl's love as not being real love, he presents himself as being implicitly unlovable. By redirecting the conversation away from such thoughts Jean-Paul represses the identity of someone who is emotionally immature, or someone who cannot handle being loved. After undermining this on-line relating Jean-Paul turns to the real relationship:

(Put into context in Appendix C)

142	Jean-Paul	now of course I don't want to meet definitely
143		uh of course that's gonna be . very exciting to to
144		to to meet some people very interesting t- you

So meeting in real life becomes the expected progression of the romantic email relationship. But Jean-Paul claims that he does not want to meet the girl, "definitely." He counters the possible assertion that he is someone who cannot handle turning an on-line relationship into an off-line relationship by again formulating it as a choice and giving a general rule. Who would disagree that is it exciting and interesting to meet certain people?

6.4 Discussion

The main theme of the analysis was to show how accounting was linked to identity. In his expressions Jean-Paul was countering any possible judgements that he might be the stereotypical male computer user. He did rhetorical work to resist being seen as lonely and without friends. This was partly accomplished through his arguing against his own experiences. For example, describing had a rhetorical import. Negative descriptions of the machine worked rhetorically to counter any implication that he might actually prefer machines to people. Furthermore, it is possible that Jean-Paul repressed an admission of his loneliness. The clues pointing to these forgotten feelings lay in what was actually said. In the account of rejecting the French people, the claim about being with his friend in France pointed to the possible experience of being friendless. The signs of avoidance were then followed up in two more sequences of talk. The sequence about saying no to the machine showed how closely intertwined the said and the unsaid can be; repressed thoughts might have entered consciousness in their negated form. In the love story sequence, Jean-Paul argued against the "girl" and the technology, but in doing this he was revealing very little about himself. Might this have been his strategy for avoiding thinking that he cannot be loved, because he is seen as a lonely person?

It is possible that Jean-Paul was using the internet because of his feelings of loneliness and isolation. The life of the international student can often be a struggle. You are in a strange country without family and friends, and the compatriots who surround you are making you feel even more homesick. A way to deal with all of this is to log on, and to make contact with the people you miss most. By attending to the details of talk one can show how thinking about the internet is dilemmatic; it is partly constructed out of the blurring notions of loneliness and socialness. Is a person isolated when they are relating with far away family and friends? This is one of the dilemmas that Jean-Paul was negotiating, and his expressions show a variability. But it seems that, while expressed thoughts can vary and change very quickly over a short period of time, feelings tend not to change so quickly. By avoiding feelings one is only pushing them slightly aside. As this analysis has shown, the feelings come back. Even in a relatively formal situation such as a research interview.

When people talk about the internet they are doing something quite special. They are constituting what the internet is, really what kind of reality it is, and what it means to them in their lives. The talk of the internet user is both novel and creative. On the face of it Jean-Paul is an example of how new technologies are affording new kinds of experiences. The claims are all there: being with his friend in France; receiving the first email from his mother; and a girl falling in love with him through email. Such experiences have only become possible and recognisable as social practices within the last 10 years or so. They are examples of the burgeoning possibilities of the internet, especially in terms of identity.

The possibilities have been praised by many authors, most notably Benedikt and Turkle [28]. However, by attending to the detail of face to face talk about these new experiences we get a slightly different version of the reality of the internet. The theorising is pulled back down to Earth somewhat. The experience of being lonely for example, is a familiar one. And so by analysing the detail of social practices, in a systematic way, we can avoid making overly optimistic theoretical accounts of technology. If we keep close to the people who are actually using the technology, they become more familiar to us. Their practices start to seem more similar to our own than we might originally have thought.

6.5 Appendices

Appendix A

00:34 to 03:16

1.	Steven	um and . let's see . i'm not sure where to start i'm
2.		gonna ask um . what do you think of um arkwright . the
3.		as a com- as a building and uh
4.	Jean-Paul	yeah uh so the building i like outside the building
5.		of course because uh it's uh i think it's neogothic uh
6.		from uh victorian period . normally the last century
7.		and uh i like this atmosphere of course because me
8.		i don't like the modern building ah an important stuff
9.		uh i i don't like the modernity but i i like uh the
10.		artistic creation it's different point . ok so uh you
11.		have you um know something in this building uh
12.		this building uh i can say that has a s- um um has
13.		a soul you know and but the computer room inside
14.		it's modern only that and uh you know it's
15.		strange the contrast you can have uh between uh the
16.		relationship you can have in email with person
17.	Steven	yeah
18.	Jean-Paul	and uh the ugly uh aspect of uh the room you know
19.		and (iszat) perhaps I pass m- um I pass my time
20.		uh uh uh longer in uh Arkwright building than
21.		in my bedroom huhuhuh
22.	Steven	yeah yeah
23.	Jean-Paul	and it's very strange it's my second house here
24.		and uh but it's ugly I hate the- the atmosphere
25.		I I hate all this atgitation around me . and uh
26.	Steven	what's that
27.	Jean-Paul	atgitation
28.	Steven	agitation yeah
29.	Jean-Paul	you have a lot of agitation and you know you
30.		have a lot of French people I no want to to
31.		meet a lot of French people I am not here
32.		for that
33.	Steven	huhuh
34.	Jean-Paul	and I heard the the because they they think
35.		I can't understand what they what uh they
36.		say and uh I can understand it uh often it's
37.		stupid um thing stupid stuff and uh
38.		pft- you know it's um not uh it's not good for that
39.		but but but I have uh strange relationship
40.		with the machine
41.	Steven	yeah
42.	Jean-Paul	and uh you know sometime i'm not in the
43.		Arkwright building
44.	Steven	um
45.	Jean-Paul	i'm with my friend uh in France sometime

46.	Steven	right
47.	Jean-Paul	in my mind I try and I forgot it I I forget and
48.		um it's very easy to to to to forget all the all what you
49.		have uh around and I can put music and uh music
50.		it's perfect to to to change the atmosphere

Appendix B

05:31 to 07:00

51.	Jean-Paul	and uh it's very interesting I was very
52.		surprised of a little story uh I know it's
53.		not the question but I receive an email from
54.		my mother the first email from my mother
55.		and uh I was very surprised . and uh you know
56.		all the reaction I can have the this I can
57.		have uh with this machine only with this
58.		machine and sometimes to to to realise it's
59.		only a machine and it's like you know a book
60.		you can have uh a big sensation a book it's
61.		not it's not beautiful or sometime you know
62.		it's artistic but you know it's not beautiful
63.		the page is not beautiful look the
64.		(stonaticisation meter) is not beautiful I prefer
65.		the natural writing but what you can have
66.		behind that it's incredible you can imagine
67.		all your friend you know and uh it . powerful
68.		machine uh uh and just because it's connected
69.		uh at internet uh I know you know some uh company
70.		some computer company try to have an
71.		(aestheticism) in the computer . you know
72.		because uh . it's ugly actually and uh it's
73.		not beautiful to to to watch that and uh it's a stra-
74.		you know I have the impression with time we
75.		realise in ten years we can say ah how we can
76.		use this t- horrible machine and have this kind
77.		of relationship you know

Appendix C

11:25 to 15:02

78	Jean-Paul	you know the freedom . uh it's important
79		if you have had the basically if you have
80		the (conscious) freedom and I think the majority of
81		the people don't have the (conscious) freedom
82		when they use internet so for me the it's a big
83		aspect and um I have always this impression
84		they are some robot on internet with the
85		mouse . people are s- like a robot I know
86		it's uh it's easy to say that when you don't
87		know the people who all the people who
88		use internet around you but me sometimes
89		I have the impression to be a robot
90	Steven	yeah
91	Jean-Paul	you know it's very strange
92	Steven	yeah
93	Jean-Paul	and uh . sometimes I don't have the impression
94		it's me i'm here and I react to to the what I see
95	Steven	huhuh

96	Jean-Paul	all but it's this little screen it's always the
97		strange relationship with the machine
98	Steven	um
99	Jean-Paul	sometime I I can say no to the machine I can
100		say no to the machine I can say no I can
101		say uh no to uh I cannot say no to the um .
102		uh yeah I cannot say no to the machine but uh I
103		can say no to a person you know and uh
104	Steven	yeah
105	Jean-Paul	uh a it's definitely it's important to don't
106		have a confusion between uh person and machine
107		and uh definitely always consider uh it's like uh
108		in music in music . the the problem of authenticity
109		of the music here is the same problem the
110		problem of the authent- the relationship
111		authenticity . because definitely . I suffer . this
112		year . to have a lot of relationship-only
113		relationship with email with some friend
114	Steven	um
115	Jean-Paul	. you know some- something uh miss me
116	Steven	um
117	Jean-Paul	and uh it's very strange uh it's um a little
118		story and I know it's a personal aspect but
119		I think for for your project it's important
120		to have personal aspect
121	Steven	yeah definitely
122	Jean-Paul	definitely because it- uh your project
123		your project if it's interesting . uh .
124		of course I- you have to . it have to try to to
125		be close to the objectivity but with the
126		subjectivity of the (person) of course you
127		know that and . the the this ye- uh this week
128		I receive an email from uh a girl . and she
129		says she fall in love uh of me . but . by internet
130		just by my message . and uh I feel very bad
131		when I receive that
132	Steven	yeah
133	Jean-Paul	. and uh what is strange is this girl is romantic
134		girl
135	Steven	um
136	Jean-Paul	and she fall in love of me just by internet
137	Steven	. how did you get in touch with
138	Jean-Paul	oh it's just uh you know uh so this girl I meet
139		three years uh in the real life you know I say
140		real life
141	Steven	yeah yeah
142	Jean-Paul	now of course I don't want to meet definitely
143		uh of course that's gonna be . very exciting to to
144		to to meet some people very interesting t- you
145	Steven	um
146	Jean-Paul	of course I meet you by internet
147	Steven	um
148	Jean-Paul	. and perhaps I think it's the first person
149		I meet directly by internet
150	Steven	um
151	Jean-Paul	you know because I try to always to eve- but
152		it's different because we live in the same
153		city
154	Steven	yeah yeah
155	Jean-Paul	and uh we are in the same university and
156		uh it's not we can perhaps uh we can uh see
157		in the street before you know it's different

6.6 References

[1] Á. J. Gordo-López and I. Parker (eds.), Cyberpsychology. Macmillan Press, London, 1999.
[2] Ibid., p. 5
[3] D. J. Haraway, Simians, Cyborgs and Women - The Reinvention of Nature, Free Association Books, London, 1991.
[4] A. J. Gordo-López and I. Parker (eds.), Cyberpsychology. Macmillan Press, London, 1999. p. 18
[5] S. Plant, Zeros + Ones - Digital Women + The New Technoculture, Fourth Estate, London, 1997.
[6] Ibid., p. 46.
[7] M. Billig, Repopulating Social Psychology - A Revised Version of Events. In: B. M. Bayer and J. Shotter (eds.), Reconstructing the Psychological Subject - Bodies, Practices and Technologies. Sage, London, 1998, pp. 126 - 152.
[8] For example T. Jordan. Cyberpower - the Culture and Politics of Cyberspace and the Internet. Routledge, London, 1999; R. Kitchin. Cyberspace - the World in the Wires. John Wiley & Sons, Chichester, 1998; B. E. Kolko, L. Nakamura and G. B. Rodman. Race in cyberspace. Routledge, London, 2000.
[9] For example M. Dery (ed.), Flame Wars - the Discourse of Cyberculture. Duke University Press, London, 1994; J. Dibbell, A Rape in Cyberspace - How an Evil Clown, a Haitian Trickster Spirit, Two Wizards, and a Cast of Dozens Turned a Database into a Society. In: M. Stefik (ed.), Internet Dreams - Archetypes, Myths, and Metaphors. MIT Press, London, 1996, pp. 293-315; D. Spender, Nattering on the Net - Women, Power and Cyberspace. Spinifex, North Melbourne, Vic., Australia, 1995.
[10] For example P. Curtis, Mudding - Social Phenomena in Text-Based Virtual Realities. In: M. Stefik (ed.), Internet Dreams: Archetypes, Myths, and Metaphors. MIT Press, London, 1996, pp. 265 - 292; S. G. Jones (ed.), CyberSociety - Computer-Mediated Communication and Community, Sage, London, 1995; S. Kiesler (ed.), Culture of the Internet. Lawrence Erlbaum Associates, Mahwah, N.J., 1995. H. Rheingold, The Virtual Community - Finding Connection in a Computerized World. Secker & Warburg, London, 1994. B. Viglizzo, Internet Dreams - First Encounters of an On-Line Dream Group. In: M. Stefik (ed.), Internet Dreams - Archetypes, Myths, and Metaphors. MIT Press, London, 1996, pp. 353-387.
[11] N. K. Baym, Tune in, Log On - Soaps, Fandom, and Online Community. Sage, London, 2000.
[12] S. Barnes, Developing a Concept of Self in Cyberspace Communities. In: S. B. Gibson and O. O. Oviedo (eds.), The Emerging Cyberculture - Literacy, Paradigm, and Paradox. Hampton Press, Cresskill, New Jersey, 2000, pp. 169-201.
[13] L. Kendall, Recontextualizing "Cyberspace" - Methodological Considerations for On-Line Research. In: S. Jones (ed.), Doing Internet Research - Critical Issues and Methods for Examining the Net, Sage, London, 1999, pp. 57-74
[14] L. S. Clark, Dating on the Net: Teens and the Rise of "Pure" Relationships. In: S. G. Jones (ed.), Cybersociety 2.0 - Revisiting Computer-Mediated Communication and Community. Sage, London, 1998, pp. 159-183.
[15] S. Stanley. Disembodiment is a Cyberspace Myth - Discourse and the Self in Real Space, CyberPsychology & Behavior, 4 (1), 2001, 77 - 93.
[16] J. Potter and M. Wetherell, Discourse and Social Psychology - Beyond Attitudes and Behaviour, Sage, London, 1987.
[17] J. Shotter, Conversational Realities - Constructing Life Through Language, Sage, London, 1993.
[18] See C. Antaki (ed.), Analysing Everyday Explanation - A Casebook of Methods, Sage, London, 1988; D. Edwards, Discourse and Cognition, Sage, London, 1997; D. Edwards and J. Potter, Discursive Psychology, Sage, London, 1992; J. Potter, Representing Reality - Discourse, Rhetoric and Social Construction, Sage, London, 1996.
[19] See M. Billig, S. Condor, D. Edwards, M. Gane, D. Middleton and A. Radley, Ideological Dilemmas - a Social Psychology of Everyday Thinking, Sage, London, 1988.
[20] M. Billig, Ideology and Opinions, Sage, London, 1991; M. Billig, Arguing and Thinking - A Rhetorical View of Social Psychology, Second Edition, Cambridge University Press, Cambridge, 1996.
[21] M. Billig. Freudian Repression - Conversation Creating the Unconscious. Cambridge University Press, Cambridge, 1999.
[22] p. 10 in S. Jones, Studying the Net - Intricacies and Issues. In: S. Jones (ed.), Doing Internet Research - Critical Issues and Methods for Examining the Net, Sage, London, 1999, pp. 1-27.
[23] J. Sterne, Thinking the Internet - Cultural Studies Versus the Millennium. In: S. Jones (ed.), Doing Internet Research - Critical Issues and Methods for Examining the Net, Sage, London, 1999, pp. 257-287.
[24] D. Edwards and J. Potter, Discursive Psychology, Sage, London, 1992.
[25] p. 141 in M. Billig. Freudian Repression - Conversation Creating the Unconscious. Cambridge University Press, Cambridge, 1999.
[26] Ibid., p. 189

[27] Ibid., p. 214
[28] M. Benedikt, Cyberspace - First Steps, MIT Press, London, 1991; S. Turkle, Life on the Screen - Identity in the Age of the Internet. Phoenix, London, 1995.

Towards CyberPsychology
G. Riva and C. Galimberti (Eds.)
IOS Press, 2001

7   Web Usability Today: Theories, Approach and Methods

Luciano GAMBERINI, Elisabetta VALENTINI

Abstract. The aim of this work is to introduce the constant transformation and evolution of the usability concept. An overview of methods, techniques and theories concerning usability is supplied. The reported review starts from the description of traditional ergonomic methods and models, coming to the suggestion of innovative theoretical and methodological proposals. We claim that usability should always take context into account when studying artifacts such as hardware and software, as they are not to be considered as mere tools, unrelated to the concrete situation in which they are used. Thus, usability has to be implemented within a cultural framework, from which actions take their meaning.

Contents

7.1   Usability: a concept in continuous evolution

The concept of "usability" is formally defined by the International Standards Organization (ISO) as: "… the effectiveness, efficiency and satisfaction with which a certain user may achieve a specific objective in a particular environment" (ISO DIS 9241-11). According to these standards, "effectiveness" represents the percentage of the use of the machine in reference to its possibilities, "efficiency" concerns the quantity of "effort" required for the purpose: the more effort that is required, the lower the efficiency of the object in question.

The concept of "satisfaction", finally, is related to the comfort that the user experiences in using a certain product. Despite this rather precise definition, various authors agree on the fact that the concept of usability is not an easy one to express. The limits of the meaning of usability are often blurred or poorly defined [1], and with their constant changes reflect the characteristics of the artifacts that we use on a daily basis. It concerns the way in which we learn to interact with the world using rapidly changing technological products that transform themselves and expand their range of characteristics and functions.

To have an idea of how vast this field of action is, we can simply observe the heterogeneity of a number of situations related to new technology, of which we have scientific demonstration. Observing the staff at Xerox when they use the web as a communicative knowledge medium, replacing a failed expert system for the recognition of faults [2], studying the suitability of a system of immersive virtual reality as preventative training for emergency situations [3], providing systems of artificial intelligence for adaptive web sites, that is, sites capable of modifying their structure and their interface according the preferences of the users [4], designing asynchronous computer networks as aids to university courses to improve the interaction between students and teachers [5], means in any case discussing usability, while not being bound by definitions that are difficult to propose.

We will run through the facts from the beginning. Traditionally, usability has been considered important in the professional field for reasons that range from safety, to annoyance, frustration, and factors of an economic nature that may involve productivity or the sale of products. Even everyday objects such as VCRs, washing machines and telephones may cause or help cause annoyance, frustration and stress, and in the worst cases even accidents [6]. Donald Norman, in his historic "*Psychology of everyday things*" [7] describes, starting from the everyday use of these objects, a model of user-world interaction, characterized by a constant cycle that recurs between the user's goal (intention, action specification), execution and evaluation of new world state. Based on his strongly cognitivistic theories, Norman argues four high-level design principles:

- Propose a *good conceptual model* with the aim of: allowing the correct planning of the actions to be performed, intervening in anomalous situations or in the event of faults, and reducing operating errors.
- *Visibility:* make the things visible. Allow the user to observe how a mechanism is made, what parts it is made of, and how these interact, showing the consequences that may arise from a certain action.
- Provide a good relationship between the parts of the product (*natural mapping*), above all between the control devices and the parts that are operated. The mapping must where possible be natural, that is, be based on physical or cultural analogies, so as to be immediately understandable by the user.
- Envisage the use of *feedback* telling the user what action they have performed and what consequences this has caused.

Another recent study on usability that has received considerable attention, regards a model whereby the usability of objects is taken apart and described in its fundamental elements.

This is the model with five components proposed by Jordan and colleagues [8], [9]. The final model [9] indeed proposes five reference concepts, which are, guessability, learnability, experienced users performances (EUP), system potential and re-usability. These are associated, respectively, with the first time use of a product for a particular task, the number of task repetitions required until an acceptable level of "competence" is reached, relatively stable level of performances, the practical best performance obtainable, and finally the level of performance achieved when a user returns to a task after a long period of non use [10].

The idea of contributing to the development of knowledge in terms of usability by building descriptive-interpretative and heuristic frameworks to support developers and designers, has accompanied the work of many researchers until the present day. It is within this interpretative framework that web usability has begun to be discussed, that is, how to make the most widespread system of Internet-based communication more usable.

7.2 Theories and approaches to WEB usability

7.2.1 Interfacing with the Internet: Web usability and Human Factor Engineering

With the advent of the computer, studies on usability have found a wide basis for application and today, following the mass introduction of the personal computer and software into the home, concepts such as "user friendly" or "ergonomic design" have become part of everyday language.

The most common perspective on usability and computers today originates from human factor engineering and human machine system engineering literature. In these studies, which include the research carried out by Nielsen [11,12] focused on the web, and the above-mentioned works by Norman, the accent is placed on human performances as the activity evaluated within contexts defined mainly or exclusively by the task and its subcomponents. The measurements made as part of these studies are typical of cognitive ergonomics, such as reaction time [13, 14] and those based on the detection of human error [15-17]. The best performance is generally the fastest and most accurate; this is commonly measured during the interaction between man and one or more products in strictly experimental situations or in more ecological conditions, such as work situations.

Various authors have subsequently built practical models and laid down guidelines based on these theories and aimed at the designers of World Wide Web sites. In this approach, focused on the concept of the interface, the importance is placed on one hand on the contribution of technology, which aims to provide hardware and software systems that are increasingly fast and reliable, and on the other, on the knowledge of the cognitive processes underlying human actions. The general focus is as mentioned the development of user-centered design techniques that can be rapidly adopted by the teams that build web sites [18], for example, provides one definition of usability by identifying five attributes of a usable interface: (1) it's easy to learn, (2) it's efficient to use, (3) it's easy to remember, (4) it causes few errors, (5) it's pleasant to use. The interdisciplinary character of Human Factor suggests the consideration of the variables of the design environment, such as the web design languages (HTML, XML, XHTML, Java) and the browser or bandwidth, which are substantially technical and psychological variables implicated in the interpretation of graphic options and colors [19], different typographic characters (fonts) in the text [20], the links and the hypertexts [18, 21], and the hierarchical structures of the sites, [22].

Studies on navigation in multimedia hypertexts represent a significant part of the studies on Web Usability deriving from the human factor approach. These studies describe the problem of usability through the examination of the cognitive skills involved during the navigation of a web site [23]. Generally, the overall purpose of such research is to provide a supplemental navigation system, also called remote navigation element, or more simply navigational aid.

These are elements that help a user to locate information on a web site, and allow the user to easily move from page to page [24]. Such aids may be separate from or included in the structure of the site. They may be made up of elements that are commonly present in the browsers (forward, back, home, bookmark) or specific elements on the web pages we visit, such as the names of the pages, the URLs, a site search engine, or a map that graphically illustrates a web site's architecture. Some works also propose specific tools that are able to simplify the users' tasks, by providing them with new and specific "instruments" [25], for example, analyze the relationship that is established between the type of client (browser) and the user's cognitive processes during navigation. What appears clear it that the users make a large number of errors due to the models of hypertext navigation facilities provided by the web client application. The authors present a system (WebNet) that extends the navigational facilities of conventional WWW through the creation of dynamic graphical overview diagrams (also see Zizi and Beaudouin-Lafon, [26]), which can provide users effective indexes for moving between the links on the Internet.

Other navigational aids have been proposed to support user browsing. Recently, Head, Archer and Yuan [27] have presented MEMOS, an on-line history tool that allows users to organize information retrieval sessions with better success compared to the traditional tools offered by the browser. Campbell [28] proposes a sort of Road-signs on Web, with the aim of letting the user know the connection speeds of the proposed links; these signs have the result of improving the performance of the users, by improving link evaluation and decision processes. Sørensen, Macklin and Beaumont [29] assume that "supporting Web navigation implies the provision of tools and techniques enabling users to access Web resources and maintain an index to these resources". These authors present the study of six experimental prototypes to support various aspects of bookmark maintenance and information filtering.

It is perhaps starting from studies on a complex activity such as navigation that we can understand how the task of making a web site useable cannot be separated from the aims of the navigator, from the new ideas that emerge during netsurfing, from the context in which information retrieval occurs or the economic transaction takes place during an e-commerce session. Navigation in these electronic environments does not imply only cognitive operations of a spatial nature: when navigating in a hypertext structure, we participate in the birth of new concepts, the sharing of meanings, the formation of new knowledge, the recontextualization of old ideas. If we try to set aside the idea of the web as a means of information broadcasting and prepare to accept its cultural validity and social dimension, the concept of usability acquires, as we will see in the next paragraph, new and interesting dimensions.

7.2.2   The situated dimension of usability

The classic metaphor of the computer used in cognitive sciences to represent the human mind clarifies the theoretical concept from which Human Factor Engineering research derives: the human cognitive system is seen as a hierarchical structure made up of various units, each of which handles a specific function. The organization of the functional components or "architecture" is what allows the system to generate suitable interactions with the world [30]. Perception, reasoning and action are thus seen as "separate" processes that allow us to find and interpret the information from the outside world and allow the creation and execution of pre-established plans present in the long-term memory. In this theoretical framework, knowledge is represented as a symbolic system and conceived as the transfer of information from one place to another, without considering the context in which this knowledge is developed and put into action.

The context is, indeed, the focus of a more recent survey paradigm, that of situated cognizance proposed by Clancey [31]. This theoretical framework encloses the psychological aspects that are closely correlated to the physical and social world. Perception, learning, reasoning and action are here proposed "in a new perspective that does not define them as independent processes that are linked in a linear fashion, but rather as coupled aspects of the mind, that is, linked by a relationship of co-determination" [30].

Knowledge too takes on a different connotation and becomes a process that develops into action, which in turn is created in the contingent circumstances, that is, situated in the context. Embracing a concept of this type means shifting the focus from processes linked to the individual, to social dynamics. As stressed in the Theory of situated action by Suchman [32], "… the dependence of the action on a complex world of objects, artifacts and other actors, situated in time and space, is no longer treated as an extraneous problem that the individual actor must face, but is rather conceived as the fundamental resource that makes knowledge possible and gives action its meaning." (p. 179) [32]. In this theoretical framework, individuals are recognized as social actors who carry their own baggage of interests and purposes, which are modified and redefined as a result of their continuous interactions with the environment. Hert [33], for example, in a study based on the retrieval of information using a system of on-line publication cataloguing (OPAC), found that the actions performed by users during the search for information were not completely defined in advance, but rather depended on the elements present in the situation. The users modified their initial objectives according to the elements that emerged during their interaction with the system. Bardram [34] also shares the view that plans, considered as forecasts of purposes, are central in human activity, and that purposes are revised and reconstructed based on the elements and circumstances of the context. The author thus proposes the redefinition of the role of plans and rules within the working activities of a hospital.

The model proposed - "The Patient Scheduler" - is a system based on the communication, planning and sharing of information relating to the care and treatment of patients. Such information, organized chronologically, is made available to all doctors in all hospital departments. Interacting with the computer network, the professionals from the various departments can gain a global view of the treatment of the patients, and work together with the other departments to organize and optimize the various activities. In this way, plans can be continually modified and redefined based on the situations that emerge during the care of the patients and the hospital's activities. The plan thus becomes socially co-constructed, and is shared between the actors, taking on a central role in the working practices of an organization; the situations become the place where the expectations of the actors and the opportunities of the environment meet and are constructed reciprocally [35].

In a wider perspective of situated action, which includes some assumptions of cultural psychology, the concept of "artifact" is also included, which is essential for studying people and the environment. Artifacts are tools that are "invented" for specific purposes, and are used to reach the objectives that such contain. Artifacts in this sense take on an essentially social role, and their meaning no longer exists separately "but emerges only through their incorporation in social procedures" [36]. Artifacts, to be shared socially, must be easy to interpret, and not create too many problems regarding their use, that is, they should be "transparent". The importance of the sharing and the "cognitive transparency" of artifacts is also stressed by Blackwell and Arnold, [37]. Their study was based on role-playing methodology in which a number of planning psychology experts had to design a software application. The task was situated in a setting conceived to be related to reality.

The simulation of the exercise was performed successfully, in that the participants had understood the characteristics of the software from the very beginning. This made it possible to shift the focus of the participants from the interaction with the artifact to the negotiation between the demands of the social context and the purposes of the individual actors, highlighting the influence of the "transparency" factor.

A subsequent assumption borrowed from cultural psychology involves that of not considering individuals as isolated, but as belonging to communities. Inside these communities the expectations, purposes and meanings of each actor are shared and negotiated on common ground. In this sense, communities of practice are a privileged space, in which the social meaning of the artifact is learned. Lave and Wenger [38] sustain that learning is essentially situated and is the result of the increasing participation by an individual inside a community of practice. Pennell, Durham, Ozog and Spark [39], sharing this view, conducted a study to confirm its validity. This study was based on the consideration that young people, during their education, do not have the possibility to learn a professional writing style suitable for communication inside a work organization. With the aim of ensuring such skills were acquired, a virtual organization was created based on the use of the web. The situated learning of the students was allowed by the interaction of each with their own tutor and a mentor from inside the organization, by carrying out interviews and by the drafting of reports to be handed in at set intervals.

The self-assessment of the participating students, as well as the assessments made by the mentors and the tutors, provided positive results, demonstrating the effectiveness of the virtual environment created. In recent years, the computing artifacts that have pervaded social communication, games, free time, companies and organizations, have forced the individuals belonging to the various communities of practice to redefine tasks, identities, roles and meanings. Computer mediated communication (CMC), is transformed from being a purely cognitive artifact into a social artifact that is able to exceed geographical barriers and allow actors from different parts of the world to relate to one another. It also changes the ways of communicating, and increasingly takes on the forms of negotiation and construction of shared meanings. "The meeting place becomes the Internet, the World Wide Web (WWW), which is increasingly considered no longer as a purely physical structure, but as a cultural space in which new forms of social relations and identity are experimented" [35].

7.3   Approaches, methods and techniques for Web usability

7.3.1   Method and context

The relationship between the theories described in the first part of this work and the methodological approaches that will be presented in this part of the article, is not strongly structured and has a rather dynamic character. It will not however be difficult for the reader to recognize how some of the methods presented do not -at least in their original version-pay particular attention to the context in which the actions of the participants are determined. According to [40], the use of decontextualized techniques in reality poses significant obstacles for the designer dealing with usability: the strongly abstract nature that the guidelines resulting from this approach assume lead to a "wide variety of interpretation in different contexts" (p. 228) [40] that may induce inappropriate choices.

Other methods that hold the context in better consideration follow rather faithfully the theoretical suggestions described in cultural psychology [41] and cognitive-cultural ergonomics [35]. These adopt the ideas behind distributed cognition and situated action [42, 32] and show interest in the analysis of the "context" in terms of social and cultural factors, including the presence of pre-existing plans or procedures, cognitive tools, organizational structures, the context where the action occurs. The fact remains, however, that even "non-contextualized" methods can be applied so as to consider "situated" aspects, or vice-versa, even the best "contextual" method can be poorly applied without respecting the theoretical framework that supports the function.

Another factor that complicates the work even further is the absence of individual methods capable of independently measuring and assessing web usability. The trend we find, above all in the aspect of works of an applicative nature, is the use of a series of methods together. These can be applied at the same time, that is to say at the same moment in the development process, or, as is more commonly the case, by spreading them across the various phases of design and development of the sites. The use of a series of methodological approaches allows more reliable assessments to be obtained by comparing the results and the suggestions that derive from the various different investigations. In reality, the apparent weakness that appears from this picture is not an indicator of methodological insufficiency as such. It rather reflects the complexity that the Internet assumes if examined not only as a reservoir of information, but also as "an environment that allows us to reconsider our way of conceiving knowledge and communication" [43].

7.3.2   Log analysis

Server log files are records of web server activity. Log files contain mainly data on the identity of the visitors, on the paths followed by the navigators through the site and the time spent navigating on the pages. These records had the original function of helping site administrators know if the bandwidth capacity of their server was consistent with the activities of the web sites they hosted. In recent years, above all due to the needs deriving from the increase in e-commerce sites, log files are used to track the activities and profiles of the users who connect to the site. The knowledge that the analysis of the log leads to, unlike all the other methods reported in this work, concerns very large numbers of people, observed for relatively long periods of time, working in perfectly natural conditions. These specific characteristics of web analysis allow "top down" evaluation of what the users as a group spontaneously do inside the entire site during navigation. On the contrary, for technical-methodological needs, most of the systems for evaluating the usability of web sites are performed on limited samples of participants, using specially prepared situations and over a normally brief time span that is restricted by the conditions of the experiment.

Using this technique, Cooper [44] has recently performed an analysis on a university's web-based library catalogue. He investigated usage patterns over 479 days, based on the traces left by 2.5 million sessions carried out by the users.

Usability specialists adopting this method should however be careful that the log files contain the complete package of data so as to be able to retrace all the actions that the users performed during their visit. The ideal data that we should obtain are therefore: who visited the site, how much time was spent in the various sections of the site, what path the visitors took through the pages of the site, where visitors left the site and data about the success of users' actions, such as the download of files or economic transactions completed. In any case, it should be stressed that the simple fact that a user has visited a page and has spent some time there doesn't allow us to claim with extreme certainty that they have read the contents of that page. Not always then is the analysis of logs useful for the purposes established. The use of log files for usability evaluation is besides an often imprecise method, for reasons that depend on the environment of the server, the client systems, and the use of tools that are "external" to the hypertext in order to reach a particular page. For example, navigating using bookmarks, addresses sent by e-mail or typing the URL in the corresponding field takes us directly to a page. This leads to a substantial failure in the recording of the paths, which no longer describe a linear structure [45]. Currently, despite the fact that the more commonly used measurements are still those involving accesses and the path followed by the users, attention is also paid to the measurements of the transit times on the pages in the site.

Fuller and De Graaff [46], for example, describe how these times can provide a path-independent measurement of the behavioral trends in a distributed and diverse community. The time spent on a page by users allows us to monitor the entire web site or some of its parts, measuring which pages have aroused more interest among the visitors, and allowing forecasts of future trends. In any case, even the measurement of the transit times on web pages cannot be considered, in our opinion, a complete indicator of the usability of a site. The method of log analysis for ergonomic purposes must in this way be integrated with other methods of investigation. Kantner and Rusinski [47], with the aim of analyzing a Beta-Version Web Site, used, together with automated data collection provided by the log files, an on-line questionnaire and a follow-up interview able to provide qualitative information on the opinions of the users. This data was added to the information on users collected using a form that the users had to fill in when accessing the site. The authors concluded their work by stressing how the combination of these methods provides results that are more reliable than those provided by any one of the methods alone.

7.3.3 Heuristic Evaluation

This is an inspection method where usability experts study the software interface by evaluating each individual element, such as the buttons or the links, and comparing these with a list of widely approved and shared design principles that take the general name of guideline checklists. Nielsen originally developed a checklist for the heuristic evaluation of the web in collaboration with Rolf Molich [48], [49]. The checklists of optimal characteristics that before these works consisted of long, all-inclusive lists, have today been reduced to just a few elements, for practical reasons.

Nielsen [18] proposes 10 elements, for example. These are: visibility of system status, match between system and the real world, user control and freedom, consistency and standards, error prevention, recognition rather than recall, flexibility and efficiency of use, aesthetic and minimalist design, help users recognize, diagnose, and recover from errors, help and documentation.

A refined version of the checklist based on a factor analysis of 249 usability problems [50] has been proposed in order to derive a set of heuristics with maximum explanatory power and to face the problems of time that often dictate the rhythms of the analysis of usability during the design of the web site [51]. Once the experts finish their work, they provide feedback to the designer.

This feedback on the status of the system may be provided in the form of a structured report, that is to say, a formal, independently written report. To make the work of the experts more accurate, they can be accompanied by an assistant to transcribe the verbalized findings.

This evaluation technique can be used at any time during the web site development cycle, but it is best suited to the earlier stages [52].

7.3.4   Cognitive walkthrough

This too is a form of expert usability evaluation. Nonetheless, while in an expert appraisal the investigator observes and studies above all the design of the site, providing comments from time to time, in cognitive walkthrough the expert navigates by assuming the point of view of a typical or inexperienced user. This method is often used to help orient designers during the creation of the sites, providing feedback on the progress of the work, and on the ease of learning of the interfaces that are proposed. De Villiers [53], for example, conducted a study to evaluate the usability of two South African e-commerce web sites - the Fortes King Hotels site, and the Cellular Shop site- using a set of techniques, including cognitive walkthrough.

The participants, computer science students, used this technique to evaluate the two sites, according to four parameters: the general characteristics of the sites, the task that the users must perform, the actions required to complete the task, and the characteristics of the users. The information collected allowed the identification not only of the sites' merits, but also of some aspects that could be improved, such as the excess of information that made the consultation of some pages boring.

This method is suitable for testing the operation of the site even with completely inexperienced users. Lisle, Dong and Isensee [54] used the cognitive walkthrough method to identify potential problems for users visiting the IBM Web Ease of Use site for the first time. The purpose was to study how the users handle the information presented and interpret the feedback from the system.

This method of investigation contributed to the development of guidelines for improving the usability of the site; some basic principles set down by the designers at IBM were: maintain the simplicity of the interface, not allow the user to make errors, and provide immediate feedback on their actions.

Pluralistic walkthroughs [55] involve a large group of end users, developers, product designers, health/safety professionals and usability professionals, generally guided by a session leader and facilitator. These navigate together, step-by-step, through a task scenario, analyzing and evaluating each element of interaction. The advantage of this pluralistic version of cognitive walkthrough is that it involves a greater number of points of view, and thus also of a larger number of comments, which, originating from quite different experiences and levels of knowledge, is assumed to be more significant in identifying the problem areas of a web site. Cognitive walkthrough too, as in the case of the heuristic evaluation above, is best used in the early stages of web site development.

Despite the fact that cognitive walkthrough is one of the most used methods in the study of Web Usability, the general orientation provided to designers should however be considered partial, in that it is now well-known that not all usability problems emerge from the application of this technique.

7.3.5   Questionnaires

Questionnaires can be used in the evaluation of the usability of web sites, in that they allow information to be obtained on the opinions, desires and expectations of the potential users of the sites. These investigation tools are made up of a list of written questions that are created and formulated according to what knowledge the team of designers considers to be useful in order to develop the web site. In this sense, questionnaires are useful and informative in all phases of the development and design of the site; indeed, they can be used: before its creation for the purpose of knowing the expectations and desires of users in advance, for the evaluation of a prototype or a site under construction in order to discover the merits and aspects that may be improved, and after the final creation of the site, to measure user satisfaction. Lisle, Dong and Isensee [54] developed an on-line questionnaire to evaluate the usability of a site on the HCI they built. They included it in a series of IBM sites with the aim of acquiring feedback from the users of such sites. They wanted to obtain new comments on the site not from the usual fixed group of designers, but rather through the participation of most of the users. The results were positive, in that they received a large quantity of feedback through the compilation of the questionnaires by the users.

7.3.6   Interviews and focus groups

These two techniques differ from questionnaires in that the experimenter interacts directly with the users, eliciting opinions and comments on the product. The participants in this type of investigation answer the questions on their experiences and preferences regarding interaction with the site. While the interviews are often structured formally, the focus group is less formal, and allows a large number of users to discuss the matters together, with the aim of eliciting common problems and important issues for the evaluation of the site in question. Vaughan and Schwartz [56] conducted a study in which a focus group was used in the construction of a web site. The participants were asked to express their opinions as potential users of the site, so as to obtain suggestions for adding new services or improving those already present. In this case, the site was tested by eight participants, each of whom was assigned tasks to be completed; in some cases, on the other hand, free navigation can also be proposed. The results of Vaughan and Schwartz demonstrated the appropriateness of the choices suggested by the group and used to orient the development of the site.

These investigation techniques can be used, as in the case of questionnaires, in all phases of the development and design of web sites and portals, in that the experimenter can sort the questions according to the information that they wish to obtain from the users.

7.3.7   Think Aloud Protocol

This method involves a participant speaking about what they are doing or thinking when they interact with an artifact. The method can be applied by assigning the subject a specific task (for example, that of finding a particular subject on a site) or even allowing free navigation, provided that a special hypertext system has been created for the participants to work on; in this sense, the think aloud protocol is used especially for the evaluation of prototypes or already existing sites.

The role of the experimenter during these work sessions is that of a group leader: they must stimulate the participant to continue to think aloud, motivating them to describe what is happening, the difficulties met, and the reasons for certain actions. This technique is especially useful, as it is able to capture a wide range of cognitive activities of the users, and is not limited to the identification of problems, but rather aims to provide information on their origins and on which cognitive mechanisms they involve. Eveland and Dunwoody [57], for example, used the think aloud protocol to analyze the activities of information processing during the learning of information contained in the hypertext. Using participants with different levels of experience and frequency of use of the web, the authors performed a quantitative analysis of think aloud protocols obtained during navigation. The authors found that users spend a substantial proportion of their cognitive effort orienting to the content and structure of the web, and this effort weighs down elaborative and evaluative processing, affecting the level of learning of the contents of the pages on the site.

One disadvantage of this method may arise in the case of interference between the participants' verbalizations and the task that they are performing [10]; in this case, people are not performing one simple task, but rather two, that is, navigating in the hypertext and verbalizing their actions, which distorts the results of the research. To overcome this problem, two variations of the protocol have been created: Critical Response, in which the users are asked to speak only during the execution of predetermined subtasks, and Periodic Report, which involves, when the task is complex, verbalization only at predetermined intervals of time. Another disadvantage of this method derives from the fact that the reports may be adapted to the interlocutor, that is, the experimenter. This could involve a "rationalization" of the report and a stiffening in the style of interaction with the web pages. Therefore, to make the results more reliable, this technique is not normally used alone, but rather integrated with other investigation protocols, such as for example the co-discovery method.

7.3.8   Co-discovery method

This method allows the usability of a site to be tested in all phases of its development: during the design, the development of the prototype, and its final use. It involves the interaction of two participants who must complete preset tasks while being observed by the experimenter. They must help each other, as if they were working together to reach a common objective using the web. As happens with think aloud protocol, they are encouraged to perform the tasks and to explain aloud what they think of their actions and the feedback received from the system. The advantage over the latter investigation protocol consists in the fact that the verbalizations of the participants occurs more naturally, and the interaction of two people working on the same task, comparing opinions, can lead to a greater amount of important information than the thoughts of a single person. This has been experimentally verified as part of a research study carried out by Lim, Ward and Benbasat [58]. These authors compared the techniques of self-discovery and co-discovery in evaluating the learning of a series of procedures during the execution of computer tasks.

The results show that the group with which the technique of co-discovery was used obtained better performance, highlighting the greater effectiveness of the social technique compared to the individual one.

7.3.9   Contextual Inquiry

Contextual inquiry is a method of analysis and investigation, a process of discovery and learning that synthesizes some aspects of ethnographic research studies and participatory design methods. Proposed by Hugh and Holtzblatt [59], this method consists of interviewing people in their own workplace while they perform their own real tasks. The methodology involves the designer teams conducting the interviews at the same time, each with one user, regarding the site in question. One of the assumptions underlying this technique is that the environment where people work influences the way in which they use artifacts. This technique thus has the purpose of providing the designers of sites with deep and detailed knowledge of the work of the user, their scenarios and the terminology that they use. These elements can then constitute the basis of the design. Traditionally, designers have obtained information about the potential users of their sites using techniques such as questionnaires or focus groups, which however do not consider the context in which the users work. Understanding how the users work, on the other hand, depends on the knowledge of the specific situations in which they act. To build a usable product, then, it is necessary to clearly understand the context in which people will use it.

In this perspective, the user is seen as a partner who contributes to the design of the site, in that they provide important data on the way in which the information is handled in their specific workplace and on the limits that this sets. Given its characteristics, the contextual inquiry method is used above all during the design or re-design of the system to correct the poorer aspects of the site emerging from the application of this technique.

Lau and Staczek [60], for example, used the contextual inquiry method to evaluate the important aspects in the maintenance of web sites. This evaluation was performed using a system designed by researchers at AT&T, called Strudel. Following the Contextual Inquiry methodology, the designers interviewed, in their workplace, six people involved in the maintenance of web sites. As expected by the Strudel system, three basic issues emerged in the maintenance of the sites: the content, the structure and the graphics. The results, overall, provided suggestions on improving the usability of each of these specific aspects.

Another interesting application of this method was reported by Ritchie and Gosbee [61], who conducted a research study to build the site of the Michigan Center for Rural Health.

The purpose of the site was to promote interaction between the experts at the various rural health clinics and between the medical and administrative staff. As the users had different degrees of expertise in the use of computers, the problem of the usability of the site was fundamental.

The subjects, members of the medical and administrative staff at eight rural health clinics, were interviewed in their workplace in relation to their problems and needs. By the application of the contextual inquiry method, it was discovered that the features required to make the site more easy to use were a simple home page, more visible distinction between links relating to the clinical area and the administrative area, and on-line instructions relating to the site search engine.

7.3.10 Object-Oriented and Scenario Based Techniques

Increasing attention to the contextual aspects of HCI has led to the development of a project-related approach known as Object-Oriented Design (OOD) [62], which is characterized by the emphasis being placed on the relationship between the tasks, the skills of the designer and the elements that the situation-problem they have to work on is made up of [36]. This model acts on two levels; at a lower level, it sets the objective of identifying classes of users and purposes, as well as the relationship that links them together and their implementation in the design of the system.

At a higher level, the objectives are the conceptualization of the most important requests of the users, the analysis of a model of their behavior, and the design of the architecture of the system to include all of these elements. As claimed by Carroll, Mack, Robertson and Rosson [63], OOD represents an important step forward in the study of software technology, because it offers new opportunities and possibilities for change. They also stress that the key idea for promoting this new form of development is to link object-oriented design to the use of scenarios.

The technique of including scenarios as a support to the design of computing artifacts takes the name of scenario-based design. In its original meaning, scenarios are stories that describe people and their activities [64]. These descriptions, which refer to concrete situations, offer information on behavior in the use of computerized systems: what the people who interact with the system try to do, which procedures they adopt or do not adopt, which tasks they complete successfully or which errors they make and what interpretations they give to what happens to them during their interaction with the artifact [65]. This method has recently been applied by a number of academics in the evaluation of web pages.

Erskine, Carter-Tod and Burton [66], for example, conducted a study to evaluate the usability of the web site of the College of Education at Virginia Tech. The methodology adopted was based on the use of scenarios built by the users. The participants in the study, who didn't have much experience with the web, were selected as potential users of the site.

Initially, they were provided with information on the functional characteristics that define the experience of the user and the importance of user input in the design process.

The scenario built by the participants was divided into three sections: context (e.g. the working environment of the user), purpose (e.g. the information required) and action (the imagined path of navigation). The users were asked to build some scenarios without referring to the elements (e.g. the links) that were effectively present on the site. In this way, the scenarios produced were authentic indicators of the information required by the users, how they planned to use it and how it should be structured.

The evaluation of the site was performed by comparing the actions imagined in the scenarios, which reflect the desires and the expectations of the users, with those effectively feasible on the site. This comparison led to the acquisition of useful information for the re-design of the site and the creation of specific guidelines concerning the hierarchical organization of the information, the basic characteristics of the home page and the characteristics of some specific contents.

Osterbauer, Köhle and Grechening [67] conducted a study on the usability of web sites based on the use of scenarios. They selected fifteen sites from the following categories: banks, newspapers and insurance companies. The thirty-five participants, potential users with different levels of web experience, were divided into five groups. Each group was asked to evaluate three sites, one per category.

The scenarios involved the simulation by the participants of real situations using the site. These simulations were videotaped. At a later time, the subjects were asked to design, based entirely on their memory, a map of the hierarchical structure of the site. The procedure used allowed the measurement of the capacity of the users to develop an understandable and aware image of the structure of the information presented. This capacity is a fundamental parameter in evaluating the usability of sites with a complex hierarchical structure.

Scholtz, Laskowski and Downey [68], on the other hand, evaluated the usability of the National Institute of Standards and Technology virtual library site, the resources of which are mostly available to the public. They collected 28 scenarios provided by the employees of the library, which included, following a scheme supplied by the researchers: a general description of the scenario, the benefits of the proposed operations, the beneficiaries of such operations, the frequency and the estimated importance of the scenario, and any negative aspects.

The results, which led to the identification of the aspects to be revised in the organization of the library, were particularly important, given the creation of an actual virtual participatory design meeting. The methodology of collecting the scenarios, in fact, involved these being made available to all the participants, the use of e-mails to advise the participants of the arrival of new scenarios, comments on the scenarios proposed by the others, and indications on the use of the information collected for the re-design of the site.

One particular approach of scenario-based design, finally, was used by Neale and Kies [69]. They analyzed a series of brainstorming sessions in which the usability of the site of the Human Factors Engineering Center at Virginia Tech was evaluated. The groups considered were made up of between two and five participants. The participants were representatives of potential users. The brainstorming task involved the generation of scenarios using the elements of a number of lists relating, for example, to the needs and the objectives of the users, or to the information to be included on the site. Scenarios useful for the evaluation of the usability of the site were obtained regardless of the background and the expertise of the participants.

7.4   Conclusion

Some more general considerations allow us to understand the importance of Web usability today, and define the role it plays or may play in the development of the Internet.

According to Riva and Galimberti [70] "...the technological evolution of the media leads us to believe that Internet could become, in the very near future, the predominant medium, or rather, it is possible that it will become a general communication interface..". It is clear that most of the interest in Internet as a medium is now focused on the World Wide Web.

The Web, which may be described as the hypertext [71] and hypermedia part of the Internet, today embraces new tools for group communication and navigation systems that are able to combine the potential of the hypertext with the advantages of virtual graphic environments [72]. The Web favours the exploration logic of the user, the multiplication of the means of access to information [73], the creation of new work environments [74], and the possibility, in the widest sense, to connect communities of practices so that they can share their expertise [43]. These are the systems that usability must guarantee, refine and make available to a growing public. In this way, it seems clear that the role of usability is today expanding and undergoing complete transformation.

Having overcome the metaphor of "the impact" of technology on society, and moved in the direction of the co-construction of social situations, the idea of web usability has acquired importance. Usability, for some time now successfully experimented within the context of interface problems, is no longer required to respond in a decontextualized manner to aspects linked to software or hardware as ends in themselves, separate from the rest of the world and in particular the context in which they are used. Motivated by the imminent mass diffusion of so-called "mobile technology", the interest in web usability is focused on the combination of "real" and "virtual", on new communication and work environments, on the hybrid nature of these [35], on the intermittence with which the social life of the individual is mediated by these technologies, on the cultural framework that surrounds actions and makes them understandable to all, and on the complexity of the cultural, political and economic accessibility of the Web within the various different contexts and range of situations.

7.5   Acknowledgment

This research was supported by the European Community funded "Telemedicine and Portable Virtual Environment for Clinical Psychology" – VEPSY UPDATED - project (IST-2000-25323; web sites: http://www.psicologia.net and http://www.vepsy.com).

7.6   References

[1]   M.G Morris and A. P. Dillon, The importance of usability in the establishment of organizational software standards for end user computing, International Journal of Human - Computer Studies 45 (1996) 243-258.
[2]   D.G. Bobrow, R. Cheslow and J. Whalen, Eureka: using the web as a community knowledge medium. Stanford University, Palo Alto. CA, 1999.

[3]   G. Mantovani, L. Gamberini, M. Martinelli and D. Varotto. Exploring the suitability of a virtual Environments for safety training: Signals, Norms and Ambiguity in a simulated virtual escape. Cognition, Technology and Work. Pp. 1-9.

[4]   M. Perkowitz and O. Etzioni, Towards adaptive web sites: Conceptual farmework and case study. Artificial Intelligence 118 (2000) 245-275.

[5]   P. Cottone, N. Zingigrian and M. Maresca, Reti di apprendimento asincrono in sussidio ai corsi universitari. Didamatica 2001. In Press, 2001.

[6]   F. Ossola, Gli infortuni domestici. Padova: Muzzio, 1989.

[7]   D. A. Norman, Psychology of everyday things. Basic Book:New York, 1998.

[8]   P. Jordan, S. W. Draper, K.K. MacFarlane and S.A. McNulty, Guessability, learnability and experienced users performances, in People and Computers VI. D. Diapere and N. Hammond, Eds. University Press: Cambridge, 1991.

[9]   P. W. Jordan, What is usability? in Contemporary Ergonomics, S. Robertson, Ed. London:Taylor and Francis, 1994, pp 454-458.

[10]   P. W. Jordan, An Introduction to Usability. Taylor and Francis. London,1998.

[11]   J. Nielsen, Usability Engineering at a Discount. In Designing and Using Human Computer Interfaces and Knowledge Based System, G. Salvendy a M. J. Smith, Eds. Elsevier: Amsterdam, 1989.

[12]   J. Nielsen, Usability Engineering. San Diego, CA, Academic Press, 1993.

[13]   M. S. Sanders and E. J. McCormick, Human Factors in Engineering and Design. Singapore: McGraw-Hill, 1993.

[14]   J.R. Wilson and E.N. Corlett (eds.) Evaluation of Human Work. Taylor & Francis, London, 1995.

[15]   J. Rasmussen, What can be learned from human errors reports? In Changes in working life, K. Duncan et al., Eds. London: Wiley, 1980.

[16]   J.T. Reason, Human Error. Cambridge: Cambridge University Press, 1990.

[17]   S. Roncato, L'errore umano e i processi di comprensione, in Ergonomia. Lavoro, sicurezza e nuove tecnologie, G. Mantovani, Ed. Bologna: Il Mulino, 2000, pp 41-80.

[18]   J. Nielsen, The art of Navigating Through Hypertext, Communications of the ACM 33, 3 (1990) 296-310.

[19]   H. Shubin, D. Falck and A. G. Johansen, Exploring colors in interface designs, Interaction 3 (4) (1996) 36-48.

[20]   J. Sklar, Principles of Web Design, Course Technology. Thomson Learning, 2000.

[21]   S. McDonald and R.J. Stevenson, Disorientation in hypertext: the effects of the three text structures un navigation performances, Applied Ergonomics 27, 1 (1996) 61-68.

[22]   J. Larson and M. Czerwinski, Web Page Design: Implication of Memory, Structures and Scent for information Retrieval, In Proceedings of the ACM CHI '97 Conference: Human Factor in Computer System (1997) 111-117.

[23]   L.A. Whitaker, Human Navigation, in Human Factor and Web development, C., Forsythe et al., Eds. Mahwah NJ, US: Lawrence Erlbaum Associates, 1998, pp. 63-71.

[24]   J.E. Alexander and M. A. Tate, Web Wisdom. How to evaluate and create information quality on the Web. Lawrence Erlbaum Associates, Mahwah, New Jersey, 1999.

[25]   A. Cockburn and S. Jones, Which way now? Analysing and easing inadequacies in WWW navigation, International Journals of Human-Computer Studies 45 (1996) 105-129.

[26]   M. Zizi and M. Beaudouin-Lafon, Hypermedia exploration with interactive dynamic maps, International Journal of Human Computer Studies 43, 3 (1995) 441-464.

[27]   M. Head, N. Archer and Y. Yuan, World Wide Web Navigation Aid, International Journal of Computer Studies 53, 2 (2000) 301-330.

[28]   C. Campbell, Facilitating Navigation in Information Space: Road Signs on the World Wide Web, International Journal of Human Computer Studies 50,4 (1999) 309-327.

[29]   C. Sørensen, D. Macklin and T. Beaumont, Navigating the World Wide Web: bookmark maintenance architectures, Interacting with computers 13 (2001) 375-400.

[30]   A. Carassa, Expertise. La conoscenza entra in azione, in Ergonomia. Lavoro, sicurezza e nuove tecnologie, G. Mantovani, Ed. Il Mulino, Bologna, 2000, pp. 123-150.

[31]   W.J. Clancey, Situated cognition. On human Knowledge and computer representation, Cambridge: Cambridge University Press, 1997.

[32]   L. Suchman, Plans and situated action, Cambridge: Cambridge University Press, 1987.

[33]   C.A. Hert, Information Retrieval as Situated Action, Proceedings of the Annual Meeting of the American Society for Information Science 32 (1995) 172-180.

[34]   J.E. Bardram, Plans and Situated Action: An Activity Theory Approach to Workflow Systems, In Proceedings of ECSCW'97 Conference, Lancaster UK, September 1997, pp.17-32.

[35]   G. Mantovani, Network. Reti elettroniche e reti di significato, in Ergonomia. Lavoro, sicurezza e nuove tecnologie, G. Mantovani, Ed. Il Mulino, Bologna 2000, pp 153-177.

[36]   G. Mantovani, La qualità dell'interazione uomo-computer, Il Mulino, Bologna, 2000.

[37] A.F. Blackwell and H.L. Arnold, Simulating a Software Project: The pop Guns go to War, In Proceedings of the 9th Annual Meeting of the Psychology of Programming Interest Group, R. Osborn and B. Khazei, Eds, 1997, pp. 53-60.
[38] J. Lave and E. Wenger, Situated learning. Legitimate peripheral participation, Cambridge, Cambridge University Press, 1991.
[39] R. Pennell, M. Durham, C. Ozog and A. Spark, Writing in Context: Situated Learning on the Web. In Proceedings of ASCILITE97, Perth Australia, 1997, pp 463-469.
[40] S. Henninger, A methodology and tools for applying context-specific usability guidelines to interface design, Interacting with Computers, 12 (2000) 225-243.
[41] M. Cole, Cultural psychology: A once and future discipline. Cambridge, MA: Belknap Press of Harvard University Press, 1996.
[42] E. Hutchins, Cognition in the Wild, Cambridge, Mass, The MIT Press, 1995.
[43] G. Mantovani, The Psychological Construction of the Internet: From Information Foraging to Social Gathering to Cultural Mediation, Cyberpsychology and Behavior, 4,1 (2001) 47-56.
[44] M.D. Cooper, Usage Patterns of a Web based library catalog, Journal of the American Society for Information Science and Technology, (2001) pp.243-267
[45] R. Stout, Web Site Stts: Traking Hits and Analyzing traffic. Berkeley, CA. Ösborne/ McGraw-Hill, 1997.
[46] R. Fuller and J.J. de Graaff, Measuring User Motivation from Server Log Files, 1998. Internet address: http://www.microsoft.com/usability/webconf/fuller/fuller.html
[47] L. Kantner and L. Rusinsky, Analizing Usability of a Beta-version Web Site Through Server Logs, user Profile data, and Online Questionnaire Responses, In Proceedings of UPA 98, Washington, DC, 1998.
[48] R. Molich, and J. Nielsen, Improving a human-computer dialogue, Communications of the ACM 33, 3 (1990) 338-348.
[49] J. Nielsen and R. Molich, Heuristic evaluation of user interfaces, In Proceedings of ACM CHI'90 Conference, Seattle, WA, 1-5 April, 1990, pp 249-256.
[50] J. Nielsen, Enhancing the explanatory power of usability heuristics, In Proceedings of ACM CHI'94 Conference, Boston, MA, April 24-28, 1994, pp152-158.
[51] J. Nielsen, Heuristic evaluation, in Usability Inspection Methods, J. Nielsen and R.L. Mack, Eds. John Wiley & Sons, New York, NY. , 1994.
[52] K. Instone, Site Usability Heuristics for the Web, 1997. Internet address http://www.webreview.com/1997/10_10/strategists/10_10_97_2.shtml
[53] C. De Villiers, using HCI tecniques to evaluate Electronic Commerce sites, Proceedings at CHI-SA 2000, South African Human-Computer Interaction Conference, University of Pretoria Conference Centre, South Africa, 2000.
[54] L. Lisle, J. Dong and S. Isensee, Case study of Development of an Ease of Use web site, Proceedings of 4th Conference on Human factors and the Web., Basking ridge, NJ, Usa, 1998.
[55] R. G. Bias, The Pluralistic Usability Walkthrough: Coordinated Emphathies, in Usability Inspection Methods, J. Nielsen, Jakob, and R. Mack, Eds. John Wiley and Sons, New York, NY, 1994.
[56] M. W. Vaughan and N. Schwartz, Jumpstarting the Information Design for a Community Network, Journal of the American Society for Information Science, 50, 7 (1999) 588-597.
[57] W.P.Jr. Eveland and S. Dunwoody, Examining information processing on the World Wide Web using think aloud protocol, Media-Psychology, 2 (3) (2000) 219-244.
[58] K.H. Lim, L.M.Ward and I. Benbasat, An empirical study of computer system learning: comparison co-discovery and self-descovery methods, Information system research 8(3) (1997) 254-272.
[59] Hugh B and Hlozblatt K. Apprenticing with the Customer. Comm. ACM, 38(5), 45-52
[60] T. Lau and J. Stazcek, A Contextual Inquiry-Based Critique of the Strudel Web Site Maintenance System, (1999). Internert address: http// www.citeseer.nj.nec.com/lau99contextual.html
[61] E.M. Ritchie and J.W. Gosbee, Design and Evaluation of a World Wide Web Site for Rural Health Practioners, The Journal of the Healthcare Information and Management Systems Society, 11 (3) (1997) 97-112.
[62] I.Jacobson, M. Christersson, P. Jonsson and G. Overgaard, Object-oriented Software engineering: A Use case Diven Approach. Addison-Wesley. Reading, MA, 1992.
[63] J.M. Carroll, R.L. Mack, S.P Robertson, and M.B Rosson, Binding objects to scenarios of use, International Journal – Computer Studies, 41 (1994) 243-276.
[64] J.M. Carroll, Scenario-based design: Envisioning Work and Technology in System Development. Wiley, New York,1995
[65] J. M. Carroll, Five reasons for scenario-based design, Interacting with Computers,13 (2000) 43-60.
[66] L.E. Erskine, D.R.N. Carter-Tod and J.K Burton, Dialogical techniques for the design of web sites. Accademic Press, 1997

[67]   C. Osterbauer, M. Köhle and T. Grechening, Web Usability Testing. In Proceedings of AusWeb2K, the Sixth Australian World Wide Web Conference, 12-17 (2000).

[68]   J. Scholtz, S. Laskowski and L. Downey, Developing Usability Tools and tecnique for Designing and testing Web Sites. In Proceedings of 4th Conference on Human factor & Web. Basking Ridge, NJ. USA. (1998)

[69]   D.C. Neale and J.K. Kies, User-Generated Scenarios for Requirements Specification and Design, Human-Computer Interaction Laboratory, On-line Report (Usability Engineering) (1997).

[70]   G. Riva and C. Galimberti Editorial, The Mind in the web: Psychology in the Internet age, Cyberpsychology & Behavior, Special Issue. 4 (1) (2001) 5 –12.

[71]   J.H. Ellsworth and M.V. Ellsworth Marketing on the Internet: multimedia strategies for the WWW. J. Wiley. New York, 1995.

[72]   L. Gamberini and S. Bussolon, Human Navigation in Electronic Environments. Cyberpsychology & Behavior. 4 (1) (2001) 57-65.

[73]   E. Rullani, Tecnologie che generano valore: divisione del lavoro cognitivo e rivoluzione digitale, Economia e Politica industriale. 93 (1997) 76-87.

[74]   G. Riva, I nuovi ambienti di lavoro. in Ergonomia. Lavoro, sicurezza e nuove tecnologie, G. Mantovani, Ed. Il Mulino, Bologna, 2000, pp. 203-226.

SECTION III

CYBERPSYCHOLOGY IN PRACTICE: VIRTUAL REALITY

Virtual environments of the not too distant future most likely will be hybrid and specialized. A computer will use headsets to stimulate the eyes and ears, as well control an array of equipment and objects in the environment that interact more physically with the person (air and mist jets; scent nozzles; passive and responsive objects like chairs, artificial trees, robotic and/or real animals and humans!). Given the complexity of the software and hardware, each system will specialize in a particular set of virtual scenarios. "Reaching the Top of Everest," "Drinks at the Ritz," "Dodgers win the World Series." Actually, this is just a few notches above the special effects rides that many of us have enjoyed (or not!) in large theme parks.

Suler, 1999
(http://www.rider.edu/users/suler/psycyber/psycyber.html)

Towards CyberPsychology
G. Riva and C. Galimberti (Eds.)
IOS Press, 2001

8   Characteristics of Interaction and Cooperation in Immersive and Non-Immersive Virtual Environments

Carlo GALIMBERTI, Sabrina IGNAZI, Pietro VERCESI, and Giuseppe RIVA

Abstract. This research presents three studies that investigate the characteristics of the interaction and cooperation activities in immersive and non-immersive virtual environments. The first study explored the characteristics of the interaction during a cooperative task; the second one investigated the characteristics of the cooperation strategies used in the cooperative task; the final one verified if and how the level of immersion in the virtual environments influenced the performance and the characteristics of the interaction/cooperation. The results of the studies showed a substantial homogeneity between immersive and non-immersive VR environments. In both environments, partners produce a reciprocal influence on their actions and seem to be able to perceive their conjoint communicative work. However, the average time used to complete the task is significantly longer in the immersive phase instead of in the non-immersive one. Moreover, our experience showed that simulation sickness is a significant problem for the immersive experience.

Contents

8.1   Characteristics of interaction and cooperation in immersive and non-immersive virtual environments

8.1.1   Introduction

Virtual Reality (VR) constitutes a three-dimensional interface that puts the interacting subject in a condition of active exchange with a world re-created via the computer. The possibility of not limiting the paradigm of interaction in a unidirectional sense represents the strong point of the new technology: man is not simply an external observer of pictures or one who passively experiences the reality created by the computer, but on the contrary may actively modify the three-dimensional world in which he is acting, in a condition of complete sensorial immersion [1, 2].

For these characteristics VR can be considered as the leading edge of a general evolution of present communication interfaces [3, 4]. But, what is a communication interface?

Biocca & Delaney [5] defined a communication interface as "the interaction of the physical media, codes and information with the sensorimotor channels of the user" (p. 59). Designers play a key role in defining the characteristics of this advanced communication interface. In order for a virtual environment to work the user has to have some idea about what the virtual reality system expects and can handle, and the environment has to incorporate some information about what the person's goals and behaviors are likely to be [6]. These two aspects, the user's "mental model" of the virtual reality system and the designer's "understanding" of the user, are just as much a part of the interface as its physical and sensory manifestations [7, 8].

However, understanding how to use virtual reality to support collaborative interaction presents a substantial challenge for the designers and users of this emerging technology. First, Virtual Environments (VEs) are designed to serve a purpose, so must be designed with intended users' tasks and goals explicitly considered [9]. Moreover, during the Internet experience the knowledge relevant to the goal should be distributed, and actions should be coordinated among the various actors. Particularly, to support collaborative activities VEs should provide task applicable information representation and communication tools embedded in the environment in which activities happen [10, 11].

Second, the possibility of negotiation, both of actions and of their meaning, has a key role in providing a satisfactory sense of cooperation. This is even truer for networked VEs where cooperation and collaboration are the key features of the experience. However, teams vary tremendously in their negotiation strategies as well as in their task achievement process [10].

Following this approach, it is rather complicated to study cooperation in VEs. Experts of the Computer Supported Cooperative Work area have tried to formalize and put in practice the structure of the human cooperation. But this approach failed when tried to model in an acceptable way the complexity of the situation and the variety of interests of the users.

Particularly, there are two basic difficulties in creating a suitable model for cooperation. The first difficulty lies in the ambiguity and unpredictableness typically present daily situations. Considering the world of experience as an open system, it soon becomes clear that it is impossible to foresee every type of situation which could be created in carrying out a series of tasks (a fixed mode if we want to build a suitable cooperation model). Another reason it is difficult to represent cooperation in a formal model is the basic diversity among the various points of views of the actors. "About rationale," says Gasser, "two agents cannot have identical representations... shared knowledge is impossible" [12]. Cooperation, according to Gasser, is simply a moment of practical understanding because the actors are good at pragmatically tuning their own activities 'as if' they had common knowledge with other actors.

Mantovani [11] partially disagrees with this view: according to this author, "The actors manage to cooperate by combining the interpretative activity with the practical one, they can make plausible *inferences* about the *meaning* that they and their interlocutors give occasionally to the situations, which they change through their intervention. Simultaneously, they define, tentatively, in which world of principles both they and their interlocutors are moving" (p. 185).

In both visions the key content of communication is the interpretation of the situations which actors are involved in [13, 14]. So, the most effective way of clearing the meaning of messages is to connect them to a shared context of meaning. However, this is more difficult in VEs than in other computer-based activities. VEs forces individuals to deal with interface constraints and time delays, adding layers of complexity to an already-overwhelming set of social constructs.

The difficulty of managing negotiation has two consequences for the design of VEs [3, 15]:

- the only way to understand negotiation is by analyzing the subjects involved in the environment in which they operate. This means that the social context in which the Internet experience happens plays a crucial role [16];
- new processes and activities will develop during interactions which challenge and change the initial relationship between subject and context. So VEs have to be flexible enough to handle these changes without imposing constraints to the interaction [17].

This paper tries to understand the characteristics of cooperative activities in networked environments. In the research we used a specific form of networked environments - shared 3D virtual worlds (metaworlds) - in three different studies:

- in the first one we used the analysis of conversations to investigate the characteristics of the interaction during the cooperative task;
- in the second one we used the analysis of conversations to investigate the characteristics of the cooperation strategies used in the cooperative task;
- the final one analyzed how the level of immersion in the networked environments influenced the communication and the interaction process within the cooperative task.

The results are analyzed to identify the psychosocial roots used to support cooperation in a digital interactive communication.

8.2 The research project

8.2.1 The research plan

8.2.1.1 Setting
The experiment was conducted in the LICENT (Laboratory of Human Interaction and New Technologies) Virtual Reality Lab., Catholic University of Sacred Heart, Milan, Italy.

8.2.1.2 Setting Sample

The complete sample included 49 couples of university students, both male and female (see Table 8.1 for details) in the 20-28 age group (mean age for the 43 males: 24.2+/-1.5; mean age for the 55 females: 23.9+/-1.2). All the subjects in the sample had not used DOOM II or other first person 3D shooting videogames before the experiment.

Table 8.1 Breakdown of the overall sample (MM-male/male; FF-female/female; MF-male/female)

First phase	MM	MF	FF	Total
Immersive phase	14,3%	20,4%	18,4%	53,1%
Non immersive phase	12,2%	14,3%	20,4%	46,9%
Total	26,5% (13)	34,7% (17)	38,8% (19)	100,0%

8.2.1.3 Objective and Instruments

Objectives of the project were:

- to verify if cooperative activities in networked environments VEs are possible;
- if yes, to understand the characteristics of cooperative activities. We also tried to identify possible differences between *immersive* and *non immersive* virtual environments.

The cooperative process used for the research is the following: by moving freely in a three-dimensional maze (see Figure 8.1), each subject of the couple had to find a key - red for the first subject and blue for the second one.

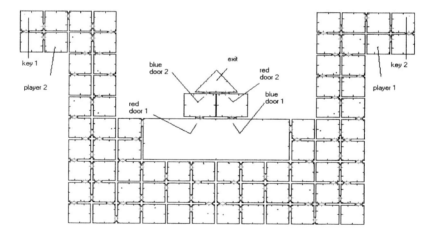

Figure 8.1 Basic maze structure. Starting point (*Player 1* and *2*); position of the keys (*Key 1* and *2*); *exit*. The smaller squares indicate the doors/passages.

After having found the right key, the subjects had to reach together the 'exit door'. No subject could reach the exit without the key found by the other one. So the couple was forced to cooperate for finding both keys.

The couples performed two consecutive phases separated by a brief pause; half of the couples were asked to do first the immersive phase and then the non immersive phase; the other half of the sample first performed the non immersive phase, then the immersive one. To avoid the possible learning effect between the phases, we used two mazes, identical in the structure and positioning of the objects, but different in visual appearance.

For this experiment two versions of the 3D Maze were built: one for each phase (immersive - non-immersive). The *layout* of the maze remains unchanged in its structural features: shape/structure of the walls, arrangement of the objects in the rooms, position of the doors to allow a comparison between the two phases. Changes were made to the starting point of each player (and therefore to the directions they would follow), the colours of the maze walls and the types of objects.

The structure is specular: the two *players* start from the two opposite sides of the *maze*, following a semi-fixed route which does not allows many variations (see Figure 8.1).

In implementing the maze structure, we referred to existing literature on the subject of creating virtual environments and the problems encountered in using virtual *hardware*. In more detail, consideration was given to the difficulty of coordinating the movements of the head and eyes. To avoid this problem we used textures on walls and objects that were highly distinguishable from one another.

8.2.1.4   Experimental procedure
For each couple of subjects, chosen in a random manner, a standard execution procedure was used:

- Welcome and presentation of the VR system.
- Assignment of codes and filling out the experiment summary sheet (performed by the experimenters).
- The signature of the informed consent.
- Handing out of the experiment - Presentation of the *Samples*.
- Phase1 - First cooperative task in the maze. During the test the experimenter took care of possible technical problems and filled out the individuals' forms.
- Phase 2 - Second cooperative task in the maze with inverted level of immersion. During the test the experimenter took care of possible technical problems and filled out the individuals' forms.
- Dismantling and completion of the data.
- Thanks and greetings.

The total duration of the experiment was about one hour.

8.2.1.5   Methods
Given the peculiar aims of this research we used as framework for our analysis the Complementary Explorative Multilevel Data Analysis (CEMDA) that integrates qualitative and quantitative procedures [18]. CEMDA incorporates complementary use of both methods, depending on the particular research stage or the initial assumptions that need to be taken in consideration. As underlined by Sudweeks and Simoff [19], "the rationale is that the weakness of any single method... is balanced by the strengths of other methods... However, the qualitative and quantitative analyses are usually distinct, mutually exclusive component of the research... The result is an integrated view that narrowly focuses on a particular social phenomenon" (p. 37). Following this approach we collected the following data during the experiment:

- codes about the subjects, personal data and remarks by the experimenter.

- transcripts of the verbal interaction of the couple during the two phases of the experimental session.
- digital recording of the behavior of the subjects within the maze.

The obtained data were analyzed separately in three different Studies. The first and the second ones investigated the cooperative process through the analysis of the transcripts (analysis of conversations - qualitative method). The second one studied the differences in the dialogical productivity between the immersive and non-immersive environments through a statistical procedure (ANOVA - quantitative approach).

A preliminary analysis of how many couples could end the proposed collaborative task, was used to verify whether networked environments could support the formation of actual cooperative processes.

8.2.2 Description of hardware

Starting from the above rationale, we used a Thunder 650/C networked virtual reality system for the studies. The Thunder 650/C is composed by two Pentium III based VR system (650mhz, 128 mega RAM, graphic engine: Matrox MGA 400, 32Mb WRam).

We used a two-button mouse to provide an easy way of motion: pressing the left button the operator moves forward; the different rotations are produced by the movement of the mouse. In the immersive phase, however, the direction of the movement is given by the rotation of operator's head. For the immersive and non-immersive phases the following hardware was also used:

8.2.2.1 Immersive phase
For the immersive phase we used two I-glasses head mounted displays (one for each subject) from Virtual I-O, USA. The I-glasses uses LCD technology (two active matrix colour LCD's) displaying 180000 pixels each. Virtual I-O has designed its I-glasses so that no optical adjustment at all is needed, aside from tightening a two ratchet knobs to adjust for the size of the wearer's head. There's enough "eye relief" (distance from the eye to the nearest lens) that it's possible to wear glasses under the head mounted display. The motion tracking is provided by an included gyroscopic tracker (Azimuth: ±180 degrees; Elevation: ±80 degrees, Refresh rate: 256Hz, Latency time: 38ms ± 2).

8.2.2.2 Non-immersive phase
For the non-immersive phase we used two SVGA Compaq Plug and Play (VESA DDC) 14'' monitors (the resolution used, 640 x 480, is the same supported by the head mounted displays).

8.2.3 Description of software

As 3D engine for the shared virtual environment we used DOOM II, a first person 3D *shoot'-em-up* videogame, produced by ID-Software.

During the game the player can explore the 3D environment in the following ways: circular movement from left to right; forwards-backwards movement. To interact with the objects (weapons, keys, *bonus*) in the 3D environment the player just has move over them.

This software supports networked play (up to 4 users) through a simple null-modem connection. DOOM II also allows the recording the games (all the movements and actions performed by the players) thus allowing them to be examined in detail later.

The two 3D virtual mazes in the experiment were developed using three different editing programmes: Deep 97 (vers. Shareware); Doom Easy Edit 2; Windeu 32 vers. 5,25 beta3.

8.3   Is collaboration possible? A positive answer with some limits

The question of whether networked environments can support the formation of real cooperative processes was the first addressed in this paper. To verify this possibility we checked how many couples of our sample could end the proposed collaborative task.

Most of the couples (41 - 83,7%) of the sample managed to complete at least one phase; 63,3% of the sample (31 couples) completed both phases (Table 8.2).

We then analysed the couples that did not manage to complete even one phase (8 - 16,3%). 62,5% of them (5) broke off while were experiencing an immersive networked environment, the other ones (3 - 37,5%) during the non-immersive experience. In this situation the main reason was a drop in interest resulting in their leaving the experiment.

The main problem for the immersive experience was simulation sickness: in each leaving couple one of the subjects, usually the female one, experienced some form of side-effects. These side-effects, usually defined "simulator sickness" [20], were characterised by three classes of symptoms: ocular problems, such as eyestrain, blurred vision and fatigue; disorientation and balance disturbances; nausea. The experienced symptoms are similar to those which have been reported during and after exposures to simulators with wide field-of-view displays [21]. The higher sensibility of female subjects to simulation sickness in our sample is a common datum in literature. In fact, females tend to be more susceptible to VR side-effects than males [22].

Table 8.2 Outcome of the couples (n=49)

Phase	1ª immersive	1ª non immersive
At least first phase	40,8%	42,9%
First and second	38,8%	24,5%
The first one only	2,0%	18,4%
No phase	12,2%	4,1%

Generally, our empirical findings suggest that networked environments support the cooperation process. A detailed analysis of the characteristics of this process will be done in the following three Studies. However, the results also underline the need, for the researchers and for the users of immersive networked environment, of addressing the effects of simulation sickness.

Table 8.3 Percentage of couplet who finished/completed: both phases, only the first one or none.

Successful Phases	1° Immersive	1° Non Immersive	Total
First and second	62,1%	37,9%	100,0%
Only the first one	10,0%	90,0%	100,0%
No phase	75,0%	25,0%	100,0%

Although there is much potential for the use of immersive virtual reality environments, this problem has still limited their application. In different studies users have experienced side-effects, during and after exposure to virtual reality environments [23]. Specifically, exposure duration of less than 15 minutes to immersive virtual reality environments has been shown to lead to significant incidences of nausea, disorientation and ocular problems [24].

8.4   Study 1: Characteristics of the cooperative process: conversation analysis of the interaction in shared environments

8.4.1   Objective and characteristics of the sample

The sample used was composed of 39 out of the 41 couples of subjects (79.6% of the original sample) who had completed at least the first phase (Table 8.4). Two couples were not in the final sample for problems with the records of their interactions.

The analysis of conversations was focussed on the structure of the interactions. In particular, main goal of this study was in to identify a series of characteristic sequences which could be considered "typical" of the cooperative process. The communicative exchanges were also analysed to identify:

- the exchanges in which the content was of an informative or collaborative nature;
- the exchanges expressing the relationship between the two subjects when one of them took the lead.
- the expressions which explain the position of the subjects in relation to the objects encountered along the path, the colour of the walls and the ability of mentally representing the environment in its specular structure.

Table 8.4 Characteristics of the sample according to the "sex" variable.

Immersive			Non immersive		
MM	MF	FF	MM	MF	FF
15,4% (6)	17,9% (7)	15,4% (6)	15,4% (6)	12,8% (5)	23,1% (9)
Total immersive on total Couples considered			Total non immersive on total Couples considered		
48,7% (19)			51,3% (20)		

8.4.2   Methodology

The sequence can be defined as a block of exchanges linked by a strong relationship of semantic and/or pragmatic coherence [25]. Hudelot [26] stated that the sequence is not well defined, which is difficult to limit at formal level. For this precise reason the distinction between the various sequences is done largely by intuition, producing different results according to the aspects that are chosen. In this specific case, to identify the sequences, we followed the same approach used in previous studies on negotiation [27].

The analysis of the interactions is concentrated specifically on four indices: 1) general information about the keys, wall and object colors; 2) spatial indications, with particular attention to the deixis; 3) collaborative exchanges; 4) the roles assumed by the two subjects in performing the task [28].

From a preliminary analysis of the conversations of the subjects in the two consecutive phases, a strong effect of habituation was noticed from the first to the second phase, due basically to three components:

- Familiarity with the game.
- Latent learning of the maze structure: in some subjects, an "instinctive" improvement of the individual performance was noticed.
- The subjects understood that the two mazes were conceived in the same way, and therefore, they no longer needed to negotiate the strategy to be used.

To eliminate the influence of the habituation process, we focussed our analysis of conversations on the first phase experienced by each couple. However, to check any possible change in the roles between the phases, we also decided to consider the interactions of the second phase (if reached).

8.4.3   General structure of the interaction

The first part of the interaction includes the first descriptive remarks exchanged by the speakers. The second part, which is more extensive and heterogeneous, includes the exchanges aimed at cooperation and solving the task. During this part the speakers become familiar with the environment, elaborating a cognitive map both through their direct experience and the information offered by the partner. Finally, the third part coincides with the end of the cooperation. This type of structure can be attributed to all the interactions taken into examination, although the proportion between the parts and their content can vary greatly. The first sequence opens usually with a brief description of the environment.

(43 IM)
G2,1(...) I'm in a wooden wall room.
G1,2 So am I (-) in a wooden wall room.

In the first sequence, just as it is normal when specifying the characteristics of a specific location, it is possible to highlight some specific features. The subjects, in this sample, find a bookcase almost immediately.

(C1 IM)
G2,1 Come in the next room (-) there should be the bookcase (.) right?
G1,2 I'm coming with pleasure (xxx).

The bookcase is a few rooms after the players' starting point and the keys have been placed in front of the furniture. When the study was handed out it was clearly specified that each player must collect the key of a certain colour and that therefore, it is never the first one which is encountered along the route.

(C42 NI)
G1,2 I've found a blue key and as it's the first I meet here I don't want pick it up
G2,2 Therefore you don't have to pick it up (.) 'cause I have the red key.

The end of the first sequence coincides with the entrance of the players in the second sector. At this point, in fact, they already reach certain conclusions. They understand that their key, and their partner, are in a zone of the maze which is similar to the one they have already left, situated elsewhere though. This hypothesis is confirmed by the description of the objects found along the route, different objects for each sector of the environment.

(C4 NI)

G1,56 Where are you?

G2,56 I'm in the wooden (-) I'm at the door (-) I'm where there are the rock and the wood, but you are not here.

G1,57 Sorry (.) don't move (-) are you halfway between wood and rock?

G2,57 Yes (-) I'm at the door.

G1,58 Ah no (.) then you must be close to another rock (-) (xxx) (.) all right (-) that's the reason way I can't find the key (.) we are talking about two different things.

The part of the maze in which the subjects pay more attention is surely the central part, where there are the exit doors.

(C1 IM)

G2,72 Excuse me (.) what are these doors (-) then (.) let's see (-) ah (.) I've found the exit doors.

The content of the central sequence is extremely varied. Typical themes are the description of the walls/objects and the hypotheses on the structure of the maze. Often the two players, after their meeting, progress together along the route that separates them from the missing keys.

(C21 IM)

G1,92 Do we go together?

G2,92 Yes (.) come with me.

G1,93 Let's go together (.) I bring you to the blue key and you bring me to the red one.

The last sequence includes the route from the key to the exit through the doors. The players, here, have crossed the entire environment. They know the sectors and the objects that appear, and they know where the doors are situated.

8.4.4   General information referring to the environment

Within the different conversations it was possible to distinguish between:

- simple monologues, during which one of the two speakers takes turns in speaking rather extensively providing extensive information;
- the alternation of interventions that are not very coherent among themselves, especially in terms of dialogue and real exchanges.

The turn that follows is an example of the first category: the speaker gives a long description of the walls and objects he encounters while he proceeds in the environment.

(C20 IM)

G1, 29

(xxx) I' m arrived (.) oh boys (.) that path (xxx) I must go back where is the blue wall (.) because there are no other ways (-) and you, you must go along the walls (.) in sequence you'll find a brown wall (.) the little wall (.) then the blue wall (.) red wall then and at his end you'll find the key at your right (.) the blue key (.) wher the bookcase is (.) (xxx) (.) the bookcase is so little (.) it's only one wall long.

The commitment of the speakers in taking so many turns in speaking seems to violate the basic general rule which says that they have to be pre-announced. In the case of a traditional conversation, in fact, such a behavior is considered a prevarication of one speaker on the other, who is not allowed to enter conversation. Here, the presence of such a phenomenon is mitigated by two considerations. The first one refers to the frequency which the speakers introduce the pauses in which the other interactor may begin to speak.

The second one concerns the particular task in which the two subjects are engaged. In fact, this needs the ability of putting at the partner's disposal the greatest amount of information possible.In this sense of a lack of intention is not reflected by the most 'exuberant' speaker but by the one who restricts his interventions to the bare minimum, inhibiting, in this way, the other partner's initiative.

The next level of analysis considers the interventions of the two speakers. While an exchange can be defined as the smallest dialogue unit, an intervention consists of a monologue-type unit emitted by a single speaker [25]. Although an intervention can be considered as a contribution by a speaker to an exchange, it is possible that a first intervention will not be followed by a second. The conversations under review often present interventions by a speaker in which exchanges are not satisfied by the other interactor.

(C1 IM)
G1,60 The other side is closed.
G2,60 The candelabrum with a green flame.
G1,61 Then (.) I think that there are two different sections (xxx)

In this example, the two speakers, in three turns, conduct a "two-some monologue". G1, is describing the room in which he finds himself. G2 is referring to the presence of a green flame candelabrum. Finally, G1, in his second intervention expresses his opinion, referring to his first intervention and not to the intervention from the other speaker. It is a well-acknowledged phenomenon, known as "connection by leaping" [29] usually typical in interviews. In current practice an interaction, composed of different apparently interconnected interventions, can be considered dysfunctional. However in the study such a behavior can in some way "support" the conversation. Speakers, in fact, are not engaged in a traditional interaction, which would call for both logical and dialogical coherence between the interventions. They are rather performing a problem solving task by trial and error, which, because of its unusual nature, puts the speakers in the position of establishing a common ground to conversation.

Following Clark and Schaefer [30] we can affirm that the two interactors are defining a common ground specifically suited for the situation they find themselves in. The commitment of the two speakers in solving the task and, indirectly, their degree of collaboration, cannot simply be inferred from the coherence of their interventions. Kerbrat-Orecchioni [25] although showing dialogic coherence as a basic requisite of dialogue, recognises to this kind of cooperative interaction the status of a gradual and ongoing phenomenon. When a question is posed, for instance, there is a whole series of intermediate possibilities between the reply that perfectly satisfies the question itself and the one that is clearly incoherent with it. In this sense it is useful to bring into the picture also the idea of conditional pertinence: once a statement is made, a system of expectations is created around the following statement. Going back to the previous example, it is greater in the case of directive speech acts rather than assertive ones. Thus the speakers, faced with a first assertive act, continue with a second one whose coherence with the previous one can be recognised in terms of its content and in relation to one's own particular situation. Following this analysis it is possible to identify a first cooperative strategy in which each of the two players attempts to make himself useful to his partner immediately, simply by describing the environment encountered in the maze route.

8.4.5 Space/time indications

This category includes interventions in which the speakers explicitly refer to their position within the environment regarding the sector in which they find themselves, an information they infer from the colour of the walls or the objects they encounter.

> (C1 IM)
> G1,54 Listen (.) I am in the blue room (.) no excuse me (.) brown bricks with this green can.

Almost all the interactions examined showed a significant use of the temporal and spatial deixis. Deixis refers to the way in which languages code the parts of the context of speech and the communication event [31]. Deixis of place or of a spatial kind concerns the indication of the positions referring to the anchor points in a communication event. There are two basic ways of referring to objects: describing them or naming them on one side and placing them somewhere, on the other [32]. The positions can be indicated in relation to the other objects or fixed reference points.

> (C40 NI)
> G1,11 My god (.) I have two doors (.) one with a tree the other with a lamp (.) I am entering the one with the tree.

Or they can be specified compared to the actual position of the participants.

> (C1 IM)
> G1,121 There is where I met you and here there is the blue door and now I wait for you (.) I stay here in front of it.

The use of the adverb here in the previous example can be considered to be symbolic and can be explained as "a pragmatic spatial unit which includes the place where the speaker is situated at the time of the statement" [32]. The adverbs *here* and *there* can be conceived in terms of contrasts on a dimension of closeness/distance, starting from the place in which the speaker is situated. In this case, *here* indicates unequivocally the place in which the speaker finds himself at the time of the statement while *there* refers to a different point, probably not far away and however, visible from the point of observation. These adverbs, as the demonstrative pronouns *this, that*, are words with a purely spatial deixis value.

Lyons [32] on this same subject specifies that the demonstrative pronouns are organized according to a linear dimension of closeness/distance where this means "the object of an area near the place where the speaker finds himself at the time of the statement" and that "the object beyond the area close to the place where the speaker finds himself at the time of the statement". The verbs of motion are another combination of deittic elements: Italian uses coming vs. going to describe the direction of movement of the participants of the communication event.

> (C1 IM)
> G2,1   Come in the next room (-) there should be the bookcase (.) right?
> G1,2 I'm coming with pleasure (xxx).

In the first turn, G2 finds himself in a room and invites G1 to join him. G1, with his intervention, shows his movement in the direction of the speaker, or rather, is moving to the place in which the interlocutor finds himself at the time of the statement. The analysis of spatial deixis is more complex when the speaker is moving and it is possible to use temporal terms to refer to places where he is positioned.

(C1 IM)
G1,109 No (.) excuse me (.) the red doors were besides the blue ones (.) so I've to go back (.) right?

Levinson [31], in this regard, raises the question if the temporal or spatial deixis has a certain priority. According to Lyons [32] the spatial deixis has the priority over the temporal one, because the spatial deittics like this and that can be used in a temporal meaning.

(C40 NI)
G2,30 No (.) I'come back to a blue bricked room but I don't know whether it is the one I was before (.) you are still in the brown?

(C40 NI)
G1,29 I (xxx) brown bricks and an eye (.) I found another eye (.) I suppose hope it is not the one I saw before (.) but I believe it is not because it is in a different position in the room (.) no and anyway in this room (xxx) the exit.

In these two examples the adverb before shows both the precedence in time, as opposed to after, and in space. The speakers, in fact, refer at the same time to a situation which happened before, both from a temporal and spatial point of view. The objects and the rooms were encountered earlier in a different place to where they are at the time of the statement, and this was possible only thanks to the speakers' movements in the environment. According to Levinson [31] the spatial deixis always includes an implicit temporal deixis, while the contrary is not true.

8.4.6 Cooperative exchanges

The dialogic coherence is seen in our analysis as the main index of the real intention to collaborate. In the conversations under examination the dialogic coherence is shown by two behaviors:

- one of conversational nature dealing with the exchange of information,
- the other as a 'practical' intervention - the two subjects accompany each other to find the keys - which is however reflected in communication.

The coherence of the subsequent exchange is proven by the fact that all the speech acts are satisfied, and the conversation proceeds in a linear manner.

(C1 NI)
G2,14 And you, what did you find?
G1,15 Wall of steel (-) with fire.
G2,15 Fire and what colour is it?
G1,16 Yellow.
G2,16 Mine is green.

G1,17 Oh yes (.) there is a can with green fire (-) no it's not a can (-) yes it's a can.

Linear exchanges of this kind are not very common. More often, different information is intertwined and the subjects show great communication skills in following the direction taken by the conversation. The exchanges are usually focused on the route. What follows is an example of negotiation on the right direction to take to get to the key.

(C10 NI)
G1,62 Where are you?
G2,62 In the brown bricked room.
G1,63 Now you have to search for green.
G2,63 No for blue (-) no (.) wait.
G1,64 No (.) I think you have to search for the green.
G2,64 Green?
G1,65 Yes.
G2,65 Oh no (.) really? Now let's go and search for green.
G1,66 'cause the blue is linked to the one of the key.

The last phenomenon taken into account happens when the two subjects, on meeting, decide to continue together to collect the two keys. Regardless of the roles assumed by the two players, it is interesting to check how, during the movement, they ensure that they do not lose sight of each other, seeking eye contact besides actually conversing. What follows is a very simple example of this behavior. Here is G1 who supports the conversation, seeking contact with G2. This is probably resulting from his position in front of G2, who can see G1 while the contrary would require G1 to turn around.

(C21 IM)
G1,159 Yes (-) here it is (.) here (.) then are you here?
G2,159 Yes I'm.
G1,160 Are you behind me? Can you see me?
G2,160 Yes I can.

As a conclusion the conversations analyzed clearly show an intention to collaborate to solve the mutual objective. This intention is witnessed and sustained by a whole series of strategies which the speakers exchange information and try to maintain contact with one another.

8.4.7　*The configuration of roles*

During the analysis a series of conversational indices was identified which could register the different roles assumed by the subjects. Normally, during an interaction, one of the two players is faster, or reaches a series of conclusions first and is more skilled in developing a mental image of the environment. Often, this difference is translated into greater level of conversation by the subject who is more skilled and who, during the interaction, has more turns in speaking than the other speaker. At a pragmalinguistic level, moreover, the player who has more difficulty tends to perform directive speech acts used to induce the other player to supply more information. In the brief sequence that follows the dominant role is assumed by G2 who, already from turn 78, has started to supply indications on the route that G1 must follow. In this first intervention G2 ensures that the other player sees him to better understand the information and to be able to follow him as requested in G2,79.

(C1 IM)
G2,78 Well (.) now I tell you where you have to go (-) then (-) can you see me?
G1,79 Yes I can.
G2,79 Follow me (.) can you see a door over there?
G1,80 Wait (.) don't go too fast (.) yes go.
G2,80 Well (.) these are the doors we have to get out.
G1,81 Ah.
G2,81 Well (.) you see over there is a door.
G1,82 Yes.
G2,82 You have to go through it and look for the blue brick area and the red one and
     when you arrive there you'll find the key.
G1,83 OK fine (.) you go in the opposite direction,
G2,83 I go the opposite direction.
G1,84 And then we meet here (-) it's non easy.
G2,84 And then we meet here coming from the opposite direction.

The next sequence is drawn from the second phase of the study by the same couple. In this example, it is clear that the roles of the subjects didn't change in moving from one phase to the next. The collaboration in the actual situation is more difficult. In fact the two subjects no longer find themselves in each other's presence and the directions that G1 asks to G2 must also bear in mind the movement of G1 in space and therefore the direction he is following. The first two turns show that G2, although not leaving his leading role, is having problems. G1, in fact, asks for some information three times, as shown by the long pauses during G1,35. At first, he simply expresses his perplexity. Then his request for help becomes more explicit, although remaining generic. In the end, he turns to G2 with a very specific question.

(C1 NI)
G1,35 Damn! (.) I don't remember if I am coming back or going on (-) I need some
     help (-) wait (.)
G2,35 Yes (.) I am in the steel area and I'm lost, me too.
G1,36 Look (xxx) if you where in the steel and there was the blue,
G2,36 No (.)you find the blue before and then the steel.
G1,37 But to go to the very centre of the maze?
G2,37 Then (.) if you go to the central part you find the steel before and then the blue
     area (.) if you come back you are likely to,
G1,38 I am going to the beginning of your maze.
G2,38 So you should find the steel after the blue.
G1,39 Ah.
G2,39 Now the blue and then the steel.
G1,40 Well and so I let the blue behind me and I am in the steel.
G2,40 Yes yes yes you are in the steel.

The two previous examples show how the same subject can have the leading role in both phases and for the entire interaction. However, not all the conversations are structured in such a rigid way and sometimes one of the two players is more skilled in carrying out a certain phase rather than another, meaning a complete reversal of their positions. In this regard, the brief exchange that follows not only explains such a phenomenon but it shows that the two subjects were aware of this fact.

(C10 NI)
G1,28 I'm starting twisting on me.
G2,28 If you need it I can come and help you and bring you back.
G1,29 Yes (.) as usual .
G2,29 No (.) you too did bring me for a while eh,

The configuration of turns of this type of interaction is not static, but tend to be a constantly changing phenomenon. Although sometimes one of the two players was more skilled than the other, this is not always true and often the roles are reversed different times during the interaction.

8.5   Study 2: Characteristics of the cooperative process: conversation analysis of the interaction in shared environments

8.5.1   *Characteristics of the sample*

As in the previous study the sample was composed of 39 couples of subjects who had completed at least the first phase (Table 8.4). To reduce the influence of the habituation process, we focussed our analysis of conversations on the first phase experienced by each couple. However, to check any possible change in the roles between the phases, we also decided to consider the interactions of the second phase (if reached).

8.5.2   *Objective and methodology*

We noticed from the transcriptions produced in the first study, that in the examined interactions the cooperation process occurred mainly in two situations:

- when the subjects met for the first time (CO1): after the meeting they tried to sum up the data acquired and agreed a strategy for the search of the keys.
- when they met in front of the doors after finding both the keys (CO2): the players began to negotiate a strategy for opening the external doors at first, and then the internal ones.

This second study aims at analysing, using Content Analysis and the Analysis of Conversations, the structure of interactions to individuate common features of cooperation in the Cooperative Parts (CO1 and CO2) considered. To identify the CO1 and CO2 sequences, we followed the same approach used in previous studies on negotiation As in the first study the sequence can be defined as a block of exchanges linked by a strong relationship of semantic and/or pragmatic coherence [25].

8.5.3   *Results*

From the analysis three conversational cooperative *microstrategies* [28] have been isolated:

1) ASSOCIATION (A): the first subject proposes a possible solution that he thinks suitable to solve the problem. The partner accepts this strategy and uses it as starting point for further reasoning, bringing new contributions that *do not clash* with the previous ones.

Example 1: CO1-IM.

G2, 79	follow me, do you see there's a door over there?
G1, 80	wait, don't go too fast, yes, go
G2, 80	so these are the exit doors
G1, 81	oh
G2, 81	you see, there's a door over there
G1, 82	yes
G2, 82	you must go there and look for the area with blue bricks and red bricks and when you reach the red bricks you'll find the key
G1, 83	all right, take the opposite direction...
G2, 83	I'll take the other direction
G1, 84	and we'll meet here again... it's easier said than done!
G1, 84	and we'll meet here again from the opposite direction
G1, 85	tell me
G2, 85	take that direction and I'll pass from here

G1 proposes the strategy and G2, *after* considering the details, accepts G2,82 in G1,83 and in turn proposing G2 to take the other direction. This passage is a still more evident example of association cooperative *microstrategy*:

Example 2: CO1-NI

G1, 26	we met at last
G2, 26	Hi
G1, 27	Here we are
G2, 27	so I have to take the opposite direction
G1, 28	I'm taking yours then
G2, 28	yes

2) NEGOTIATION (N): the different starting positions are compared and one of the two parts conforms itself to the solution proposed by the other.

Example 3: CO1 IM

G1, 40	you're over there
G2, 40	hi, there are the doors...
G1, 41	we found a door....
G1,42	it is blue
G2, 42	...it is blue
G1, 43	here it is
G2, 43	here it is
G1, 44	(...)
G2, 44	yes, there's the red door behind you, go
G1, 45	here it is (...)
G2, 45	Are you going on?
G1, 46	where are we going?

G2, 46	I don't know
G1, 47	what did you find in your area?
G2, 47	more or less the same things you saw
G1, 48	shall we take this direction? shall we continue together or...
G2, 48	why don't we exchange/swap directions? I'll take yours and you'll take mine
G1, 49	so we would find, we already found them at the beginning of the game, wait, you should, you should try to turn and it seems to me that the key was in the brown, wooden scratched walls
G2, 49	you must come back too...
G1, 50	where was your key?
G2, 50	my key was in the wooden walls at the beginning, the one I mentioned, can you remember?
G1, 51	mm
G2, 51	at least it seems to me (...), wood, I think

Example 4: CO2-NI

G1, 35	all right
G2, 35	here you are (...) you're beautiful, I can see you, shall we follow this direction, can you see me?
G1, 36	no, but I think you should take my direction to get to the key and I'll take your direction... that's right, in fact I see now the green pillars If I'm not wrong
G2, 36	yes, the green pillars in the beige wall
G1, 37	that's right
G2, 37	I'm getting into the grey stones
G1, 38	yes, it's right, the two doors are there
G2, 38	there are two doors, I can see them, I see the doors but the keys are not there
G1, 39	no, you must reach the area I'm coming from, go through a green area, then a beige area... did you have seen the red torches before?
G2, 39	yes

3) DOMINANCE (D): one of the two subjects clearly prevails over the other. Dominance has two patterns:

- the person who decides, *forces* his partner to follow the strategy he proposes without giving any explanation
- the second subject accepts the suggested strategy, verbally expressing his total inability to solve the problem, thus relying on the other.

Example 5: CO1-NI

G1, 67	Hi
G2, 67	let's take this direction
G1, 68	take me out
G2, 68	just a moment, the keys, where did you come from? why did you have my key and I had yours?
G1, 69	turn and look at me... can you see me? no, let's take that direction to go out...
G2, 69	no, Chiara, Chiara, listen, we are coming from opposite directions
G1, 70	yes

G2, 70   so we must now take opposite direction, I have to take your direction, in my opinion, to get to my key, and you must take the direction I was coming from
G1, 71   is that right?
G2, 71   mhh
G1, 72   ....
G2, 72   yes, and remember, is that right?
G1, 73   I don't know
G2, 73   well, let's have a try and remember... I know where the doors are
G1, 74   let's go then...
G2, 74   grey walls, let's go, take the other direction
G1, 75   which direction?
G2, 75   the opposite of the direction you were coming from

After presenting the three strategies, we codified the different interaction to calculate how many times the sample used every strategy employed (see Table 8.5).

Table 8.5 Percentage of Microstrategy used during the Cooperative Parts (CO1 e CO2)

Microstrategy used	CO1 Cooperative part/Phase/Level of Immersion		CO2 Cooperative part/Phase/Level of Immersion
	CO1 (1st Phase Immersive)	->	CO2 (1st Phase Immersive)
ASSOCIATION	63,16%		68,42%
NEGOTIATION	21,05%		21,05%
DOMINANCE	15,79%		10,53%
TOTAL	100,00% (19)		100,00% (19)
	CO1 (1st Non-immersive)	->	CO2 (1st Phase Non-immersive)
ASSOCIATION	50,00%		70,00%
NEGOTIATION	30,00%		25,00%
DOMINANCE	20,00%		5,00%
TOTAL	100,00%		100,00%
	CO1 (independently from level of immersion)	->	CO2 (independently from level of immersion)
ASSOCIATION	56,41%		69,23%
NEGOTIATION	25,64%		23,08%
DOMINANCE	17,95%		7,69%
TOTAL	100,00% (39)		100,00% (39)

If we check Table 8.5 we can verify that *Association* is the favourite strategy both in CO1 and in CO2 (in this case, the use of *Association* strategy is a little higher): the subjects listen to the other's proposal, respecting his/her experience in terms of/as being the result of a greater knowledge of the labyrinth. This choice is essentially due to two reasons: an "economic" one (finding an agreement on the *modus operandi* saves time), and a "conversational" and "cooperative" one (keeping in touch helps reaching the main aim).

The reduced importance of the *Dominance* and "*Negotiation* strategies, seems to underline the strong cooperative nature of the task (less time devoted to discussion means more time to devote to the exploration of the labyrinth).

Also interesting is the influence of the level of immersion on the cooperation strategy. The data show that in CO1 we have a significant reduction in the choice of the Association strategy counterbalanced by an increase in the *Dominance* and in the *Negotiation* ones. The influence of the level of immersion is not significant in CO2.

We also verified whether the subjects who used the *Association* (the most used) strategy in the CO1 also used it in CO2 (Tables 8.7, 8.8, 8.9). In general the sample maintained in CG2 the strategy previously chosen, independently from the level of immersion: percentages of conservation of strategy A are respectively 75% (IM) and 80% (NI).

Table 8.6 Changes of strategy from CO1 to CO2 (only first phase – Immersive VR - n. 19)

First Phase: Immersive	From Association in CO1 to Association in CO2	From Association in CO1 to Negotiation in CO2	From Association in CO1 to Dominance in CO2	Total %
ASSOCIATION (A)	75,00%	16,67%	8,33%	100,00
	From Negotiation to Association	*From Negotiation to Negotiation*	*From Negotiation to Dominance*	*Total %*
NEGOTIATION (N)	50,00%	50,00%	0,00%	100,00
	From Dominance to Association	*From Dominance to Negotiation*	*From Dominance to Dominance*	*Total %*
DOMINANCE (D)	66,67%	0,00%	33,33%	100,00

Table 8.7 Changes of strategy from CO1 to CO2 (only first phase – Non Immersive VR - n. 20)

First Phase Non-Immersive	From Association in CO1 to Association in CO2	From Association in CO1 to Negotiation in CO2	From Association in CO1 to Dominance in CO2	Total %
ASSOCIATION (A)	80,00%	20,00%	0,00%	100,00
	From Negotiation to Association	*From Negotiation to Negotiation*	*From Negotiation to Dominance*	*Total %*
NEGOTIATION (N)	50,00%	33,33%	16,67%	100,00
	From Dominance to Association	*From Dominance to Negotiation*	*From Dominance to Dominance*	*Total %*
DOMINANCE (D)	75,00%	25,00%	0,00%	100,00

Table 8.8 Changes of strategy from CO1 to CO2 (only first phase - n. 39)

Independently from level of immersion	From Association in CO1 to Association in CO2	From Association in CO1 to Negotiation in CO2	From Association in CO1 to Dominance in CO2	Total %
ASSOCIATION (A)	77,27%	18,18%	4,55%	100,00
	From Negotiation to Association	*From Negotiation to Negotiation*	*From Negotiation to Dominance*	*Total %*
NEGOTIATION (N)	50,00%	40,00%	10,00%	100,00
	From Dominance to Association	*From Dominance to Negotiation*	*From Dominance to Dominance*	*Total %*
DOMINANCE (D)	71,43%	14,29%	14,29%	100,00

8.6   Study 3: The influence of the level of immersion on the communication and the interaction process

8.6.1   *Objective and characteristics of the sample*

As in the previous study the sample was composed of 39 couples of subjects who had completed at least the first phase (Table 8.4). The Main goal of Study 2 was to verify if a significant change in the dialogical productivity (turns in speaking) happened between the immersive *and* non-immersive *phases.*

8.6.2   *Methodology*

On a preliminary basis, we divided each of the 39 transcriptions of the verbal comments made by the couple during the first phase into six parts (PA), three of which referred to the turns in speaking of the first player (G1), three referring to the second one (G2).The single PAs included respectively:

PART 1 *(P1): P1 included the route from the moment the subjects "enter" the maze, to they arrive to the central part (where the doors are situated).*
PART 2 *(P2): P2 includes the route from the doors to the required key (on the opposite side of the maze).*
PART 3 *(P3): P3 includes the route from the key back to the doors. The players had to follow all three PAs at least once.*

8.6.3   *Results*

Objective 1: verifying if there are significant differences in the time that took the couples to get out of the maze with reference to:

- Order of presentation (First phase/Second phase);
- Level of immersivity.

Conclusion: there is a significant difference (Sig.=.001; df =1; p =.05) in the time used to get to the end of the maze regarding the order of presentation. Specifically, the average time used is significantly longer in the first presentation instead of in the second one (learning process).
    There is a significant difference in the time used to reach the end of the maze with reference to the type of immersivity. Particularly, the average time used is significantly longer in the immersive phase instead of in the non-immersive one.
    There is a quite significant interaction (Sig.=.089; df = 1; p =.05) between the two independent variables (order of presentation and level of immersivity). In particular, the time necessary to get to the end of the maze is significantly shorter in the phase of immersion, when the couple tests the phase of non-immersivity first (learning process, from immersivity to non-immersivity).
    The simple survey of the time used doesn't allow to estimate the differences in the communicating process. Therefore, we have proceeded to further series of analysis:

Objective 2: verifying if there are significant differences between the immersive and non-immersive situation with reference to the inducement of the activity of speaking. The comparison is made using an index that expresses the relation between time of speaking and total time of the performance. The relation "dialogue over the totality" expresses a measure free from the temporal variations of performance among the couples on the basis of the hypothesis that anyhow there is a relation between word and action, between speaking(recording) and time of decision.

Conclusion: the difference immersive/non-immersive has no influence on the determination of the percentage of time of speaking, calculated on the overall time of the test (coherence with substantial homogeneity).

Objective 3: verifying if there are significant differences between the first and the second phase (when the first one is immersive) regarding the activity of speaking. The comparison is made using an index that expresses the relation between time of speaking and total time of the performance. The relation "dialogue over the totality" expresses a measure free from the temporal variations of performance of the same couple between the two tests on the basis of the hypothesis that anyhow there is a relation between word and action, between speaking (recording) and time of decision.

Conclusion: when the first test is immersive, there is no significant difference between time of speaking of the first phase and time of speaking of the second one (we suppose the exclusion of the effect of getting used to).

Objective 4: verifying if there are significant differences between first and second phase (when the first one is non-immersive) regarding the inducement of the word activity. The comparison is made using an index that expresses the relation between time of speaking and total time of the performance. The relation "dialogue over the totality" expresses a measure free from the temporal variations of performance of the same couple between the two tests on the basis of the hypothesis that anyhow there is a relation between word and action, between speaking (recording) and time of decision.

Conclusion: when the first test is non-immersive, there is a significant difference (Sig. 0,26; $p = .05$) between time of speaking of the first phase and time of speaking of the second one (in the immersive phase they talk less: 0,64 VS 0,49); this fact shows that starting with the non-immersive phase, the subjects have a better perception of the structure of the environment. This hypothesis has to be examined more closely.

Objective 5: verifying if there are significant differences between the number of turns of speaking produced by every single subject in each of the three parts of the maze. Particularly, we tried to verify if the turns of speaking were influenced by the level of immersivity (immersive/non-immersive), by the order of presentation (First phase-Second phase) and by the interaction of the two variables.

Conclusion: A) There is a significant difference between the number of turns of speaking produced by every single subject in the three parts. Specifically, the average of the turns of speaking produced in the First Part (Average PA1= 40,76) is more than the double of the turns of speaking produced in the other two parts (Average PA2= 18,56 - Average PA3= 16,1). So, It seems confirmed the hypothesis that the subjects interact using the first part of the way both to get used to the new environment and to co-construct a common ground *to be based on for the following conversations, also in absence of physical co-presence.* B) There is a significant difference (Sig.=.02; p=.05) between the number of turns of speaking produced by every single subject in the three parts, with reference to the order of presentation. In particular, apart from the parts taken into consideration, the number of turns in speaking of the first phase is significantly greater than that of the second phase.

Finally, there is no significant difference between the number of turns of speaking produced by every single subject in the three parts. Particularly, apart from the parts taken into consideration, the number of turns of speaking of the immersive mode is always greater than that of the non-immersive mode, even if it is not significant. However, the analysis of the statistical power (0,237) let us suppose that the lack of significance should be resulting from the limited size of the sample.

8.7   Conclusions

In this chapter we tried to reach two different goals:

- to verify if cooperative activities in networked virtual environments are possible;
- if yes, to identify the characteristics of the cooperation process. We also tried to identify possible differences between immersive and non immersive virtual environments.

We used as framework for our analysis the Complementary Explorative Multilevel Data Analysis (CEMDA) that integrates qualitative and quantitative procedures [18]. In particular, the obtained data were analyzed separately in three different Studies:

- Study 1 investigated the cooperative process by means of the analysis of the transcripts of the verbal interaction of different couples (analysis of conversations - qualitative method);
- Study 2 investigated the characteristics of the cooperation strategies used in the cooperative task;
- Study 3 analyzed the differences in the dialogical productivity between the immersive and non-immersive environments by means of a statistical procedure (ANOVA - quantitative approach).

The question of whether networked VEs can support the formation of real cooperative processes was the first addressed in this paper. To verify this possibility we checked how many couples of our sample could end the proposed collaborative task: most of the couples (41 - 83,7%) of the sample managed to complete at least one phase; 63,3% of the sample (31 couples) completed both phases. These empirical findings can be interpreted as an indication that in networked environments cooperation is possible even if individuals have to deal with interface constraints and limited interaction.

However, the results of Study 1 clearly stated that the couple has to tune its communicative approach to the characteristics of the experienced environment. For example, simple monologues, in which one of the two speakers takes turns in speaking rather extensively providing extensive information, are very common. If in traditional conversations, we can consider such a behavior a prevarication of one speaker on the other, in this situation simple monologues "support" the conversation: the specific collaborative task calls for the ability of putting at the partner's disposal the greatest amount of information possible.

Other characteristic of the specific communicative approach is a significant use of the temporal and spatial deixis. As a conclusion the conversations analyzed clearly show an intention to collaborate to solve the mutual objective. As showed in the second study, this intention is witnessed and sustained by specific strategies – Association, Negotiation and Dominance. Using them the speakers exchange information and try to successfully reach their common goal.

On the basis of the results of the studies, both quantitative and qualitative analysis showed a substantial homogeneity between immersive and non-immersive VR environments. In both environments, partners produce a reciprocal influence on their actions and seem to be able to perceive their conjoint communicative work. However, the average time used to complete the task is significantly longer in the immersive phase instead of in the non-immersive one. Moreover, our experience showed that simulation sickness is a significant problem for the immersive experience: in each leaving couple one of the subjects, usually the female one, experienced some form of side-effects. These side-effects were characterised by three classes of symptoms: ocular problems, such as eyestrain, blurred vision and fatigue; disorientation and balance disturbances; nausea. The experienced symptoms are similar to those which have been reported during and after exposures to simulators with wide field-of-view displays [21]. The higher sensibility of female subjects to simulation sickness in our sample is a common datum in literature. In fact, females tend to be more susceptible to VR side-effects than males [22].

In the end, our empirical findings suggest that networked environments can support the cooperation process. The way the description of the environment and space and time indications are shared, the co-construction of roles, and the characteristics of the exchanges, are examples of how social interaction can be mastered in virtual environments. We can consider them paradigm of cooperative action facing complex tasks. On the basis of results we can argue that studies in this field are worthwhile and useful to reach a sufficient knowledge about ways to control and master complexity of interaction in virtual environments.

However, the results also underline the need, for the researchers and for the users of immersive networked environment, of addressing the effects of simulation sickness. Although there is much potential for the use of immersive virtual reality environments, this problem is still limiting their real-life applications.

8.8 Acknowledgments

Although this article is based on a strong collaboration between the four authors, each of them developed more in depth different parts of the article. Galimberti and Riva together took charge of the theoretical discussion, the definition of the methods and the elaboration of the general results. Galimberti and Ignazi performed Studies 1 and 2 and were responsible for the conversation analysis of the collected data. Vercesi performed Study 3 and was responsible for the statistical analysis of the collected data. Riva defined the research context, the Complementary Explorative Multilevel Data Analysis procedure, and prepared the final discussion.

The present work was supported by the Commission of the European Communities (CEC), in particular by the by the IST programme (Project VEPSY UPDATED, IST-2000-25323 - http://www.vepsy.com).

8.9   Appendix: transcription codes

In the transcriptions the capital letter followed by a full stop indicates the name of the subjects, which is omitted for confidential reasons.

* o # (in both turns)	start of a superimposition
+ o / (in both turns)	end of a superimposition
(.)	pauses up to 2"
(-)	pauses between 2" and 5"
,	slightly raised intonation
?	interrogative intonation
.	ending or downward intonation
x-	incomplete words
(xxx)	incomprehensible words
(word)	uncertain interpretations
(...)	omission

8.10   References

[1]   G. Riva, Virtual reality as assessment tool in psychology, in *Virtual reality in neuro-psycho-physiology: Cognitive, clinical and methodological issues in assessment and rehabilitation*, G. Riva, Ed. Amsterdam: IOS Press, 1997, pp. 95-112.

[2]   F. Vincelli and E. Molinari, Virtual reality and imaginative techniques in clinical psychology, in *Virtual environments in clinical psychology and neuroscience: Methods and techniques in advanced patient-therapist interaction*, G. Riva, B. Wiederhold, and E. Molinari, Eds. Amsterdam: IOS Press, 1998, pp. 67-72.

[3]   G. Riva, Virtual Reality as a communication tool: a socio-cognitive analysis, *Presence, Teleoperators, and Virtual Environments* 8 (1999) 460-466.

[4]   G. Riva and G. Mantovani, The ergonomics of virtual reality: Human factors in developing clinical-oriented virtual environments, in *Medicine meets virtual reality. The convergence of physical & informational technologies: Options for a new era in healthcare*, J. D. Westwood, H. H. Hoffman, R. A. Robb, and D. Stredney, Eds. Amsterdam: IOS Press, 1999, pp. 278-284.

[5]   F. Biocca and B. Delaney, Immersive virtual reality technology, in *Communication in the age of virtual reality*, F. Biocca and M. R. Levy, Eds. Hillsdale, NJ: Lawrence Erlbaum Associates, 1995, pp. 57-124.

[6]   T. Bardini, Bridging the Gulfs: From Hypertext to Cyberspace, *Journal of Computer Mediated-Communication [On-line]* 3 (1997) Available: http://www.ascusc.org/jcmc/vol3/issue2/bardini.html.

[7]   B. Laurel, Interface agents: Metaphors with character, in *The art of human computer interface design*, B. Laurel, Ed. Reading, MA: Addison-Wesley, 1990, pp. 355-365.

[8]   B. Laurel, *Computers as theater*. Reading, MA: Addison-Wesley, 1991.

[9]   T. Rodden, J. Mariani, and G. Blair, Supporting cooperative applications, *International Journal of Computer Supported Cooperative Work* 1 (1992) 1-2.

[10]   E. F. Churchill and D. Snowdon, Collaborative virtual environments: an introductory review of issues and systems, *Virtual Reality* 3 (1998) 3-15.

[11]   G. Mantovani, *New communication environments: from everyday to virtual*. London: Taylor & Francis, 1996.

[12]   L. Gasser, Social conceptions of knowledge in action: Distributed Artificial intelligence foundations and open systems semantics, *Artificial Intelligence* 47 (1991) 107-138.

[13]   G. Riva and C. Galimberti, The psychology of cyberspace: a socio-cognitive framework to computer mediated communication, *New Ideas in Psychology* 15 (1997) 141-158.

[14]   G. Riva and C. Galimberti, Computer-mediated communication: identity and social interaction in an electronic environment, *Genetic, Social and General Psychology Monographs* 124 (1998) 434-464.

[15]   G. Riva, From technology to communication: Psycho-social issues in developing virtual environments, *Journal of Visual Languages and Computing* 10 (1999) 87-97.

[16]   G. Mantovani, Social context in HCI: A new framework for mental models, cooperation and communication, *Cognitive Science* 20 (1996) 237-296.

[17]   G. Mantovani and G. Riva, "Real" presence: How different ontologies generate different criteria for presence, telepresence, and virtual presence, *Presence, Teleoperators, and Virtual Environments* 8 (1999) 538-548.

[18]   G. Riva, The mind over the Web: The quest for the definition of a method for Internet research, *CyberPsychology and Behavior* 4 (2001) 7-16.

[19]   F. Sudweeks and S. J. Simoff, Complementary Explorative Data Analysis: The reconciliation of quantitative and qualitative principles, in *Doing Internet research: Critical issues and methods for examining the Net*, S. Jones, Ed. Thousand Oaks, CA: Sage Publications, Inc., 1999, pp. 29-56.

[20]   R. S. Kennedy and K. M. Stanney, Postural instability induced by virtual reality exposure: Development of a certification protocol, *International Journal of Human Computer Interaction* 8 (1996) 25-47.

[21]   R. S. Kennedy, L. J. Hettinger, D. L. Harm, J. M. Ordy, and W. P. Dunlap, Psychophysical scaling of circular vection (CV) produced by optokinetic (OKN) motion: individual differences and effects of practice, *J Vestib Res* 6 (1996) 331-41.

[22]   M. J. Griffin, *Handbook of Human Vibration*. London: Academic Press, 1990.

[23]   J. R. Lackner, Multimodal and motor influences on orientation: implications for adapting to weightless and virtual environments, *J Vestib Res* 2 (1992) 307-22.

[24]   E. C. Regan and A. D. Ramsey, The efficacy of hyoscine hydrobromide in reducing side-effects induced during immersion in virtual reality, *Aviat Space Environ Med* 67 (1996) 222-6.

[25]   C. Kerbrat-Orecchioni, *Les interactions verbales*. Paris: Armand Colin, 1990.

[26]   C. Hudelot, Dialogue et monologue dans l'èchange mère-enfant, *Journée d'études* 6 (1983) 13-23.

[27] M. E. Holmes, Phase structures in negotiation, in *Communication and negotiation*, L. L. Putnam and M. E. Roloff, Eds. Newbury Park: Sage, 1992, pp. 83-105.

[28] C. Galimberti, *La conversazione [Conversation]*. Milan: Guerini e Associati, 1992.

[29] C. Galimberti, Dalla comunicazione alla conversazione [From communication to conversation]. *Ricerche di Psicologia* 18 (1994) 113-152.

[30] H. H. Clark and E. F. Schaefer, Contributing to discourse, *Cognitive Science* 13 (1989) 259-294.

[31] C. S. Levinson, *Pragmatics*. Cambridge, MA: Cambridge University Press, 1983.

[32] C. Lyons, *Semantics*. Cambridge, MA: Cambridge University Press, 1977.

Towards CyberPsychology
G. Riva and C. Galimberti (Eds.)
IOS Press, 2001

9 Using Virtual Reality in Experimental Psychology

Andrea GAGGIOLI

Abstract. The major aim of the present study is to emphasize the potential offered by Virtual Reality (VR) to develop new tools for research in experimental psychology. Despite several works have addressed cognitive, clinical and methodological issues concerning the application of this technology in psychological and neuro-psychological assessment and rehabilitation, there is a lack of discussion focusing on the role played by Virtual Reality and 3D computer graphics in experimental behaviour research. This chapter provides an introduction to the basic concepts and the historical background of experimental psychology along with a rationale for the application of Virtual Reality in this scientific discipline. In particular, the historical framework aims at emphasizing that the application of VR in experimental psychology represents the leading edge of the revolution that informatics has operated into the traditional psychology laboratory. We point out that the use of VR and Virtual Environments (VEs) as research tool might discover new methodological horizons for experimental psychology and that it has the potential to raise important questions concerning the nature of many psychological phenomena. In order to put the discussion on a concrete basis, we review the relevant literature regarding the application of VR to the main areas of psychological research, such as perception, memory, problem solving, mental imagery and attention. Finally, fundamental issues having important implications for the feasibility of a VR approach applied to psychological research are discussed.

Contents

9.1   Introduction

9.1.1   The history of scientific psychology and of its experimental instruments

The emergence of scientific psychology in the period 1855–1914 constituted an important advance in the history of human understanding. For centuries issues such as the characteristics of human and animal mind, the relationship between mind and body, the relative roles of cognition, and the nature of mental healing were the subject of philosophical speculation and debate. The adoption of the experimental method by psychological research can be considered as the point of transition of the psychological investigation, which moved from a speculative approach of the great philosophers to the empirical approach of the modern scientific method. The method of this new science was to be experimental. As Wundt [1] phrased it, "Psychological introspection goes hand in hand with the methods of experimental physiology, and the application of the latter to the former has given rise to the psychophysical methods as a separate branch of experimental research. If one wishes to place major emphasis on methodological characteristics, our science might be called *experimental psychology* in distinction from the usual science of mind based purely on introspection".

Physiology made an important contribution to the emergence of scientific psychology through its development of experimental apparatus. In order to study physiological processes with the care and precision required for the generation of reliable findings, experimental physiologists developed a wide array of instrumentation. The function of these instruments was to control variation in stimulus presentation or to register and measure response. Among the instruments designed for the control of variation in stimulus presentation, for example, were the color mixer (for varying wavelength composition and/or brightness of a visual stimulus), the aesthesiometer (for varying tactile stimuli), the accoumeter (for varying amplitude of sound), and the tonometer (for varying frequency of sound). Apparatus designed to register and measure response included the kymograph (which allowed analogue registration of a continuous response), the cardiograph (for heart rate), the plethysmograph (for pulse), the ergograph (for effort expended and fatigue), and the chronoscope [2].

At the end of the 19th century, as psychologists began to set up laboratories for experimental research, it was natural for them to look to physiology for basic apparatus; and items of the sort listed above became standard fixtures in these laboratories. In addition, psychologists began to develop specialized apparatus of their own. Often these instruments were designed for research on higher or more complex mental processes.

Examples might include Georg Elias Myller's *memory apparatus*, Felix Krueger's *larynx sound recorder*, Karl Marbe's apparatus for the melody of speech, and Emil Kraepelin's writing apparatus.

The informatics revolution of the second half of the 20th century increased the diffusion of the use of the computer in psychology research. Although initially experimental psychologists used the computer mainly for gathering and processing experimental data, later it became an important support of all phases of the experimental procedure, from task presentation to on-line storage and recording of subject's responses.

(9a)   (9b)

(9c)   (9d)

Figure 9.1 Early psychology instruments: a) Hipp chronoscope; b) Aesthesiometric Compasses; c) Vertical Kymograph; d) Tonometer (*courtesy of the University of Toronto Brass Instrument Collection*).

Legrenzi [3] indicated four main factors by which the beginning of the informatics era might have characterized the revolution of the traditional psychology laboratory:

1. *Dehumanisation.* One of the most important methodological innovations introduced by Wundt was the division of roles between the observer and the subject. The subject, according to Wundt, was merely the source of the data while the observer was charged with manipulating the stimuli and measuring/interpreting subject's responses. In this way, the result of the investigation became the product of a social interaction following a system of rules defined by a scientific procedure. The introduction of the computer restricted even more the role of the subjects, by constraining them to give their response in very bound tasks.

2. *Simulation.* The possibility of simulating the investigated phenomena by using the computers offered a new tool for experimental research. The use of the computer-simulation of natural phenomena assumed a fundamental role not only in psychology, but also in several other scientific disciplines, like physics, chemistry, biology and meteorology.

3. *Creation of artificial phenomena.* The development of new methods for the creation of artificial phenomena offered the researchers the opportunity of using artificial systems (i.e. neural networks) to emulate the response of a human being. This determined a radical transformation of the concept of "division of roles" as was intended by Wundt, since the subject was beginning to be replaced by artificial systems. However, this replacement was - and currently is - limited to a restricted range of phenomena, because due to their complexity most part of psychological effects cannot be simulated or re-created by using artificial systems.

As Legrenzi points out, the emergence and growth of information technology transformed the traditional psychological laboratory. The laboratory was not any longer understood as an environment where the subject's response could be observed under controlled conditions, but as an environment where a set of natural phenomena, classified as "cognitive events", could be created and/or simulated. Moreover, the development of new computer software and hardware for the controlled presentation of stimuli and the accurate recording and measurement of reactions strengthened the belief that experimentation could yield progress in the description and explanation of psychological phenomena. Finally, it should be emphasized that the impact of the computer on psychology was not only circumscribed to the laboratory research. In fact the adoption of the computer as a metaphoric/symbolic model of the human mind [4] determined the beginning of a new scientific movement, the *cognitive science*, which represents the leading theoretical model of present experimental psychology.

9.1.2   A brief historical outline of Virtual Reality technology

The technology of Virtual Reality is not as recent as one might suppose. The first VR system appeared early in the 1962, as Morton Heilig presented a first prototype of multi-sensorial simulator called *Sensorama*. The prototype was a simulator of a real experience (a motorcycle ride through New York) complete with fan-generated wind, the smells and the noise of the metropolis. The *Sensorama* had all main features of a modern Virtual Reality system with one exception: there was no possibility of interaction by the user, because the route was fixed and pre-recorded. Few years later Ivan Sutherland, one of the pioneers of computer graphics (Sutherland's first computer-aided design program, called *Sketchpad*, opened the way for designers to use computers to create blueprints of automobiles, cities, and industrial products), described and realized the first head-mounted display, a visual device which can display an image in front of the user's eyes, no matter where the user may be looking. Key innovative features of Sutherland's HMD were the implementation of stereoscopic vision, the fact that the visual images were computer-generated (and not produced by a video cam) and the adaptation of the user's view according to the head's movements (visual feedback) [5]. He wrote also about force-feedback-devices.

The introduction of flight simulators was one of the most important precursors to Virtual Reality. By the 1970s, computer-generated graphics replaced videos and models that had been used since the Second World War. Fight simulations were operating in real time, though the graphics was primitive. In 1979, the military started to experiment fight simulation systems that used head-mounted displays. These innovations were driven by the greater dangers associated with training on and flying the jet fighters that were being built in the 1970s. In the mid-1980's, a limited three-dimensional virtual workspace in which the user interactively manipulated three-dimensional graphical objects spatially corresponding to hand position was developed. In 1984, NASA started the VIVED project (Virtual Visual Environment Display) and later the VIEW project (Virtual Interactive

Environment Workstation). The goal of both projects was to develop a multipurpose, multimode operator interface to facilitate natural interaction with complex operational tasks and to augment operator awareness of large-scale autonomous integrated systems [6]. Virtual Reality was introduced to the general public first in 1989, at two trade shows organized by two companies (AutoDesk and VPL Research) involved with NASA projects.

The term "Virtual Reality" was originated at that time by J. Lanier, defining it as "a computer generated, interactive, three-dimensional environment in which a person is immersed". Through the 1990s, faster computers provided the key to interactivity; scientists developed advanced visualization software programs and many research centres started at working on VR applications in education, medicine, industry, military training and entertainment. At present, the number of human activities that benefit of VR technology is constantly increasing and further positive expectations are made thanks to the growing diffusion of wireless devices and wearable computing, which represent the new frontier of the research concerning VR interfaces.

9.2   The application of VR technology in Experimental Psychology: the rationale

While many Virtual Reality applications have emerged in several human activities, only recently Virtual Reality technology has been recognized as a useful medium for the study, assessment, and rehabilitation of cognitive processes and functional skills [7]. The opportunity offered by Virtual Reality technology to create interactive three-dimensional stimulus environments, within which all behavioural respondings can be recorded, offers experimental psychologists options that are not available using traditional techniques.

The main benefits offered by the application of VR technology to experimental psychology can be summarized as follows:

1. *Ecological validity.* A clear advantage of a Virtual Reality system is the capacity to record and measure naturalistic behaviour within a simulated functional scenario. This asset offers the potential to collect reliable data which might be otherwise lost to methods employing behavioural ratings from trained observers of behaviour in "real" world settings [8]. Virtual Reality allows researchers to carry out dynamic testing and training in an ecologically valid or "real-world" manner, while still maintaining strict control over all aspects of the experimental situation.

2. *Flexibility.* Virtual environments are highly flexible and programmable. They enable researchers to present a wide variety of controlled stimuli and to measure and monitor a wide variety of responses made by the subject [9]. Furthermore, both the synthetic environment itself and the manner in which this environment is modified by the user's responses can be tailored to the needs of each experimental setting.

3. *Sensorial Feedback.* Our sense of physical reality is a construction derived from the symbolic, geometric, and dynamic information directly presented to our senses. The output channels of a Virtual Reality application, thus, should correspond to our senses: vision, touch and force perception, hearing, smell, and taste. At the present time a good choice of commercial products exists for visual, tracking and user input interfaces. Auditory and haptic interface technologies are becoming ready for use in practical applications, while olfactory interface is the least mature of all the feedback technologies. Despite of the immaturity of some of these input devices, the ones available at present can represent a powerful tool for behavioural research, in particular for studies requiring the simulation of complex sensorial effects otherwise difficult – if

not impossible - to reproduce with traditional methods (i.e., the translation of one sense into different senses).

4. *Performance Recording.* VR and related technologies allow the complete performance recording. This can avoid the loss of important experimental data, which is a common drawback, for example, of traditional pen-pencil based observational methods.

The next section will present a summary of the VE literature targeting cognitive/functional processes in experimental psychology.

9.3   Empirical work in behaviour research involving Virtual Reality technology

Having set out the rationale for the application of Virtual Reality in experimental psychology, we will now try to make these ideas more concrete. Rather than attempt to a global review, we shall concentrate on a small number of influential studies to draw out some general issues pertinent to our aim of assessing the pros and cons of this new tool for behaviour research.

9.3.1   Perception

The study of sensation and perception involves not only the anatomy and physiology of the sensory system, but also behavioural measures. Psychophysical data obtained from tasks in which observers are asked to detect, discriminate, rate or recognize stimuli provide information about how the properties of the sensory system relate to what is perceived.

Behavioural measures also provide considerable information about the function of higher-level brain processes for which current knowledge of the physiological bases is rudimentary. The sensory information must be interpreted by these higher-level processes, which include mental representations, decision-making, and inference. Thus, perceptual experiments provide evidence about how the sensory input is organized into a coherent percept. Methods for investigating sensation and perception include *anatomical-physiological methods* and *psychophysical methods*. The former are represented by a wide variety of specific techniques for analysing and mapping out the pathways associated with sensation and perception and include both neuropsychological and psychophysiological techniques, which are used to investigate issues concerning information processing.

Psychophysical methods aim at obtaining some estimate of sensitivity to detect either the presence of some stimulation or differences between stimuli. In this framework, VR should be interpreted as a useful tool, which can *support* and *improve* both anatomical-physiological and psychophysical methods. Taken for granted that the simulation of reality in its infinite complexity is far beyond the possibility of present Virtual Reality systems, the major advantage offered by the use of VR in perception research is represented by the possibility of investigating the perceptual mechanisms using specific virtual stimuli tailored to the needs of each experimental task.

It is interesting to point out that Virtual Reality technology was developed by implementing many perceptual laws discovered by experimental psychologists during the last century. To some extent, one might say that 3D computer graphics has recapitulated the development of psychological knowledge in this area. Now experimental psychology has the opportunity to use this technology to reach a deeper understanding of some perceptual phenomena, which otherwise might not be investigated at all. This not only demonstrates that findings in one scientific discipline are often easily applied to others, but also that the relationship between the questions scientists ask and the apparatus that they have available for research is bi-directional. Theoretically derived questions may motivate the search for adequate apparatus; and apparatus, once developed, not only permits but in some cases also drives the search for additional questions. Actually, beyond the scientific questions raised by the possibilities offered by VR technology regarding known perceptual and cognitive phenomena, the experience of being immersed in a synthetic environment itself might represent a new theoretical construct (the sense of *presence*) that is worth being investigated.

The range of perceptual phenomena investigated using Virtual Reality is quite heterogeneous, demonstrating that VR has the potential to be applied to several fields of perceptual research. Therefore, the best approach for a review would be to classify the studies according to the perceptual processes targeted by VR applications. The review is not meant to be complete, rather to illustrate examples of relevant studies where the added value of VR technology to traditional anatomical-physiological and psychophysical methods can be emphasized.

9.3.1.1   Visual perception

Seeing is the process of decoding the image information conveyed by patterns of light. 3D computer graphics simulates the process of encrypting scene information into the image.

By presenting subjects with computer-generated 3D stimuli, we can gain powerful insights into the constraints used by the visual system to decode image information and assess the roles of specific visual cues in determining the visual percept. Conversely, knowledge of the minimal conditions for the perception of visual environmental properties can be used in the design of more effective optical displays. This bi-directional relationship between perception research and advance in VR technology is well represented, for instance, by studies which examined the effectiveness of using perceptual criteria to select the amount of detail that is displayed in an immersive Virtual Reality (VR) system. Based upon this determination, Reddy et al. [10] developed a principled, perceptually oriented framework to automatically select the appropriate level of detail (LOD) for each object in a virtual scene, taking into consideration the limitations of the human visual system. They applied knowledge and theories from the domain of visual perception to the field of VR thus optimising the visual information presented to the user based upon solid metrics of human vision. The rationale of this approach was that, if one could describe one object in terms of its spatial frequencies, this would enable to select the lowest LOD available without the user being able to perceive any visual change.

Another example of the bi-directional relationship between perception research and advance in VR technology is represented by research on distance perception. Perceived distance judgments have been previously studied in both naturalistic and laboratory settings. The initial investigations of distance estimation in VEs have been carried out to determine how accurately people perform distance estimation tasks under tightly controlled conditions and to assess how selected distance cues influence their estimates. By assessing the contribution of the various distance cues to distance perception, researcher can not only gain insights to the processes underlying spatial perception, but they can also investigate factors that may have potential to improve the visual fidelity of a VE [11]. Surdick et al. [12] compared the effectiveness and accuracy of multiple depth cues across viewing distances to examine which cues should be implemented in a visual display in order to minimize costs while maximizing the effectiveness of depth information. For example, the binocular displays required for stereopsis (a depth cue based on stimulation of disparate locations on the retinae) are more costly and complex than biocular displays. If stereopsis provides effective and accurate depth information for task performance (e.g., in performing surgery), then perhaps it should be included in the display. However, if other cues (e.g. perspective depth cues) are just as effective and accurate but less costly, then perhaps these perspective depth cues should be incorporated into the display instead. Results of this study showed that the use of perspective cues in simulated displays may be more important than other depth cues tested because these cues are the most effective and accurate, can be easily perceived by all subjects, and can be readily incorporated into simpler displays (e.g., biocular HMDs).

Figure 9.2 An experiment on visual perception performed in a full-immersive Virtual Reality system (*courtesy of Fraunhofer IAO, Stuttgart, Germany*).

In another study, Gaggioli and Breining [13] investigated how stereo vision and different monocular coding techniques (Wireframe, Flat-Shading and Gouraud Shading) affect the ability to estimate the depth of a 3D computer-generated object displayed on the front wall of a four-walls CAVE (a projection-based VR system that surrounds the viewer with 4 screens) capable of both stereoscopic and monoscopic modes. Results showed a significant positive effect of binocular disparity on perceptual performance, but when concave 3D-shapes were used as stimuli. Furthermore, perceptual estimates were found more accurate and easier when the 3D object's surface was rendered with less realistic monocular coding techniques, like Wireframe and Flat-Shading.

Servos et al. [14] assessed stereo-motion thresholds with high-resolution computer monitor. Stereo-motion thresholds for a rectangle oscillating in depth were determined with the use of a dual randomly interleaved staircase design. By assessing the thresholds for a rectangle that was defined either by lateral motion or by changing size in a group of experienced observers, the authors were able to show that any potential residual translational motion present in the display would not have influenced the stereo-motion thresholds. These findings suggest that this computer-graphics-based technique may be a reasonable alternative to optics-based methods of assessing stereo-motion thresholds.

Harris et al. [15] used a VR display to assess the role of visual and vestibular cues in determining the perceived distance of passive, linear self-motion. Subjects were given cues to constant-acceleration motion: either optic flow presented in a Virtual Reality display, physical motion in the dark or combinations of visual and physical motions. Subjects indicated when they perceived they had traversed a distance that had been previously given them either visually or physically. Results showed a dominance of the physical cues in determining the perceived distance of self-motion in terms of capture by non-visual cues.

The authors related these findings to emerging studies showing the importance of vestibular input to neural mechanisms that process self motion.

Distler et al. [16] investigated the effect of velocity constancy in a Virtual Reality environment. In this study the authors used a virtual environment (VE) to investigate how cues to speed judgments are integrated. The results of this research suggest that both low-level cues to spatio-temporal structure and depth, and high-level cues, such as object familiarity, are integrated by the brain during velocity estimation in real-world viewing.

Shikata et al. [17] used a 3D computer graphics display to identify a group of neurones in the posterior parietal cortex of the monkey that responded preferentially to a flat stimulus in a particular 3D orientation. By using this methodology the authors were able to provide evidence that SOS neurones extract surface orientation signals from the binocular disparity signals and play an important role in the perception of 3D shape and the visual guidance of hand movement.

9.3.1.2 Visuospatial navigation

Research on human spatial cognition aims at investigating the cognitive mechanisms that are triggered in environmental perception and in the representation of spatial information in the environment. The methodology used in this research is usually based on static measures of spatial behaviour, either in real settings or in laboratory simulations (such as film or slide projections). The limits of this approach are that it is difficult to control all environmental parameters in real settings and, on the other side, laboratory simulations are often unrealistic [18]. Virtual Reality has the potential to override such problems. In fact, it allows to make continuous measurements during navigation and to design three-dimensional environments of varying complexity and realism levels. Moreover, real-time interactivity (and head-tracking) in three-dimensional spaces can give the feeling of actual immersion.

Finally, the use of virtual environments can be combined with functional brain imaging techniques, which are useful to identify the neural basis of navigation [19]. For example, Gron G. et al. used functional MRI (*Magnetic Resonance Imaging*) to observe brain activation in male and female subjects as they searched for the way out of a complex, three-dimensional, virtual-reality maze [20]. Results of MRI showed that navigation activated the medial occipital gyro, lateral and medial parietal regions, posterior cingulated and parahippocampal gyri as well as the right hippocampus proper. Gender-specific group analysis revealed distinct activation of the left hippocampus in males, whereas females consistently recruited right parietal and right prefrontal cortex. According to the authors, these findings demonstrate a neural substrate of well-established human gender differences in spatial-cognition performance.

Sandstrom et al. [21] used a computer-generated virtual environment to study sex differences in human spatial navigation. Adult male and female participants navigated through a virtual water maze where both landmarks and room geometry were available as distal cues. Manipulation of environmental characteristics revealed that females rely predominantly on landmark information, while males more readily use both landmark and geometric information. The authors discussed these results as a possible link between recent human research reporting hippocampus activation in spatial tasks and animal work showing sex differences in both spatial ability and hippocampus development.

A fundamental property of the human brain is the ability to make predictions of future sensory and motor events. Grasso et al. [22] simulated navigation along a multi-legged virtual corridor in order to understand whether a time-related or space-related signal triggers anticipatory head orienting movements. Results showed that anticipatory orienting movements are triggered (in standing subjects) by reaching specific locations rather than by the time to the approaching corridor's bend. Similar to what happens in car driving, specific spatial features of the route rather than time to collision seem to drive steering.

9.3.1.3 Sensorimotor transformation

Carrozzo et al. [23] investigated viewer-centred and body-centred frames of reference in direct visuomotor transformations. A Virtual Reality system was used to present visual targets in different three-dimensional (3D) locations in two different tasks, one with visual feedback of the hand and arm position (Seen Hand) and the other without such feedback (Unseen Hand). The findings from these and previous experiments support the hypothesis of a two-stage process, with a gradual transformation from viewer-centred to body-centred and arm-centred coordinates. Retinal, extra-retinal and arm-related signals appear to be progressively combined in superior and inferior parietal areas, giving rise to egocentric representations of the end-point position of reaching.

In a research published in *Nature Neuroscience*, Rushton and Wann [24] used a Virtual Reality task to verify a computational model for timing hand closure to catch a ball. The model is sensitive to the relative effectiveness of size and disparity and implicitly switches its response to the cue that specifies the earliest arrival and away from a cue that is lost or below threshold. The authors demonstrate the model's robustness by predicting the response of participants to some very unusual ball trajectories.

Blakemore et al. [25] have examined the role of sensorimotor context estimation in predicting the consequences of our own actions. They postulated that an efference copy of the descending motor command, in conjunction with an internal model of both the motor system and environment, enables us to predict the consequences of our own actions. In order to test this hypothesis, the authors used two robots to simulate virtual objects held in one hand and acted on by the other. Precise predictive grip force modulation of the restraining hand was highly dependent on the sensory feedback to the hand producing the load. The results show that predictive modulation requires not only that the movement is self-generated, but also that the efference copy and sensory feedback are consistent with a specific context; in this case, the manipulation of a single object.

VR has been also successfully applied to the study of the regulation of human locomotion. Buekers et al. [26] investigated how human locomotion is regulated under externally paced temporal constraints. In this study, a virtual hallway in which a pair of doors was presented that continuously opened and closed at a rate of 1 Hz was projected on a screen placed in front of a treadmill. Subjects were attached to a locometer and instructed to regulate walking pace such that the doors were passed correctly. Performance outcome, movement kinematics (stride duration, stride length and synchronization of stride and door cycles) and flow patterns (change in visual angle of door aperture) were used to examine the data. The findings of this study showed that regulations of locomotion under externally paced temporal constraints are postponed until the final stage of the approach during which adaptations are made according to the requirements of the current situation.

9.3.1.4 Haptic perception

Haptic displays are devices for presenting tactile and force sensations. These displays are being developed in several laboratories, but are not yet widely used elsewhere. Most of the haptic displays available are electro-mechanical devices that deliver force feedback to the hand or arm within limited ranges of movements. For both these reasons, few researches used VR to investigate haptic perception.

Using a visuo-haptic Virtual Reality environment, Atkins et al. [27] tested the hypothesis that observers can use haptic percepts as a standard against which the relative reliabilities of visual cues can be judged, and that these reliabilities determine how observers combine depth information provided by these cues. The results suggest that observers can involuntarily compare visual and haptic percepts in order to evaluate the relative reliabilities of visual cues, and that these reliabilities determine how cues are combined during three-dimensional visual perception.

9.3.2 Attention

Traditional methods for the study of attention usually include pencil and paper techniques, motor reaction time tasks in response to various signaling stimuli and flat-screen computer programs. As Rizzo [28] suggests, within a VR setting a person could be systematically tested and trained on attentional tasks that incorporate settings and response requirements that could simulate real-world functional environments beyond what currently exists.

Virtual Reality, in particular, is well suited to investigate *selective attention* (the ability to maintain behavioural or cognitive set in the face of distracting or competing stimuli) since this cognitive ability is best studied under conditions similar to the three-dimensional, real-world action in which humans typically engage.

Maringelli et al. [29] investigated the shift of visuo-spatial attention in a virtual three-dimensional space. A Virtual Reality set-up was used to study attentional orienting within a three-dimensional visual world. Near and far stimuli were used. Half of the subjects were provided with a virtual representation of their body, whereas half were not. Results showed a different distribution of attentional resources in the two conditions, suggesting a dissociation between attentional systems controlling the proximal and the distal visual space. In particular, the authors found that attention was focused close to the subject's body when a virtual representation of it was present, whereas attention was focused away from the body when a virtual representation of the body was not present.

Lyons J. et al. [30] performed three experiments to assess the predictions of an action-centred model of selective attention. Participants were required to direct action to intended targets located within a computer-generated virtual environment. Using this methodology, the authors found evidence that human selective attention is predominant influenced by the degree to which perception and action space are aligned.

9.3.3 Memory

The main applications of Virtual Reality technology into the field of memory research are concerned with topographical memory and the representation of spatial knowledge.

Environmental psychology models propose that knowledge of large-scale space is stored as distinct landmark (place appearance) and survey (place position) information. Studies of brain-damaged patients suffering from "topographical disorientation" tentatively support this proposal. In order to determine if the components of psychologically derived models of environmental representation are realized as distinct functional, neuroanatomical regions, Aguirre and Desposito [31] performed a functional magnetic resonance imaging (fMRI) study of environmental knowledge. During scanning, subjects made judgments regarding the appearance and position of familiar locations within a Virtual Reality environment. A direct comparison of the survey position and landmark appearance conditions revealed a dorsal/ventral dissociation in three of four subjects. According to the authors, this experiment confirms that environmental knowledge is not represented by a unitary system but is instead functionally distributed across the neocortex.

Virtual Reality was also used to test cognitive models of environmental learning (for a survey, see Wilson [32]). These models ascribe a key role to salient landmarks in representing large-scale space. In order to further investigate this hypothesis, Maguire et al. [33] examined the neural substrates of the topographical memory acquisition process when environmental landmarks were specifically identifiable. Using positron emission tomography (PET), they measured regional cerebral blood flow changes while normal subjects explored and learned in a Virtual Reality environment. One experiment involved an environment containing salient objects and textures that could be used to discriminate different rooms. Another experiment involved a plain empty environment in which rooms were distinguishable only by their shape. Learning in both cases activated a network of bilateral occipital, medial parietal, and occipitotemporal regions. The presence of salient objects and textures in an environment additionally resulted in increased activity in the right parahippocampal gyrus. This region was not activated during the exploration of the empty environment. According to the authors, these findings suggest that encoding of salient objects into a representation of large-scale space is a critical factor in determining parahippocampal involvement in topographical memory formation in humans.

In another experiment, Astur et al. [34] used a computerized version of the Morris water task to examine whether sex differences exist in this domain of topographical learning and memory. This task represents the standard for measuring place learning ability in non-human mammalian species and requires subjects to use the spatial arrangement of cues outside of a circular pool to swim to a hidden goal platform located in a fixed location.

Across three separate experiments, varying in attempts to maximize spatial performance, the authors consistently found males navigate to the hidden platform better than females across a variety of measures. The authors emphasize that these results show a robust sex difference in virtual place learning and demonstrate the effectiveness and utility of the virtual Morris water task for humans.

Gender differences in acquisition of navigational knowledge were found also by Cutmore et al. [35]. The authors performed five experiments to examine the influence of gender, passive/active navigation, cognitive style, hemispheric activation measured by electroencephalography and display information on the acquisition route and survey knowledge using a virtual environment. The results showed that males acquired route knowledge from landmarks faster than females and that proficiency in visual-spatial cognition is associated with better performance in situations where survey knowledge must be used. Furthermore, EEG showed that the right cerebral hemisphere appears to be more activated than the left during navigational learning in a VE. According to the authors, these results have a number of implications in the use of VEs for training purposes and may assist in linking processes involved in navigation to a more general framework of visual-spatial processing and mental imagery.

Richardson et al. [36] investigated spatial knowledge acquisition from maps and from navigation in real and virtual environments. In this experiment, participants first learned the layout of a simple desktop VE and then were tested in that environment. Then, participants learned two floors of a complex building in one of three learning conditions: from a map, from direct experience, or by traversing through a virtual rendition of the building. The authors found that VE learners showed the poorest learning of the complex environment overall. However, all the conditions showed similar levels of performance in learning the layout of landmarks on a single floor. Learning the initial simple VE was highly predictive of learning a real environment, suggesting that similar cognitive mechanisms are involved in the two learning situations.

The specificity of spatial memory performance in a virtual environment was studied by Brooks et al. [37]. Two experiments investigated differences between active and passive participation in a computer-generated virtual environment in terms of spatial memory, object memory, and object location memory. The authors found that active participants, who controlled their movements in the virtual environment using a joystick, recalled the spatial layout of the virtual environment better than passive participants, who merely watched the active participants' progress. Conversely, there were neither significant differences between the active and passive participants' recall and recognition of the virtual objects, nor in their recall of the correct locations of objects in the virtual environment.

According to the authors, these findings emphasize the specificity of memory enhancement in virtual environments.

Gamberini [38] performed two experiments to analyse the effects of immersive and nonimmersive (desktop) VR displays for a three-dimensional environment on memory performance. The tasks consisted in: a) the recognition of the objects perceptual characteristics after exposure to the virtual environment and 2) the recollection of the objects locations in the virtual environment. Quite surprisingly, results showed that subjects performed better in the nonimmersive (desktop) condition for both objects recognition and objects location recollection memory tasks. The author attributed the lack of a positive effect of the immersive display to the inadequacy of the surfing-command interface available for the subjects in such condition, thus emphasizing the importance of the usability issues concerned with the input instruments in navigating in electronic environments.

9.3.4 Cognitive performance

As means of representing and interacting with information, Virtual Reality is at the forefront of technological development. Despite claims that much can be gained from interacting with virtual environments and graphical animation, however, researchers did not consistently demonstrate benefits for cognitive performance. For example, it is not yet clear why particular graphical representations which change response to user interaction should be more effective at facilitating problem solving than static graphical representations, or why three-dimensional representations are better than two-dimensional ones. Scaife and Rogers [39] have developed an analytic framework from which these and other questions regarding graphical representations might be explained. In this framework three central characteristics are emphasized:

- *Computational offloading*. This refers to the extent to which differential external representations (referred both to linguistic and graphical forms) reduce the amount of cognitive effort required to solve informationally equivalent problems.

- *Re-Representation.* This refers to how different external representations, that have the same abstract structure, make problem solving easier or more difficult. The authors report as an example how Zhang and Norman [40] describe carrying out the same multiplication task using roman or Arabic numerals. Both represent the same formal structure, but the former is much harder for people, used to working with the decimal system, to manipulate to reach the solution (e.g. LXVII × X is much more difficult to solve than 68 × 10).

- *Graphical constraining.* This final feature of the framework refers to the way graphical elements in a graphical representation are able to constrain the kinds of inferences that can be made about the underlying represented world. The authors' central idea about this characteristic is that the relations between graphical elements in a graphical representation are able to map onto the relations between the features of a problem space in such a way that they restrict (or enforce) the kinds of interpretations that can be made. The closer the coupling between the elements in the visual display and the represented world, the more tractable the inferencing. Scaife and Rogers point out that computational offloading and re-representation are not overlapping, but complementary. In fact, the former highlights the cognitive benefits of graphical representations while the latter relates to their structural properties and graphical constraining to possible processing mechanisms.

By using this framework, Scaife and Rogers identify some problems that could drive further empirical research concerning human cognitive performance in Virtual Reality.

First, the authors emphasize that the value of Virtual Reality should not be assumed to come about through a structural and spatial equivalence between the Virtual Reality simulation and the real world. In fact, preliminary findings from studies investigating transfer of training in VR systems show that performance characteristics of a task learnt in a VR context are of limited utility when carrying out the same task in the real world. So, instead of considering VR immersion in terms of the value gained from attaining higher levels of perceptual fidelity with the real world, the authors consider more useful to determine what aspects of the represented world need to be included in the virtual environment, what aspects should be omitted and what additional information needs to be represented that is not visible in the real world but enhance task's performance. From a cognitive perspective, this approach enables researchers to assess the benefits of VR in terms of the processing mechanisms that operate at different levels of abstraction of information.

Another way in which the value of VR can be characterized is in terms of "steering" the interaction, in that VR simulations provide more opportunities to visualize and manipulate the behaviour of abstract data structures or processes which are not otherwise visible (for example, the simulation of virtual smoke stream for fluid dynamics, which enables a scientist to manipulate the fluid by using finger tips). The assumption here is that better mental models of the abstract processes will develop through making these kinds of processes more concrete and that on-line problem solving will be facilitated [41]. Scaife and Rogers, however, emphasize that this approach of defining the value of VR does not fully explain how experts, who are supposed to be highly familiar with abstract representations and have to interact with them in their work, are able to transfer between these forms of representation and the concretised visual representation of the same problem space in the Virtual Reality simulation. For the authors, therefore, the value of being able to "steer" a physical simulation should be analysed in relation to how it integrates with ways of interacting with other existing forms of external representations in professional practice.

9.3.5   Mental imagery

Mental imagery is the cognitive process that resembles perceptual experience, but which occurs in the absence of the appropriate stimuli for the relevant perception [42]. Mental imagery is centrally involved in visuo-spatial reasoning and inventive or creative thought. Indeed, it has usually been regarded as crucial for *all* thought processes, although, during the 20th century in particular, this has been called into question. Cognitive psychologists have hypothesized two main models that describe how images are processed and represented in human memory: these are known as the *analogue* model and the *propositional* model [43].

The analogue model asserts that visual information is stored as images, which correspond closely with actual visual images as received by the retina. This correspondence is maintained during mental transformation as if the real object was itself being transformed.

According to the propositional model, images are stored as set of propositions, which are memory representations structured according to specified rules of formation and must be either true or false with respect to the image. To explore mental images more objectively, researchers give subjects tasks that seem to require the use of mental images.

As a critical part of the task is varied, some characteristics of mental images can be deduced. Roger Shepard and his colleagues designed one of the most often used tasks. In the original task subjects were shown two novel visual stimuli projected on a tachistoscope and were asked to determine whether the stimuli had the same shape or different shapes. The shapes (random block shapes) were rotated either in the plane or in depth. Subjects reported that they mentally rotated an image in their head until the two stimuli were oriented the same way, and then made their judgment. When subjects were asked to make their response as quickly as possible, the reaction time increased with the angle of rotation between the shapes. This suggests that it takes time to mentally rotate an image, and implies that mental images are much like real images (thus providing evidence for the analogue model) [44]. With the advance of 3D computer graphics, it became possible to adapt the mental rotation paradigm to study the effect of several shape and realism cues in order to achieve a better comprehension about how visual images are processed and stored in human memory. Barfield and Salvendy [45] investigated the effects of object complexity (three levels, all shown as wireframe images with hidden edges) on mental rotation rates. Reaction times indicated that mental rotation rates were significantly longer for wireframe images than for standard Shepard-Metzler figures and that the reaction time functions were non-linear and related to image and task complexity. The authors used these results to provide preliminary evidence for a third model of mental imagery, called the *hybrid* model for mental rotation, which contains features of both the analogue and propositional positions. In a later study Barfield, Sanford and Foley performed one experiment to investigate the effect of computer-generated realism cues (hidden surfaces removed, multiple light sources, surface shading) on the speed and accuracy with which subjects performed the mental rotation task [46]. Results indicated that mean reaction times were faster for shaded images than for wire frame images (with hidden surfaces removed) and evidenced significant effect for object complexity. According to the authors, these results are consistent with the hybrid model described above.

Gallimore [47] investigated differences in subjects' ability to discriminate between the shape of two 3d objects (a task similar to the classic mental rotation paradigm except that subjects were provided with the ability to rotate one of the objects using a two-dimensional joystick) for various levels of monocular coding techniques and stereopsis. Results indicated that interposition enhanced performance and that stereopsis did not help subjects in performing the visualization task used in this experiment. Brown [48] used a modified version of the standard rotation paradigm in order to consider long-term memory characteristics. In the modified study, subjects were forced to compare a visible stimulus to an object existing in memory. The manipulated variables were interposition and stereoscopic vision. Results showed a positive effect of interposition on performance and a significant, albeit limited, positive effect of stereopsis. Actually, the effect of stereopsis was only measurable for trials with rotated stimuli lacking in clear cues to object structure.

The authors interpreted this result by supposing that stereopsis represents a useful visual cue when other cues to stimulus structure are insufficient and/or ambiguous.

9.4 Conclusion

Virtual Reality is becoming a commonly used research tool in experimental psychology, and the studies of those researchers who apply this technology are acknowledged and even encouraged by the scientific community. In addition, this trend is reinforced by reduced computer size, lower costs and significant increase in computing power, which are likely to make advanced computer systems available in many psychology laboratories. However, for this technology to be successfully applied to the available behaviour research methodologies, efforts must be made both by behaviour and computer scientists in order to override some methodological and technical problems.

A fundamental issue having important implications on the feasibility of a VR approach applied to psychological research concerns the concept of generalization of measurement. In fact, it is not fully understood whether, and to which extent, results concerning a hypothesis tested in a virtual environment setting can be extended to day-to-day, real-world life [49]. Experiences offered in Virtual Reality are restricted to what perceptual cues we can reproduce and are much more limited than the sensorial-rich experiences available to an individual going about daily routine. This limitation, therefore, should be taken in account when attempting to generalize results obtained using a Virtual Reality simulation to explain the behaviour observable in a natural setting.

A second problem concerns the limitations of the current sensorial output devices. In fact, although devices with 3D sound and tactile feedback are available, virtual environments are mainly designed around the visual modality and do not account for interactions among the sensorimotor systems. This constrain, thus, reduces drastically the range of experimental situations where VR could be applied.

Another technical problem is represented by the lack of reference standards. In fact, almost all the VR applications in behaviour research are "one-off" creations tied to their development hardware and software. This makes it difficult to use them in context others than those in which they were developed [7].

Finally, the issues related to the user interface should be not disregarded. The essence of Virtual Reality is the ability to interact with a three-dimensional computer-generated environment. If this technology has to become an effective research tool in experimental psychology, the goal is to build applications that allow a person to interact with the electronic environment in a naturalistic fashion. Furthermore, the development of more naturalistic interfaces could have positive implications for the concerns on generalization discussed above.

In conclusion, although Virtual Reality technology represents a promising tool in areas of experimental research such as those described above, a need is identified for more fundamental systematic research about methodological, technical and human factors issues so as to improve understanding of the potential offered by this innovative technology to scientific psychology.

9.5   References

[1]   Wundt, W., Contributions to the theory of sensory perception. In T. Shipley (Ed.). *Classics in Psychology*. New York: Philosophical Library, 1961

[2]   Robert H. Wozniak, Rudolph Schulze, Experimental Psychology and Pedagogy. In *Classics in Psychology, 1855-1914: Historical Essays*. Robert H. Wozniak (Eds). Bristol: Thoemmes Press, 1998.

[3]   Legrenzi, P. *Storia della Psicologia*. Bologna: Il Mulino, 1999, pp.22-23.

[4]   Vera, A.H., Simon, H.A., Situated action: a symbolic interpretation, *Cognitive Science* 17(7) 1993.

[5]   Sutherland, I. The ultimate display. In *Proceedings IFIP Congress*, 1965.

[6]   Fisher, S.S., MacGreevy, M., Humphries, J., and Robinnet, W. Virtual Environment Display System. In *Proceedings 1986 ACM Workshop on Interactive 3D Graphics*. Chapel Hill, NC: 1986, pp. 77-87.

[7]   Riva, G., From Toys to Brain: Virtual Reality Applications in Neuroscience, *Virtual Reality*, 3 1998 pp. 259-266.

[8]   Rizzo, A.A., Buckwalter, J.C., Neumann, U., Kesselmann, C., Thiebaux, M., Basic Issues in the Application of Virtual Reality for the Assessment and Rehabilitation of Cognitive Impairments and Functional Disabilities. *Cyberpsychology and Behavior*, 1(1) 1998 pp. 59-78.

[9]   Riva, G., From Technology to Communication: Psycho-Social Issues in Developing Virtual Environments. *Journal of Visual Languages and Computing*, 10(1) 1999 pp. 87-97.

[10]   Witmer, B.G., Kline, P.B., Judging Perceived and Traversed Distance in Virtual Environments, *Presence-Teleoperators and Virtual Environments*, 7(2) 1998, pp. 144-167

[11]   Reddy, M., Watson, B., Walker, N., Hodges, LF., Managing Level of Detail in Virtual Environments - A Perceptual Framework, *Presence-Teleoperators and Virtual Environments*, 6(6) 1997, pp. 658-666.

[12]   Surdick, R.T., Davis, E.T., King, R.A., Hodges, L.F., The Perception of Distance in Simulated Visual Displays: A Comparison of the Effectiveness and Accuracy of Multiple Depth Cues Across Viewing Distances, *Presence-Teleoperators and Virtual Environments*, 6(5) 1997, pp. 513-531.

[13]   Gaggioli, A., Breining, R., Perception and Cognition in Immersive Virtual Reality. In *Emerging Communication: Studies on New Technologies and Practices in Communication*. Riva, G., Davide, F. (Eds) Amsterdam: IOS Press, 2001.

[14]   Servos, P., Symons, L.A., Schmidt, W., Goodale, M.A., Assessing Stereo-Motion Thresholds With High-Resolution Computer Monitor, *Behavior Research Methods, Instruments, and Computers*, 30(3) 1998, pp. 449-453.

[15]   Harris, L.R., Jenkin, M., Zikovitz, D.C., Visual and Non-Visual Cues in the Perception of Linear Self Motion, *Experimental Brain Research*, 135(1) 2000, pp.12-21.

[16]   Distler, H.K., Gegenfurtner, K.R., van Veen, H.A.H.C., Hawken, M.J., Velocity Constancy in a Virtual Reality Environment, *Perception*, 29(12) 2000, 1423-1435.

[17]   Shikata, E., Tanaka, Y., Nakamura, H., Taira, M., Sakata, H., Selectivity of the Parietal Visual Neurones in 3D Orientation of Surface of Stereoscopic Stimuli, *Neuroreport*, 7(14) 1996, pp. 2389-2394.

[18]   Peruch, P., Gaunet, F., Virtual Environment as Promising Tool for Investigating Human Spatial Cognition, *Cahiers de Psychologie*, 17(4-5) 1998, pp. 881-899.

[19]   Maguire, E.A., Burgess, N., O'Keefe, J., Human Spatial Navigation: Cognitive Maps, Sexual Dimorphism, and Neural Substrates, *Current Opinion in Neurobiology*, 9(2) 1999, pp. 171-177.

[20]   Gron, G., Wunderlich, AP., Spitzer, M., Tomczak, R., Riepe, MW., Brain activation during human navigation: gender-different neural networks as substrate of performance, *Nature Neuroscience*, 3(4) 2000, pp. 404-408.

[21]   Sandstrom, N.J., Kaufman, J., Huettel, S.A., Males and Females Use Different Distal Cues in a Virtual Environment Navigation Task, *Cognitive Brain Research*, 6(4) 1998, pp. 351-360.

[22]   Grasso, R., Ivanenko, Y.P., McIntyre, J., Viaud-Delmon, I., Berthoz, A., Spatial, Not Temporal Cues Drive Predictive Orienting Movements During Navigation: a Virtual Reality Study, *Neuroreport*, 11(4) 2000, pp. 775-778.

[23]   Carrozzo, M., McIntyre, J., Zago, M., Lacquaniti, F., Viewer-Centered and Body-Centered Frames of Reference in Direct Visuomotor Transformations, *Experimental Brain Research*, 129(2)1999, pp. 201-210.

[24]   Rushton, S.K., Wann, J.P., Weighted Combination of Size and Disparity: a Computational Model for Timing a Ball Catch, *Nature Neuroscience*, 2(2) 1999, pp. 186-190.

[25]   Blakemore, S.J., Goodbody, S.J., Wolpert, D.M., Predicting the Consequences of Our Own Actions – The Role of Sensorimotor Context Estimation, *Journal of Neuroscience*, 18(18) 1998, pp. 7511-7518.

[26]   Buekers, M., Montagne, G., de Rugy, A., Laurent, M., The Regulation of Externally Paced Human Locomotion in Virtual Reality Source, *Neuroscience Letters*, 275(3) 1999, pp. 171-174.

[27] Atkins, J.E., Fiser, J., Jacobs, R.A., Experience-Dependent Visual Cue Integration Based on Consistencies Between Visual and Haptic Percepts, *Vision Research*, 41(4), 2001, pp. 449-461.

[28] Rizzo, A.A., Buckwalter, J.G., Virtual Reality and Cognitive Assessment and Rehabilitation: The State of the Art. In G. Riva (Eds), *Virtual Reality in Neuro-Psycho-Physiology – Cognitive, Clinical and Methodological Issues in Assessment and Rehabilitation.* Amsterdam: IOS Press, 1997, pp. 123-145.

[29] Maringelli F., McCarthy J., Steed A., Slater M., Umilta C., Shifting visuo-spatial attention in a virtual three-dimensional space, *Cognitive Brain Research* 10(3) 2001, pp. 317-322.

[30] Lyons, J., Elliott, D., Ricker, K.L., Weeks, DJ., Chua, R., Action-Centred Attention in Virtual Environments, *Canadian Journal of Experimental Psychology*, 53(2) 1999, pp. 176-188.

[31] Aguirre, G.K., Deposito, M., Environmental Knowledge is Subserved by Separable Dorsal/Ventral Neural Areas, Journal of Neuroscience, 17(7) 1997, pp. 2512-2518.

[32] Wilson, P.N., Use of VR Computing in Spatial Learning Research. In Foreman, N., Gillet, R. (Eds), *A Handbook of Spatial Research Paradigms and Methodologies, Vol. 1. Spatial Cognition in the Child and Adult.* London: Taylor and Francis, 1997, pp. 181-206.

[33] Maguire, E.A., Frith, C.D., Burgess, N., Donnett, J.G., Okeefe, J., Knowing Where Things Are – Parahippocampal Involvement in Encoding Objects Locations in Virtual Large-Scale Space, *Journal of Cognitive Neuroscience*, 10(1) 1998, pp. 61-76.

[34] Astur, R.S., Ortiz, M.L., Sutherland, R.J., A Characterization of Performance By Men and Women in a Virtual Morris Water Task – A Large and Reliable Sex Difference, *Behavioural Brain Research*, 93(1-2) 1998, pp. 185-190.

[35] Cutmore, T.R.H., Hine, T.J., Maberly, K.J., Langford, N.M., Hawgood, G., Cognitive and Gender Factors Influencing Navigation in a Virtual Environment, *International Journal of Human-Computer Studies*, 53(2) 2000, pp. 223-249.

[36] Richardson, A.E., Montello, D.R., Hegarty, M., Spatial Knowledge Acquisition From Maps and From Navigation in Real and Virtual Environments, *Memory and Cognition*, 27(4) 1999, pp. 741-750.

[37] Brooks, B.M., Attree, E.A., Rose, F.D., Clifford, B.R., Leadbetter, A.G., The Specificity of Memory Enhancement During Interaction with a Virtual Environment, *Memory*, 7(1) 1999, pp. 65-78.

[38] Gamberini, L., Virtual Reality as a New Research Tool for the Study of Human Memory, *Cyberpsychology and Behaviour*, 3(3) 2000, pp. 337-342.

[39] Scaife, M., Rogers, Y., External Cognition: How Do Graphical Representations Work? *International Journal of Human-Computer Studies*, 45 1996, pp. 185-213.

[40] Zhang, J., Norman, D.A., Representations in Distributed Cognitive Tasks, *Cognitive Science*, 18 1994, pp. 87-122.

[41] Gigante, M. A., Virtual Reality: Definitions, History and Applications. In R.A Earnshaw, M.A. Gigante and H. Jones (Eds), *Virtual Reality Systems.* London: Academic Press, 1993, pp. 3-15.

[42] Finke, R.A., *Principles of Mental Imagery.* Cambridge, MA: MIT Press, 1989.

[43] Yuille, J.C., Steiger, J.H., Nonholistic Processing in Mental Rotation: Some Suggestive Evidence, *Perception and Psychophysics*, 31 1982, pp. 201-209.

[44] Shepard, R., Metzler, J., Mental Rotation of Three-Dimensional Objects, *Science*, 171 1971, pp. 701-703.

[45] Barfield, W., Salvendy, G., Discriminating the Structure of Rotated Three-Dimensional Figures, *Perceptual and Motor Skills*, 65 1987, pp. 453-454.

[46] Barfield, W., Sanford, J., Foley, J., The Mental Rotation and Perceived Realism of Computer-Generated Three-Dimensional Images, *International Journal of Man-Machine Studies*, 29 1988, pp. 669-684.

[47] Gallimore, J.J., Brown, M.E., Visualization of 3-D Computer-Aided Design Objects, *International Journal of Human-Computer Interaction*, 5 (4) 1993, pp. 361-382.

[48] Brown, M.E., Gallimore, J.J., Visualization of Three-Dimensional Structure During Computer-Aided Design. *International Journal of Human-Computer Interaction*, 7(1) 1995, pp. 37-56.

[49] Rizzo, A.A., Buckwalter, J.G., Virtual Reality and Cognitive Assessment and Rehabilitation: The State of the Art. In G. Riva (Eds), *Virtual Reality in Neuro-Psycho-Physiology – Cognitive, Clinical and Methodological Issues in Assessment and Rehabilitation.* Amsterdam: IOS Press, 1997, pp. 123-145.

Towards CyberPsychology
G. Riva and C. Galimberti (Eds.)
IOS Press, 2001

10   An Investigation into Physiological Responses in Virtual Environments: An Objective Measurement of Presence

Brenda K. WIEDERHOLD, Dong P. JANG, Mayumi KANEDA, Irene CABRAL, Yair LURIE, Todd MAY, In Y. KIM, Mark D. WIEDERHOLD, Sun I. KIM

Abstract. The purpose of this study was to investigate the relationship between subjective ratings of presence and physiological responses to a virtual environment. To measure subjective presence, Immersion, Presence, and Realism questionnaires were used. As measures of physiological response, heart rate and skin resistance readings were acquired. Seventy- two participants (36.4±15.5 years of age) were presented with a virtual environment depicting an airplane flight. The results show a correlation between Presence Questionnaire scores and both heart rate and skin resistance: -0.232 (95% confidence), -0.306 (99% confidence) respectively. In the study, heart rate and skin resistance appeared to indicate the participant's degree of immersion.

Contents

10.1 Introduction

Virtual Environments have been employed as tools for working applications in the mental health field for the past 8-10 years. One of the most important aspects of a virtual environment is to induce a state of "Presence," which is defined as "the observer's subjective sensation of 'being there' in a remote environment" [1]. The importance of the construct has generated multiple views for the quantitation and measurement of presence.

These measurements can be broadly classified into two types: subjective and objective measures. Questionnaires that have previously been developed have been used as subjective measures in a majority of studies [2, 3, 4, 5]. They include such questions as: "How aware were you of events occurring in the real world around you?" or "How strong was your sense of presence, 'being there,' in the virtual environment?" While analyses of presence questionnaires may elucidate the phenomenology of immersive experiences, they largely remain post-test measures that are dependent on memory of the event. Presence has, also, been measured during the virtual experience by using a hand-held sliding scale [1, 6].

However, it is unclear exactly what participants were responding to and how responses were affected by the disruption of continuously assessing one's own experience.

Objective measures involve monitoring the impact of a virtual environment on physiologic processes such as heart rate, respiration rate, skin resistance, skin temperature and peripheral brain wave EEG activity. Unfortunately, there are only a few studies that examine the relationship between presence and physiological responses [7, 8, 9]. Meehan found a high and significant correlation between presence and skin conductance level with 10 participants exposed to a virtual height environment. The goal of the study was to investigate the relationship between subjective ratings of presence and physiological responses [13]. Heart rate and skin temperature did not prove to be good measures of presence and results of their correlation with presence were inconclusive. The results support the findings of presence by Wiederhold, Wiederhold, & Davis. Four non-phobic participants and one phobic participant had physiology measured while exposed to a virtual flight environment both in a head-mounted display and on a two-dimensional flat computer screen. Heart rate, respiration, skin resistance and peripheral skin temperature were measured during baseline, relaxed conditions, and during the virtual flight condition. Skin resistance seemed to correspond with self-report measures of anxiety. In addition, the more immersive and interactive experience of a head-mounted display increased physiological arousal and self-report scores of presence and immersion during the exposure. There was an obvious difference in arousal between the phobic participant and non-phobic participants.

10.2 Method

10.2.1 Participants

Seventy-two persons attending a local computer expo in August 1998 in San Diego served as participants. All participants had the study characteristics explained to them fully and gave written informed consent before the protocol began. Table 10.1 shows the characteristics of study participants (gender, ethnicity, and phobic/non-phobic status based on Diagnostic and Statistical Manual of Mental Disorders, Fourth Edition (DSM-IV) criteria).

Table 10.1 Characteristics of Participants

Total (n)	72		
Gender	N		%
(Male/Female)	30/42		42/58
	M	SD	Range
Age	36.4	15.5	18~73
Ethnicity (White/Hispanic/ African-American /other)	N 44/13/4/11		% 61/18/6/15
Non-Phobic/Phobic	N 62/10		% 86/14

10.2.2 Virtual Environments

The flying system being used was designed by Drs. Hodges and Rothbaum of Virtually Better, Inc. (Atlanta, Georgia) who have previously performed VR treatment for acrophobia and fear of flying [10, 11]. The system is run on a high-end Intel Processor-based personal computer and contains advanced audio and Diamond Monster-3D graphics cards, external multimedia speakers and subwoofer, a Polhemus INSIDETRAK position Tracker, and customized software. Audio was delivered to the participants through earphones on the head-mounted display. Vibratory sensations were delivered via a subwoofer mounted under the participant's chair.

10.3 Measures

10.3.1 Self-report questionnaires

The following questionnaires were administered to all participants:

- The Tellegen Absorption Scale (TAS) assesses a person's ability to become deeply absorbed into what one is doing or one's environment. Scores on the 34-item True/False inventory may range from 0-34 [12].
- The Dissociative Experiences Scale (DES) is a brief, self-report measure of one's frequency of dissociative experiences. All 28 items are scored from 0 to 100 according and an average score is determined by dividing the total score by 28 [13].
- The Simulator Sickness Questionnaire (SSQ) measures a participant's somatic response to the virtual environment [14, 15]. Each of the items is scored from 0 to 3.
- The Questionnaire on Presence and Realism rates the sense of presence and degree of realism [14, 7]. It is measured on a scale from 0 to 100.

10.3.2   Physiological measures

The following physiological parameters were measured:

- Skin Resistance (SR), which changes in relation to change in sweat gland activity-as sweat gland activity increases;
- Skin resistance decreases, and
- Heart Rate (HR), measured by electrocardiography.

SR was monitored with two silver/silver chloride electrodes placed on the ring and index fingers of the left hand. HR was collected with two sensors, one on each wrist. An I-330 C-2 computerized biofeedback system manufactured by J&J Engineering (Poulsbo, Washington) was used to collect physiological data.

10.4 Procedure

After signing an informed consent, the participant's two wrists, and left ring and index fingers were swabbed with a cotton ball soaked in to remove any dead skin cells and skin oils that might cause artifact and interfere with accurate readings. For SR, a small amount of electrode gel was placed on each electrode. The electrodes were attached to the ring and index fingers of the participant's left hand with Velcro tabs. For HR, a small amount of electrode gel was placed on each disposable electrode attached to the participant's right and left wrist. A 1-minute eyes closed baseline was then taken. The participant was then placed in a MRG4 Head-Mounted Display (HMD) by Liquid Image. The Polhemus head tracker allowed the participant to move his/her head and view various parts of the virtual environment. The virtual environment shows the participant seated in the left window seat over the wing in the passenger cabin of a commercial aircraft. The participant was instructed to look around the virtual plane to become oriented before beginning the flight sequence. During a 6-minute VR flight, the following sequence was performed: engines on, taxi, take-off, flying in good weather, and landing. After the plane landed, physiological recording was ended and the HMD was removed. Participants were then asked to fill out the self-report questionnaires previously described.

10.5 Analysis

Baseline physiology levels often vary widely between individuals so the percentage change from baseline was used for analyses rather than absolute values. Therefore, before comparing physiological recordings with presence measures, the percentage change of heart rate (ΔHR) was calculated as follows:

$$\Delta HR = (MeanVR - MeanBaseline)/MeanBaseline,$$

with:
 MeanVR: Mean of Heart Rate during the VR exposure, and
 Mean Baseline: Mean of Heart Rate during baseline

Percentage change of skin resistance (ΔSR) was also obtained using the same method. A Spearman correlation was then used to evaluate the relationship among the various presence measures (questionnaires, physiological parameters) due to its suitability for non-linear relationships.

10.6 Results

As was predicted, the TAS and DES were highly correlated, as were the SSQ and DES. The expected significant relationship between the Presence questionnaire and Realism questionnaire was also shown, with both also showing a high degree of correlation with the DES (Table 10.2).

Table 10.2 Spearman Correlation of Dissociative Experiences Scale (DES) to other questionnaires

Measurements	Spearman Correlation
Tellegen Absorption Scale & DES	.353 (p < 0.01)
Simulator Sickness Questionnaire & DES	.289 (p < 0.05)
Presence & DES	.293 (p < 0.05)
Realism & DES	.271 (p < 0.05)

Also noted were changes in physiology based on degree of immersion. Table 10.3 shows the relationship among the presence, absorption, and dissociation measures.

Table 10.3 Spearman Correlation among the presence measures and physiology (Correlation / Sig.)

	PRESENCE	REALISM	TAS	•SR	•HR
PRESENCE		.813(.000)**	.229(.053)	-.306(.009)**	-.232(.050)*
REALISM	.813(.000)**		.255(.031)*	-.307(.009)**	-.250(.034)*
TAS	.229(.053)	.255(.031)*		.061(.612)	-.264(.025)*
ΔSR	-.306(.009)*	-.307(.009)**	.061(.612)		.004(.973)
ΔHR	-.232(.050)*	-.250(.034)*	-.264(.025)*	.004(.973)	

** : Correlation is significant at the 0.01 level (2-tailed).
 * : Correlation is significant at the 0.05 level (2-tailed).

Percentage change of skin resistance (ΔSR) and heart rate (ΔHR) both had a high correlation with the Presence questionnaire and Realism questionnaire. When placed in a virtual environment, a new and novel stimulus, skin resistance levels decreased, indicating some physiological arousal. In 1907, Carl Jung discovered that skin resistance was a means to objectify emotional tones previously thought to be invisible. Skin resistance, unlike EMG and skin temperature, tends to reflect mental events more quickly and with more resolution than other physiological measures [16]. Before the experiment, it was predicted that heart rate would also increase to reflect arousal when the participant experiences the virtual environment. However, contrary to this expectation, heart rate had a negative correlation with the realism questionnaire as shown in Table 10.3. That is, heart rate decreased as the participant felt the virtual environment was more realistic. Figure 10.1 illustrates the scatter plot of heart rate and realism.

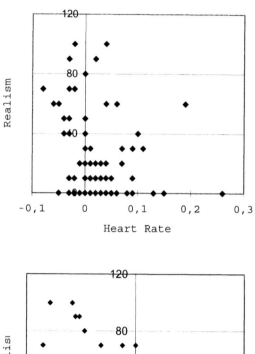

Figure 10.1 Scatter plot: Realism and Heart Rate (ΔHR), Realism and Skin Resistance (ΔSR)

From previous work on experiences to novel situations, two types of reactions are described: an orientation reaction (OR) that was automatically elicited by novel stimuli, and a defense reaction (DR) that was evoked by high-intensity stimulation and had the opposite effect on stimulus discrimination [17]. Previous research shows some of these reactions (i.e., the skin conductance response) are common to both reactions but HR and general motor activity distinguish between the reactions [18]. That is, in reaction to unexpected stimuli, heart rate deceleration has been correlated with the orienting response to novelty and accelerations with defensive responses such as fear and anxiety [19, 20].

Therefore, the well-immersed participants who had no fear of flying react to the virtual environment as an unexpected, novel stimulus. This results in an increase in parasympathetic activity and resulting in a decrease in heart rate. It may be that a relaxed and focused physiological tone allows for more careful and full exploration of a new experience, such as that seen with intense but enjoyable concentration. Analysis of heart rate was not significantly different between phobics and non-phobics, however, it is clear that heart rate measures are probably not sensitive enough to discriminate between groups, or sensitive enough to illustrate differences. For this reason, other measures of cardiovascular reactivity must be used, and are currently being measured at the Virtual Reality Medical Center. We are currently measuring systolic and diastolic blood pressure, heart rate variability, and cardiac output. Skin resistance levels, however, delineate the phobic and non-phobic participants (see Figure 10.2).

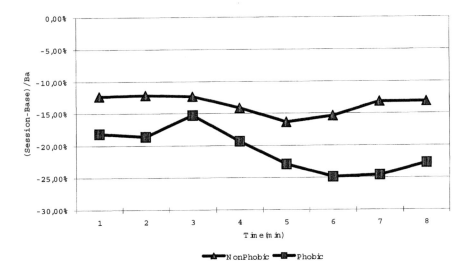

Figure 10.2 The average display of Skin Resistance in non-phobic and phobic participants

This has been found also in previous work comparing phobic and non-phobic participants [9, 20, 21-24].

Another interesting finding, although not significant, is that non-phobics did not rate the virtual environment as realistic as phobics (Table 10.4).

We need to bear in mind when constructing new virtual reality environments for additional mental health applications that patients with disorders may have unexpected reactions to novel virtual worlds. Results obtained with normal participants can be a useful guide for predicting of how patients might react, but graded exposure of patients to new environments is prudent.

Table 10.4 Summary of results obtained from both non-phobics' and phobic's measurements

Measurement	Phobic	Non-Phobic
Presence & Realism	M=28.5 (SD=24.7)	M=23.1 (SD=25.4)
Simulator Sickness Questionnaire	M=11.3 (SD= 8.4)	M=7.2, (SD= 8.2)
Tellegen Absorption Scale	M=7.10 (SD=2.42)	M=6.29 (SD=2.51)
Dissociation Experiences Scale	M=19.2 (SD=11.5)	M=18.3 (SD=19.2)
Δskin Resistance (%)	M=-23.6 (SD=29.9)	M=-12.8 (SD=24.8)
Δheart Rate (%)	M=-0.1 (SD=2.8)	M=2.85 (SD=6.15)

10.7 Conclusion

This study revealed that percentage change in heart rate and skin resistance had a high level of correlation with presence, degree of realism, and immersiveness. The two physiological parameters may therefore be useful as an objective measure of presence and real-time measure of immersiveness. In future work, other physiological measures such as, EEG, blood pressure, heart rate variability, and cardiac output could provide additional important indicators of responses to virtual worlds. In addition, presence questionnaires need to be modified for use in clinical practice. We have as yet incomplete understanding of how those with mental health disorders fully perceive, react, and interact within virtual environments.

10.8 Acknowlegement

Partial support was provided by a grant from the National Research Laboratory Program (2000-N-NL-01-C-159).

10.9 References

[1]   Freeman, J., Avons, S.E., Pearson, D.E., & Ijsselsteijn, W.A. Effects of sensory information and prior experience on direct subjective ratings of presence. *Presence: Teleoperators and Virtual Environments*, 8(1), 1999, 1-13.
[2]   Regenbrecht, H., Schubert, T. Measuring the sense of presence and its relations to fear of heights in virtual environments. *International Journal of Human-Computer Interaction*, 10(3), 1998, 230-250.
[3]   Slater, M., Usoh, M. Depth of presence in virtual environments. Presence: Teleoperators and Virtual Environments, 3(2), 1994, 130-144.
[4]   Usoh, M., Catena, E., Arman, S., & Slator, M., Using Presence Questionnaire in Reality. *Presence: Teleoperators and Virtual Environments*, 9(5), 497-503, 2000.
[5]   Witmer, B.G., & Singer, M.M., Measuring presence in virtual environments: A presence questionnaire. *Presence: Teleoperators and Virtual Environments*, 7(3), 1998, 224-240.
[6]   Ijsselsteijn, W., Ridder, R.H., Hamberg, R., Bouwhuis, D., & Freeman, J., Perceived depth and the feeling of presence in 3DTV. *Displays*, 18, 1998, 207-214.
[7]   Dillon, C., Keogh, E., Freeman, J., & Davidoff, J., Aroused and immersed: the psychophysiology of presence. *Presence 2000 - 3rd International Workshop on Presence*, 2000.
[8]   Meehan, M., An Objective Surrogate for Presence: Physiological Response. *Presence 2000-3rd International Workshop on Presence*, 2000 [online]. Available: http://www.presence-research.org (May 29,2001)
[9]   Wiederhold, B.K., Davis, R., & Wiederhold, M.D., The effect of immersiveness on physiology. In Riva, G., & Wiederhold, M.D. (Eds.), *Virtual environments in clinical psychology and neuroscience*. Amsterdam: IOS Press, 1998.
[10]   Hodges, L.F., Kooper, R., Rothbaum, B.O., Opdyke, D., de Graaff, D.D., Williford, J.S., & North, M.M. Virtual Environments for treating the fear of heights. *Computer Innovative Technology for Computer Professionals*, 28(7), 1995, 27-34.
[11]   Rothbaum, B.O., Hodges, L.F., Watson, B.A., Kessler, G.D., & Opdyke, D. Virtual reality exposure therapy in the treatment of fear of flying: A case report. *Behavior Research & Therapy*, 34(5), 1996, 477-481
[12]   Tellegen, A. & Atkinson, G. Openness to absorbing and self-altering experiences ("absorption"), a trait related to hypnotic susceptibility. *Journal of Abnormal Psychology*, 83, 1974, 268-277
[13]   Carlson, E.B., & Putnam, F.W. An update on the dissociative experiences scale. *Dissociation*, 6(1), 1993, 16-27.
[14]   Parent, A. Unpublished questionnaires. [online]. Available: http://www.trytel.com/~aparent (May 29, 2001)
[15]   Kennedy, R.S., Lane, N.E., Berbaum, K.S. & Lilienthal, A simulator sickness questionnaire (SSQ): A method for quantifying simulator sickness. *International Journal of Aviation Psychology*, 3(3), 1993, 203-220
[16]   Schwartz, M.S. (Eds.), Biofeedback: A Practitioner's Guide. New York: Guilford Press, 1995.

[17] Sokolov, E.N. Perception and the conditioned reflex. New York: MacMillan, 1963.

[18] Graham. F.K., & Hackley, S.A., Passive and active attention to input. In J.R. Jennings & M.G.H. Coles (Eds.), Handbook of cognitive psychophysiology (pp. 251). Sussex, England: Wiley, 1991.

[19] Graham, F.K., Attention: The heartbeat, the blink and the brain. In Campell, B.A., Hayne, H., & Richardson, R. (Eds.), Attention and information processing in infants and adults: Perspectives from human and animal research. Hilldale, New Jersey: Lawrence Erlbau Associates, 1992.

[20] Wiederhold, B.K., & Wiederhold, M.D., Clinical Observations During Virtual Reality Therapy for Specific Phobias. CyberPsychology & Behavior, 2(2), 1999, 161-168.

[21] Wiederhold, B.K., A comparison of imaginal exposure and virtual reality exposure for the treatment of fear of flying. (Doctoral dissertation, California School of Professional Psychology, May, 1999). *Dissertations Abstracts International*, 1999.

[22] Wiederhold, B.K. & Wiederhold, M.D., Lessons learned from 600 virtual reality sessions. *CyberPsychology & Behavior: The Impact of the Internet, Multimedia and Virtual Reality on Behavior and Society, 3*(3), 1999, 393-400.

[23] Wiederhold, B.K., Gevirtz, R., & Wiederhold, M.D., Fear of flying: A case report using virtual reality therapy with physiological monitoring. *CyberPsychology & Behavior: The Impact of the Internet, Multimedia and Virtual Reality on Behavior and Society,* 1 (2) 1998, 97-104.

[24] Wiederhold, B.K., Gevirtz, R.G., & Spira, J.L., *A controlled study comparing imaginal exposure and virtual reality exposure for the treatment of fear of flying.* Manuscript submitted for publication, 2000.

Towards CyberPsychology
G. Riva and C. Galimberti (Eds.)
IOS Press, 2001

11   Communities' Development in CVEs and Sustaining Functions of On-line Tutorship

Alessandra TALAMO, Cristina ZUCCHERMAGLIO, Maria Beatrice LIGORIO

Abstract. The impact of Collaborative Virtual Environments (CVEs) on communities' development is a topic still rather unexplored. All the interaction processes mediated by these technological environments are characterised, from both psychosocial and discursive points of view, by absolutely new practices and by the absence of some communication features, typical of face-to face. The "Community of Practice" model, allows us to analyse the growth of virtual communities along the construction of a *shared repertoire*, the involvement in a *common enterprise* and the sharing of a *mutual engagement*. Communities of practice use technology in social and material contexts, sharing meanings about the technology uses and peculiarities through a continuous negotiating process. The analysis is aimed at describing how a community of practice is established in a virtual world where both textual and graphical interactions are allowed. Conversational and quantitative results show: a) how the community of practice evolves over the time, b) the specificity of the interactions mediated by the virtual environment; c) the role of different participants in the management of discourse in interaction, with a detailed analysis of the on-line tutorship impact on the development of the community.

Contents

11.1 Technology and communities

Technological innovation makes problems that were central no long ago in the ergonomics of human-computer interaction rapidly obsolete. Information and Communication technology and virtual reality environments underline the theoretical and empirical limits of a purely cognitive ergonomic perspective, focussed on interaction between user and technological system. The adoption of new theoretical and empirical approaches able to analyse the social complexity of technology mediated communication and interaction processes is nowadays required. The main characteristic of telematic and virtual technology is that of sustaining and mediating our interaction and communication with others: they mediate a complex person-computer-person-computer-person system.

From these considerations a perspective, defined as social and cultural ergonomics, has been developed [1, 2, 3, 4]. Cultural perspective considers as central units of analysis the social contexts of interaction and communication mediated by technological systems, observing carefully how different technological systems are developing new communicative and interactive contexts. "Each online communication system structures interaction in a particular way, in some cases with dramatic effect on the types of social organizations that emerge from people using them" [5, pag.4].

From this point of view, technological artefacts are not only neutral tools able to develop tasks already defined: on the contrary, they prescribe determinate working and communicative practices sustaining specific social actions [6, 7]. Technology should not be analysed as simply technical and material tools but as cultural artefacts mediating the social, distributed and situated construction of communicative and interactive practices [8, 9]. The central concept to understand the result of interaction among shared practices and technology is that of "mediation" [10, 11, 12]. Communicative and interactive practices are always developed in *inter-subjectivity* and *inter-objectivity* contexts: in social contexts (with others members) and through the mediation of artefacts, nearly exclusively technological, sustaining the communication processes and the information sharing and coordination.

Speaking of mediated practices, it should be underlined that communicative practices cannot have a meaning outside a repertoire shared within a community. An electronic mail system, a text chat or a Collaborative Virtual Environment (CVE) will never be used in equal ways in different communities of practice: they will assume specific meanings and they will sustain peculiar social communicative practices through the mediation of the pre-existing practices system [13].

The Community of Practice model [14, 15, 16] allows us to focus on communities where the participants co-construct a *shared repertoire*, are engaged in a *joint enterprise*, and are involved in *mutual engagement*. In previous studies we showed how the communities of practice at work use discourse in interaction for negotiating social identity of self and others [17] and for sharing some dimensions related to the development of work projects as for example time boundaries [18].

The use of "community of practice" as central unit of analysis of cultural ergonomic research leads to consider human action as always built by answering to other persons, in social contexts of inter-subjectivity. In fact it is only the interaction among individuals that makes possible "the existence of a "discourse world", defined as repertoire of social and shared meanings [19]. Human action, even when mediated by technological artefacts, is always a social action: an action whose meaning is interactively and discursively built in the course of the social practices that we share with other individuals [20, 21]. Such actions are implemented through discursive interaction and during the course of shared practices. Both processes are culturally elaborated [22] and constitute the meaningful actions repertoire of a specific community of practice that should be known in order to understand (and anticipate) how the technology would be used in that community [23].

Communities of practice use technology in their social and material context, attributing to them shared meanings that are developed and defined through the continuous negotiation of their possible uses (and not-uses), benefits, disadvantages and peculiarity.

This negotiation process explains how the use of each technology is shaped and developed by different communities of practice. Pre-existing shared practices act as essential mediators among the intended (by technical developers) meaning of technology and their actual use in the daily practices of each specific community.

The focus of an ergonomic analysis becomes then the negotiation and development of such shared meanings through the interaction with others among specific communities of practice. The main aim is to describe how, through a negotiation process, a repertoire of shared practices is built. This is essential to understand how the community uses the technological artefacts [24]. The shared repertoire of practices in a community - even when technologically mediated - is not the starting, but rather the arrival point of a common activity. A community is incessantly engaged in the negotiating activity about meanings in order to build and widen the shared repertoire (even tacit) and to adapt it to the contingent needs of the community itself. In this way the community can be efficient and collaborative and can ground the basis for further negotiations.

All the interactive processes mediated by technological environments are characterised by the presence of absolutely new practices from the psychosocial and discursive points of view, and by the absence of some communicational practices typical in face-to face settings. It is also essential to distinguish among different mediating technological systems: the multiplicity of technological systems forces us to distinguish more deeply among different types of virtual communities. Recent studies [25] show the relationship between the distinctive characteristics of different mediating systems, in terms of communication channels and resources offered to the interacting participants, and the task performed.

Some authors [26, 5] propose some classifications of the different mediating environments sustaining the development of community of practice based on the synchronicity and on communication channel available:

a) E-mail and discussion list: asynchronous communication, only textual;
b) Usenet and BBS: asynchronous communication, only textual;
c) Text chat, internet relay chat MUD's: synchronous communication, text based;
d) Metaworlds (3D MUDs, 3D Collaborative Virtual Environments): synchronous communication, textual, sharing of a "graphical space", realistic identity (avatar);
e) Interactive video and voice (synchronous communication, verbal and not verbal communication sharing of a real interactive space, real identity).

These mediating environments are greatly differentiated in the temporal aspects of communication (asynchronous or synchronous), in the textual constraints of exchanges, in the presence of a virtual space in which to represent social encounters and in the presence of real voice and identity.

Each of these aspects would pose some specific constraints (both positive and negative) on the style of interaction as well as on community development. Every time the characteristics of the interaction within a community working inside different technologically mediated environments should be identified and described. Nowadays, the specialist literature is still focussed on "describing and analysing patterns of online social interaction and organization as they exist" [5, pag.4] in the virtual environments created by each technological system, without any evaluative and comparative aims. Researches about the potentiality, constraints and limits of technology for mediation of collaborative interaction and coordination of the groups would be advisable.

Besides the limited effort on comparing different technological environments, when speaking of virtual communities another theme is even less present in the literature: differences in the story, structure and aims of each community. Most of the literature presents data on "free" communities, not stable (members can join and leave at any moment), based on poorly defined aims and with no shared objectives [5]. Even if these virtual communities have very interesting aspects for a social and psychological analysis, it is of remarkable interest to analyse the development of interactive patterns inside stable and definite community, such as work communities [13] and communities formed around a specific project [27]. Those communities are characterized by a stable composition, assigned communicative and organizational roles, members identities declared and strategically used to accomplish the task and a common effort to achieve shared aims.

These features make those communities privileged loci for the analysis of the technology mediation on the negotiation of the fundamental dimensions of a community of practice: mutual engagement, joint enterprise and shared repertoire. This is the case of the Metaworlds virtual community based on a 3D Collaborative Virtual Environment that is analysed in this paper.

11.2 The Euroland project

Euroland is a research project involving students, teachers, and researchers from two European countries (Italy and The Netherlands). The main research goal was to design and implement an educational virtual reality environment fostering collaborative learning at a distance and enabling students from schools apart to work together, collaborate, and communicate. The principles used in designing the projects were inspired by the community of learners [28] and practice [14], where knowledge is built through computer supported collaborative learning [29]. All participants — students, teachers and researchers — collaborate actively on the design, building and evaluation of Euroland exchanging information and ideas with the partners at a distance. During the project, that lasted eight months, three weekly meetings were scheduled in order to let at least two groups of participants located at a distance meet synchronously. Several cultural houses populated Euroland: the house of music, art, sport, food and a travel agency. The collaborative construction was guaranteed by the "interdependence" principle [30] according to which each participant had to take charge of the cultural content of the partner country.

The software used for this project is a CVE named Active Worlds (AW) (www.activeworlds.com). AW is a three-dimensional, desktop, non-immersive virtual reality software, very user oriented. It is based on collaborative and constructive learning principals. In facts, it allows participants to design and build virtual objects and any type of web-based tools can be embedded into the virtual environment created by AW. There are two different types of "universes" AW based: one of them is entertainment oriented, the other (called Eduverse) has an educational vocation and it is composed only by virtual worlds monitored by research centres, schools, and universities. Euroland is part of this universe, which sustains a broader community with a common interest about the educational value of this type of technology and protects the virtual worlds from unwanted visitors. In fact, only people registered within Eduverse can visit the virtual worlds and several cross-virtual worlds exchanges and activities were planned during the project.

11.3   The social actors

Seven schools, four from Italy and three from The Netherlands, participated to the project.

The youngest students participating were 9 years old and the oldest 14. In each participating classroom a small group of students (from 2 up to 10) were selected and enabled to connect to the virtual worlds as citizenships with building rights. For each group of citizens, at least one teacher was actively involved on-line and often other teachers supported the in-classroom activities related to the project.

The staff was composed by seven researchers. Four of them acted as on-line or in classroom observers and three of them acted as tutors on-line. One of the tutors (Bea) was also the project manager. She is a researcher with a strong background in educational psychology and about mediated communication in educational contexts. Clarence is the tutor expert in using the software AW and he has a particular talent in teaching building strategies to kids on-line. Lp (short name for Little Prince) was in charge of the start up of the project and later he was mainly dedicated to the server control and monitoring.

Table 11.1 Differences in participation

Type of participants	n. of participants	n. of interventions	Ratio int./participants
tutors	3	16821	5607,00
researchers	4	2407	601,75
teachers	13	3323	255,62
students	40	6490	162,25
occasional guests	27	331	12,26
Total	87	29372	337,61

Euroland was also populated by occasional guests coming from the other virtual worlds belonging to Eduverse, by kids' parents connecting from home, by citizens' classmates and friends curious to see what Euroland was about.

The three tutors, among which there was also the project manager, participated with a great amount of interventions. The others participants seem to participate quantitatively in accordance with their responsibility and engagement in the organisation of the project: the collective impact of researchers and teachers on the total amount of chat talk is greater than students' impact. This result is due to the fact that the Euroland project has been conceived as a pilot project and all the adults, according to their roles, spent a lot of time in discussing its development.

11.4 The objectives

The main aim of this study is to show how both formal and informal aspects of the communication and participation to the community are longitudinally defined by the members through discourse in interaction, using the tools available within the virtual environment the group is building. We will focus in particular on:

1. How the dimensions of a community of practice (mutual engagement, shared repertoire, joint enterprise) develop and are negotiated within a stable and educational community, such as Euroland;

2. How the specificity of the virtual environment mediates the participants' interactions. Special attention will be given to some phenomena related to the explicit use of technical features and software related characteristics as interactive resources, and

3. The role covered by the different participants in managing the discourse in interaction. Since the most active participants were the tutors on-line, a closer look will be given to the tutors' impact on the development of the community.

11.5 Looking at virtual communities as natural groups: ethnomethodology of the virtual meetings

Ethnomethodology and conversation analysis, integrated by the recent methodological research about on-line interactions, and especially the studies on discursive interactions in CMC environments, are more and more considered as the appropriate methods to analyse data collected in research like the one presented in this paper. In using these methods will be taken in consideration that Internet "provides a level of access to the details of social life and a durability of the traces of social interaction that is unprecedented" [5, pag. 4].

From a methodological point of view, this implies the analysis of the negotiation of shared meaning in the discursive interaction within members of a "natural community".

The ethnographic and discursive perspective [20, 22] is able to grasp the social complexity of the negotiation practices, considering as unit of analysis the activity system of the community of practice (instead of single individuals). Conversation analysis [31] looks for order and regularity in human actions, in the place of they observable intersection, that is in the forms that persons give at their encounters with others, in the empirical methods with which they regulates the shared activity and with which attribute meaning to artefacts, even technological, with which they go into contact. The corpus of data comprises all the chat interactions over a period of eight months, 29372 total turns collected in eight months (about 80 chatting hours).

11.5.1   *The analysis of the development of the Virtual Community*

The first part of the study is aimed at describing how Euroland participants became a community of practice. Based on Wenger's theory [14] we started analysing the chats by identifying the topics[1] of discussion according to the three fundamental dimensions: a) mutual engagement, b) shared repertoire, c) common enterprise.

Topics belonging to these dimensions were isolated within the chats. Each turn inside the identified topic has been codified according with the related dimension. Once discarded turns in Dutch (none of the researchers knew that language), digressions and not comprehensible utterances, 28802 turns have been codified in total. A qualitative research has also been carried out in order to show the interactive processes that lead to the development of each dimension in the lifetime of the community.

11.5.2   *The analysis of tutors' impact*

As said before, the Euroland community emerged around specific educational aims. The project was built defining different roles for each participants according with two

---

[1] We use the term *topic* according to the definition of Conversation Analysis, as a sequence of at least three turns on the same argument developed by at least two participants.

integrated aims: a) a research aim, that is verifying whether 3-D software can be used for educational purposes, and b) a didactical aim, tat is trying to enhance learning of specific topics through collaboration among distant classrooms. Teachers' and researchers' aims shared even if they were not always overlapping. This particular condition is interesting to see how the researchers leading the community as a whole offered their tutorship over the time and sustained the development of the community.

Starting from the work proposed by Shathon et al. we developed a category system for the tutors' functions. All the tutors' interventions in chat were analysed through that category system. Three independent researchers checked the interventions' categorisation. The uncertain cases were discussed till an agreement has been reached. The category system of tutorship comprises four different functions, each of them composed by sub-functions, presented in details in Ligorio, Talamo and Simons [33].

The main tutoring functions are:

1. MANAGERIAL: all the attempts to coordinate the activities and to keep the project coherent to its general aims.
2. SOCIAL: interventions aimed at supporting social and interpersonal relationships between community members through the consideration of personal expression, needs, requests, and feelings.
3. TECHNICAL: all the interventions related to specific technical problems (computer connections, server availability, etc…)
4. PEDAGOGICAL: explicitly aimed at sustaining the learning process about the specific didactical contents as well as the building strategies of the virtual objects with whom Euroland has been built.

11.6 First outcomes: How did the Euroland community develop in the CVE?

Graph 11.1 gives an overview, as it emerges from the chats analysis, of the longitudinal development of the three fundamental dimensions of the Euroland as a community of practice. Graph 11.1 shows that each of the three dimensions follows different evolution paths over the time.

a) Mutual Engagement. The Reciprocal Engagement is the only dimension whose trend is based on a very low percentage of interventions during the whole project. The starting level (around 15% of total interactions) quickly decreases after two months. These data suggest that the mutual engagement is a dimension that is negotiated at the very beginning of the project, in order to verify that all the participants have satisfactory conditions to carry the collaborative work. The low level of interaction dedicated to mutual engagement can be explained by considering the nature of the community itself. As already said, the Euroland project raises from common interests of both researchers and teachers to test and implement the three-dimensional environments in a didactical way. This interest was negotiated before the chats on-line started, through personal contacts between researchers and teachers that took place during face-to-face meetings, phone calls and e-mail exchanges, as found in previous ethnographic survey [34]. The mutual engagement was negotiated outside the virtual environment. The students' engagement is negotiated within the classrooms, among teachers and students, built mainly during the pedagogical relationship that each teacher developed inside her/his classroom.

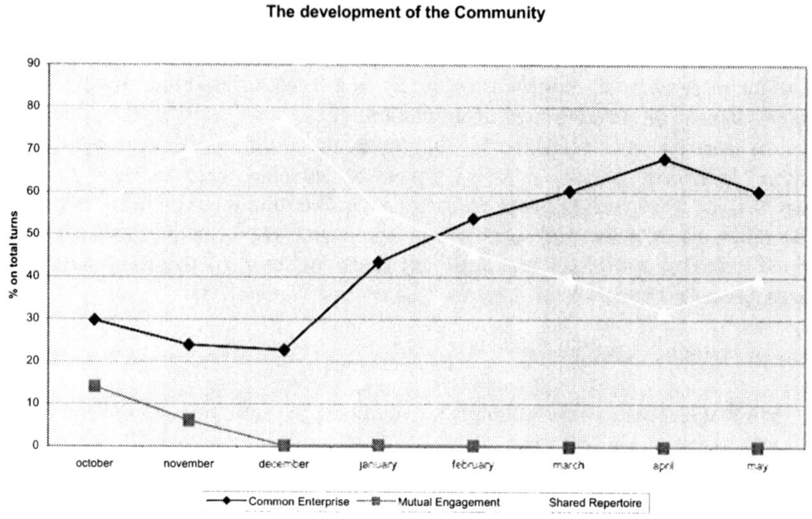

The development of the Community

Graph 11.1 The development of the community's dimensions along the project

During the recruitments phase, even when teachers and/or principles declared their availability to participate to the project, the project manager always assessed and stated the conditions for a mutual engagement. In the chat excerpt below, recorded during a very initial state of the project when participants were still wanted, one of the tutors (LP) organized an on-line meeting between the project manager and a few new candidates:

Excerpt n. 1 (October 13, 1999)[2]

11. LittlePrince:	*Bea listen to me.. .*
12. LittlePrince:	*I am right now at a meeting with school principals ...*
13. LittlePrince:	*there are some interested ...*
14. LittlePrince:	*is it still possible for new schools to participate to the project?*
15. Bea:	*yeeeeees... to whom are you thinking of?*
16. LittlePrince:	*There is a art school and a few junior schools ...*
17. LittlePrince:	*the art school is interested in particular in organizing an art exhibition in The Netherlands...*
18. Bea:	*and this a school is right now there?*
19. LittlePrince:	*paintings, sculpture, and architecture exhibition...*
20. LittlePrince:	*what do you think about it?*
21. Bea:	*It seems a great idea!*
22. LittlePrince:	*can I eventually collect new participants?*
23. Bea:	*Sure, but under certain conditions*
24. LittlePrince:	*what conditions?*
25. Bea:	*1) they have to fill a questionnaire, both students and teachers*
26. LittlePrince:	*ok.*
27. Bea:	*2) they give to me their weekly agenda with when they can connect and with how many students*

---

[2] This chat was originally in Italian and it has been traslated by one of the authors of this paper.

28. *Bea:*   *3) they have to be active in the mailing list*
29. *LittlePrince:* *ok.*
30. *LittlePrince:* *I think it is fair.*
31. *Bea:*   *4) the task has to be discussed in the classroom*
32. *LittlePrince:* *ok.. but what abut the exhibition? Do you think it can be done?*
33. *Bea:*   *The exhibition, sure, of course!*

Bea's interventions are aimed at fixing the pre-conditions to participate to the project but at the same time is made explicit the engagement required to any one wants to be part of this community. LP (one of the online tutors) proposes the entrance of some newcomers as an additional resource for the project itself. The rhetorical presentation of the new interested schools in fact stresses some possible outcomes that could provide more visibility to the project (as an offer from the "counterpart" to the Euroland community). Bea (the project manager) starts the negotiation process by stating the conditions for participating according to some aspects specifically connected with the rules established by the community.

b) Shared Repertoire. As shown in graph 11.1, the other two dimensions of the community, the shared repertoire and the common enterprise, have different and opposite trends. At the beginning of the project the community spends a lot of interaction in co-constructing a shared repertoire while the negotiation of the common enterprise is rather low. In the case of Euroland, most of the participants were not used in interacting in such an environment so the repertoire had to be shared under several aspects. Several communicational dimensions have to be explained by expert members to the novices before they could use the communication tools in a proper way and interact with a reciprocal understanding. In the excerpt below, one of the tutors is introducing to a researcher some technological terms.

Excerpt n. 3 (december 15, 1999)[3]

115. *Clarence:* *this can be caused by a short interruption of the ISP[4]*
116. *[...]*
117. *ale:*   *(to Clarence) what is the ISP?*
118. *[...]*
119. *Clarence:* *internet service provider*
     Clarence: *TIn, Tiscali, IOl etc etc*

This excerpt reports one of the simplest aspects of sharing a specialist meaning related to the ICT use. The expert only untangles the acronym and makes some examples to make clear what he is talking about. The next example introduces another aspect of the shared repertoire, closely related to the language used during the chat interactions:

Excerpt n. 4 (November 25, 1999)[5]

207. *Clarence:*   *wb Elena*
208. *Elena:*   *what does it mean WB Elena?*

---

[3] The original chat was in Italian and it has been translated.
[4] When marked in blue and in italic it means that the sentence has been whispered between the two users and the dialogue is not visible in the public chatroom.
[5] Chat originally in Italian language.

| 209. *Clarence:* | =*welcome back=bentornata*[6] :o) |
| 210. *Clarence:* | *it is more convenient to use these abbreviations in a chat* |

This example shows how the shared repertoire of chat-based communities strongly depends on how constrains and resources of the communication tool are used. Communication via chat supports a fast follow up of utterances, thus a concise language is required. Clarence uses an expression which is very common in the chat style of talking.

Since Elena does not understand it, the tutor not only clarifies the term but he also adds some information related to the culture of chatting such as the reasons for using that symbolic system: the chat talk is a written talk and it has to respond to the speed of talk even if it is typed. This type of interactions greatly influences the dictionary used by the chat-based communities and transforms radically the linguistic terms used. This aspect has to be learned by novices in order to have them interacting in an effective way inside the community.

But there are other communicative dimensions that have to be learnt by the newcomers who enter in a cybercommunity. All the aspects discussed above are related to the shared repertoire and are aimed at introducing the newcomers into chat culture.

In the following excerpt, it is highlighted the complementary process of co-constructing some of the features of the community repertoire. This kind of process arises in dependence of specific interactive situations, when specific needs community are evident:

Excerpt n. 6 (February 8, 2000)

268	Rob	*I call MarcoMichela MM ok?*
269	*MarcoMichela:*	*yes*
270	Rob	*THANK YOU mm i AM VERY FINE*
		oops my capslock :))
271	*MarcoMichela:*	*i'm very happy*
272	Rob	*What are you doing MM ?*
273	*Clarence:*	*remember kids :o) THIS IS SHOUTING in a chat :o)*
274	Rob	*Good Clarence !! That's the netiquette-rule*
275	*Clarence*	*:o)*
276	*MarcoMichela:*	*we are exploring Euroland*
277	*FrancoPierPaolo:*	*at first, we'll ask information about the trip*
278	Rob	*Aha and how far did you came yet?*
		Aha FrancoPieroPaolo I will call you FP ok?
279	*Bea:*	*(to Ale) are we attending to a just born rite???*

The students connected during this chat were in front of the computers in dyads. This generated a misunderstanding about who was actually interacting during the online connection. The nickname that the project manager stated for them (and they continued to use it for all the duration of the project) is made by combining the names of the students composing the dyads. One of the Dutch teachers, Rob, proposes the abbreviation of those nicknames, again in accordance with the general role of chat talk to shorten the word. The project manager (Bea) notices the creation of a new element in the repertoire of the community and underlines this event whispering to the other connected researcher (Ale).

Sometimes solving practical matters via the construction of a shared repertoire could affect also the cohesion within the participants. When many users were connected at the

---

[6] This is the corresponding Italian expression for welcome.

same time, it became hard to say goodbye since everybody wants to send greetings and wait for a reply. Euroland greetings were very long sequences of reciprocal "Hello!". Even if the system was equipped by an automatic boot (Cicoje) reporting who was entering and leaving the chat, the desire of being polite made difficult to leave the virtual environment in a quick way. Clarence found a way to remark the very last interaction before logging out of the system and, implicitly, to notify that further text addressed to the leaving user would not be read:

Excerpt n. 7 (November 24, 2000)[7]

817. Clarence: Hello alessandra :o)) see you later!
818. Clarence: ;)
819. Clarence: again :o) *click*
820. [Cicoje]: Bye Clarence

The *click* was a quick and effective way to say goodbye, it was addressed to everybody and it was a good way to solve a relational problem which could affect the personal needs of the users (funny as it can look it allowed users to feel free from politeness rules). The success of the new procedure was immediate and all the users quickly adopted it when they intended to leave the system.

The community interactively constructed further communication symbols and words. Many chat interactions took place at a relational level and different kinds of emotions were shared. For example, the need to have a community built upon strong interpersonal relationships and individual support was expressed by the project manager introducing the costumes of kissing by typing the word "smacks", that emulates the kisses sounds, in a cartoon style. The co-construction of the common repertoire affected the community at different levels and contributed to empower the other dimensions.

d) Common Enterprise. The chat talk related to the common enterprise is rather low at the beginning of the project. After three months from the start of the project, the trend reversed (see graph 11.1). It may be not a coincidence that at that point most of the repertoire was already shared and negotiated, therefore the language could be finally used to achieve the declared aim (building Euroland). It seems that having a shared repertoire is a pre-requisite before really starting to work for a common enterprise. In fact, only when the effort to have a shared repertoire decreases then the community focuses on the common enterprise.

As soon as the building activity becomes the main activity, the staff has to agree on some fundamental dimension for the building activity itself. Monitoring the building activities means comparing different classrooms' strategies, various building aims, dissimilar pedagogical points of view, and a variety of ideas coming from each participant that have to be negotiated and shared. Having those issues in the foreground changes the content of the chat: main concern is now the project itself and how the building activities can affect the pedagogical goals. In the following excerpt the staff is busy discussing the common enterprise and Clarence, trying to explain his point of view, took Ale and Bea in another 3-D world realized along his line of thinking.

---

[7] Chat originally in Italian language.

Excerpt n. 7 (January 21, 2000)[8]

308. Clarence:	*lets wait the download*
309. Clarence:	*then we can take a look around*
310. Clarence:	*maybe trying to identify us with kids around 11 years*
311. [...]	
312. [...]	
313. Clarence:	*what do I see ?*
314. Clarence:	*a background with big and funny faces ...who are they?*
315. Clarence:	*ahh Madonna!*
316. [...]	
317. Clarence:	*and how is this other guy?*
318. Clarence:	*do you see how many coloured teleports[9]*
319. Clarence:	*it is really professional*
320. Clarence:	*but at the same time friendly, like a merry-go-round*
321. Clarence:	*for sure more successful than the Euroland GZ[10]*
322. Clarence:	*more functional, but kind of cold*
323. Bea:	*I understand but our goal (at least mine) is not to build splendid worlds*
324. Bea:	*but to understand how do they do it...*
325. Clarence:	*I am talking about the involvement*
326. Clarence:	*Sorry Bea, I give you an example about music*
327. Clarence:	*I kind of play*
328. Bea:	*Tell me*
329. Clarence:	*I often listen to very good bands*
330. Clarence:	*(but it is the same about movies and books)*
331. Bea:	*yes*
332. Clarence:	*Why some of them make me saying "what do I play for, what do I write for?"*
333. Clarence:	*and others, still very good, may be even better*
334. Clarence:	*make me feel like I want really badly play?*
335. Bea:	*clarence what you are saying is not possible in this project*
336. ale:	*I agree with Bea*
337 Bea:	*We would need more technical support ... more time*
338. Clarence:	*Bea this is a brainstorming, I just say what I think, if it is doable is another question*
339. ale:	*I am not sure it should make sense here*
340. Bea:	*I am not looking for a marvellous world*
341. Bea:	*I want to understand what are the problems when using AW in classrooms*

Again as for the mutual engagement, most of the issues related to the common enterprise were negotiated out of the technology-mediated environment. However, as soon as the online work started to be considerable, the leading staff (tutors and researchers) had to state and agree again on some organisational matters, which aroused from the real practice.

The agreement about the pedagogical aims is mainly constructed by two members (Ale and Bea) that already shared a common pedagogic culture on cooperation inside schools

---

[8] Chat originally in Italian

[9] Virtual objects able, when clicked, to take the user directly to a certain virtual location, usually advised on the object itself

[10] Ground Zero = is the point where users land when connecting to the virtual world

and supported by computers. Clarence, the technical tutor in charge of teaching how to build, was forced at assuming a pedagogical view based on his teaching activity. Initially, his vision was driven by an esthetical paradigm, not shared by the other two researchers.

Lately in the project, both counterparts (esthetical and strictly pedagogical) were combined and an agreement was reached.

11.7 How did tutorship impact the community?

During the project tutors, provide to the community, four different types of functions: social, pedagogical, managerial, and technical.

The impact of these functions on community life is significant with 39% of the total interventions coming from the tutors performing these functions. Within the four functions, and from the data collected, the most relevant is the managerial function (see graph 11.2).

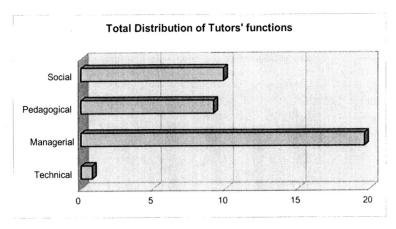

Graph 11.2 Distribution in percentage of the four tutorship functions.

Comparing this result to the information gathered from other studies [34], it can be inferred that the relevance of the managerial function is due to the specificity of the chat content.

On-line synchronous communication is more suitable for discussing the organization of the sub-tasks, to make decisions about who and when is taking charge of specific activities, and to assign and share responsibilities. The typical interventions of this function concern those issues.

The other functions are relevant in different types of settings and through other communication tools available: within the classroom, in the discussion forum embedded into Euroland, and through the mailing list available for all the participants. In particular, the technical function is performed off-line most of the time, by technicians that provide this type of support without necessarily taking part in Euroland life. The pedagogical function is more central in the classroom context, where there is face-to-face discussion between teachers and students. The pedagogical function is relevant in this community since it has a clear educational nature, but it is discussed only during a few chats. These chats are exclusively dedicated to researchers and teachers and exclude the students. During those meetings, researchers introduced their aims to the teachers and once a shared vision is reached, teachers were delegated to carry out the pedagogical function in their classrooms.

When looking at the longitudinal development of the four tutors' functions (see Graph 11.3), each function appears in a specific pattern changing little over the time. From this graph, is clearly visible that after the first month, all the tutor functions developed rapidly and reached their plateau in January/February. Those months were actually marked by a crisis: the Dutch students dropped the project and new participants were sought. The tutorial effort seems to be meant to support the community in such a difficult moment. As soon as newcomers arrived (in February) and the cross-national exchange, which was based on the construction of the virtual houses, was restored the tutorial effort started to decrease.

Analysing each tutors' function, it becomes evident that the managerial function is more relevant from the second month on, but drops dramatically toward the end of the project.

The social and pedagogical functions appear to remain stable throughout the project. The technical function is very low as most of the technical problems are solved at computer schools within the real school's setting or by technicians operating directly on the server. This function however, does have a slightly higher frequency during the second month that corresponds with the entrance into the project of newcomers.

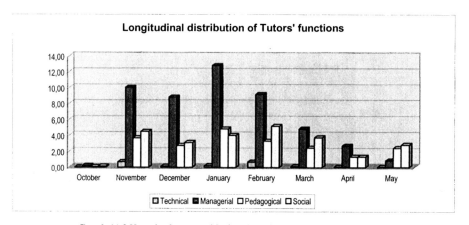

Graph 11.3 How the four tutorship functions developed during the project.

To better analyse this trend, a further investigation was carried out comparing the tutorial function of each tutor (Graph 11.4).

As already mentioned, the managerial function is the most relevant in the project and the graph above provides a further reason for this: all the tutors were initially prepared to undertake this function. Even Lp that was responsible for commencing the project maintained a reasonable high managerial function within his overall performance.

By examining the chats where this function appears, it also becomes clear that there are different types of management incorporated within this role. The excerpt selected and reported below is a good example of the various ways in which the managerial function is used.

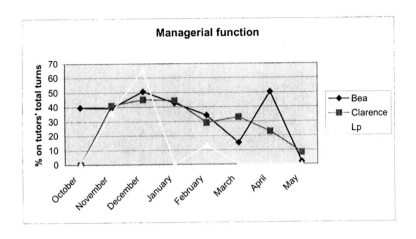

Graph 11.4 Managerial function covered by each tutor throughout the project.

Excerpt n. 8 (April 19, 2000)

258	Bea	*clarence can you help danilo ??*
259	Clarence	*danilo tell me. Manta, coccolini wait the bridge should begin where*
		is your arch
260	Manta	*ok*
261	Clarence	*here :o)*
262	Danilo	*yes, so: I am on the 883[11] web site and I would like to listen to a*
		song but I am not able to do it, how do I do it?[12]
263	Clarence	*so it ends right on the entrance of other building*
265	Manta	*ok*
266	Bea	*ehi Bart..*
267	Bart	*yes Bea....*
268	Bea	*you may think of a bridge between your building and the NL*
		music
269	Bart	*Yes I will. I am already thinking..... How is the house of NL music?*
270	Bea	*who is now connected from Modena??? Let's take a look*

In line 258, Bea fulfils her managerial function toward the other tutor (Clarence), asking him to help one of the on-line students. Later, in line 268, Bea is playing the managerial function toward one of the teachers connected, suggesting to him a possible activity to be performed in the virtual world. In the following line (269), Bea is checking who is connected, accomplishing yet another aspect of this function.

The managerial function seems to decrease over the time, with the only exception being Bea who experiences an increase in this function in April. The event that increased Bea's managerial function was the imminent closure of the project. This required the accomplishment of all the virtual houses and, given her role as project manager, Bea actively encouraged all the participants to finish this task on time. The last month of the project comprised an evaluation of the project outcomes and as a consequence Bea's managerial function was not required.

[11] This is an Italian band. Those students are building the house of music
[12] This utterance was in Italian and it has been translated in English by the authors of this chapter.

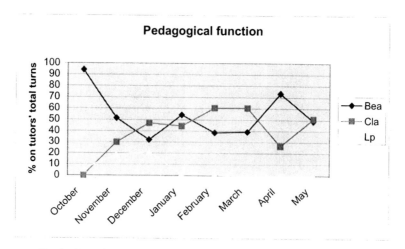

Graph 11.5 Pedagogical function covered by each tutor throughout the project.

With respect to the pedagogical function, at the commencement of the project Bea is more dominant in this area. This could be due to her role of project manager and because she is acknowledged by her peers as an educational expert. Within a few months Clarence is also able to perform the pedagogical function at the same level as Bea does. This enables the pedagogical function to be kept at a constant level, as the two tutors are able to alternate an online presence with each other.

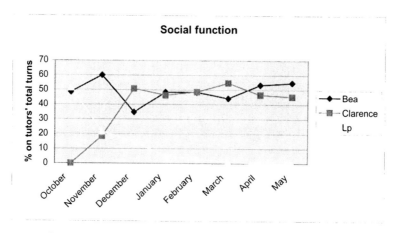

Graph 11.6 Social function covered by each tutor throughout the project.

The same balance found for the pedagogical function characterizes the development of the social function. After a few months from project commencement Bea and Clarence are again able to support each other in this function (see graph 11.6). The tutors are interchangeable along the social and pedagogical functions and this makes stable the trend of both functions during the project (to compare the social and pedagogical functions see graph 11.2). Graph 11.6 displays how from mid project on, the technical function becomes a specialized function of the tutor Clarence. This is in fact, the only function within this community that becomes exclusive to one of the tutors.

One of the aims of the community was to create specializations and specific roles but it should not necessarily be linked to one person. The intention was to have functions clearly identified but interchangeable so that the efficiency of one function was not dependent on the presence of a certain tutor. Beside the technical function, this result has been achieved for all other functions. In fact the two tutors working on the project (Lp, after the start up, monitored the project mainly off-line) were able to substitute each other and to use different functions simultaneously. The excerpt below contains an interesting example of this.

Excerpt n. 9 (January 21, 2000)[13]

24. bea:	lets see ... you are already able to build, aren't you ?
25. Valentina:	well ...
26. bea:	but it is very easy
27. bea:	lets go to the Rome area
28. bea:	(to EDUHML Ivo) would you have some time to help one of the students from Rome?
29. Valentina:	yes, I know the theory ... but is the practice that makes me worry
30. bea:	(to EDUHML Ivo) Valentina .. she is really nice
31. bea:	click on the panel with the word Rome on it
32. Valentina:	ok, lets go
33. Valentina:	tell me if it is right
34. bea:	if it is right what?
35. Valentina:	I click on an object, I duplicate it
36. bea:	very good
37. bea:	lets duplicate one now
38. Valentina:	and I « transform » it in the object I want
39. bea:	ehi you are very good, do you see that you know it
40. bea:	for the rest you need only some practice
41. EDUHML Ivo:	I suppose she is from History :)
42. bea:	you know how to look for the objects, right ?
43. Valentina:	yes, yes, so far yes
44. bea:	(to EDUHML Ivo) well from Art - I am talking about Valentina
45. bea:	(to EDUHML Ivo) come over :)
46. bea:	(to EDUHML Ivo) join us
47. EDUHML Ivo:	OK
48. EDUHML Ivo:	whisper
49. Immigration Officer:	You are being joined by EDUHML Ivo.
50. bea:	so, valentina how is it going?
51. bea:	Hello Ivo !!
52. bea:	Hei Valentina this is Ivo (ti presento Ivo)
53. bea:	Ivo this is Valentina from Rome
54. EDUHML Ivo:	I did understand that!
55. EDUHML Ivo:	Pleased :)
56. Valentina:	well, I tried to build a wall
57. bea:	she is not that familiar with building

---

[13] This excerpt was originally in Italian

58. EDUHML Ivo:	*Me neither :))*
59. Valentina:	*hello ivo!!*
60. bea:	*(to EDUHML Ivo) this is one of the things you are supposed to do here: tutoring novel builders*
61. bea:	*(to EDUHML Ivo) right?*
62. EDUHML Ivo:	*OK*
63. bea:	*Ivo is very good in building*
64. bea:	*he is an expert*

This excerpt shows how Bea, at the beginning, replaces Clarence in giving instruction about how to build virtual objects. Bea also used the social function when asking Ivo (one of the Dutch students) to support Valentina (an Italian student) in building. Ivo was an expert student since he was previously involved in a similar school experience based on AW. For this reason Ivo agreed to function as a peer-tutor. This was congruent with the aim of the project *not* to create a rigid leadership but rather to transfer as many different competencies to all participants and to have *active* students. Within the same excerpt Bea carried two functions simultaneously: the pedagogical one used with Valentina and replacing Clarence that was usually in charge of teaching how to build, and the social function supporting the interaction between the two students.

11.8 How do the on-line tutors sustain the development of the community?

Tutors supported the community of practice dimensions by facilitating its development in different ways. As well as in face-to-face communities, the tutors act as expert members who can legitimate the participation of the peripheral ones. By doing this, tutors act as cultural mediators inside the community by guiding novices, showing rules, and defining the common enterprise. How is tutors' action carried on? How do tutors sustain in a concrete way the community? This section will show how tutors' intervention have effects on all the fundamental dimensions of the community: infact they act in specific ways defined both by the features of context and by the culture of that particular community.

11.8.1   Legitimating the novices' contribution to the shared repertoire.

The promotion of novices' interventions is one of the core strategies used to support the newcomers' sense of belonging to the community. This is illustrated in the following excerpt.

Excerpt n. 10 (December 15, 1999)[14]

81	Ale	*=:0*
82	Clarence	*ahahahhhahahaa !!!!!!!!*
83	Ale	*does it work to express wonder ?*
84	Clarence	*see, you started creating !!! Ok I'll go back*
85	Ale	*Am I good?*
86	Clarence	*do join to me if you like*
87	Ale	*ok*
88	Clarence	*Yes, you are good:o)*

---

[14] This excerpt was originally in Italian

For the first time Ale is producing new *emoticons* – symbols used to smile ☺ or to express sadness ☹ – and she asks for feedback about the interlocutor's comprehension. The personal contribution to the shared repertoire is legitimated by the tutor's intervention also allowing participants to create new symbols, introduced into the community repertoire via "permission" of the tutors. A previous phase of this tutors' role concerned the sharing of meanings of the repertoire used. For example, the "join" request (line 86) that refers to an option offered by the software, is already in use and does not need to be negotiated anymore.

11.8.2   Using leadership to define a common enterprise.

The managerial function is used to strengthen consensus around the ideas presented via chat to improve individual involvement in the shared enterprise. Tutors know that awareness about a common general enterprise has to be fostered in order to facilitate the interaction between participants carrying on different sub-tasks and diverse building projects.

The common enterprise is mostly intended as a dimension that has to be shared first at the adults' level. In this sense Bea collects students' proposals and then asks for consensus directly addressing all the teachers who are connected at that time:

Excerpt n. 11 (October 13, 1999)[15]

120. Bea:	Now I am taking notes of your ideas and ....
121. Bea:	I will post a message about it into the mailing list
[...]	
125. Bea:	I will ask to all the others what they think
[...]	
127. Bea:	what do you think of this idea?
128. Mantastrega:	it sounds good... I like it
129. Bea:	ehi Giovanni we would like also to have your opinion
130. Bea:	Did you hear the ideas proposed by mantastrega?
131. Bea:	and you Modena??? Do you have any suggestion?

The project manager tries to share the proposal of one classroom with the whole community by starting a discussion around the proposal. In the tutor's representation, the chat is not a suitable "place" to deepen the discussion, because of the speed of interaction.

So she tries to keep the users' attention (also that of those not connected at that time) by moving the discussion to another medium, the mailing list, where each "speaker" can find "voice" and "space" to intervene.

11.8.3   Defining some behavioural rules affecting the mutual engagement.

Mutual engagement arises in the community as a need expressed by members. The mutual engagement in the Euroland community has been built around affective involvement of the members. The online tutors sustained the development of this dimension in many ways (like creating warm ways of saying hallo and goodbye, addressing to young students like

---

[15] This excerpt was originally in Italian

pets). But sometimes the definition of the boundaries of this involvement is not agreed and the definition of the mutual engagement is turned in a more concrete perspective.

In the excerpt below some Dutch students are expressing their good feelings to all connected users:

Excerpt n. 12 (November 3, 1999)

463. popeye:	*I love you bea*
464. bea:	*I love you too :))*
465. zorro:	*Are you crazy norm ?????*
466. Mantastrega:	*bea, do you have a bew love ;-))?*
467. Mantastrega:	*new..sorry*
468. norm:	*I love you I love you I love you little prince*
469. zorro:	*Do you really love them little Prince*
470. popeye:	*I love you not norm*
471. norm:	*I love you not popeye*
472. popeye:	*Hello mantastrega*
473. Mantastrega:	*hello popeye...*
474. norm:	*Hello little prince*
475. Milano:	*little prince, we can see you*
476. Mantastrega:	*but I'm Arianna...*
477. LittlePrince:	*so....what's going here?!? what is all this loving stuff?!? we are*

supposed to learn here!! :))

The way the two on-line tutors are managing what is going on in this moment shows some core problems about sharing tutorship in a community. Bea and LP have (according to their own roles among the community) different responsibilities and they respond to the students' utterances in a different way. Bea picks up the students' game about sharing warm feelings for each other and legitimates the game by participating and replicating to the "love affaire". After Bea's intervention a lot of "love" continues to be shared among students. LP, the technical supporter, makes a humoristic intervention that stops the love sequence. The intervention of LP states the main aim of meeting and by using the pronoun "we" he addresses everybody connected. LP's focus on the project in terms of learning requirements shows a personal view of the mutual engagement different from that of the other tutor[16].

11.9 Conclusions

The study presented in this paper describes the development of a community of practice in a virtual environment. The results showed how the fundamental dimensions of the community develop and shift according to the community needs and life. The conversation analysis allowed demonstration of how these dimensions are co-constructed via chat interactions and how newcomers are supported by expert members in the project culture and in the communicative rules. Results show that the development of the fundamental dimensions of the community are strongly dependent on the life and needs of the

---

[16] For the analysis of the specialist interventions of each tutor see also Ligorio, Talamo, Simons (in progress).

community itself. The technological solutions are used in a strategic way according to the members' aims time by time.

The analysis of the interactions showed also the relevance of the tutors' role in leading and sustaining the community and its development. For example, based on their special status, tutors have the power to legitimate others' interventions and to define the modalities of participation. These results are on line with the studies on non-mediated communities [9, 18], but in the case we presented here tutors, as expert members, have the possibility of using specific interactive resources offered by the 3D CVE and by participating to the chatters' culture.

The analysis of tutors' functions showed that during on-line interactions different functions were recognizable but not enacted as rigid specializations. This was especially true after the community basic dimensions had been established and the repertoire of all members (including that of the tutors) had been shared. The specialist function became visible only along the technical dimension, where a specific competence is more recognisable. More studies seem to be necessary about the integration of multiple sharing of tutoring functions.

The Euroland project is an example of how a "natural" group, still virtual in the sense that it is composed by people resident at a distance and populating CVEs, realises a common project, shares activities and aims and becomes a real community. Some of the dimensions are co-constructed outside the virtual environment, but data show how the specific interactive tools can be used by the members as new and additional resources to sustain and develop basic dimensions.

11.10 Acknowledgements

The Euroland project was funded by the European Community, Training and Mobility of Research (TMR) Programme Marie Curie Research Training Grants (7th call) Proposal n. ERB4001GT975495.

The data presented in this article were categorized with the help of Katia Iorio and we thank her for the fine and patient job. We also like to thank Prof. Robert-Jan Simons (University of Nijmegen) for his supervision on the project and the Garamond Company for its technical support.

Although this paper is based on a strong collaboration among the three authors, we like to specify that each of them took particularly charge of certain parts. The first author designed the whole article and presented the results about the community development, the support offered by tutors to the community, and the conclusions. The second author wrote the theoretical discussion and the objectives. The third author described the Euroland project and elaborated the results about the tutorship impact.

11.11 References

[1] G. Mantovani, Exploring Borders. Routledge, London, 2000.
[2] C. C. Heath, and , P. K. Luff, Technology in action. Cambridge University Press Cambridge, N.J., 2000.
[3] C. Galimberti, and G. Riva, La comunicazione virtuale. Dal computer alle reti telematiche: nuove forme di interazione sociale. Guerini e Associati, Milano, 1997.
[4] C. Zucchermaglio, S. Bagnara, & S. Stucky (eds.). Organizational learning and technological change. Springer Verlag, New York, 1995.
[5] M.A. Smith, and P. Kollock (eds.). Communities in Cyberspace. Routledge, London, 1999.

[6]   L. Suchman. Plans and Situated Actions. The Problem of Human-Machine Communication. Cambridge University Press, Cambridge, 1987.

[7]   L. Suchman. Constituting shared workspaces. In Y. Engestrom & D. Middleton (eds.) Cognition and Communication at Work. Cambridge University Press, Cambridge, MA, 1996.

[8]   Y. Engstrom, and D. Middleton (eds.). Cognition and communication at work. Cambridge University Press, Cambridge, 1996.

[9]   C. Zucchermaglio. Vygotsky in azienda. Apprendimento e comunicazione nei contesti di lavoro. La Nuova Italia Scientifica Roma, 1996.

[10]   M. Cole. Culture and Cognitive Development: From Cross-cultural Research to Creating Systems of Cultural Mediation. *Culture & Psychology*, **1**, 1995, 25-54.

[12]   G. Mantovani. L'elefante Invisibile. Giunti, Firenze, 1998.

[13]   C. Zucchermaglio. Gruppi di lavoro: tecnologie, pratiche sociali e negoziazione. In G. Mantovani (ed.) Ergonomia.Le tecnologie nel contesto sociale. Il Mulino, Bologna, 2000.

[14]   E. Wenger, Communities of Practice. Learning, Meaning and Identity. Cambridge University Press, Cambridge, Mass., 1998.

[15]   E. Wenger. Communities of Practice and Social Learning Systems. *Organization*, **7**, 2, 2000, 225-246.

[16]   J.S. Brown, P. Duguid. Organizational Learning and Communities of Practice: Toward a Unified View of Working, Learning and Innovation. *Organization Science*, 2/1, 1991, 40-57.

[17]   C. Zucchermaglio, A. Talamo. Identità sociale e piccolo gruppo. *Giornale Italiano di Psicologia*, XXVII, 3, 2000, 57-86.

[18]   C. Zucchermaglio, A. Talamo. The social construction of worktimes: Negotiated Time and Expected Time, *Time and society*, , 9(2/3), 2000, 21-38.

[19]   G.H. Mead. Mind, self and society. Chicago University Press, Chicago, 1934.

[20]   A. Duranti. Linguistic Anthropology. Cambridge University Press, Cambridge, Mass., 1997.

[21]   M. Bachtin. L'autore e l'eroe. Teoria letteraria e scienze umane. Einaudi, Torino, 1979.

[22]   E. Ochs. Becoming a speaker of culture. Paper presented at Dipartimento di Psicologia dei Processi di Sviluppo e Socializzazione, University of Rome " La Sapienza", Rome, April 1999.

[23]   S. Gherardi Organizational Learning, In M. Zeleny. (ed.), The IEBM Handbook of Information Technology in Business. Business Press, London, 2000.

[24]   L. Suchman,. Technologies of accountability. Of lizards and aeroplanes. In G. Button (ed.), Technology in Working Order. Routledge, London, 1993, 113-126.

[25]   G.C. Bowker, and S. Leigh Star. Social Science, technical Systems and Cooperative Work: Beyond the Great Divide. Lawrence Erlbaum, Hillsdale, N.J. 1997.

[26]   G. Riva, C. Galimberti, Mind in the Web, Special Issue of *Cyberpsychology and Behavior*, in press.

[27]   A. Talamo, M.B. Ligorio. Strategic Identities in Cyberspace. In Riva, G. and Galimberti, C. (eds.) Mind in the Web, Special Issue of *Cyberpsychology and Behavior*, in press.

[28]   A.L. Brown, J.C. Campione, Communities of Learning or a Context by any other name. in D. Kuhn (ed.) Contributions to Human Development, 21,1990, 108-126.

[29]   M.Scardamalia, C. Bereiter, Computer support for knowledge-building communities. *The Journal of the Learning Sciences*, 3, 1994, 265-283.

[30]   G. Salomon. Novel constructivist learning environments and novel technologies: some issues to be concerned with. *Research Dialogues in Learning and Instruction*, 1 (1), 1998, 3-12.

[31]   J. Schegloff. Harvey Sacks' lectures on conversation: an Introduction/memoir, *Human Studies*, 12, 1989, 185-209.

[32]   S. Ashton, T. Roberts, and L. Teles. Investigating the Role of the Instructor in Collaborative Online Environments. Poster presented at the Computer Supported Collaborative Learning, Stanford, 12-15 dec. 1999.

[33]   M.B. Ligorio, A. Talamo and R.J. Simons (in progress) Tutoring a on-line community.

[34]   M.B. Ligorio, D. Cesareni, A. Talamo et al., Euroland: a virtual community. Research report presented at the Computer Supported Collaborative Learning Conference. Maastricht, 22-24 March, 2001.

Towards CyberPsychology
G. Riva and C. Galimberti (Eds.)
IOS Press, 2001

12   VR Learning: Potential and Challenges for the Use of 3D Environments in Education and Training

Fabrizia MANTOVANI

Abstract. There is some evidence that Virtual Reality (VR) can contribute to raise interest and motivation in students and to effectively support knowledge transfer, since the learning process can be settled within an experiential framework. However, the practical potential of VR is still being explored: understanding how to use Virtual Reality to support training and learning activities presents a substantial challenge for the designers and evaluators of this learning technology. This chapter has the main aim of discussing the rationale and main benefits for the use of virtual environments in education and training. A number of key attributes of VR environments will be described and discussed in relationship to educational theory and pedagogical practice, in order to establish a possible theoretical basis for VR learning. Significant research and projects carried out in this field will be also presented, together with suggestions and guidelines for future development of VR learning systems. However, further research is required, both on technological side and on key issues such as transfer of learning, appropriate curriculum implementation, elements of effective VR design, and the psychological and social impact of the technology use.

Contents

12.1 Introduction

"Learning is the development of experience into experience." (James, 1892), [1]

In education and training, Computer–Based Learning (CBL), or Computer-Assisted Learning (CAL) has been representing since the '70s an important source of innovative learning tools [2, 3]. With the diffusion of the World Wide Web and many other hardware and software technologies, this influence is reaching a wider and wider audience and is no more limited to providing support and aid tools for learning: as Bonk and colleagues [4] point out, "recent technological developments have converged to dramatically alter conception of teaching and learning process" (p.25).

As suggested by several authors [5-8], Virtual Reality (VR) represents a promising area with high potential of enhancing and modifying the learning experience: Virtual Environments (VEs) can provide a rich, interactive, engaging educational context, supporting experiential learning. As Bruner underlined [9], performing the task enhances the learning process; VR can provide a medium to learn by doing, through first-person experience.

Current use of Virtual Reality Environments (VREs) extends to a wide range of activities, from training people to acting in dangerous environments (e.g. training for space missions or military interventions) to experiencing contexts that in physical reality would be too expensive or impossible to access (e.g. travelling around Mars or visiting a castle in the Middle Age).

The use of Virtual Reality gradually broadened from teaching simple tasks to the acquisition of complex skills, such as abstract reasoning, visualization and management of complex information spaces [10]. This shift has brought new challenges to educators and developers, since it becomes more and more important to understand what characteristics and features such environments should have in order to fit established educational goals.

As Osberg [11] underlines: "Technology does not, by itself, improve education, and even the most promising educational innovation needs skilful application to be effective."

In order to build effective VR learning systems, collaborative and iterative design is key issues: educators, developers and students should be cooperatively involved, at different development stages.

According to Osberg [11], "The role of educators, in this context, is to keep the focus on the needs of learner, not on the technology itself. The general aim is that of empowering the learner by maximizing the opportunity for learning; creating environments, materials, and processes to make learning interesting, motivating and effective for everyone". In this process, the main tasks are: fixing precise learning objectives and educational goals; reflecting on the rationale of use of VR; evaluating what VR features are more pertinent and useful for learning enhancement within "that" specific application.

Designers and developers, on the other hand, should be concerned with the creation of ergonomic and usable environments, as well as with the integration of educational and pedagogical guidelines. These guidelines will come from interaction with teacher and students according to a user-centred and goal-based design [12].

Although "there is clearly the potential that VR learning environments can be powerful educational experiences" [11], many technological, theoretical, economical and cultural challenges still have to be faced for further integration of VR into educational and training contexts.

This chapter has the main aim of discussing the rationale and main benefits for the use of virtual environments in education and training. A number of key attributes of VR environments will be described and discussed in relationship to educational theory and pedagogical practice, in order to establish a possible theoretical basis for VR learning.

In order to transform the potential of VR features into educational efficacy, a number of issues will be investigated, focusing on the complex web of relationships within which VR learning occurs. The link between VR and learning outcome will be analysed through a model [10] which considers the influence and interaction of many other factors such as the concepts to be learned, learners' characteristics, usability, motivation, etc.

Significant research and projects carried out in this field will be then presented, and insights and guidelines suggested by the review of these examples will be provided.

12.2 "Learning by constructing knowledge": a rationale for the use of Virtual Reality in education and training

12.2.1   Experiencing learning in Virtual Environments

What is Virtual Reality? And how can its use enhance the learning process? Gaddis [13] defined Virtual Reality (VR) as:

"a computer-generated simulation of the real or imagined environment or world"

According to Fitzgerald and Riva [14], "the basis for the *Virtual Reality* idea is that a computer can synthesize a three-dimensional (3D) graphical environment from numerical data. Using visual and auditory output devices, the human operator can experience the environment as if it were part of the world. This computer generated world may be either a model of a real-world object, such as a house; or an abstract world that doesn't exist in a real sense but is understood by humans, such as a chemical molecule or a representation of a set of data; or it might be in a completely imaginary science fiction world" (p.327).

Key feature of the VR experience is also the possibility to actively interact with the created environment; this is allowed by the use of external input devices responding to the user's reactions and motions.

Although many authors have defined VR essentially as a technology [15], more recent approaches [16] forward a more complex vision, considering VR as a human experience [17] and underlining how "the essence of VR is the inclusive relationship between the participant and the virtual environment" [14] (p.328).

In this context, the concept of presence is a crucial one: according to Slater [18] it includes three aspects:

- "the sense of being there in the environment depicted by the VE
- the extent to which the VE becomes the dominant one, i.e. that participants will tend to respond to events in the VE rather than in the real world
- the extent to which participants, after the VE experience, remember it as having visited a place rather than just having seen images generated by a computer" (p.550-561)

As we can note from this description, the sense of presence relies on two different factors: immersion and interaction.

- *Immersion* in the Virtual Environment can be defined as an "intense feeling of self-location within the computer-generated reality with which the user interacts" [19]. But what are the elements contributing to this feeling? Immersion can be considered as the product of the match between the technologies and the subjective feeling of involvement experienced by the user in the interaction process.

Immersion can be also defined, following Cronin [19], as a human factor:

"Effective immersion requires the ability on the part of the participant to control attention and focus on what is going on in the VE while simultaneously excluding all interference from the outside world".

- *Interaction*: According to Sastry and Boyd [20], the feeling of presence, especially within real world applications, is more influenced by the level of interaction/interactivity that actors experience within the simulated environment than by the richness and faithfulness of available images. The focus is much more on the possibility for the user "to navigate, select, pick, move and manipulate an object much more naturally". (p.235)

This is very important within educational contexts, since it highlightens how the added-value is represented by the experiential and intuitive nature of learning in the VR environment.

12.2.2   Looking for a theory of VR learning

Actually, we cannot say that there is a general theory of VR learning. Nevertheless, as Winn [5] suggested, constructivist theory provides a valid and reliable basis for a theory of learning in virtual environments. Adapting what Gabbard [21] said about hypermedia, VR provides a tool for developing instruction along constructivist lines and an environment in which learners can actively pursue their knowledge needs. The attraction that constructivists have for Virtual Reality is that VR provides the perfect tool or technology to apply their theories in the "real world". The attraction that VR supporters have for constructivism is that it provides a philosophical foundation for their activities.

Trying to give a comprehensive definition of constructivism is not an easy task: according to Scheurman [22], constructivism can be considered as a group of theories dealing with the nature of knowledge; their common ground relies on the idea that people, grounded in a societal and cultural setting, actively create knowledge.

McGuire [23] suggests that "constructivist learning theorists purport that there is no true representation of knowledge but that each individual constructs sense out of new information as it is encountered." (p. 257)

Constructivism [24] claims that we construct our own reality through interpretation of personal perceptual experiences and that reality is in the mind of the knower rather than in the object of our knowing. According to this perspective, each of us builds up a personal model of reality, which we can communicate but not entirely share with other people.

According to Winn, [5] the key to the compatibility of VR with constructivism lies in the possibility for students, by the means of interaction and immersion, to learn through first-person, non-symbolic experience. First-person experiences play a central role in our activity in the world and our learning about it. Within first-person experiences, our interaction with the world does not involve conscious reflection or the use of symbols.

Learning process, as suggested by Osberg [11], is about the development of meaning: "meaning about the world, about patterns and relationships, about themselves". According to this point of view [11], "meaning may be constructed from information outside of the learner, or may be constructed by each individual using information from the environment, and from within".

VR provides exactly this opportunity of making first-person, non-symbolic experiences: immersive environments allow to construct knowledge from direct experience by giving the participants the "perceptual illusion of nonmediation" [25] between them and the computer. VR technology provides learners with the possibility to reflect and get a deeper understanding of the process through which a person can reach a knowledge of the world.

In order to better focus this convergence between VR and Constructivism, we point out a few key concepts of constructivist theory and show how these principles and practices of learning and teaching can be found in Virtual Environments [5, 7].

*   *Constructionism*: constructivism [26, 27] holds that students learn best when they build their own understanding of content by directly interacting with it, rather than receiving pre-structured content from an external source, such as a teacher or a text. According to Papert et al. [28], the term "constructionism" is used to describe knowledge construction arising from physical interaction with objects in the world. Nicaise and Crane [29] point out how, within constructivist perspective, physical engagement with material is central in the learning process. Students reach an understanding of the material under study through object manipulation and building of physical artifacts. To the extent that "immersion in a virtual world allows the same kind of natural interaction with objects that participants engage in the real world" [5], action in VEs can support this process of knowledge construction. Furthermore, since this process and its output are highly individual and can be only partially shared with other people, the possibility to experience different points of view and frames of reference is very important. Virtual Reality environments provide learners with the possibility to take up multiple perspectives and can thus represent a valuable support to develop awareness of the constructed nature of our own reality.

*   *Exploratory learning*: students assimilate knowledge more effectively when they have the freedom to move and engage in self-directed activities within their learning context. Finding and structuring content authonomously, they invest mental effort for the construction of conceptual models that are both consistent with what they already understand and with the new content presented. According to McGuire [23], this active process allows students to reach understanding of the world through an "ongoing process of making sense out of new information- by creating their own version of reality instead of simply receiving the author's view" (p.257). The effective adaptation of old knowledge to new one leads to understanding and, when the students are in charge of this process of "accomodation", success is also intrinsically motivating. Simulation of the real world provided by VR offer students the opportunity to learn while they are situated in the context where what they learn is to be applied; this results in more meaningful and effective learning, as compared with learning out of context [30, 31].

*   *Collaboration:* as noted by Roussos et al. [7], "one of the most important purposes of an education environment is to promote the social interaction among children located in the same physical space" (p.251). Vygotsky underlined the central importance of social interaction in cognitive growth [32] and suggested that efficacy of collaborative learning is to be considered in a broader framework, where the final creation of a learning product is but one element. Constructivists emphasize the importance of providing opportunities for learning where students are involved to work in groups and reach a consensus about meaning [33]. Within distributed multi-user environments, there is the possibility for a group of students to interact and take part into the learning activity at the same time. This is possible through the use of *avatars*, representing users geographically separated but simultaneously present in the virtual environment; through activities such as verbal interaction, collective decision making, conflict

resolutions, peer teaching, undestanding is reached through negotiation and consensus-building.

12.2.3   Potential benefits from the use of Learning Virtual Environments

The possibilities provided by the use Virtual Environments, such as 3D immersion, multiple perspectives and multisensory cues [10] offer a number of potential benefits to education and training [8, 34]:

- *Experiential and active learning.* VR provides experience with new technologies through actual use: learning in VEs requires interaction, thus encouraging active participation rather than passivity.

- *Visualization and reification.* VEs can be an alternate method for presentation of material, new forms and methods of visualization. Its use can be very important in domains where information visualization is needed, such as manipulating and rearranging information using graphic symbols; it is useful also when it is needed to make perceptible the imperceptible (for example, using and moving solid shapes to illustrate clashes of ideas in group processes).

- *Learning in contexts impossible or difficult to experience in real life.* Virtual reality allows observation and examination of areas and events unavailable (such as underwater, historical scenes, reconstructions of archaeological sites) or impossible (for example, exploring Mars, traveling inside human body, moving among molecules) by other means. Furthermore, it allows extreme closeup examination of an object, as well as observation from a great distance. VEs can also be a good solution when teaching or training using the real thing is dangerous, (for example, there is risk of injury to learner, bystanders, and/or instructor is possible), or for logistic reasons (for example, training about a process during working hours: travel, cost, and/or logistics of gathering a class for training make an alternative attractive). VR can furthermore provide effective training in situations requiring the use of equipment prohibitively expensive or impossible to obtain otherwise. Another potential of learning is in Virtual Environments is that it allows the disabled to participate in an experiment or learning environment when they cannot do so otherwise.

- *Motivation enhancement.* Interacting with a VR model can be as motivating or more motivating than interacting with the real thing, for example, using a game format. It can be a good solution to make learning more interesting and fun, for example, when working with boring material or with students who have attention problems.

- *Collaboration fostering.* Shared VR can encourage collaboration and foster the learning of skills that can be better developed through shared experiences of a group in a common environment. It is most useful when the experience of creating a simulated environment, or model is important to the learning objective.

- *Adaptability.* VR learning offers the possibility to be tailored to learner's characteristics and needs (different students are characterized by different learning rates and styles). Learners are allowed to to proceed through an experience at their own pace, and during a broad time period not fixed by a regular class schedule. Furthermore, well-designed Virtual Environments can flexibly present students a broader, deeper set of experiences than those that can be found in the "standard" educational environment.

- *Evaluation and assessment.* VR itself offer a great potential as a tool for evaluation, since every session in the virtual environment can be easily monitored and recorded by teachers, thus facilitating assessment tasks.

12.3 From technological components to educational features: towards a model for design and implementation of educational VEs

How to develop an effective educational virtual environment? What properties and features should it have in order to enhance the learning experience and to provide a real added-value as compared to traditional classroom? Answers to these questions are essential to provide designers and educators with useful guidelines to drive their practice.

Dillon [35] underlines how "theoretical insights into learning are crucial to improve our designs and understanding how we can advance education... [since]... there can never be a purely empirical approach to design" (p.100). Nevertheless, it seems that current theories could not yet provide a reliable basis upon which build up practice, whether design, assessment or teaching. This essentially because they were more concerned with offering broad conceptual frameworks of learning than with explaining the findings of learning outcome with various media, thus failing to provide concrete guidelines that could inform practice.

On the other hand, too little research was carried out up to now and there is no common framework for effective integration of their results. As Salzman underlined [10], "unfortunately, although researchers have many ideas concerning how VR might facilitate the understanding of complex concepts, the field has little information concerning which of virtual reality's features provide the most leverage for enhancing understanding or how to customize those affordances for different learning environments" (p.294). The investigation of a more complex web of relationship than the one between VR features and learning outcome is especially required when the focus shifts from the training of specific abilities and contents to teaching more abstract contents and higher-level skills.

Designing and delivering VR learning requires thoughtful analysis and investigation on how to use the VR's potential in concert with instructional design principles. Facilitation of the design of meaningful learning environments and relevant learning opportunities can be achieved by gaining an understanding of the (real) capabilities of VR components and features (and how they relate to learning efficacy) and by carefully examining crucial issues.

What is clear is that VEs are not effective or ineffective by themselves. The point is no more to establish whether VR is useful or not for education; the focus is instead on understanding how to design and use VR to support learning process. Many research questions are of great importance for the development of VEs for education and training; among these are the following:

- What kind of learning contents can be better conveyed through the use of VR environments?
- What kind of skills can be enhanced through VEs (cooperation and negotiation)?
- How to do this? What are the technical requirements (Head-Mounted Display or not, etc.)?
- How does cognition-transfer from VEs to real-life contexts vary with learner's characteristics such as age, experience and gender?

- How can VR offer specific (and competitively effective) solutions in different areas and for different people (e.g. the disabled)?

Before we can build effective Virtual Environments (VEs) for education and training, we must understand the nature of this technology. Following Fitzgerald and Riva [14], VR can be presented in at least five ways:

1) *"Desktop VR.* Uses subjective immersion. The feeling of immersion can be improved through stereoscopic vision. Interaction with the interface can be made via mouse, joystick or typical VR peripherals such as Dataglove.
2) *Fully Immersive VR.* With this type of solution the user appears to be fully inserted in the computer generated environment. This illusion is rendered by providing a head mounted display (HMD) with 3-D viewing and a system of head tracking to guarantee the exact correspondence and co-ordination of user's movements with the feed-backs of the environment.
3) *CAVE.* A Cave is a small room where a computer generated world is projected on the walls. The projection is made on both front and side walls. This solution is particularly suitable for collective VR experience because it allows different people to share the same experience at the same time.
4) *Telepresence.* Users can influence and operate in a world that is real but in a different location. The users can observe the current situation with remote cameras and achieve actions via robotic and electronic arms.
5) *Augmented.* The user's view of the world is supplemented with virtual objects, usually to provide information about the real environment. In military applications, for instance, vision performance is enhanced by providing the pictograms that anticipate the presence of other entities out of sight." (p.329)

We can see that VR systems differ a lot according to many technological components, such as hardware and software configurations (obviously with different costs and usability issues), interaction modes, the use of the Internet, support of single/multi-user interaction, multimedia components embedded in the 3D worlds. These components influence many VR features such as the levels of immersion, graphic fidelity and interactivity, multisensory cues, possibility of collaboration, number and complexity of tasks supported.

How well these feature are conducive to learning and instruction depends a lot on the quality and sophistification of the VE design. In fact, features of a learning environment do not act in isolation. Elements such as the concepts to be learned, individual characteristics, the learning experience and the interaction experience all play a role in shaping the learning process and learning outcomes.

A very good example of the efforts in this direction is represented by the work of Salzman and colleagues [10]: according to their model, the link between VR's affordances and learning occurs within a web of other relationships. The first important factor is surely the *concept* the student/user is trying to understand.

Different VR features are appropriate for different concepts. In other words, the relative effectiveness of VR features such as immersiveness or multisensory representations may depend on the concept being learned.

Moreover, *learner characteristics* (e.g., domain knowledge), play an important role in shaping the learning process and may also interact with VR's features in influencing the student/user experience. A number of important learner characteristics have been identified: age, gender, domain experience, spatial ability, computer experience, motion sickness history, and immersive tendencies. As Gabbard [21] points out, "instructional designers must take into account the range of kinds and types of [...] users when designing. Users may or may not be able to make use of the "advantages" of hypermedia in the learning environment. Instructional professionals must also be aware that not all students will be able to make effective use [...] in the learning environment" (p.107).

Evaluations to date also suggest that the *interaction experience* is affected by VR features: Designing effective and ergonomic strategies for navigation, object selection and manipulation, as well as trying to minimize sickness is a central task for designers. As far as "simulator sickness" [36] is concerned, some users have experienced side effects (such as ocular problems, disorientation and balance disturbances, and nausea) during exposure to VR environments [37]. Although the latest VR tools have fewer or no side effects [38, 39], further research is needed to confirm these results.

Another important factor in this complex framework was pointed out by Owston [40] and concerns *teaching style*. In his study about two online programs' efficacy, he underlined how teacher-related dimension play a key role in determining success or failure of a program. "These factors were (1) the teachers' perceptions of the value of the program for students and (2) the congruence between the pedagogy implicit in the program and the teachers' own practices" (p. 81).

12.4 VR learning applications

In recent years, a number of virtual reality platforms were designed and implemented to support education and training in different learning domains.

Identifying the situations where learning in VEs can represent a real added value to traditional education and understanding how to use and adapt virtual reality to support the learning of different concepts and skills has represented (and actually still represents) a challenge involving educators and developers at the same time.

12.4.1   VR in training

As Stansfield [41] underlines, the use of VR-based trainers for structured task training is being explored in many application areas. In addition to the long-standing use of partial trainers for training vehicle operation (aircraft, tanks, helicopters, and the like) within both the military and civilian sectors, researchers have begun to explore VR as a means to train other, fairly structured, tasks. Tate et al. [42] explored VR-based training of shipboard fire-fighting. Johnson et al. [43] developed a VR system for training equipment operation, with an emphasis on incorporating intelligent agents for tutoring and feedback.

Training concerning more complex processes were explored by Loftin and Kenney [44], who developed an immersive VR system to train the flight team on the procedure for repairing the Hubble Space Telescope, and by Stansfield [45], who describes a VR system for training teams in the disassembly of a subcomponent of a nuclear weapon.

Most of these systems, while providing an experiential learning environment, are still focused primarily on the training of the specific steps that are involved in accomplishing a fairly structured procedure.

Two areas that received relevant interest in these years are the military and the medical, as far as individual training, distributed system and model simulators are concerned.

12.4.1.1   Military training

The military has long used simulation-based experiential training systems to augment live exercises: a number of applications in this field concern the design and implementation of flight simulators, distributed battlefield environments and simulation-based acquisition models.

Within the training systems focusing on critical decision-making in unpredictable environments, we can cite the SIMNET/DIS, an architecture [46] for training and rehearsing battlefield operations, which has been in use now for many years. Closely related systems, such as the High-Level Architecture [47] and NPSNET [48], continue the research into large scale, distributed mission training systems for warfighting.

12.4.1.2   Medical training

Satava and Jones [49] presented a possible categorization of virtual environments in (medical) education and training based upon application and distinguished individual training, medical crisis training, and medical virtual prototyping.

According to the authors, individual training systems represent at the moment the majority of VR medical applications. These task-specific individual medical trainers,which are also referred to as "partial trainers", seek to train a single (or a limited) set of skills within a simulation that is highly realistic and anatomically correct. Kaufman and Bell [50] discuss the potential of VR-based partial trainers for teaching and assessing task-specific clinical skills. It is a promising area, which is being addressed by researchers working in a number of different clinical areas. Common to all such partial trainers is their focus on a specific task and anatomical region: VR-based training system for debridment of a gunshot wound to a leg [51], simulator for temporal bone dissection [52], virtual endoscopy simulator [53, 54], trainer for arthroscopic knee surgery [55], simulation for training palpation of subsurface breast tumors [56].

Medical crisis raining systems focus on complex training tasks in which the individual must act directly and manually on the environment and in which the responses to an action may be very subtle (such as a change in skin colour). Doing so requires the design and implementation of several interaction and simulation methodologies, from distributed-system support for high-fidelity simulations to the development of clinically realistic virtual patients and, perhaps most importantly, to the creation of techniques that permit a user to act naturalistically upon the virtual environment. Stansfield and colleagues [6] developed BioSimMER, a fully immersive distributed virtual reality platform developed to train medical emergency-response personnel. Small and his team [57] presented an emergency medical trainer similar a flight simulator: a customizable mannequin with realistic anatomical features represents the patient, whom users act upon using physical instruments that interface the mannequin to a computer control system that drives the appropriate clinical state and response. Such systems, although highly sophisticated, can be expensive and limited in their programmability. Other researchers [41, 58, 59] developed the entire training scenario via software, with dynamic virtual patients presenting changing physical condition and responding to the clinician/trainee, who interacts with the system via a series of menus.

12.4.2   VR in education

12.4.2.1   Virtual Environments for Science

The use of VR as a means to teach abstract physics concepts was investigated by researchers at George Mason University and the University of Houston [60] who developed "NewtonWorld" and "MaxwellWorld". These systems provide immersive learning environment in which students may explore the kinematics and dynamics of motion, electrostatic forces, and other physical concepts. VEs' potential to help students develop correct mental models of the abstract material is identified in three key features: multisensory cues, multiple frames of reference and multimodal interaction.

Researchers at the Computer Museum [61] developed an immersive VR application designed to teach children about biology concepts, in particular the structure and function of cells. In the application, users were asked to construct cells from component parts, with successful completion indicated by an animation of internal cell function.

NICE ("Narrative-based, Immersive, Constructionist/Collaborative Environments") project [7] was the first immersive, multiuser learning environment designed specifically for children. Started in 1996, it was designed to support children's learning of simple relationships between plant growth, sunlight and water. NICE implements a persistent virtual garden in which children may collaboratively plant and harvest fruits and vegetables, cull weeds, and position light and water sources to differentially affect the growth rate of plants.

An exhibit-based research project, the Virtual Gorilla Project [62] was aimed at teaching middle-school students about gorilla behaviors, vocalizations, and social interaction. The study re-created the gorilla exhibit at Zoo Atlanta, allowing users to adopt the role of an adolescent gorilla, navigating the environment and observing other gorilla's reactions to their approach.

12.4.2.2 Virtual environments for design

A further application developed from the Atlanta Virtual Zoo was designed in order to teach college students about habitat design. The learning goal in this case thus shifted to fostering students' understanding of the philosophy of environmental design and of the specific design decisions made for the exhibit.

The Human Interface Technology Laboratory (HITL) at the University of Washington has been one of the early educational seedbeds for VR, with projects such as the Virtual Reality Roving Vehicle (VRRV) [5, 63] and summer camp programs in VR for students [64]. The VRRV was experienced by a large number of students, while the summer camp focused on "world-building" activity, in which students conceived and created the objects of their own virtual worlds, using a 3-D modeling software on desktop computers. This gave the opportunity for students to understand the process involved in creating a virtual setting.

12.4.2.3 Augmented reality and educational toys

As far as augmented and mixed reality systems are concerned, we can cite "EQUATOR-Technical innovation in physical and digital life" [65], a EPSRC Funded Research Project running for 6 years as an interdisciplinary collaboration between 8 academic institutions in UK. Its central goal is to promote the integration of physical and digital worlds by uncovering and supporting the development of Mixed Reality Environments (MREs). They affect different aspects of people's everyday life, such as education, leisure, home, work, community etc. For what concerns educational technologies the University of Sussex, Bristol and Nottingham are exploring and extending current forms of playful interaction by developing a combination of digital toys and collaborative playgrounds for young children.

Researchers' interest is also focused on evaluating, from a psychological point of view, the potential of MREs for learning and education at different levels: how easily children can discover new relationships between actions and effects in MR spaces, what kind of concepts and causal links they might develop and use to produce creative behaviours, how MREs provide external support to the experiences of traversing viewpoints and spaces so as to improve children's decentring/authoring abilities and socio-cognitive development.

12.4.2.4 Virtual Environments for Second-Language Learning

Researchers at the HITL (Human Interface Technology Laboratory) of the University of Washington, have designed and developed "Zengo Sayu", an immersive educational environment for Japanese Language Instruction [66]. It is an immersive, interactive VE designed to teach Japanese prepositions to students with no prior knowledge of the language. The immersive aspects of this virtual environment are aimed at helping students to develop an understanding of Japanese through natural, physical interaction. This should strenghten both linguistic acquisition and recall abilities, while reducing the need for translation into their first language. The prototype application uses full immersion with a head-mounted display, digitized voice samples for natural speech reproduction, voice recognition and body tracking technology to allow the user to interact and affect the world.

12.4.2.5 VR in ethical education

Another interesting application domain was suggested by Ruggeroni [67]. The purpose of his study was to investigate the possibility to support the activity of ethical education by the means of VR softwares, assessing whether the use of a life-simulation game could enhance understanding and learning the ethical principles found in everyday life.

In "The Sims", a people simulator, users can interact with characters and environments and are involved in a non-immersive 3D scenario to experience and act on ethical dilemmas, observing potential consequences and take part in the decision making to solve concrete situations where ethical dilemmas need a response.

12.4.2.6 Special-Needs Education

As noted before, VR can be very useful in Special-Needs Education [68, 69]: students with Special Educational Needs (SEN) can experience problems in dealing with abstracts and often learn directly through experience with the real world. On the other hand, the ability to learn directly from experience depends on the range and complexity of the experiences that are offered. In an educational environment, these experiences may be restricted due to the limited number of real-world artifacts that can be provided in a classroom setting, and there are certain logistical problems in regulaly taking a group of SEN students out of school in search of richer environments. The LIVE project, from the Sheperd School in Nottingham, UK, developed twenty VEs in three application areas: experiential environments in which students can practice everyday life skills; communication environments in which students are encouraged to develop their speech, signing and symbols skills; personal and social education environments, in which students can investigate appropriate behavior in public situation.

Obviously, such experiences are not intended to replace their real-world counterparts, but they "could be used to prepare the students for them by filling in educational "experience gaps" that are caused by factors such as overprotective parenting, mobility problems and cognitive deficits" [69] (p. 265).

12.5 Transforming the potential of Virtual Reality into Real Educational Efficacy: insights and guidelines

12.5.1 Evaluation and assessment

Evaluation is undoubtedly a crucial issue for future integration of VEs in educational and training contexts.

Given both the intrinsic multidimensionality of learning and the novelty and dynamic nature of VR learning tools, the evaluation of VR learning efficacy requires "a sound conceptual framework that would encompass, rather than restrict, the multiple dimensions of the issues that need to be examined in a virtual learning environment" [7] (p. 254).

What is required is a shift of focus from learning outcomes to learning process; Windschitl [70] very clearly pointed out the limits of "black-box-type" classroom research, where "inputs are operationally defined (e.g., learner characteristics or instructional interventions), learning experiences occur (unexamined), then the outputs are measured (e.g., objective achievement tests, posthoc interviews)" (p. 90). Shifting the attention to the dynamics of the learning experience provides evaluators with precious information for the comprehension of *"why* rather than simply *if* certain learning contexts are more robust than others" (p. 90). Of course, such a perspective requires researchers to assume as object of their analysis a much more complex web of relationships, involving people and not just variables.

In order to capture this complexity, it is important to apply multiple measures of learning and performance [63]. Measuring different aspects of learning and interaction experiences may help explaining outcomes beyond what VR's affordances explain, and help understand the strengths and weaknesses of VR's capabilities in shaping the learning process and learning outcomes. As suggested by a number of authors [7, 71] different technical, orientational, affective, cognitive, pedagogical issues should be included.

- The *technical aspect* examines usability issues, regarding interface, physical problems, and system hardware and software.
- The *orientation aspect* focuses on the relationship of the user to the virtual environment; it includes navigation, spatial orientation, presence and immersion, and feedback issues.
- The *affective parameter* evaluates the user's engagement, likes and dislikes, and confidence in the virtual environment.
- The *cognitive aspect* identifies any improvement of the subject's internal concepts through this learning experience.
- Finally, the *pedagogical aspect* concerns the teaching approach: how to gain knowledge effectively about the environment and the concepts that are being taught.

As far as the methodological approach is concerned, integration of quantitative and qualitative methodologies seems the best way to face and to catch this complexity. Riva and Galimberti [72], in this book, presented a complex model of data analysis for Internet research called CEMDA (Complementary Exploratory Multilevel Data Analysis) and supported the value of the mixed use of quantitative and qualitative tools: different techniques can highlight different and complementary features of the VR experience, and they are thus suitable to different levels of analysis. As Windschitl [70] suggests, "research methods act as lenses to reveal or obscure, and [...] drawing upon a variety of methods can help clarify phenomena that are not interpretable using a single paradigm" (p. 90).

A last issue to be addressed concerns standardization of assessment techniques in order to allow researchers in the area to confront themselves on crucial themes. To this aim, a valuable approach could be the one proposed by Kozma and Quellmalz [73] for Web-Based Instruction, consisting in clustering network-based projects with generally similar goals for evaluation. This would allow evaluators to make use of common instruments and data collection procedures, and aggregate the projects for most analyses and interpretations. "Cluster evaluation" could not only represent a cost-effective method of evaluating several projects simultaneously, but also a way to promote sharing of information among the projects' stakeholders to improve performance and effectiveness. Furthermore, this approach is likely to foster the development of communities of practice "that can share effective project strategies and lessons learned" [73].

12.5.2 Tuning the learning environments

Experience gained in past projects makes it possible to propose some general reflections useful to design and implementation of VEs in educational contexts. Analysis of these issues, in fact, is important for designers and educators in order to manage VR potential and transform it into an effective learning tool.

First of all, as Roussos [7] suggests, in VEs' design for education, "the *balance among reality, abstraction and engagement* is particularly difficult to achieve" (p. 260) and this often requires a trade-off among these elements. Especially when designing for young children, it is important to carefully define the level of abstraction. When teaching science concepts, for example, great attention should be payed to the adequacy of the underlying model; the introduction of familiar and simplified elements for children to enhance engagement and fun (such as, in the NICE project [7], umbrellas or sunglasses on the plants to signal the wet/dry status) can, at the same time, risk to engender misconceptions and reductive bias about the concepts taught.

The focus of the teachers should be to support complementary discussion and instruction in order to contextualize the use of VEs; this to help students to understand general principles underlying the virtual experience and creating relationships between the VE and their previous knowledge background.

On the other hand, Draper and colleagues [74] remind us that despite the ability of a VE to develop a rich computer-mediated world, designers have a great responsibility in tailoring interfaces to meet the task-dependent needs of the user. The possibility for rich and immersive interfaces to display much more information and in a more compelling way as compared to non-immersive technology introduce a question about *whether* this is always useful. In fact, we should not forget that, "in some cases, simple map reading ...[can be]... more effective in imparting knowledge about an environment than experience in a virtual representation of that environment" [74].

A second issue to be considered [7, 75] concerns the *open-ended exploratory nature* of many educational environments; the basic assumption that the learning process will take place naturally through the simple exploration and discovery of the Virtual Environment should be reviewed. Despite the undoubtful value of the exploratory learning provided by VR, when the knowledge context is too unstructured, learning process can become very difficult. This is especially true for younger students [21]. Experience by itself is not enough: as constructivism underlines, learning takes place when students can build conceptual models that are both consistent with what they already understand and with the new content. As suggested by Bowman et al. [75] "it seems that experience can take a student only part of the way to learning and understanding a subject. In most cases, it is necessary to have background knowledge, peripheral information, reflection, and experience before the subject can be comprehended by the student" (p.317). In order to ensure successful adaptation of old knowledge to new experience, flexible learning direction should be provided; this can be done in two ways: a) through the integration of other types of information and educational supports other than the 3D representation (such as audio and text annotations, images etc.) and/or b) in carefully defining specific tasks to the users/students through interaction with the teacher.

A last concern is about *collaboration* in distributed educational environments: as noted above, VR can encourage collaboration and foster the acquisition of skills developed through shared experiences of a group in a shared environment. Networked, web-shared Virtual Environments, where more users can experience a common learning context, represent one of the most promising applications of VR. These systems have all the potential to enhance VR efficacy by meeting the main constructivist principles of both experiential learning ("learning by doing") and collaborative learning (learning by sharing and negotiating knowledge).

Nevertheless, as Roussos [7] points out, this can prove a double-edged sword. The presence of avatars representing remote users is a strong boost to social interaction, sometimes at the expense of the intended concept learning. As distributed VEs support collaboration through the provision of a shared virtual space, it is necessary to make efforts to structure cooperative learning [76, 77] in a way that fosters positive interdependence among learners, or supports reflection and planning. Social interaction is intended as a mechanism to support learning and thus should not become an end by itself.

12.6 Conclusions

Technological advances have made it available to the educational and training world a wide set of innovative learning tools. Among these, Virtual Reality seems to have a great potential to enhance the learning process [8, 10].

First of all, VEs can provide modes of *experiential learning*; to the extent that VR provides *high-level interaction* with the learning content, it can foster *active engagement* by students. This contributes to raise *motivation* and interest, conditions which are recognized as crucial in the learning process. VR learning also allows entirely new capabilities and experiences, that would be too difficult, too costly or simply impossible to have in the real world. Finally, VR environments can be tailored to individual learning and performance style. They are highly *flexible* and programmable, thus enabling the teacher or the trainer to present a wide variety of controlled stimuli and to measure and monitor a wide variety of responses made by the user.

Current educational theories such as constructivism seem to present convergence and be consistent with learning in VEs, and this surely represents a further strenght for the use of this technology in education and training [5].

Nevertheless, the potential of each VR feature needs careful reflection in order to be actually translated into educational efficacy. The matter is not establishing whether VR is useful or not to enhance learning, but understanding how to effectively exploit its potential.

In order to design effective learning environments, a model is needed to integrate the theoretical insights about VR educational potential and the principles of design and development; such a model could be useful to generate research questions, stimulate new studies and should be gradually implemented by their results.

When looking at the current use and integration of VR tools in educational and training contexts, we can see how a number of problems limit their actual application and effectiveness. These problems represent challenges for future development of learning VEs and encompass various VR-based learning issues, including: pedagogical, technological, institutional, cultural, economical, management, interface design.

- *Costs*: At the moment, cost surely represents one important limit to VR penetration into educational context. Although some attempts have been made to use PC-based VR systems (and current efforts in this direction are encouraging), most of the existing VEs are based on VR systems such as CAVEs or high-end platforms (such as Onyx Sylicon Graphics) whose cost is beyond the reach of the average school, university, not to talk about single students.

- *Lack of reference standards*: almost all applications in this sector can be considered "one-off" creations tied to a proprietary hardware and software, which have been tuned by a process of trial and error. This makes them difficult to use in contexts other than those in which they were developed. Furthermore, this lack of reference standards does not only concerns technological aspects but extends to the lack of common reference framework in design, implementation, evaluation and assessment.

- *Educational culture*: 3-D graphics technology is not intended to entirely replace conventional classroom teaching techniques; nevertheless, as Dean and colleagues [78] point out, "properly implemented virtual environments can serve as valuable supplemental teaching and learning resources to augment and reinforce traditional methods" (p.505). Anyway, good design and implementation are surely not enough to ensure effective results: the learning potential of the actual VR experience must be constantly integrated and managed by the teachers within the actual educational context. Teachers themselves must develop specific expertise and sufficient practical experience of VR learning in order to effectively support learning process in 3D environments.

- *Safety*: some users have experienced certain side effects during and after exposure to immersive VR environments [37], collectively referred to as "simulator sickness" [79]: ocular problems (e.g. eyestrain, blurred vision, and fatigue), disorientation and balance disturbances, and nausea. Though the latest VR tools seem to have minor or no side effects, future researchers have to confirm these results.

- *Usability*: another crucial issue for integrating VR into classrooms is system *usability* - by students of various ages, by teachers, and by curriculum developers. This is surely not an easy task, seen the multidimensional nature of learning process and the complexity and novelty of VR technology. Interface experts stress the value of involving end-users in the development of computer technology during the design phase. There is a need for collaborative and iterative design of these environments, that should involve, repeatedly at different stages of the project, designers, teachers, and end-users.

Professionals in this field must be aware of the crucial importance of *research and co-development*: by sharing information about their experience as they continue to explore, observe, evaluate and refine VR, they can expedite suitable developmental work in this field and increase professional and public understanding of the technology.

Further research is required, both on technological side and on VR issues such as transfer of learning, appropriate curriculum implementation, elements of effective VR design, and the psychological and social impact of the technology use.

12.7 Acknowledgments

I thank Giuseppe Riva, Andrea Gaggioli and Gianluca Castelnuovo for their help and support, as well as for their useful comments on earlier versions of this chapter.

The present work was supported by the Commission of the European Communities (CEC), in particular by the IST programme (Project VEPSY UPDATED, IST-2000-25323 – http://www.psicologia.net; http://www.vepsy.com).

12.8   References

[1]   W. James, *Talks to Teachers*. New York: W.W. Norton, 1958. (originally published, 1892).
[2]   National Research Council, *How people learn: Building research and practice*. Washington, D.C.: National Academy Press, 1999.
[3]   J. E. Newhagen, Why communication researchers should study the Internet: A dialogue, *Journal of Communication* 46 (1996) 4-13.
[4]   C. J. Bonk, N. Hara, V. Dennen, S. Malikowsky, and L. Supplee, We're in TITLE to Dream: Envisioning a Community of Practice, The Interplanetary Teacher Learning Exchange, *CyberPsychology & Behavior* 3 (2000) 25-39.
[5]   W. Winn, A Conceptual Basis for Educational Applications of Virtual Reality, *Technical Report TR 93-9: http://www.hitl.washington.edu/publications/r-93-9/* (1993).
[6]   S. Stansfield, D. Shawver, A. Sobel, M. Prasad, and L. Tapia, Design and Implementation of a Virtual Reality System and Its Application to Training Medical First Responders, *Presence* 9 (2000) 524-556.
[7]   M. Roussos, A. Johnson, T. Moher, J. Leigh, C. Vasilakis, and C. Barnes, Learning and Building Together in a Immersive Virtual World, *Presence* 8 (1999) 247-263.
[8]   V. S. Pantelidis, Reasons to Use Virtual Reality in Education, *VR in the Schools: http://www.soe.ecu.edu/vr/reas.html* 1 (1995 (Revised 2000)).
[9]   J. Bruner, *Towards a theory of instruction*. New York: WW Norton, 1966.
[10]   M. C. Salzman, C. Dede, R. B. Loftin, and J. Chen, A Model for Understanding How Virtual Reality Aids Complex Conceptual Learning, *Presence* 8 (1999) 293-316.
[11]   K. M. Osberg, Virtual Reality and Education: A Look at Both Sides of the Sword, *http://www.hitl.washington.edu/publications/r-93-7/* (1992).
[12]   R. C. Schank, The Virtual University, *CyberPsychology & Behavior* 3 (2000) 9-16.
[13]   T. Gaddis, *Virtual reality in the school. Virtual reality and Education laboratory*: East Carolina University, 1998.
[14]   M. Fitzgerald and G. Riva, Virtual Reality, in *Telemedicine Glossary*, L. Beolchi, Ed.: European Commission-DG INFSO, 2001, pp. 327-329.
[15]   M. Heim, *Virtual Realism*. New York: Oxford University Press, 1998.
[16]   G. Riva and G. Mantovani, The Need for a Socio-Cultural Perspective in the Implementation of Virtual Environments, *Virtual Reality* 5 (2000) 32-38.
[17]   J. S. Steuer, Defining virtual reality: dimensions determining telepresence, *Journal of Communication* 42 (1992) 73-93.
[18]   M. Slater, Measuring presence: a response to the Witmer and Singer Presence Questionnaire, *Presence* 8 (1999) 560-565.
[19]   P. Cronin, Report on the application of virtual reality technology to education, University of Edinburgh 1997.
[20]   L. Sastry and D.R.S. Boyd, Virtual environments for engineering applications, *Virtual Reality* 3 (1998) 235-244.
[21]   R. B. Gabbard, Constructivism, Hypermedia, and the World Wide Web, *CyberPsychology & Behavior* 3 (2000) 103-110.
[22]   G. Scheurman, From behaviorist to constructivist teaching, *Social Education* 62 (1998) 6-9.
[23]   E. G. McGuire, Knowledge representation and construction in hypermedia and environments, *Telematics and Informatics* 13 (1996) 251-160.
[24]   D. H. Jonassen, Objectivism vs. constructivism: Do we need a new paradigm?, *Educational Technology: Research and Development* 39 (1991) 5-14.
[25]   M. Lombard and T. Ditton, At the heart of it all: the concept of presence, *Journal of Computer Mediated Communication* 3 (1997).
[26]   J. Dewey, *Democracy and Education*. New York: Free Press, 1966.
[27]   S. Papert, *Mindstorms: Children, Computers and Powerful Ideas*. New York: Basic Books, Inc., 1980.
[28]   S. Papert, Situating Constructionism, in *Constructionism*, I. Harel and S. Papert, Eds. Norwood, NJ: Ablex, 1991.
[29]   M. Nicaise and M. Crane, Knowledge constructing through hypermedia authoring, *Educational Technology, Research and Development* 47 (1999) 29-50.
[30]   J. S. Brown, A. Collins, and P. Duguid, Situated cognition and the culture of learning, *Educational Researcher* 18 (1989) 32-43.
[31]   J. Lave and E. Wenger, *Situated learning: Legitimate peripheral participation*. Cambridge: Cambridge University Press, 1991.
[32]   L. Vygotsky, *Mind in society*. Cambridge, MA: Harvard University Press, 1978.
[33]   H. McMahon and W. O'Neill, Computer-mediated zones of engagement in learning, in *Designing environments for constructive learning*, T. Duffy, J. Lowyck, and D. Jonassen, Eds. New York: Springer, 1993.

[34]   V. S. Pantelidis, Suggestions on When to Use and When Not to Use Virtual Reality in Education, *VR in the Schools* 2 (1996 (Revised 2000)).

[35]   A. Dillon, Designing a better learning environment with the Web: Problems and prospects, *CyberPsychology & Behavior* 3 (2000) 97-101.

[36]   R. S. Kennedy and K. M. Stanney, Postural instability induced by virtual reality exposure: Development of a certification protocol, *International Journal of Human Computer Interaction* 8 (1996) 25-47.

[37]   J. R. Lackner, Multimodal and motor influences on orientation: implications for adapting to weightless and virtual environments, *J Vestib Res* 2 (1992) 307-322.

[38]   G. Riva, *Virtual Reality in neuro-psycho-physiology: Cognitive, clinical and methodological issues in assessment and rehabilitation.* Amsterdam: IOS Press, 1997.

[39]   G. Riva, B. K. Wiederhold, and E. Molinari, *Virtual Environments in clinical psychology and neuroscience: Methods and techniques in advanced patient-therapist interaction.* Amsterdam: IOS Press, 1998.

[40]   R. D. Owston, Evaluating Web-Based Learning Enviornments: Strategies and Insights, *CyberPsychology & Behavior* 3 (2000) 79-87.

[41]   S. Stansfield, D. Shawver, and A. Sobel, MediSim: A prototype VR system for training medical first responders, presented at Virtual Reality Annual International Symposium, 1998.

[42]   D. Tate, L. Silbert, and T. King, Virtual environments for shipboard firefighting training, presented at IEEE Virtual Reality Annual International Symposium, 1997.

[43]   W. Johnson, J. Rickel, R. Stiles, and A. Munro, Integrating pedagogical agents into virtual environments, *Presence* 7 (1998) 523-548.

[44]   R. Loftin and P. Kenney, Training the Hubble Space Telescope Flight Team, *IEEE Computer Graphics and Applications* 15 (1995) 31-37.

[45]   S. Stansfield, Applications of virtual reality to nuclear safeguards, presented at Joint ESARDA/INMM Workshop on Science and Modern Technology for Safeguards, 1998.

[46]   J. Calvin, A. Dickens, R. Gaines, P. Metzger, D. Miller, and D. Owen, The SIMNET virtual world architecture, presented at IEEE Virtual Reality Annual International Symposium, 1993.

[47]   J. Dahmann, J. Calvin, and R. Weatherby, A reusable architecture for simulations, *Communications of the ACM* 42 (1999) 79-84.

[48]   M. Macedonia, M. Zyda, D. Pratt, P. Barham, and P. Zeswitz, NPSNET: A network software architecture for large-scale virtual environments, *Presence* 3 (1994) 265-287.

[49]   R. Satava and S. Jones, Virtual environments for medical training and education, *Presence* 6 (1997) 139-146.

[50]   D. Kaufman and W. Bell, Teaching and assessing clinical skills using virtual reality, *Medicine Meets Virtual Reality/Studies in Health Technology and Informatics* 39 (1997) 467-472.

[51]   S. Delp, P. Loan, C. Basdogan, and J. Rosen, Surgical simulation: An emerging technology for training in emergency medicine, *Presence* 6 (1997) 147-159.

[52]   R. Kuppersmith, R. Johnston, D. Moreau, R. Loftin, and H. Jenkins, Building a virtual reality temporal bone dissection simulator, *Medicine Meets Virtual Reality/Studies in Health Technology and Informatics* 39 (1997) 180-186.

[53]   R. Robb, Virtual endoscopy: Evaluation using the visible human datasets and comparison with real endoscopy in patients, *Medicine Meets Virtual Reality/Studies in Health Technology and Informatics* 39 (1997) 195-206.

[54]   G. Wiet, R. Yagel, D. Stredney, P. Schmalbrock, D. Sessanna, Y. Kurzion, L. Rosenberg, M. Levin, and K. Martin, A volumetric approach to virtual simulation of functional endoscopic sinus surgery, *Medicine Meets Virtual Reality/Studies in Health Technology and Informatics* 39 (1997).

[55]   S. Gibson, J. Samosky, A. Mor, C. Fyock, E. Grimson, T. Kanade, R. Kikinis, H. Lauer, N. McKenzie, S. Nakajima, H. Ohkami, R. Osborne, and A. Sawada, Simulating arthroscopic knee surgery using volumetric object representations, real-time volume rendering and haptic feedback (Technical Report TR96-19), (1996).

[56]   M. Dinsmore, N. Langrana, G. Burdea, and J. Ladeji, Virtual reality training simulation for palpation of surface tumors, presented at IEEE Virtual Reality Annual International Symposium, 1997.

[57]   S. Small, R. Wuerz, R. Simon, N. Shapiro, A. Conn, and G. Setnik, Demonstration of high-fidelity simulation team training for emergency medicine, *Academic Emergency Medicine* 6 (1999) 312-323.

[58]   M. Stytz, B. Garcia, G. Godsell-Stytz, and S. Banks, A distributed virtual environments prototype for emergency medical procedures training, *Medicine Meets Virtual Reality/Studies in Health Technology and Informatics* 39 (1997) 473-485.

[59]   D. Chi, J. Clarke, B. Webber, and N. Badler, Casualty modeling for real-time medical training, *Presence* 5 (1996) 359-366.

[60] C. Dede, M. C. Salzman, and B. Loftin, ScienceSpace: Virtual realities for learning complex and abstract scientific concepts, presented at IEEE Virtual Reality Annual International Symposium (VRAIS '96), 1996.

[61] E. Gay and D. Greschler, *Is virtual reality a good teaching tool?*: Boston Computer Museum, 1994.

[62] D. Allison, B. Wills, D. Bowman, J. Wineman, and L. F. Hodges, The virtual reality gorilla exhibit, *IEEE Computer Graphics and Applications* (1997) 30-38.

[63] H. Rose, Assessing learning in VR: Towards developing a paradigm virtual reality roving vehicles (VRRV) project. (Technical Report TR-95-1), Human Interface Technology Laboratory-University of Washington 1995.

[64] M. Bricken and C. Byrne, Summer students in VR: A pilot study, *Virtual Reality: Applications and Explorations* (1993) 178-184.

[65] M. Scaife and R. Y., Traversing between the digital and the physical: what does it mean?, presented at Abstract of the talk presented at the 1st Equator Workshop, Porto, Portugal, 2001.

[66] H. Rose and M. Billinghurst, Zengo Sayu: An Immersive Educational Environment for Learning Japanese, *Technical Report No. TR-95-4: http://www.imprintit.com/Publications/HRPubs/TR-95-4/* (1995).

[67] C. Ruggeroni, , and E. by, Virtual Reality in Ethical Education, in *Communications through Virtual Technologies. Identity, Community and Technology in the Communication Age*, F. Davide and G. Riva, Eds. Amsterdam: IOS Press, 2001, pp. 119-133.

[68] D. J. Brown, P. J. Standen, and S. V. Cobb, Virtual Environments: Special Needs and Evaluative Methods, in *Virtual Reality in Clinical Medicine*, G. Riva, B. K. Wiederhold, and E. Molinari, Eds. Oxford: IOS Press, 1998, pp. 91-102.

[69] H. R. Neale, D. J. Brown, S. V. G. Cobb, and J. R. Wilson, Structured Evaluation of Virtual Environments for Special-Needs Education, *Presence* 8 (1999) 264-282.

[70] M. Windschitl, Using the WWW for teaching and learning in K-12 classrooms: What are the interesting research questions?, *CyberPsychology & Behavior* 3 (2000) 89-96.

[71] C. Lewin, Test driving CARS: Addressing the issues in the evaluation of computer assisted reading software, presented at International Conference on Computers in Education, 1995.

[72] G. Riva and C. Galimberti, Complementary Explorative Multilevel Data Analysis, in *Towards Cyberpsychology*, G. Riva and C. Galimberti, Eds. Amsterdam: IOS Press, 2001.

[73] R. B. Kozma and E. Quellmalz, Issues and needs in evaluating the educational impact of the National Information Infrastructure, *Online document: http://www.ed.gov/Technology/Futures/kozma.html* (1996).

[74] J. V. Draper, D. B. Kaber, and J. M. Usher, Speculations on the value of telepresence, *CyberPsychology & Behavior* 2 (1999) 349-362.

[75] D. A. Bowman, L. F. Hodges, D. Allison, and J. Wineman, The Educational Value of an Information-Rich Virtual Environment, *Presence* 8 (1999) 317-331.

[76] R. E. Slavin, Cooperative learning, *Review of Educational Research* 50 (1980) 315-342.

[77] D. W. Johnson and R. T. Johnson, *Cooperative learning*. New Brighton, MN: Interaction Book Co., 1984.

[78] K. L. Dean, X. S. Asay-Davis, E. M. Finn, T. Foley, J. A. Friesner, Y. Imai, B. J. Naylor, and S. R. Wustner, Virtual Explorer: Interactive Virtual Environment for Education, *Presence* 9 (2000) 505-523.

[79] R. S. Kennedy, L. J. Hettinger, D. L. Harm, J. M. Ordy, and W. P. Dunlap, Psychophysical scaling of circular vection (CV) produced by optokinetic (OKN) motion: individual differences and effects of practice., *J Vestib Res* 6 (1996) 331-341.

SECTION IV

CYBERPSYCHOLOGY IN PRACTICE: TELEMEDICINE AND E-HEALTH

Psychologists do not have to become technology specialists to be competent providers of telehealth services. The complexities and explosive growth of telehealth may prevent one from ever completely "learning" telehealth. However, to best know when and how to use technology to support healing, I believe that psychologists will need more technology proficiency, particularly with computers, than has been the norm. This is particularly true for those who will be establishing their practices in the coming decades. Thus, the present challenge is to examine critically the telehealth options available, imagine and test new ones, and determine how we can use them to administer the best possible treatment.

Stamm, 1998
(http://www.apa.org/journals/pro/pro296536.html)

13 CyberPsychology Meets Clinical Psychology: The Emergence of e-Therapy in Mental Health Care

Gianluca CASTELNUOVO, Andrea GAGGIOLI, Giuseppe RIVA

Abstract. Clinical psychologists have traditionally shied away from technology, perhaps because many of the therapeutic elements of psychotherapy rely on verbal and nonverbal interpersonal communication. Although nothing will ever replace face-to-face communication as the key element of psychological practice, the advance of technology is now offering new communication tools that psychologist and their patients feel comfortable using for clinical care.
This chapter presents the concept of e-therapy and examines the possible role of Internet and related media in psychotherapy. Current clinical applications are presented including equipment, research, and examples of direct clinical care. Different modes of online mental health care, including e-mail counselling, self-help therapy and self-help groups are analysed and discussed. The chapter also focuses on the technology used in e-therapy – email, IRC, videoconference - providing information about the equipment and its clinical use. A particular focus is given to the analysis of shared hypermedia, new Internet tools in which different users, who are simultaneously browsing the same Web site, can communicate and share files. The chapter concludes with suggestions for evaluating the value of adding e-therapy to existing clinical practices.

Contents

13.1 Introduction

Clinical psychologists have traditionally shied away from technology, perhaps because many of the therapeutic elements of psychotherapy rely on verbal and nonverbal interpersonal communication.

Although nothing will ever replace face-to-face communication as the key element of psychological practice, the advance of technology is now offering new communication tools that psychologist and their patients feel comfortable using for clinical care.

As noted by Jerome and Zailor [1]: "emerging technology will perpetually alter the health care environment, continuously changing the tools and options that are available to therapists. It is thus important to study the impact of these changes as they occur, and it is imperative that new technological competencies be developed as clinicians integrate these technologies into their research and practice" (p. 478). In general, distributed communication media could become a significant enabler of consumer health initiatives. In fact they provide an increasingly accessible communications channel for a growing segment of the population. Moreover, in comparison to traditional communication technologies, shared media offer greater interactivity and better tailoring of information to individual needs.

Nickelson [2] defined as *telehealth* the use of telecommunications and information technology "to provide access to health assessment, diagnosis, intervention, consultation, supervision, education and information, across distance" (p. 527).

Telehealth means "medicine at distance" where "medicine" includes not only medical activities - involving ill patients - but also public health activities - involving well people [3]. In other words telehealth is *process* and not a technology, including many different health care activities carried out at distance.

E-therapy, the use of Internet and related media in clinical psychology is the next logical step. Although e-therapy is a branch of telehealth, it is differentiated in several important ways. As noted by Allen [4] telehealth to date has been largely non-Internet based and has been characterized by point-to-point (e.g., T1) and dial-up (e.g., telephone, ISDN) information exchange. E-therapy, on the other hand, is more accessible due to its increasingly affordable ability to communicate through a common set of standards and across operating systems.

The basic idea is to use the power and convenience of Internet to allow simultaneous (synchronous) and time-delayed (asynchronous) communication between an individual and a professional. From this point of view, e-therapy represents neither a substitute to traditional psychotherapy nor an alternative to psychological counselling [5]: it provides different innovative, powerful tools that have the potential to *enhance* the effectiveness of the communication within the therapeutic process. In addition, the Internet can allow the provision of appropriate health assistance in remote areas where there are not specialized staff and facilities.

As the availability of new communication technologies expands the ways in which treatment can be provided, psychologists will incorporate these innovations into their practice and research. The purpose of this chapter is to review the effects of the Internet and related media on the field of psychology and to discuss the implications of these changes for the clinical practice.

However, different types of Internet media, such as chat, e-mail and video teleconferencing may present differing challenges and opportunities [1, 6]. Thus, the first section of this chapter introduces the reader to the rationale of e-therapy by providing an overview of the current applications in this field. In the second section a critical analysis of e-therapy tools currently available for psychotherapy is provided. Starting from the results of this analysis, the third section discusses how *shared hypermedia*, the most innovative of the e-therapy tools presented, could be used in mental health care. Finally, fundamental issues having important implications for the feasibility of the application of Internet media in psychotherapy are discussed.

13.2 The use of e-therapy in mental health care: Rationale and applications

The rapid technological evolution of the media suggests that Internet - a global computer network that connects ever-growing numbers of local networks and computers - will become the predominant communicational tool in the next future. Psychology is now discovering the great opportunities inherent in this medium. A number of psychological resources are already available for professionals and common users, covering all kinds of information on psychological concepts and issues, scientific research, clinical testing and assessment [1, 6, 7]. Among these applications, Internet-aided psychotherapy is rapidly emerging as one of the most interesting one [8]. In fact, during last years mental health professionals worldwide are pioneering new services that offer to establish a therapeutic relationship over the Web, sometimes on a fee basis. There are two main psychotherapy areas where the Internet has been applied so far: individual therapy and self-help therapy.

13.2.1   Individual telepsychotherapy

The first area in which the Internet can offer significant advantage is telepsychotherapy.

Remote psychological consultation, for example, could give clients greater access to skilled mental health professionals regardless of geographical proximity. Although efficacy of the use of remote consultation in psychotherapy is not yet fully understood, the technological advances have allowed the publication of some pioneering works with good and promising results. Klein and Richards, for example, investigated the effectiveness of an Internet-based intervention for people with panic disorder [9]. Participants meeting criteria for panic disorders were randomly assigned to either the treatment or a self-monitoring control condition. After the study, participants were assessed on measures pertaining to panic, negative affect, body vigilance, anxiety sensitivity and self-efficacy in managing panic. The treatment condition was associated with significant reductions in all variables except anxiety sensitivity and depressive affect [9].

Botella et al. [10] developed a telepsychology system for the treatment of public speaking fear. The system is composed of three main parts. The first component is a structured assessment protocol that gives the patient a diagnosis of his/her problem; the second component is represented by a structured treatment protocol, organized in separate blocks reflecting the patient's progress. The third part is an outcome protocol that assesses treatment effectiveness, not only at its end, but also at every intermediate step [10].

Murdoch and Connor-Greene reported two clinical cases where e-mail was used as an adjunction to therapy to enhance patient's involvement in treatment [11]. In both cases, patients' reports suggest that therapeutic alliance and therapeutic impact improved with the use of e-mail homework reporting. The authors attribute this improvement to the fact that some patients have fewer problems when they talk about personal issues using e-mail than when they are in a face-to-face setting. For this reason the use of email makes more likely that unknown aspects of the patient personality will emerge. In fact, patients may use their e-mail communication to reveal more about themselves, without having to be reactively attentive on a moment-to-moment basis to clinicians' comments or body language [11].

Yager has used e-mail like a therapeutic adjunct in the outpatient treatment of anorexia nervosa [12]. Results of this study showed a clinical improvement for all patients included in the experimental group. Furthermore, patients accepted the rationale of using e-mail as therapeutic adjunct and they considered it helpful.

In another study, Bouchard and colleagues [13] used videoconference to deliver cognitive behaviour therapy (CBT) to patients suffering from panic disorders with agoraphobia.

Participants received several sessions of CBT by trained therapists according to a standardized treatment manual. The remote site was located at 130 Km north of the local site and both were linked by ISDN lines. According to the authors, telepsychotherapy demonstrated statistically and clinically significant improvements of target symptoms (frequency of panic attacks, panic apprehension, severity of panic disorder, perceived self-efficacy) and measures of global functioning (trait anxiety, general improvement).

Furthermore, the authors noticed that a very good therapeutic alliance was built after only the first telepsychotherapy session [13].

13.2.2   Self-Help therapy

Self help material can be defined as any means (written, recorded etc.) whose content is a treatment program (or part of it) that may be self-administered by patients with or without the therapist's guidance [10]. The utility of self-help procedures has been acknowledged for a wide variety of psychological problems, like phobias, obesity, sexual dysfunctions and tobacco addiction. Scogin, Bynum, Stevens, & Calhoon, performed a meta-analysis review of 40 well designed outcome studies of self-help treatments [14]. The focus was on written or audiotaped material used by persons with various problems (bad habits, fears, depression, poor skills) without regular contact with a therapist or a teacher. The overall conclusions were that self-help is clearly more effective than no treatment at all and just as effective in most cases as treatment administered by a therapist.

Nonetheless, it has been remarked that there is a need of conducting more research in this area, in order to avoid indiscriminate use of self-help material which might even strengthen the problem rather than reduce it [15]. For instance, a person who self-applies an inadequate treatment may get the result of worsening the trouble instead of alleviating it. As noted by Botella [10], this risk depends on the fact that the information is offered in one go, that is, without taking precautions regarding whether every step along the therapeutic process is given in the appropriate way.

Useful self-help information can be found in books and on the Internet. Of course, the 50,000 self-help books published over the last 50+ years contain much more information than the current Internet, but the gap is narrowing [16]. In fact, the Internet is growing rapidly with more and more people getting access to free advice within seconds or minutes.

13.2.2.1   Online Self-Help groups

By the terms "on-line self-help groups", we refer to bulletin boards, chat rooms, news and discussion groups operated within health-related web pages, listservs (groups in which each individual message is copied and E-mailed to all subscribers), and other electronic forums focused on the sharing and solving of psychological disturbances [17]. Some are simply unstructured discussion groups, others are led by an individual (usually a nonprofessional) who shares the problem that the group addresses.

The last few decades have seen an enormous growth of self-help groups. The principle at the core of this approach is the sharing of experiences, strengths and hopes between members in order to solve their common problem. These groups offer both an alternative and adjunct to the traditional psychotherapy approach. A summary of what online self-help groups offer its members is provided by Madara [18]. Madara explains that social support, practical information, shared experiences, positive role models, helper therapy, empowerment, professional support, and advocacy efforts are all factors that operate online, just a they do in face to face groups [18].

The asynchronous nature of email online support groups provides the additional advantages of 24 hour availability, selective participation in entering and responding to messages, anonymity and privacy, immediate and/or delayed responding, and recording of transmissions. Members can save notes for later study, decide which sub-topics to engage in, and know that other group members are not judging them based on physical appearance [19]. According to Hsiung [20] the best option for online support is an online self-help group hosted by a mental health professional. In this way the mental health professional focuses on maintaining the supportive milieu and the members of the group focus on providing the support for each other.

In general the effectiveness of online self-help groups is high: different researches proved their efficacy as support tools in the treatment of eating disorders [21, 22], depression [23] and headache [24].

Nevertheless, as noted by Humphreys and colleagues [17] challenging ethical situations can arise for psychologists in Internet-based groups (p. 494):

- *Location*: on-line group members usually come from a broad geographical area, which makes it unlikely that a psychologist would be able to competently execute ethical responsibilities in the event of an emergency (e.g., a client residing in another state becomes suicidal);
- *Identity*: individuals cannot be reliably identified over the Internet. So, an individual with access to a client's computer (e.g., a family member or a coworker) could sign into on-line group psychotherapy by using the password and the name of the actual client.
- *Privacy*: because by definition everything "said" in Internet group therapy is typed, recorded, copied, and distributed, ensuring clients' privacy is difficult.

However, as underlined by these authors, future technological developments (e.g., improved encryption systems) and practical adjustments (e.g., restricting on-line group psychotherapy membership to local residents who can be screened personally before therapy begins) will help solving these problems.

13.2.2.2 Online Self-Help resources

In the following table, different services for seeking specific online self-help information and online support groups are summarized.

Table 13.1 Online Self-Help resources

Type of service	Name of service	Web-Address
Online support groups	Psychcentral	http://www.psychcentral.com/mail.htm
	Self-Improvement Online	http://www.selfgrowth.com/newsgrp.html
Information about psychiatric diagnoses	Mental Health Net	http://mentalhelp.net/disorders/
	Psych Web	http://www.psychwww.com/
	Internet Mental Health	http://www.mentalhealth.com/fr20.html
	American Psychiatric Association	http://www.appi.org/pnews/pnhome.html
Information about treatment methods	Internet Mental Health	http://www.mentalhealth.com/
	Psych Web	http://www.psywww.com/
	Mental Health Net	http://mentalhelp.net/dxtx.htm
	Knowledge Exchange Network	http://www.mentalhealth.org/

13.3 The use of e-therapy in mental health care: The tools

Although these preliminary studies and applications of clinical telepsychology seem very promising, other aspects apart scientific and clinical issues are to be taken in account. As noted by Stamm [8] "Psychologists do not have to become technology specialists to be competent providers of telehealth services... However, to best know when and how to use technology to support healing... psychologists will need more technology proficiency, particularly with computers, than has been the norm. This is particularly true for those who will be establishing their practices in the coming decades." (pp. 536-537).

However, as showed by a recent survey on a sample of 213 Californian psychologists, only a fraction of psychologists is making use of computers for anything other than simple word processing [25]. Even though 52% of the samples were using their computer to maintain client financial records, only one in four who kept computerized client records were using office management systems designed for mental or medical health professionals. The rest were using general spreadsheets or word processing programs that did not have the capability to perform all functions required by a mental health practice.

In fact, in order to ensure appropriate development of mental telehealth applications, psychologists and other mental health professionals must have a clear understanding of the benefits and drawbacks (including costs) of different e-therapy tools, in order to choose the most suitable and convenient technologies to start with. In the next sections, these issues are examined in details.

13.3.1   Interaction modalities between client and therapist in telepsychotherapy

As compared to in-person therapy, telepsychotherapy is unique in how it offers the opportunity to use the computer to interact with clients via different pathways, each one having its advantages and drawbacks. These different interaction modalities are included in two distinct types of computer mediated communication (CMC): synchronous and asynchronous [26, 27]. Synchronous CMC is produced when communication occurs simultaneously between two or more users, as in any normal telephonic or face-to-face conversation. In synchronous communication, the client and therapist are sitting at their computer at the same time, interacting with each other at that moment.

Asynchronous CMC is produced when communication is not simultaneous. This means, simply stated, that there is a stretching of the time frame in which the interaction occurs.

The commonest form of asynchronous CMC is E-mail, in which a sender leaves a message in a receiver's electronic letterbox, which the receiver must open before he can read the message. Another more sophisticated type of asynchronous CMC is Newsgroup, an electronic notice-board on which users can post messages referring to a specific topic or area of interest. Users can read the messages by opening the notice-board, and send their own messages in turn. As with E-mail, there is no real-time link between the computers of the interacting subjects. Unlike asynchronous CMC, the most important feature of synchronous CMC is that it does provide a real-time link between users' computers [26].

Although the most frequently cited example is the video-conference, the most widespread system is in fact Internet Relay Chat, or IRC. IRC is a form of synchronous CMC which enables a group of users (a chat) to exchange written messages and interact with each other in two different ways, by sending a message either to a specified user, or to all members of the chat [27].

13.3.2   Pros and cons of synchronous and asynchronous CMC in telepsychotherapy

Suler [28] has analysed the pros and cons of synchronous and asynchronous communication in telepsychotherapy. Results of this evaluation are reported in the following table (13.2).

13.3.3   E-mail

E-therapy tools can be used to facilitate electronic communications between patients and care providers, typically in the form of electronic mail (e-mail). It could prove to be an effective mechanism for improving care and lowering costs because more frequent communications might enable better tracking of a patient's progress or eliminate the need for an office visit. As we have just seen, psychologists are already incorporating the use of E-mail into their professional activities.

Table 13.2 Pros and cons of different types of CMC according to Suler [28]

Type of CMC	Pros	Cons
Synchronous	• The ability to schedule sessions defined by a specific, limited period of time; • A feeling of presence created by being with a person in real time; • Interaction may be more spontaneous, resulting in more revealing, uncensored disclosures by the client. • Making the effort to be with the person for a specific appointment may be interpreted as a sign of commitment and dedication; • Pauses in the conversation, coming late to a session, and no-shows are not lost as psychologically significant cues.	• The difficulties and inconvenience in having to schedule a session at a particular time, especially if the client and therapist are in very different time zones; • There is less "zone for reflection" - the time between exchanges to think and compose a reply – with the possible exception of lag, which offers a small zone for reflection • In the mind of the client, "therapy" may be associated specifically with the appointment and be less perceived as an ongoing, daily process.
Asynchronous	• There are no difficulties in having to schedule a specific appointment time; different time zones are not a problem; • There is the simple convenience of replying when you are ready and able to reply; • There is an enhanced "zone for reflection" that allows the therapist and client to think and compose a reply.	• The professional boundaries of a specific, time-limited "appointment" are lost. • There is a reduced feeling of "presence" because the client and therapist are not together in the moment. • Some of the spontaneity of interacting "in the moment" is lost, along with what spontaneous actions can reveal about a person. • There may be some loss of the sense of commitment that "meeting with me right now" can create. • Pauses in the conversation, coming late to a session, and no-shows are lost as psychologically significant cues (although pacing and length of replies in asynchronous communication may serve as cues).

A representative survey of California psychologists in 1997 revealed that 36% used E-mail, a 50% increase since 1995 [5]. By using e-mail, various types of data (text, psychological tests, photographs etc.) can be stored in a computer and forwarded to another user. Equipment needs are minimal: a moderately fast computer and a connection to a network are adequate. In the e-mail therapy participants can use only the verbal channel because it is not possible to communicate with paraverbal or not verbal elements.

Emotions can be simulated, to some extent, by using symbolic or graphics expressions (i.e. the emoticons). According to Yager, [12] who has made a pioneering attempt to use e-mail in a clinical procedure, there are several reasons for which e-mail can be considered as a positive adjunct in therapy. Firstly, e-mail increases the frequency and amount of time contact with clinicians and therapeutic processes. Briefing feedback several times per week between sessions lets the patient know that the clinician is present, listening, and thinking about the patient. Secondly, the emotional value of e-mail is relevant because patients can initiate contacts when they feel most inspired and need most to be in contact with their clinician. A third factor is represented by the observation that quasi-daily e-mail reports require patients to be constantly aware of their behaviours and of being in therapy. Finally, e-mail can reduce the emotional burden of patients by encouraging and enabling them to say whatever they care to say. However, the use of e-mail as an adjunct in psychotherapy can have also some drawbacks. As underlined by Yager [12], potentially negative effects are:

1. Unwanted disclosures resulting from lack of privacy for receiving e-mail messages;
2. Clinician failure to respond in a timely and adequate fashion;
3. Clinician failure to recognize urgent and troubled communications meriting phone and/or face-to-face contact;
4. Inappropriate or excessive use of electronic messages.

As noted by Maheu and Gordon, [5], current findings regarding the use of E-mail by physicians suggest increasing utilization rates, although there is much debate about its clinical efficacy. For example, a recent study revealed that 69% of medical consultation requests by E-mail were limited to answering simple questions about particular symptoms, diagnostic tests, and therapeutic interventions [29].

13.3.4 Internet Relay Chat

The most widespread tool in psychotherapy for written synchronous communication is the Internet Relay Chat (IRC). As e-mail IRC allows more frequent patient-therapist communications, facilitating the tracking of a patient's progress and eliminating the need for an office visit [5]. IRC enables a group of users to exchange written messages and interact with each other in two different ways, by sending a message either to a specified user, or to all members of the chat. IRC has been successfully used by self-help organizations. The principle of the self-help group is that members are allowed to share experiences, strengths and hopes in order to solve their common problems. These groups offer both an alternative and adjunct to the traditional psychotherapy arena. They have in common the fact that members participate with the expectation of receiving emotional support and finding new ways to help themselves cope with their shared problems. By far the largest segment of these groups deal with substance abuse problems (i.e. Alcoholics Anonymous).

13.3.5   Video teleconferencing

Video teleconferencing (VTC) is considered by many as a synonym for telehealth [1, 6].

Simply stated, video teleconferencing allows participants to conduct visually interactive electronic meetings between one or more distant locations using video cameras, monitors and communications.

VTC can be a possible solution to limited rural mental health services [1, 6]. Especially in remote areas, patients tend to be under treated, receiving mental health services only in emergencies. Moreover, VTC can provide opportunities for clinical consultation, assessment, diagnosis, supervision, home health care, medication management, continuing education, and administrative review.

Patient acceptance in using VTC is high, even when individuals are acutely or chronically psychotic or agitated [1, 6]. This result is confirmed by the results obtained by Ghosh and colleagues [30], who found no differences in the therapeutic alliance when they compared 10 psychotherapy sessions conducted by video conference with 10 sessions conducted face to face.

Unlike conventional telephone communications, where parties are limited to only hearing each other, video teleconferencing utilizes both audio and video communications enabling participants to see and hear each other as if they were in the same room. VTC operates with a camera, a monitor and a computer processor. There are four basic types of VTC on the market:

1. dedicated VTC units;
2. desktop computer VTC units that pass data via telephone lines;
3. desktop computer VTC units that pass data via the Internet, and
4. retrofit units that use existing televisions and telephones.

A good measure of the quality of the unit is frames per second (fps): the faster the speed, the better the quality but, concomitantly, the higher the cost. The target is 30 fps (broadcast quality) but to keep costs down many units have a maximum of 15-20 fps, which allows fairly clear resolution as long as there is little movement. Determining appropriate speed (and price) should be based on the improvement over current clinical options and the clinical demands on the system [31]. For example, if it is important to see movement, as might be appropriate for seeing hearing-impaired patients who communicate by signing, higher frame rates are necessary. However, slower frame rates might be a better application in an underserved rural or frontier clinic where the choice is between no VTC and slower VTC. Slower frame rates are not a deterrent in situations where a still image is the most important clinical information. The next table provides an overview of the approximate costs per unit of different VTC systems along with the specification of transmission rate.

Tab. 13.3 Principal VTC systems and related costs

VTC type	Frame Rate (fps)	Price (per unit)
dedicated VTC	up to 30 fps	between $7,000 and $50,000
desktop computer VTC (telephone data transfer)	15 fps	$1,000-5,000
desktop computer VTC (Internet data transfer)	up to 30 fps	$100 and $500
Retrofit VTC	up to 20 fps	$350-500.

13.3.6   Shared Hypermedia Tools

Hypermedia can be described as "on-line setting where networks of multimedia nodes connected by links are used to present information and manage retrieval" [32]. While a hypertext consists of textual information in the first place, hypermedia include multiple information formats, such as visual, musical and animation elements. When hypermedia are used as communication tools, they are defined *Shared Hypermedia* [33, 34] tools (SHs).

SHs have the unique feature of integrating the communication potential offered by Internet with the richness of different multimedia contents. Different users, who are simultaneously browsing the same website, can communicate with each other and share files or web addresses. Furthermore, each user can get a constantly updated list of all the other online users who are visiting the same website [34]. Usually, a SH allows the user to conduct group and private chats, to exchange information and files, and even to share the same web-pages. On any website, SH users can see a list of other users and talk with them on group and private levels. SHs further enhances the user's experience by consolidating different forms of computer-mediated-communication (e-mail, IRC etc.) into one fully integrated interface. Many SHs also have a search engine that can be used to find a user who meets specific requirements (i.e. age, interests etc.). In this way, it is relatively easy for a therapist e.g. to set up a group with common interests, such as eating disorder or other mental illnesses. Some SHs have a feature called "web tour" that is very interesting for the possibility given to the therapist to provide patients who are not familiar with search/surf techniques in the Internet with relevant information tailored to their needs [34].

The next section provides a detailed description of the main features of most common SHs. In order to put the description of these software on a concrete basis, two possible scenarios are identified for their potential use in psychotherapy. According to the first scenario, the end-user (patient) can use a high-bandwidth internet connection (> 56 Kbps) and a middle/high-level PC workstation. According to the second scenario, the end-user can use only low-bandwidth internet connection (56 Kbps) and an entry-level workstation. For each scenario is provided a selection of the most suitable software along with an analysis of the application's technical specifications, the system's requirements, the estimated costs and the user-interface features. Furthermore, the main pros and cons of each application are discussed.

13.3.6.1 Scenario 1: high-bandwidth connection (> 56 Kbps), middle-high level PC workstation

According to the first scenario, the end-user (patient) can use:

- A PC workstation equipped with a Pentium III-IV-Athlon (1.3 Ghz or better) processor or equivalent, at least 20 GB hard disk, at least 256 MB RAM memory, graphic card with at least 32 MB memory, full-duplex sound card (price: 2000-2500 Euros)
- A USB Web-Cam, headset, speakers, microphone (price: about 150 Euro);
- ISDN connection or faster (price variable depending on the Internet Service Provider)

This equipment supports the use of advanced (video) Shared Hypermedia Tools. As, we have seen before, these tools enable different users, who are simultaneously browsing the same website, to communicate with each other through audio/video conferencing and share files or web addresses. In the following section a description of the main features of these tools is provided, along with a critical evaluation of their functionalities and usability.

13.3.6.1.1   Microsoft NetMeeting 3.0

13.3.6.1.1.1   Developer and web-site
Microsoft Corporation (http://www.microsoft.com/windows/NetMeeting)

13.3.6.1.1.2   System's requirements
For Windows 95, Windows 98, or Windows Me, a Pentium II processor with 128 MB of RAM (recommended). ISDN, or LAN connection. Sound card with microphone and speakers (sound card required for both audio and video support). Video capture card or camera that provides a Video for Windows capture driver (required for video support).

13.3.6.1.1.3   Features
NetMeeting is a freeware shared hypermedia tool developed and distributed by Microsoft Corp. NetMeeting delivers a complete Internet conferencing solution for all Windows users with multi-point data conferencing, text chat, whiteboard, and file transfer, as well as point-to-point audio and video. The following features are supported by the release 3.0: Video/audio conferencing, Remote desktop sharing, Program sharing, Whiteboard, Chat, File Transfer and Advanced security setting.

13.3.6.1.1.4   Video/Audio conferencing
Using the feature of video/audio conferencing, the user can share ideas by talking with a remote user, send and receive real-time video images and send video and audio to a user who doesn't have video hardware.

13.3.6.1.1.5   Remote desktop sharing

Remote Desktop Sharing allows the user operating a computer from a remote location. Users activate the feature, then close NetMeeting - the feature doesn't work if NetMeeting is open. Remote sharing also only works with secure calls, and there is password protection.

13.3.6.1.1.6   Program sharing

Application sharing provides the ability to give control of a program to callers who don't have that program on their computer. Only one user can control an application at a time, and if "Controllable" appears in the title bar of the shared application, then callers know that the application is available for them to control. Other application sharing features include the ability to "unshare" specific programs or to "unshare" all programs, a feature for automatically accepting control requests or for requiring manual acceptance, and a "do-not-disturb" feature for temporarily disabling non-host control without actually switching the feature off. Users who have been granted control by the host can pass control to other users, as long as they are also using version 3.0, and the host can take control again at any time.

13.3.6.1.1.7   Whiteboard

With the Whiteboard, the user can review, create, and update graphic information, manipulate contents by clicking, dragging, and dropping information on the whiteboard with the mouse, cut, copy and paste information from any Windows-based application into the Whiteboard. Whiteboard pages can be saved and loaded in a second time, enabling the user to prepare information before a conference, then drag and drop it into the Whiteboard during a meeting.

13.3.6.1.1.8   Chat

Using the chat feature, the user can type text messages to communicate with other people during a conference and chat with one person or a group of people across multiple computers. The "Whisper" mode allows sending private messages with another person during a group chat session. The contents of the dialogue can be saved from the chat session to a file for future reference.

13.3.6.1.1.9   File Transfer

The feature "file transfer" enables the user to send a file in the background to conference participants. The file can be sent to everyone in the conference, or to one or more selected participants. The transferred files can be accepted or rejected.

13.3.6.1.1.10 Advanced security setting

Security is an important feature of NetMeeting 3.0. At the basic level, all calls can be secure or non-secure, which is the default setting. Options for secure calls include data encryption, certificate authentication, and password protection, but in secure calls, the audio and video options are disabled. In meetings, all calls are either secure or non-secure; calls between meeting participants can not be of different types. Another security option that's unique to meetings is the host's ability to limit what features participants can enact.

For example, meeting hosts can disable the right of anyone but themselves to begin any of the six main features (application sharing, text chat, audio, white boarding, file sharing, and video), and hosts can make themselves the only participant who can invite or accept others into the meeting. Hosts can also enable meeting names and - finally - meeting passwords.

Fig. 13. 1 Screenshot of Netmeeting's Whiteboard

13.3.6.1.2 Paltalk

13.3.6.1.2.1   Developer and Web-Site
Paltalk (www.paltalk.com)

13.3.6.1.2.2   System's requirements
Windows 95/98/NT4/2000, Pentium 120 MHz, 64 MB RAM (recommended 128 MB), Internet Explorer 4.0, ISDN or LAN connection. Sound card with microphone and speakers, USB video camera.

13.3.6.1.2.3   Features
Paltalk is a freeware tool that combines the functionality of an instant messaging and internet telephony. The user can create his/her personal contacts-list and know who is online at any time. Anyone who has access to a PC and the Internet can make local and long distance calls for free, or simply chat with other people. The installation process is easy and does not require the user to fill in private information. The configuration wizard lets the user set the microphone in an intuitive way. Further features supported by Paltalk are the following:

13.3.6.1.2.4   Video/audio conferencing
Using the feature of video/audio conferencing, the user can share ideas by talking with a remote user, send and receive real-time video images and send video and audio to a user who doesn't have video hardware.

13.3.6.1.2.5   Voice mail
The user can record and send voice-mail messages. This feature is useful when the user is offline and another user is trying to contact him/her.

13.3.6.1.2.6   Hand rising
For moderated groups, the Administrator can control the microphone, and the participants can click the "raise the hand" to ask a question or add comments. This feature enables constructive discussions with a large number of people.

13.3.6.1.2.7   Group voice
The user can join ongoing group voice discussions or create a forum of his/her own.

In the next section some screen-shots of Paltalk are provided in order to illustrate the main features of this software.

13.3.6.1.2.8   Contacts list / Control Panel
The user can use this screen to access many of the features in Paltalk. For example, the user can see who is online and offline and can call them by double clicking on their name. The user can also see a group list by clicking on the Groups button.

13.3.6.1.2.9   One-to-One Video Screen
This is the screen used to communicate with another Paltalk user. The interface enables text chat, voice or video communication.

13.3.6.1.3 Eyeball chat

13.3.6.1.3.1   Developer and Web-Site
Eyeball Networks (www.eyeball.com)

13.3.6.1.3.2   System's requirements
Windows 98, ME or 2000; Microsoft DirectX 7.0, Pentium 166 MHz, at least 64 MB RAM (128 MB recommended), Internet Explorer 4.0, ISDN or LAN connection. Sound card with microphone and speakers, USB video camera.

13.3.6.1.3.3   Features
Eyeball is a shared hypermedia tool that enables distance communication by using different channels, as video, audio and text messages. The quality of video is high, even using a slow internet connection. Another interesting feature of this software is the user-friendliness of the interface, which requires a relatively short learning time. Eyeball chat can be used either as video-chat or video-messenger communication tool. This last feature allows the user to send and receive video-messages and it is useful especially when the other users are temporarily offline.

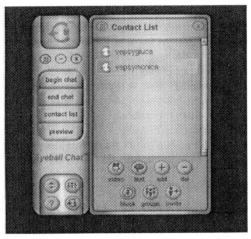

Fig. 13.2 Screenshot of Eyeball's main menu

Furthermore, the software enables the user to optimise the configuration of the hardware supporting video communication. In fact, it is possible to give more or less weight to the image quality, frame-rate and audio fidelity, so that each user can define the most suitable configuration according to his/her needs. The video quality is dynamically and automatically optimised according to the bandwidth and the computational power available at any moment. The contacts list shows the users online, who can be directly contacted by selecting their nickname with the mouse. The graphic interface can be positioned everywhere in the screen and overlapped to other applications. This makes it possible to keep on working with other applications during the chat-session. Moreover, the web-version of the software allows the user to begin a chat session directly from the web browser. This feature is useful, for example, when the user needs to access the service from other locations. Of particular interest, finally, is the group video chat. The group video chat enables multiple users to share ideas and sending and receiving real-time video images.

13.3.6.2 Scenario II: slow bandwidth, entry-level workstation

According to the second scenario, the end-user (patient) has:

- A PC workstation equipped with at least a Celeron 800/Pentium III 800/Duron 800 processor, 10 GB Hard Disk, graphic card with at least 16 MB memory, sound card, at least 64 MB RAM memory (price: 700-1000 Euros)
- Headset, speakers, microphone (price: about 50 Euro);
- 56 Kbps internet connection.

This equipment supports the use of simple (text/voice) Shared Hypermedia Tools. The tools most suited to this equipment are the *Instant Messengers (IM)*. These applications have one common feature: they allow users, who are simultaneously online, to send each other's text messages in real time. From a technical point of view, the underlying mechanism is the same: after the connection to the internet, the user is assigned with a numerical address. Then the software connects to its own network and communicates the system which IP address has been assigned to the user. In this way, a direct connection between two users is enabled.

Most IMs provide the user with the option to decide his/her *status* (i.e. online, offline, away, etc.) and the degree of privacy he/she wishes to maintain. In this way, one can either communicate with the users who are included in the contacts list, or be visible to all users of the network. If compared with standard e-mail client applications, the added value of the IMs is that such applications enable the users to know whether friends or colleagues are simultaneously online and, in this last case, to communicate with them instantaneously.

Another common feature of most IMs is represented by their low complexity. In fact, these software can be easily integrated both in the desktop (by an icon in the system tray) and in other software. Actually, such tools are conceived primarily to remain active while the user keeps on working with other applications.

In order to evaluate the potential of the IMs for a clinical application, issues such as user-friendliness, simplicity of use, facility of contacts management, compatibility with other systems, richness of features and network's stability are examined in detail.

13.3.6.2.1   AOL Instant Messenger

13.3.6.2.1.1   Developer and Web-Site
America Online Corporation (http://www.aol.com/aim)

13.3.6.2.1.2   System's requirements
Internet Explorer 4.5, Internet connection, Pentium I processor or higher, 16 MB RAM, 5 MB Hard Disk, sound card with microphone and speakers, Windows 95, 98, o NT, Microsoft Virtual Machine.

13.3.6.2.1.3   Features

The interface of this IM is represented by an icon in the system tray and a window, which displays the contacts list. The contacts list can be easily organized by categories. A useful feature is the possibility to check new e-mail messages on multiple accounts, which can be set in the "general options" panel. In addition, AIM can automatically check the incoming mail and the user is informed as soon as a new e-mail message is downloaded. Other communication features are:

- sending and receiving e-mail messages;
- text chat;
- voice chat;
- telephone calling over IP (PC to PC and PC to telephone)

There is also an "express" version of AIM available, which can be loaded from the web browser. The main cons of AIM are that this IM comes with few features and that its user interface is too essential.

13.3.6.2.2 ICQ

13.3.6.2.2.1 Developer and Web-Site
Icq Inc. (www.icq.com)

13.3.6.2.2.2 System's requirements
Internet Explorer 4.5, Internet connection, Pentium I processor or higher, 8 MB RAM, sound card with microphone and speakers, Windows 95, 98, o NT.

13.3.6.2.2.3 Features
ICQ is a widespread IM with over 100 million downloads since its launch, five years ago.

The program's kernel is the messages management system, which is represented by the classic icon in the system tray. The messages management system is linked to the control panel, which collects the main features of the application. The control panel can be displayed in two modalities: *advanced* and *simple*.

The *simple* modality displays the basic features only, which are the *contacts list* and *messages management*. The *advanced* modality allows the user to configure his/her *status*: online, offline, standby, etc. A sound and a flashing icon announce the incoming messages.

Further features provided by this application are: sharing file and web-addresses, sending and receiving e-mail messages, sending chat request, sending contacts list, voice chat and telephone over IP. ICQ represents an effective choice especially for those users who need to efficiently coordinate the communication between many people, especially if they are working in different geographical locations. Furthermore, ICQ provides the web-site administrators with the opportunity to include in the home page a real communication centre, which allows the visitor to contact the web-site administrator in real time. In conclusion, ICQ is a very interesting application, rich of features and well organized. The main drawback of this software is represented by the user interface, which is a bit complex and not easy to learn, especially for novices.

13.3.6.2.3   MSN Messenger

13.3.6.2.3.1 Developer and Web-Site
Microsoft Corporation (www.msn.com)

13.3.6.2.3.2   System's requirements

Internet connection, Microsoft Internet Explorer 4.0, Netscape Navigator 4.0, Pentium I processor or higher, full-duplex sound card with microphone and speakers, 8 MB RAM, 2 MB Hard Disk, Windows 95, 98, Me, 2000, NT 4.0.

13.3.6.2.3.3   Features

MSN Messenger Service is an easy way to take advantage of the full power of instant messaging. It is a simple, not invasive application that allows the users to exchange messages with friends or colleagues, but only if they are also registered users. The range of services offered by this IM is reduced to the minimum, and consequently the user interface results very simplified. Installing MSN is easy: on Windows 98, the entire program installs in just a few seconds, even while several applications are open, and it requires just one reboot. The MSN icon, always active in the system tray, indicates the *status* of the user (online, offline, busy, away etc.) and when the icon is double-clicked a window pops up and displays the contacts list. The window is the kernel of MSN, and it allows the user to manage the contacts list, to change *status* and to check the incoming mail. The incoming messages are automatically announced by a sound and by a small-sized window that pops out and provides a brief description of the message's features. Further features of MSN are:

-   searching contacts by using Microsoft Passport™
-   sending instant messages
-   sharing file
-   telephone over IP
-   voice chat
-   sending SMS (this service is limited to devices registered at msn.com)

In conclusion, MSN messenger is well-suited for a professional use, thanks to its simplicity and its high stability.

13.3.6.2.4 Odigo

13.3.6.2.4.1   Developer and Web-Site

NovaWiz (www.odigo.com)

13.3.6.2.4.2   System's requirements

Internet connection, Pentium I processor or higher, full-duplex sound card with microphone and speakers, Windows 95, 98, Me, 2000, NT.

13.3.6.2.4.3   Features

Odigo is a IM application easy to use and features-rich. Installing Odigo is easy and the installation can be customized, so that the user can choose which features are to be downloaded. The registration process is included in the installation, and it does not require to exit from the wizard. An icon placed in the system tray represents the basic interface.

Double-clicking on this icon can activate the control panel. The appearance of the window of the control panel can be customized and the user can choose between several different *skins*. An unique feature of Odigo is the possibility to define the "mood": in fact, the user can choose the *emoticon* that fits best according to his/her current mood (i.e. happy, tired, bored, etc.). Odigo's kernel is represented by the *Communication Centre*, the dialog window that allows the management of the messages and of the other communication options.

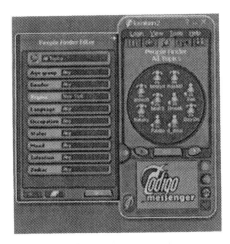

Fig. 13.3 Screenshot of Odigo

The *Communication Centre* is divided in two parts. The upper part tracks the text of the dialogue, while messages are written in the lower part. The *Communication Centre* is also the control panel of the other program's features, which include file sharing, text/voice chat, and co-surf. This last characteristic of Odigo is very intriguing, because it allows two or more users to co-surf simultaneously in the same web-site. Furthermore, Odigo can be interfaced with other IMs (ICQ, AIM, Yahoo Messenger) by downloading and installing the appropriate plug-ins. However, a drawback of this application is that the user is burdened by communication requests coming from all over the world, and there is no way to reduce the visibility to the rest of the community. Another drawback is that the Odigo displays continuously commercial banners tailored to the user's profile.

13.3.6.2.5 Yahoo Messenger

13.3.6.2.5.1   Developer and Web-Site
Yahoo Inc. (http://messenger.yahoo.com)

13.3.6.2.5.2   System's requirements
Internet connection, Pentium I processor or higher, full-duplex sound card with microphone and speakers, Windows 95, 98, Me, 2000, NT.

13.3.6.2.5.3   Features
Yahoo Messenger is a very simple application full integrated with the services of the web-portal yahoo.com. The installation process is easy but requires the registration to the Yahoo! services. YM offers two different modalities of use of its services: the YM *window*, which gives access to all the application's tools, and the YM *browser*, which is direct linked with all the services offered by the web-portal yahoo.com. The application allows the user to create and to organize a personal contacts list, which can be upgraded at any time. To add new contacts to the list, there is a search tool integrated into the web-portal that offers advanced search options, i.e. searching a new contact by name, by keyword or simply by nickname. The incoming messages are automatically announced by a sound and by a small-sized window that pops out and provides a brief description of the message's features. The communication features include text chat and voice mail.

Tab. 13.4 Synoptic chart of software features, system's requirements and usability

Software	Features	Usability	System's requirements
NetMeeting	• Video/audio conferencing; • Files/programs sharing; • Desktop sharing; • Whiteboard; • Text chat.	User interface: easy Learning rate: fast	Win 95, Win 98, or Win Me, Pentium II processor with 128 MB of RAM (recommended). 10 MB of free hard disk space, ISDN or LAN connection. Sound card with microphone and speakers. Video capture card or camera that provides a Video for Windows capture driver (required for video support).
Paltalk	• Video/audio conferencing; • Voice mail; • Text chat; • Voice chat.	User interface: easy Learning rate: fast	Win 95/98/NT4/2000, Pentium 120 MHz, 64 MB RAM (recommended 128 MB), Internet Explorer 4.0, ISDN or LAN connection. Sound card with microphone and speakers, USB video camera.
Eyeball chat	• Video/audio conferencing; • Group video conferencing; • Video mail; • Text chat.	User interface: easy Learning rate: fast	Win 98, ME or 2000; Microsoft DirectX 7.0, Pentium 166 MHz, at least 64 MB RAM (128 MB recommended), Internet Explorer 4.0, ISDN or LAN connection. Sound card with microphone and speakers, USB video camera.
AOL Instant Messenger	• E-mail; • Text chat; • Voice chat; • Telephone over IP.	User interface: easy Learning rate: fast	Internet Explorer 4.5, Internet connection, Pentium I processor or higher, 16 MB RAM, 5 MB Hard Disk, sound card with microphone and speakers, Windows 95, 98, o NT, Microsoft Virtual Machine.
ICQ	• File sharing; • E-mail; • Text chat; • Contacts list sharing; • Voice chat; • Telephone over IP; • SMS.	User interface: complex Learning rate: slow	Internet Explorer 4.5, Internet connection, Pentium I processor or higher, 8 MB RAM, sound card with microphone and speakers, Windows 95, 98, o NT.
MSN Messenger	• File sharing; • Telephone over IP; • Voice chat; • SMS.	User interface: easy Learning rate: fast	Internet connection, Microsoft Internet Explorer 4.0, Netscape Navigator 4.0, Pentium I processor or higher, full-duplex sound card with microphone and speakers, 8 MB RAM, 2 MB Hard Disk, Windows 95, 98, Me, 2000, NT 4.0.
Odigo	• File sharing; • Text chat; • Contacts list sharing; • Voice chat; • Web co-surf; • SMS.	User interface: easy Learning rate: slow	Internet connection, Pentium I processor or higher, full-duplex sound card with microphone and speakers, Windows 95, 98, Me, 2000, NT.
Yahoo Messenger	• Voice mail; • Text chat; • Organizer; • File sharing.	User interface: easy Learning rate: fast	Internet connection, Pentium I processor or higher, full-duplex sound card with microphone and speakers, Windows 95, 98, Me, 2000, NT.

Tab. 13.5 The audio/video quality of the software has been assessed by using an Acer Travelmate 521TE, OS Win. 98, equipped with ATI Rage 8 MB AGP video card, full-duplex sound card, 128 MB SDRAM memory, Pentium III 800 MHz processor. Quality rates (1 = low; 2 = acceptable; 3 = high) are strictly related to the available bandwidth.

Software	Bandwidth	Audio Quality	Video Quality
NetMeeting	< 56 Kbps	2	1
	> 56 Kbps	3	2
Paltalk	< 56 Kbps	1	1
	> 56 Kbps	2	2
Eyeball Chat	< 56 Kbps	1	2
	>56 Kbps	1	3
AOL Messenger	< 56 Kbps	1	-
	> 56 Kbps	2	-
ICQ	< 56 Kbps	1	-
	> 56 Kbps	3	-
MSN Messenger	< 56 Kbps	2	-
	> 56 Kbps	3	-
Odigo	< 56 Kbps	2	-
	> 56 Kbps	3	-
Yahoo Messenger	< 56 Kbps	1	-
	> 56 Kbps	2	-

Finally, an interesting characteristic of YM is the virtual organizer, which can be used to schedule activities and to fix appointments. The virtual organizer can be shared with other users by selecting them in the contacts list.

In conclusion, YM is a very effective shared hypermedia tool particularly suited for workgroups. The main drawback of YM is the lack of the voice chat, which has become a standard feature in most IMs.

13.4 The use of e-therapy in mental health care: The possible future

13.4.1 How to integrate shared hypermedia in the clinical procedure

Taken together, the results of this review suggest that shared hypermedia are well-suited for a telemedicine application in psychotherapy [33]. However, the real effectiveness of such tools depends largely on the ability of therapists to coherently integrate the features of SHs in the clinical procedure.

For this reason, it would be useful to provide the reader with some insights regarding potential ways of using SHs in psychotherapy. The following considerations are not meant to be exhaustive, rather to stimulate the creativity and the curiosity of mental health professionals who are particularly interested in promoting new solutions for using Internet related technologies in the clinical practice.

By using SHs, the therapist and the patient are able to share pictures, screenshots and videos captured by a video camera installed on their workstations and to communicate their ideas and impressions using both the text chat and voice chat features. The "application sharing" feature enables the therapist to send to the patient a psychometric questionnaire for assessment purposes and receive the result in real time. Consequently, the therapist is able to provide the patient with a feedback in a fraction of the time that this process normally requires.

Remote desktop sharing is a powerful new feature which, when perfected, could allow the therapist to help novice patients to configure their system remotely. The "virtual whiteboard" is another interesting feature that has promising applications. For example, the therapist can use the whiteboard to enrich his/her explanations with diagrams and drafts, which can be exported to other applications. Finally, the text-chat feature allows the therapist to save the content of the dialogue as text file, making it available for future reference.

Less complex SHs (IMs) represents an acceptable compromise between simplicity of use and richness of communication features. Although few exceptions, IMs have a very intuitive and easy-to-learn interface. This last feature is very important, because it makes IMs well-suited also for end-users who are not very familiar with Internet technologies.

Another advantage of most IMs is that therapist can send the patient a request for a communication session using either the IM feature (if the patient is online and logged in) or the e-mail. Once the session is open, the therapist can chat with the patient privately or in group, by sending a request to the other patients that are online at that moment. In some IMs, the users can rapidly move from the text chat to the voice chat, which has often a valuable quality even if the users are using a slow connection (56 Kbps). Furthermore, even using simple IMs applications the therapist is able to send the patients files (i.e. assessment questionnaires) and to receive the results even within the same session.

13.4.2   How to evaluate the effectiveness of Shared Hypermedia as Telemedicine tools

The clinical effectiveness of telemedicine tools can be measured and compared at several levels. In fact, it is possible to look for effects on the process care or for effects on the outcomes of care or both [3]. Fineberg and colleagues [48] distinguish several process and outcome dimensions that might appropriately be assessed by evaluators. According to these authors, these dimensions include:

- Technical capacity – whether a technology is safe, accurate, and reliable;
- Diagnostic accuracy – whether a technology contributes to a correct diagnosis;
- Diagnostic impact – whether a technology provides diagnostic information that is useful in making a diagnosis (e.g., after the telemedicine consult, is face-to-face consultation still necessary?);
- Therapeutic impact – whether a technology influences patient management or therapy;
- Patient outcome – whether a technology improves patients' health and well-being.

Could the clinical effectiveness of SHs be assessed by using such dimensions? In order to answer this question, a point-to-point analysis is needed.

Technical capacity

The technical capacity of SHs is well demonstrated. In fact, these software are developed for commercial purposes and are conceived for massive distribution (actually most of them are freeware or shareware) over the Internet. They are first intended to be effective, safe, accurate and reliable communication tools. Their success - and that of the developer - depends primarily on these aspects, including human-interface and ergonomic issues. Of course, there are some differences concerning the degree to which each particular SH meets these requirements (i.e., not all SHs have a user-friendly interface).

Diagnostic accuracy and diagnostic impact

This issue is strictly dependent on the type of hypermedia that the mental health professional might choose. However, there are boundaries to the accuracy with which SHs can be used for diagnostic purposes. Despite of the great range of communication features that characterize most of these software, they can not remotely convey the richness of information (verbal and non verbal) provided by direct, face to face (f2f) interaction. The real challenge for SHs is to allow the remote reconstruction of the clinical setting.

Therapeutic impact
The therapeutic impact of SHs could be very significant. In fact, such tools have the potential to influence both patient management and therapy. This forecast is supported by the observation that simpler Internet-related technologies (i.e. e-mail or text-chat) have significantly and positively affected the outcomes of mental health sessions [e-mail in eating, etc.].

Patient outcome
Up to now, the majority of programs that have applied Internet related technologies for the treatment of mental disorders have encountered positive, if not even enthusiastic, reactions by patients. This is not sufficient, of course, to demonstrate whether this technology (and related ones, like SHs) can really improve patients' health and well-being. To our knowledge, the only ongoing project that is currently experimenting SHs-based telemedicine solutions for clinical psychology is the EU-funded VEPSY Updated (Telemedicine and Portable Virtual Environments for Clinical Psychology) project (IST-25323 – http://www.vepsy.com). However, there are several studies in different therapeutic areas that reported significant improvements of patient who were included in Internet-supported therapy programs [Yager, Murdock, King e Moreggi]. So, although there is still a lack of experimental and clinical outcomes evidencing the effectiveness of SHs in psychotherapy, these preliminary results are encouraging.

13.5 Conclusion

The emergence of e-therapy could have a strong effect on mental health care. As we have seen, the key characteristic of e-therapy is the use of shared media. Using the Internet, therapists can present, from a remote site, a wide variety of stimuli and to measure and monitor a wide variety of responses made by the user. In the near future psychotherapists will probably use e-therapy tools that support advanced communicational features like real time video connections, audio, exchange of text and video messages etc. From this point of view, shared hypermedia tools represent the evolution and the natural candidate to replace email and telephone, which are currently the most widespread telehealth tools [33].

However, at this stage, there are different short-comings that delimit the potential of this approach. The main problem is non-technical and is related to the personal and organizational changes needed to introduce e-therapy in healthcare organizations [35].

Although the introduction of shared media has been successful and become accepted practice in many areas of industry, traditional methods have tended to prevail in health-care. Telehealth and e-therapy have been adopted by enthusiasts who recognize the potential benefits of these new media. However, the more widespread introduction of e-therapy requires considerable organizational change in the way health-care is delivered [36]. This requires a modification of established factors such as consultations and referral patterns, ways of payment, specialist support for primary healthcare, co-operation between primary and secondary healthcare, defining geographical catchment areas and the "ownership" of the patients [37].

A further problem is the technology of e-therapy. Actual technology – hardware, software and transmission – is far from perfect [38]: insufficient image quality, low framing rate, flickering and delays makes working in front of a video terminal unattractive and in particular very tiring.

Fortunately the quality of technology in this area is increasing while costs are falling down. Prices are declining by about 25 per cent per year [39]. Simple telephone-based videoconferencing system are now available for under $500 while high quality board-based ISDN systems can cost less than $1000. New transmission technologies, including Digital Subscriber Line (xDSL) and cable modem, promise to provide order-of-magnitude increases in dependable bandwidth for a small increment of price. For the success of e-therapy applications widespread access to the Internet is also required. Many applications currently demand only moderate bandwidth and latency, meaning that standard modem access to the Internet, at 28.8 to 56 kbit/s may suffice.

A recent research evaluated a low-bandwidth e-health system in eight community hospitals connected to a central hospital via the Internet. PCs were used with videoconferencing software and modem connections to the telephone network. Even if the average live video frame rate was 1 frame/sec. (at the best image quality), with an average latency of 3 seconds, the results suggested that Internet-based videoconferencing is acceptable for certain telemedicine applications [40]. Successful results with a limited bandwidth have also been obtained by an e-health teleconsultation application developed in Croatia: a 33 kbit/s link was established between a team of specialists in the General Hospital 'Sveti Duh' in Zagreb and a general practitioner's clinic in Selca, on the island of Brac using $700 computer systems [41]. Another relevant issue is that of ensuring equitable access to health resources by different demographic groups. There are already considerable differences in access to health care in the world. Ensuring that differential access to the Internet along demographic lines does not exacerbate this imbalance could become an increasingly important issue, especially if the provision of health care moves online [42].

Security and legal protection are two more key issues for the diffusion of e-therapy [43, 44]. In fact this approach involves three fundamental types of relationship [45] in which a duty is owed by one party to another: the relationship between the clinician and the patient, the relationship between clinicians and the relationship between the provider of the telemedicine system and the user. The situation may be complicated by the involvement of multiple clinicians and/or the providers of the telemedicine systems (call centres, telecommunications network, etc). As noted by Stanberry [45], if "a patient is harmed during a teleconsultation (the healthcare centre) could choose to name a number of these organisations or individuals as defendants to a legal action for negligence if it is unclear what went wrong or where responsibilities are" (p. 24). Moreover e-therapy can hide severe privacy and security risks, because patient data and hospital data stored on a secure Intranet can be manipulated by connecting it to the Web. This is even truer for e-mail consulting. Most e-mail exchanges between patient and provider involve discussions of personal health information, which must be suitably protected from breaches of confidentiality and, to a lesser extent, alteration [46]. However the establishing of a firewall and the introduction of HPC (Health Professional Card) can drastically reduce the risk of un-authorized access to the hospital server. For secure e-mail, PGP (Pretty Good Privacy) can be easily used as a standard protocol [43]. In general, planning all activities exactly as well as introducing advanced form of data protection are important requisites for reduction of security risks in Internet [47].

To spread the diffusion of e-therapy, further research is needed. More evaluation is required of clinical outcomes, organizational effects, benefits to health-care providers and users, and quality assurance. The absence of empirical research at this time makes it impossible to objectively evaluate the benefits and the efficacy of e-therapy [5]. Each Internet technology requires thoughtful and flexible research, legislation, and ethical guidelines to make it safe and effective as a service delivery vehicle. As clearly underlined by Maheu and Gordon, "it is crucial for professional psychologists to give proper attention to empirical research and current standards of practice before attempting to deliver counselling or psychotherapy via the Internet" (p. 489). It is also very important that professionals in this field share information about their experience and examine the results of evaluations so that the suitable development work can be speeded up.

13.6 References

[1] L. W. Jerome and C. Zaylor, Cyberspace: Creating a therapeutic environment for telehealth applications, *Professional Psychology: Research and Practice* 31 (2000) 478-483.

[2] D. Nickelson, Telehealth and the evolving health care system: strategic opportunities for professional psychology, *Professional Psychology: Research and Practice* 29 (1998) 527-535.

[3] R. Wootton, European Telemedicine 1998/99. London: Kensington Publications Ltd, 1999.

[4] A. Allen, When the ship comes in, *Telemedicine Today* 7 (1999) 7.

[5] M. M. Maheu and B. L. Gordon, Counseling and therapy on the Internet, *Professional Psychology: Research and Practice* 31 (2000) 484-489.

[6] L. W. Jerome, P. H. DeLeon, L. C. James, R. Folen, J. Earles, and J. J. Gedney, The coming of age of telecommunications in psychological research and practice, *American Psychologist* 55 (2000) 407-21.

[7] G. Riva, The mind in the Web: Psychology in the Internet age, *CyberPsychology and Behavior* 4 (2001) 1-6.

[8] B. H. Stamm, Clinical applications of telehealth in mental health care, *Professional Psychology: Research and Practice* 29 (1998) 536-542.

[9] B. Klein and J. C. Richards, A brief Internet-based treatment for panic disorder, *Behavioural & Cognitive Psychotherapy* 29 (2001) 113-117.

[10] C. Botella, R. M. Banos, H. Villa, C. Perpina, and A. Garcia-Palacios, Telepsychology: Public speaking fear treatment on the internet, *CyberPsychology and Behavior* 3 (2000) 959-968.

[11] J. W. Murdoch and P. A. Connor-Greene, Enhancing therapeutic impact and therapeutic alliance through electronic mail homework assignments, *Journal of Psychotherapy Practice & Research* 9 (2000) 232-237.

[12] J. Yager, E-mail as a therapeutic adjunct in the outpatient treatment of anorexia nervosa: Illustrative case material and discussion of the issues, *International Journal of Eating Disorders* 29 (2001) 125-138.

[13] S. Bouchard, R. Payeur, V. Rivard, M. Allard, B. Paquin, P. Renaud, and L. Goyer, Cognitive behavior therapy for panic disorder with agoraphobia in videoconference: Preliminary results, *CyberPsychology and Behavior* 3 (2000) 999-1007.

[14] F. Scogin, J. Bynum, G. Stevens, and S. Calhoon, Efficacy of self-administered treatment programs: Meta-analytic review, *Professional Psychology: Research and Practice* 21 (1990) 42-47.

[15] V. Prasad and D. Owens, Using the Internet as a source of self-help for people who self-harm, *Psychiatric Bulletin* 25 (2001) 222-225.

[16] C. E. Tucker-Ladd, *Psychological self-help*. online: http://mentalhelp.net/psyhelp/: Mental Health Net, 2000.

[17] K. Humphreys, A. Winzelberg, and E. Klaw, Psychologists' ethical responsibilities in the Internet-based groups: Issues, strategies, and a call for dialogue, *Professional Psychology: Research and Practice* 31 (2000) 493-496.

[18] E. J. Madara, Maximizing the potential for community self-help through clearinghouse approaches, *Prevention in Human Services* 7 (1990) 109-138.

[19] S. A. King and D. Moreggi, Internet therapy and self-help groups-the pros and cons, in *Psychology and the Internet: Intrapersonal, interpersonal, and transpersonal implication*, J. Gackenbach, Ed. San Diego, CA: Academic Press, 1998, pp. 77-109.

[20] R. C. Hsiung, The best of both worlds: An online self-help group hosted by a mental health professional, *CyberPsychology and Behavior* 3 (2000) 935-950.

[21] M. F. Zabinski, M. A. Pung, D. E. Wilfley, D. L. Eppstein, A. J. Winzelberg, A. Celio, and C. B. Taylor, Reducing risk factors for eating disorders: Targeting at-risk women with a computerized psychoeducational program, *International Journal of Eating Disorders* 29 (2001) 401-8.

[22] A. A. Celio, A. J. Winzelberg, D. E. Wilfley, D. Eppstein-Herald, E. A. Springer, P. Dev, and C. B. Taylor, Reducing risk factors for eating disorders: comparison of an Internet- and a classroom-delivered psychoeducational program, *Journal of Consulting & Clinical Psychology* 68 (2000) 650-7.

[23] K. A. Dyer and C. D. Thompson, Internet use for Web-education on the overlooked areas of grief and loss, *CyberPsychology and Behavior* 3 (2000) 255-270.

[24] L. Stroem, R. Pettersson, and G. Andersson, A controlled trial of self-help treatment of recurrent headache conducted via the Internet, *Journal of Consulting & Clinical Psychology* 68 (2000) 722-727.

[25]   L. D. Rosen and M. M. Weil, Psychologists and technology: A look at the future, *Professional Psychology: Research and Practice* 27 (1996) 635-638.

[26]   G. Riva and C. Galimberti, Computer-mediated communication: identity and social interaction in an electronic environment, *Genetic, Social and General Psychology Monographs* 124 (1998) 434-464.

[27]   G. Riva and C. Galimberti, The psychology of cyberspace: a socio-cognitive framework to computer mediated communication, *New Ideas in Psychology* 15 (1997) 141-158.

[28]   J. R. Suler, Psychotherapy in Cyberspace: A 5-dimensional model of online and computer-mediated psychotherapy., *CyberPsychology and Behavior* 3 (2000) 151-159.

[29]   S. M. Borowitz and J. C. Wyatt, The origin, content, and workload of email consultations, *Journal of the American Medical Association* 280 (1988) 1321-1324.

[30]   G. J. Ghosh, P. M. McLaren, and J. P. Watson, Evaluating the alliance in video-link teletherapy, *Journal of Telemedicine and Telecare* 3 (1997) 33-35.

[31]   J. V. Hill, L. R. Allman, and T. F. Ditzler, Utility of real-time video teleconferencing in conducting family mental health sessions: two case reports, *Telemedicine Journal and e-Health* 7 (2001) 55-59.

[32]   P.-A. Federico, Hypermedia environments and adaptive instructions, *Computers in Human Behavior* 15 (1999) 653-692.

[33]   G. Riva, From Telehealth to E-health: Internet and distributed virtual reality in health care, *CyberPsychology & Behavior* 3 (2000) 989-998.

[34]   G. Riva, Shared Hypermedia: Communication and interaction in Web-based learning environments, *Journal of Educational Computing Research* 25 (2001) 205-226.

[35]   E. J. Cardno, Managing the 'fit' of information and communication technology in community health: a framework for decision making, *J Telemed Telecare* 6 (2000) S6-8.

[36]   K. Birch, M. Rigby, and R. Roberts, Putting the 'tele' into health-care effectively, *J Telemed Telecare* 6 (2000) S113-5.

[37]   S. Olsson and J. Calltrop, Telemedicine: a tool for organisational and structural change in healthcare, in *European Telemedicine 1998/99*, R. Wootton, Ed. London: Kensington Publications Ltd, 1999, pp. 26.

[38]   S. L. Lou, H. D. Lin, K. P. Lin, and D. Hoogstrate, Automatic breast region extraction from digital mammograms for PACS and telemammography applications, *Comput Med Imaging Graph* 24 (2000) 205-20.

[39]   A. Allen, Telemedicine: a global perspective, in *European Telemedicine 1998/99*, R. Wootton, Ed. London: Kensington Publications Ltd, 1999, pp. 13-15.

[40]   E. D. Lemaire, Y. Boudrias, and G. Greene, Technical evaluation of a low-bandwidth, Internet-based system for teleconsultations, *J Telemed Telecare* 6 (2000) 163-7.

[41]   V. Ostojic, A. Stipic-Markovic, Z. Tudman, N. Zivkovic, B. Cvoriscec, T. Trajbar, C. L. Donnelly, M. Grgic, P. Matek, M. Lusic, and M. Iskra, A feasibility study of realtime telemedicine in Croatia using Internet videoconferencing, *J Telemed Telecare* 6 (2000) 172-6.

[42]   E. H. Shortliffe, Networking health: Prescriptions for the Internet. Washington, DC: National Academy Press, 2000.

[43]   K. DeVille and J. Fitzpatrick, Ready or not, here it comes: the legal, ethical, and clinical implications of E-mail communications, *Semin Pediatr Surg* 9 (2000) 24-34.

[44]   W. R. Hirsch, Policing the electronic frontier: an introduction to E-health legal issues, *J Cardiovasc Manag* 11 (2000) 9-11.

[45]   B. Stanberry, Legal and ethical issued in European telemedicine, in *European Telemedicine 1998/99*, R. Wootton, Ed. London: Kensington Publications Ltd, 1999, pp. 20-25.

[46]   P. Sogner, K. Goidinger, D. Reiter, A. Stoeger, and D. zur Nedden, Security aspects of teleradiology between the university centre and outlying hospitals in Tyrol, *J Telemed Telecare* 6 (2000) S160-1.

[47]   R. M. Seibel, K. Kocher, and P. Landsberg, Security aspects on the Internet, *Radiologe* 40 (2000) 394-9.

[48]   Fineberg HV, Bauman R, Sosman M. Computerized cranial tomography: effect on diagnostic and therapeutic plans. Journal of the American Medical Association 1977; 238: 224-227.

Towards CyberPsychology
G. Riva and C. Galimberti (Eds.)
IOS Press, 2001

14 Virtual Reality Exposure Therapy vs. Imagery Desensitization Therapy in the Treatment of Flying Phobia

Brenda K. WIEDERHOLD, Richard N. GEVIRTZ, James L. SPIRA

Abstract: This study examined the value of virtual reality graded exposure therapy (VRGET) compared to standard graded exposure therapy using imagery alone for patients with flying phobia. Thirty subjects were randomized into either VRGET with physiological feedback of skin resistance, peripheral skin temperature, heart rate, and respiration; VRGET with no physiological feedback, or imagery conditions. Patients in all conditions were first taught to relax (for two sessions) and then exposed in six subsequent sessions to flying stimuli (either through a virtual airplane with visual and somatic stimuli, or through producing mental images). Results showed that subjects in all three conditions were equally physiologically and subjectively aroused throughout the exposure series. However while only 20% of imagery patients flew after 8 weeks of therapy, 80% of VR patients receiving no physiological feedback and 100% of VR patients receiving physiological feedback were able to fly without using medications (p<.001). This is the first study to compare the benefit of virtual reality graded exposure therapy to graded exposure using imagery alone.

Contents

14.1 Introduction

An estimated 10-20% of the general population are affected by a fear of flying, although this fear may not always reach the intensity to meet Diagnostic and Statistical Manual of Mental Disorders, Fourth Edition (DSM-IV) criteria for classification as a specific phobia [1,2]. Of those who do fly, approximately 20% use sedatives or alcohol to deal with their anxiety [3]. Fear of flying not only results in social stigmatization for some, but may result in lost job opportunities due to an inability to travel. The cost to the airline industry alone has been estimated at $1.6 billion per year [4], while the costs to individuals for lost productivity and opportunities is incalculable.

Although fear of flying has been shown to be quite prevalent in the general population, few controlled studies exploring treatment for this disorder have been conducted. The first controlled study of fear of flying with a civilian population was by Solyom, Shugar, Bryntwick, and Solyom in 1973 [5]. Subjects were treated with one of four treatments: 1) habituation, 2) systematic desensitization, 3) aversion relief , 4) or group therapy. All three behavior therapies were forms of "exposure therapy" and proved equally effective in reducing fear of flying. Group therapy, however, proved ineffective.

Several controlled studies have shown that exposure-based treatments are effective for fear of flying [5-8]. In fact, since Solyom et al's 1973 study, all other fear of flying studies found in the literature have included an exposure-based technique, either used alone or as part of a comprehensive treatment package intended to manage arousal, such as cognitive restructuring, thought stopping, and relaxation training [9-14]. Systematic desensitization has been the most common clinical method for treating fear of flying. Systematic desensitization consists of pairing relaxation skills with imaginal exposure to the phobic stimuli [15]. In a study by Howard, Murphy, and Clarke (1983), fifty-six subjects were treated in groups of two or three with seven sessions of systematic desensitization, flooding, implosion, or relaxation alone. Forty-four subjects completed the flight. All treatments proved equally effective in reducing anticipatory fears. Fear of the actual flight – takeoff, being in the air, and landing – was not reduced. The authors hypothesized that in vivo exposure might work better at helping overcome actual in-flight fears [8].

In Solyom, Shugar, Bryntwick, and Solyom's 1973 study mentioned earlier, behavior therapy techniques including systematic desensitization, aversion relief, and habituation worked equally well in decreasing fear of flying compared to group psychotherapy, which employed discussion only and proved ineffective in reducing fear. Since aversion relief and habituation worked as well as systematic desensitization, the need for the relaxation component unique only to systematic desensitization was questioned [5]. However, a 1979 study done by Borkovec and Sides found that heart rate data provided evidence for the hypothesis that relaxation used in desensitization with speech phobics increased imagery vividness, increased physiological arousal to imagery, produced a decline in arousal over repeated exposures, and resulted in the most positive outcome for subjects in their study. Thus, vividness of imagery and not relaxation per se may be a critical element of laboratory exposure therapy [16].

Other studies have attempted to approximate laboratory flight experiences through advanced audio-visual sensations. Enholtz & Mann (1975), used a combination of techniques (desensitization, modeling, and positive reinforcement) as part of an automated audiovisual program to treat flight phobics. Phobics were allowed to complete up to twenty-four sessions of treatment. Results of the study revealed that sixty-five percent of those in a relaxation group with progressive audio-visual exposure were able to fly alone on a free post-treatment flight, compared to only 15% of a relaxation group with full exposure, 27% of a group with no relaxation but progressive exposure, and 0% of a relaxation-only group. However, there were significant problems with dropouts in this study (37%), compromising its generalization. It is also not known if patients were selected based on ability to visualize, so the group chosen may have only been those with good imagery abilities [6].

At 3 1/2-year follow-up, Denholtz, Hall, & Mann (1978) ascertained subjects continued ability to fly alone. Forty-three of the fifty-one subjects from the 1975 study were contacted. Of those who had taken the post-treatment flight, eighty-eight percent had maintained their ability to fly as measured by a telephone interview, although forty-three percent still continued to use alcohol or tranquilizers before flying [7].

14.2 Virtual Reality Graded Exposure Therapy

Recent case studies have appeared in the literature using virtual reality graded exposure to successfully treat fear of flying [17-24]. It has long been known that individuals vary in their imagery ability. A major benefit of VRGET over visualization is that the patient need not rely on internal imagery or their abilities to visualize well [25]. Immersive virtual reality consists of a computer-generated real-time graphical display accessed by the subject through the use of some type of head-mount display, tracking mechanism, and other sensory input devices [26]. In an immersive virtual reality system, the headset worn by the user allows projection of the virtual world through liquid crystal displays mounted in the headset. This presents the illusion of actually being in the virtual world and allows the brain to combine the images into a three-dimensional picture [27]. Virtual reality graded exposure was used to successfully treat ten undergraduate students suffering from acrophobia [28, 29]. This study compared computer-generated (virtual reality) graded exposure (n=10) to a waiting-list control group (n=7). Seven of the 10 students who completed the virtual reality graded exposure treatment exposed themselves to actual height situations during treatment though not specifically asked to do so. No behavioral change was reported for those in the wait-list control group. Other studies have also shown VRGET to be efficacious in the treatment of fear of heights [30, 31].

Other phobias that have responded well to VRGET include claustrophobia [32-35]; arachnophobia [36]; agoraphobia [37]; public speaking [38, 39]; driving [23, 40]; and social phobia [23].

Virtual reality exposure therapy offers several advantages over both imaginal and in vivo exposure therapies. In comparison to in vivo, VR is safer since the exposure is entirely under the patient's and therapist's control and can be "switched off" any time it becomes intolerable. With virtual reality, there is also an added benefit of being able to expose a patient over and over to the specific part of a scenario that causes fear. For example, a patient who only fears airplane landings, but is comfortable with all other aspects of air travel, would be able to practice landings over and over as many times as necessary in the virtual world.

In comparison to imaginal exposure, VR may be more realistic. It offers an advantage over imaginal exposure of bringing in several different sensory modalities, such as sight and sound. Vestibular clues such as motion and vibration can also be included to allow the patient to feel more present in the experience. VR is also interactive and provides constant stimuli versus the patient perhaps "drifting" from the imaginal scene. VR offers the advantage of allowing the therapist to see exactly what the client is seeing so that therapy can be tailored to what is activating the fear structure for the client. This flexibility should allow therapy to proceed more efficiently [41]. VR, versus something like television, provides a more immersed and richer experience.

This study was designed to explore the use of virtual reality graded exposure therapy in the treatment of fear of flying. When this study was undertaken, no studies had compared virtual reality graded exposure to more standard exposure. The only fear of flying studies using virtual reality exposure had been case studies lacking empirical rigor. Since that time, however, a controlled study by Rothbaum, et al [42] has shown VR to be equally effective to in vivo exposure for fear of flying when compared at six month post-treatment follow-up.

The goal of this study was to determine if VRGET was equally efficacious, more efficacious, or less efficacious, than IET in the treatment of fear of flying. Physiology was measured to give an objective measurement of improvement over the course of exposure therapy. In addition, self-report questionnaires, subjective ratings of anxiety (SUDs), and behavioral observations (included here as flying behavior before beginning treatment and at a three-month post treatment follow-up) were included to provide several different measurement techniques, from subjective to objective. This was based on emotional processing theory which indicates that treatment success depends on the occurrence of both physiological and subjective activation of fear during exposure [43, 44].

14.3 Method

14.3.1 Participants

Volunteers over 18 years of age with confirmed DSM-IV diagnosis of Specific Phobia Fear of Flying were chosen for this study. Participants were recruited through advertisements at CSPP-San Diego, through advertisements in local newspapers, and were referred by clinicians in the San Diego area. After an initial phone screening, qualified participants were scheduled for an initial intake session. A participant was excluded from the study if he or she had a history of heart disease, migraines, seizures, or concurrent diagnosis of severe mental disorders such as psychosis or major depressive disorder as determined by the intake interview.

14.3.2 Demographics

The sample included thirty participants, ranging in age from 24 to 55, who met the DSM-IV criteria for fear of flying. Means, standard deviations and percentages are listed in Table 14.1 for age, ethnicity, gender, occupational status, and marital status.

14.3.3 Group Assignment

Participants were randomly assigned to one of three groups when they arrived for the initial intake session, based on a previously generated random numbers table. The three groups were: Group A: virtual reality graded exposure therapy with no physiological feedback (VRGETno); Group B: virtual reality graded exposure therapy with physiological feedback (VRGETpm); and Group C: systematic desensitization with imaginal exposure therapy (IET). All three groups received an initial intake session, instruction in diaphragmatic breathing, and a relaxation tape to be used for home practice. In addition, all groups received a second forty-five minute session to answer further questions about the study and to practice breathing techniques prior to beginning desensitization training.

Table 14.1 (a) Demographic Characteristics of the Study Sample

Participants N.	30	Occupational Status	%
Age, mean years (s.d.)	39.80 (9.69)	Blue Collar Workers	3
Demographic Variables	%	Retirees	7
Ethnicity		Students	10
Caucasian	93	Unemployed	7
Hispanic	7	White Collar/Professional	73
Gender		Marital Status	
Female	60	Never Married	30
Male	40	First Marriage	47

Table 14.1 (b) Demographic Characteristics by Experimental Groups

	VRGETno	VRGETpm	IET
Age, mean years (s.d.)	35.8 (9.26)	40.1 (9.89)	43.5 (9.28)
By Percentage	VRGETno	VRGETpm	IET
Ethnicity			
Caucasian	30%	33%	30%
Hispanic	3%	0%	3%
Gender			
Female	13%	23%	23%
Male	20%	10%	10%
Marital Status			
Never Married	13%	7%	10%
First Marriage	17%	17%	13%
Remarried	0%	3%	3%
Separated/Divorced	3%	7%	7%
Widowed	0%	0%	0%
Occupational Status			
Blue Collar Workers	3%	0%	0%
Retirees	3%	3%	0%
Students	3%	3%	3%
Unemployed	0%	0%	7%
White Collar/Professional	23%	27%	23%

IET = imaginal exposure therapy without physiological feedback; VRGETno = virtual reality graded exposure therapy without physiological feedback; VRGETpm = virtual reality graded exposure therapy with physiological feedback

14.4 Measures

14.4.1 Physiological Measures

All three groups had the following physiological measures recorded during the six sessions of desensitization: SR Skin Resistance (SR), Heart Rate (HR), Peripheral Skin Temperature (ST), Respiration Rate (RR), and electroencephalogram (EEG) at both 01 and CZ.

14.4.2 Self-Report Measures

Visual Analog Scales. After an explanation of the therapy procedure, but before receiving any actual therapy sessions, participants were asked to fill out a form adapted from [45]

rating the relative efficacy of the therapy. This was done with a series of five ten-centimeter Visual Analog Scales (VAS), with anchors: 1) not logical and very logical for scale 1, 2) not confident and very confident for scales 2 and 3 3) not willing and very willing for scale 4, and 4) not successful and very successful for scale 5.

Demographic Information Survey. Individuals were asked to fill out a standard demographic survey that included such items as racial/ethnic background, age, and gender.

In addition, items pertinent to this study included questions concerning heart problems and seizures. Three times during the protocol – prior to any training, after two weeks of relaxation training, and after completion of six sessions of exposure therapy - participants were asked to complete the following self-report measures:

Questionnaire on Attitudes toward Flying (QAF) [46]. This questionnaire was used to assess the participants' flying histories and attitudes, as well as to ascertain how much fear different aspects of the flying experience caused. Scores may range from 0 to 360, with 36 scoreable items on the scale. Test-retest reliability has been reported at .92.

Fear of Flying Inventory (FFI) [47]. This 33-item questionnaire was used to measure how much anxiety various aspects of flying such as landing and taking off cause, from no anxiety at all to very severe anxiety. Scores on the questionnaire may range from 0 to 264. Test-retest reliability is reported at .92.

Self-Survey of Stress Responses (SSR) [48]. This questionnaire was used to determine a person's pattern of physiological responses to stress, whether it is autonomic (A), somatic motor(M), or central nervous system (CNS). An example of an autonomic response item would be, "I feel nausea." An example of a somatic motor response item would be, "My hands tremble or my head quivers". And an example of a CNS response item would be, "I continuously have the same or many thoughts running through my head." Each item is rated from 0 to 5, with a maximum score of 70 for each sub-scale, and there are 38 items to the scale.

State-Trait Anxiety Inventory (STAI)   [49]. This inventory measures a person's situational (or state) anxiety, as well as the amount of anxiety a person generally feels most of the time (trait) anxiety. Individuals were instructed to answer the "state" questions as how their anxiety was currently about flying and to answer the "trait" questions as how their anxiety was generally about every day life and situations. Trait anxiety has a test-retest reliability of .81 and state of .40, with internal consistency of between .83 and .92.

VR Scenarios Sheet. A checklist of the different scenarios used in the VR environment was given to participants to determine the subjective anxiety caused by "sitting on the plane, engines off; sitting on the plane, engines on; taxiing; takeoff; smooth flight; turbulent flight and thunderstorm; and landing". This self-rating scale, developed by Rothbaum & Hodges [19] is scored from 0 to 100 for each item. Maximum and minimum scores were assessed to determine if these changed over treatment.

14.4.3   Subjective Ratings of Anxiety

Subjective Units of Distress. Subjective Units of Distress (SUDs) ratings, from 0 = no anxiety to 100 = maximal anxiety, were taken every two minutes during the training sessions for participants in the VRGETno group and the IET group. One SUDs rating was taken after twenty minutes for participants in the VRGETpm group. Participants in the VRGETpm group were progressed through the VR scenarios based on SR levels and therefore were not asked for SUDs ratings during the exposure sessions.

14.4.4   Behavioral Observation

Patients were telephoned three-months post treatment and asked about their flying behavior. They were asked if they could still not fly, could now fly with the use of medication or alcohol, or could now fly without the use of medication or alcohol.

14.5 Procedure

Participants were recruited from CSPP-San Diego, newspaper advertisements, and San Diego area clinicians. Potential participants who inquired about the study were contacted by telephone. At this time, the purpose of the study was indicated, as well as an initial assessment to see if any exclusion criteria were met. Those who met the research criteria and agreed to participate were given an individual initial appointment time. Each participant was called the night before his or her appointment and asked to refrain from exercise for two hours prior to the appointment, and caffeine for four hours prior to the appointment. This was done so that no participant's physiology would be affected by either stimulant. At the initial appointment, the purpose of the study was again explained to each participant who was asked to read and sign an informed consent form indicating that they had voluntarily agreed to participate in this investigation. The consent form also acknowledged that they were able to withdraw from the study at any time if they so chose.

Session 1 was comprised of consenting to participate and history taking to ascertain comorbid mental disorders, physical illnesses, and specificity of fear (whether relating to a fear of crashing or a fear of panic attacks and inability to escape from an enclosed place).

This session was also used to convey instructions on diaphragmatic breathing, along with the making of a relaxation tape for home use by all participants. Only participants in the VRGETpm group were allowed to view the physiological data on the computer monitor with instructions to try and reduce their arousal and were given an explanation of what each numerical value and graph meant. Following standard protocol, Skin Resistance electrodes were attached with velcro, and were placed on the pads of the first and third fingers, on the palmer surface of the left hand. The pneumograph strain gauge was placed over the participant's clothing around the abdomen. The thermistor was placed on the palmer surface of the participant's middle finger and attached with cloth tape at the fingertip and just above where the finger attaches to the hand. A positive electrode was placed on the left wrist, and a negative electrode was placed on the right wrist to measure heart rate.

An individualized fear hierarchy was constructed for each participant randomized into the IET group during the first meeting. Participants in the IET group were told that they would be in the IET group and that IET had been used successfully for the treatment of phobias for over forty years. They were also told that an "individualized" hierarchy would be constructed for them with the therapist's help. The participants in the IET group were told that the VR therapy, which had not been proven effective in a controlled study, would be offered to them at the end of their treatment and a three-month follow-up period for free if they so desired.

Persons in both VRGET groups were told that the VR therapy was still considered experimental and had not been proven effective in a controlled study. They were told that they would be given IET for free at the end of treatment and a three-month follow-up period if they so desired.

Immediately following the first session, each participant filled out the first set of self-report questionnaires. Although the participants were shown diaphragmatic breathing procedures during session 1, questionnaires were filled out before leaving the office, so no practice in the procedures had occurred. Questionnaires were collected and the participants were instructed to practice breathing each day for fifteen to twenty minutes using the relaxation tape made in session 1 as a guide.

During Session Two, a five-minute eyes open and a five-minutes eyes closed baseline physiology recording were taken. This was done to allow participants the chance to further become comfortable with having non-invasive sensors attached to their fingers and wrists, and a strain gauge placed around their abdomen. This session also allowed participants the opportunity to ask any questions that they might have as well as a chance for the therapist to further review breathing techniques with them. Participants were then instructed on the format for desensitization training, whether imaginal or virtual, and an appointment time to begin desensitization training the following week was secured.

Thirty minutes prior to Session 3, each participant was asked to again fill out the self-report questionnaires. This allowed each participant to have experienced two weeks of relaxation training. For the remaining six sessions, Sessions 3-8, the exposure therapy sessions, the following procedure was followed:

The participant arrived at the clinic and was escorted to the treatment room. Following alcohol swabbing, surface electrodes were attached to both the individual's wrists, and to the middle, ring, and index fingers of the left hand to measure physiology. A baseline reading was then taken for five minutes while the participant remained in a sitting position with eyes open. Participants only in the VRGETpm group received visual feedback on physiology at this time. Participants then received twenty minutes of desensitization training, either imaginally or in virtual reality. A recovery reading was then recorded for five minutes following the desensitization training. The above procedures were done once a week for six weeks.

Participants in the IET group and the VRGETno group did not receive information on their physiology during the sessions. Participants in these two groups were asked for a SUDS rating every 2 minutes during exposure therapy. Participants in the VRGETpm group received visual feedback on physiology during baseline and recovery periods of the session, and verbal feedback from the therapist concerning their skin resistance levels while in the virtual environment. Participants in this group were asked for an average SUDS rating after the conclusion of each exposure session.

Three-months post-treatment, all participants were contacted by phone to assess number of flights taken, number of flights avoided, and flight opportunities experienced since completion of treatment.

14.6 Results

14.6.1 Group Equivalence at Baseline

14.6.1.1 Demographics: The three groups were compared on demographic characteristics. Chi-square analyses showed no statistically significant differences in age, [$F_{(2,27)} = 1.66$, $p = .21$], gender, [$\chi^2(2) = 2.5$, $p = .29$], ethnicity, [$\chi^2(2) = 2.22$, $p = .33$], marital status, [$\chi^2(6) = 2.21$, $p = .90$], occupation, [$\chi^2(8) = 7.36$, $p = .50$], or flying behavior at intake [$\chi^2(2) = .27$, $p = .87$].

14.6.1.2 Baseline Distress Level: A one-way ANOVA was used to compare the three groups at baseline across self-report questionnaire scores. In this and all subsequent ANOVAs, to correct for the Type I error created by violation of the sphericity assumption, the Huynh-Feldt correction was used. The degrees of freedom associated with this correction are reported as appropriate [50].

Table 14.2 Pre-treatment scores on self-report questionnaires

Questionnaire	Group	N	Mean	S.D.
FOF	VRGETno	10	128,20	50,21
	VRGETpm	10	106,55	37,81
	IET	10	133,40	45,26
	Total	30	122,72	44,74
SSR-Tot	VRGETno	10	74,10	34,68
	VRGETpm	10	73,50	23,03
	IET	10	78,60	25,07
	Total	30	75,40	27,17
SSR-A	VRGETno	10	26,50	13,18
	VRGETpm	10	25,10	10,62
	IET	10	31,40	9,67
	Total	30	27,67	11,20
SSR-M	VRGETno	10	20,90	12,67
	VRGETpm	10	20,70	9,99
	IET	10	21,70	11,61
	Total	30	21,10	11,08
SSR-CNS	VRGETno	10	26,70	10,89
	VRGETpm	10	27,70	6,80
	IET	10	25,50	6,69
	Total	30	26,63	8,12
STAI-S	VRGETno	10	46,00	18,12
	VRGETpm	10	42,00	14,39
	IET	10	52,40	12,00
	Total	30	46,80	15,16
STAI-T	VRGETno	10	43,20	16,43
	VRGETpm	10	38,00	7,72
	IET	10	39,10	8,61
	Total	30	40,10	11,42
QAF	VRGETno	10	213,80	71,27
	VRGETpm	10	193,50	73,57
	IET	10	211,90	54,81
	Total	30	206,40	65,38
VR-Low	VRGETno	10	15,00	12,47
	VRGETpm	10	24,60	23,39
	IET	10	28,60	20,40
	Total	30	22,73	19,52
VR-High	VRGETno	10	97,40	4,20
	VRGETpm	10	93,50	6,26
	IET	10	95,00	9,43
	Total	30	95,30	6,92

STAI-T = state-trait anxiety inventory (trait); QAF = Questionnaire on attitudes toward flying; VR-Low = VR scenario sheet low score; VR-High = VR scenario sheet high score; VRGETno = virtual reality graded exposure therapy without physiological feedback; VRGETpm = virtual reality graded exposure therapy with physiological feedback; IET = imaginal exposure therapy without physiological feedback; FOF = Fear of Flying Inventory; SSR-Tot = self-survey of stress responses – total; SSR-A = self-survey of stress responses – autonomic; SSR-M = self-survey of stress responses – motor; SSR-CNS = Self-survey of stress responses – CNS; STAI-S = state-trait anxiety inventory (state)

To correct for Type I error due to multiple dependent variables, a modified Bonferroni correction was used. Therefore, group differences were considered significant if $< .02$ [50,51]. There were no statistically significant differences between the scores on the Fear of Flying Inventory [F (2,27) = 1.01, p = .38], Self-Survey of Stress Responses Total Score [F (2,27) = .10, p = .91], Self-Survey of Stress Responses Autonomic Score [F (2,27) = .86, p = .43], Self-Survey of Stress Responses Motor Score [F (2,27) = .02, p = .98], Self-Survey of Stress Responses Central Nervous System Score [F (2,27) = .17, p = .84], State-Trait Anxiety Inventory, State Score [F (2,27) = 1.21, p = .31], State-Trait Anxiety Inventory, Trait Score [F (2,27) = .56, p = .58], Questionnaire on Attitudes Towards Flying [F (2,27) = .28, p = .76], VR Scenario Sheet Low Score [F (2,27) = 1.31, p = .29], and VR Scenario Sheet High Score [F (2,27) = .80, p = .46] (See Table 14.2).

14.6.2   Manipulation Checks

14.6.2.1   Objective Arousal
In order to verify that participants became aroused during each exposure session, skin resistance was used as a measure of sympathetic arousal [52]. Change scores were computed by subtracting skin resistance average for the 20-minute exposure session from a 5-minute baseline skin resistance level. A Group (3) x Time (6) ANOVA revealed no significant effect of Time (p = .47), and no significant Group x Time Interaction (p = .50).

Since there was no difference in arousal by Group, individual t-tests were conducted to determine increases in arousal level at each time session. Paired samples t-tests were computed for baseline vs. the first exposure session, [t(29) = 5.25, p < .001]; second exposure session, [t (29) = 3.37, p = .002]; third exposure session, [t (25) = 4.47, p < .001]; fourth exposure session, [t(22) = 2.556, p = .018]; fifth exposure session , [t(22) = 1.863, p = .076]; and sixth exposure session, [t (22) = 2.74, p = .012]. Although during the fifth exposure session significance was not reached, it did approach significance (see Table 14.3).

Table 14.3 (a) Skin Resistance Averages for 5-minute baseline compared to 20-minute flight. Skin Resistance is measured in microohms

	Mean	S.D.	t	p	df
Session 3	85,72	89,42	5,25	< .001	29
Session 4	70,04	113,94	3,37	0,002	29
Session 5	87,78	100,23	4,47	< .001	25
Session 6	81,87	153,59	2,56	0,018	22
Session 7	43,24	111,32	1,86	0,076	22
Session 8	72,32	126,67	2,74	0,012	22

Table 14.3 (b) SUDS Average for 5-minute baseline compared to 20-minute flight (baseline = 1)

	Mean	S.D.	t	p	df
Session 3	27,58	21,33	7,08	< .001	29
Session 4	28,89	22,24	7,12	< .001	29
Session 5	29,19	25,90	5,85	< .001	26
Session 6	24,40	22,54	5,19	< .001	22
Session 7	18,85	13,51	6,39	< .001	20
Session 8	12,25	9,55	6,15	< .001	22

SUDS = subjective units of discomfort, from 0 = no anxiety to 100 = maximum anxiety

14.6.2.2 Subjective Arousal

In order to verify if there was subjective arousal during exposure, subjective units of discomfort (SUDs) scores were computed by subtracting SUDs average for the 20-minute exposure session from a 5-minute baseline SUDs level (with all subjects reporting they felt "very relaxed," SUDS = 1 by the end of the baseline). A Group (3) x Time (6) ANOVA revealed a significant effect of Time (p<.001), and a significant Group x Time Interaction (p = .008), however, no significant main effect for group was found (p = .05). The VR group receiving physiological feedback reported the highest level of subjective arousal, however, all groups showed arousal during all six exposure sessions. Single sample t-tests (vs. 1) were computed for the first exposure session, [t(29) = 7.08, p < .001]; second exposure session, [t(29)=7.12,p<.001]; third exposure session, [t(26)=5.85,p<.001]; fourth exposure session, [t(22)=5.19,p<.001]; fifth exposure session, [t(20)=6.39,p<.001]; and sixth exposure session, [t(22)=6.15,p<.001]. Means and standard deviations for SUDS scores across Sessions are shown in Table 14.3. Based on skin resistance and SUDS data, it was concluded that arousal, both subjective and objective, was achieved using the stimulus at hand.

14.6.2.3 Treatment Expectancy

Groups rated the treatments as being efficacious after having heard a description of the proposed treatment, but prior to the beginning of treatment. As several prior research studies have demonstrated, patient expectancy for improvement is thought to be a significant variable that may affect treatment outcome [45]. It was predicted that VRGETno, VRGETpm, and IET would be rated as potentially equally efficacious by participants on a series of five 10-centimeter line visual analog scales (VAS) adapted from Borkovec and Nau [45]. As in Borkovec's study, scores were summed over the five items. A one-way ANOVA compared the three groups at baseline. No significant differences were found, indicating that all three groups felt treatment would be equally efficacious in any of the groups they participated in [F (2,24) = .29, p = .75]. It was; therefore, a significant finding to know that participants in all treatment groups showed no difference in their expectancy for improvement based on the explanation of the treatment they received.

14.7 Clinical Outcomes

14.7.1 Subjective Ratings

Group (3) x Time (3) ANOVAs were used to test whether self-report questionnaire scores (QAF, FFI, SSR, STAI, VR Scenarios) varied due to intervention condition (VRGETpm, VRGETno,or IET) over three time periods (prior to treatment, after two sessions of relaxation training, and after six sessions of exposure therapy). All self-report questionnaires showed decreases in distress scores over Time (see Table 14.6). However, no main effect for Group or Group x Time interaction was found among any of the self-report questionnaires (see Table 14.4).

A Group (3) x Time (6) ANOVA was performed to assess Subjective Units of Distress (SUDs - with 0 indicating no anxiety and 100 indicating maximum anxiety) during exposure sessions 1, 2, 3, 4, 5, and 6. No significant main effect for group was found [F(2,18) = 3.69, p = .05]. However, there was a significant main effect for Time [F(3.51,63.14) = 7.93, p < .001]. Group x Time Interaction was also found to be significant [F(7.02, 63.14) = 3.06, p = .008] (see Table 14.5). Planned comparisons revealed that both the VRGETno group and the VRGETpm group were significantly improved on SUDS ratings compared to the IET group over the course of the six exposure sessions (VRGETno vs. IET p = .009; VRGETpm vs. IET p = .04). The two VR groups also differed from each other over time (p = .03).

14.7.2   Behavioral Outcome

Flying behavior was assessed three months post treatment. Chi-square analysis compared the groups at three-months post-treatment to determine how many participants could fly with medication, without medication, or could not fly.

Prior to training, there was no difference between subjects' ability to fly with or without medications between the three groups (see Table 14.6).

Participants were telephoned to determine how many flights they had taken since the end of treatment, how many flight opportunities they had since treatment ended, and how many flights they had avoided since treatment ended. They were also asked if they had taken medication prior to or during the flights to control anxiety.

The chi-square revealed a statistically significant difference in flying behavior between the groups $[\chi^2(4) = 19.41, p < .001]$.

14.8 Discussion

The goal of this study was to determine if Virtual Reality Graded Exposure Therapy (VRGET) was equally efficacious, more efficacious, or less efficacious, than IET in the treatment of fear of flying. Physiology was measured to give an objective measurement of degree of arousal caused by exposure therapy. In addition, self-report questionnaires, subjective ratings of anxiety (SUDs), and behavioral observations (included here as flying behavior before beginning treatment and at a three-month post treatment follow-up) were included to provide both subjective to objective measurements.

Table 14.4 (a) Questionnaire scores at Session 1, 3, and 8.

	Group	*Mean*	*S.D.*	*N*
VR-High	VRGETno	97,38	4,57	8
	VRGETpm	93,89	6,51	9
Session 1	IET	94,44	9,82	9
	Total	95,15	7,25	26
VR-High	VRGETno	85,63	20,26	8
	VRGETpm	93,33	8,66	9
Session 3	IET	96,00	5,39	9
	Total	91,88	12,94	26
VR-High	VRGETno	47,50	22,36	8
	VRGETpm	81,11	21,47	9
Session 8	IET	75,56	31,77	9
	Total	68,85	28,75	26

VR-High = VR scenario sheet high score; VRGET = Virtual reality graded exposure therapy; IET = Imaginal exposure therapy; Sess 1 = Session 1; Sess 3 = Session 3; Sess 8 = Session 8

First examined was whether self-report questionnaires scores would change differently over treatment for the Virtual Reality Graded Exposure Therapy with physiological feedback (VRGETpm) group, Virtual Reality Graded Exposure Therapy with no physiological feedback (VRGETno) group, and Imaginal Exposure Therapy (IET) groups.

Although all groups showed improvement, they did not change differentially over time based on self-report questionnaire scores. Previous studies have found that participants given IET do show a decrease in self-report questionnaire scores [46, 21].

Table 14.4 (b) Questionnaire scores at Session 1, 3, and 8.

	Group	Mean	S.D.	N
FOF: Sess 1	VRGETno	115,38	37,27	8
	VRGETpm	108,72	39,44	9
	IET	132,44	47,89	9
	Total	118,98	41,57	26
FOF: Sess 3	VRGETno	119,50	29,83	8
	VRGETpm	112,78	38,93	9
	IET	141,61	46,82	9
	Total	124,83	39,98	26
FOF: Sess 8	VRGETno	83,38	32,95	8
	VRGETpm	91,44	35,00	9
	IET	111,44	57,49	9
	Total	95,88	43,57	26
SSR-Tot: Sess 1	VRGETno	77,13	35,17	8
	VRGETpm	71,56	23,54	9
	IET	80,11	26,10	9
	Total	76,23	27,48	26
SSR-Tot: Sess 3	VRGETno	64,75	40,58	8
	VRGETpm	76,56	31,88	9
	IET	74,56	31,35	9
	Total	72,23	33,58	26
SSR-Tot: Sess 8	VRGETno	59,88	36,36	8
	VRGETpm	72,83	22,77	9
	IET	68,67	34,11	9
	Total	67,40	30,62	26
SSR-A: Sess 1	VRGETno	27,50	12,87	8
	VRGETpm	23,89	10,51	9
	IET	32,00	10,06	9
	Total	27,81	11,23	26
SSR-A: Sess 3	VRGETno	21,13	13,90	8
	VRGETpm	24,11	13,62	9
	IET	29,67	9,31	9
	Total	25,12	12,42	26
SSR-A: Sess 8	VRGETno	18,13	10,40	8
	VRGETpm	22,67	9,89	9
	IET	27,22	11,39	9
	Total	22,85	10,82	26

FOF = Fear of Flying Inventory; SSR-Tot = self-survey of stress responses – total; SSR-A = self-survey of stress responses – autonomic; VRGET = Virtual reality graded exposure therapy; IET = Imaginal exposure therapy; Sess 1 = Session 1; Sess 3 = Session 3; Sess 8 = Session 8

Table 14.4 (c) Questionnaire scores at Session 1, 3, and 8.

	Group	Mean	S.D.	N
SSR-M: Sess 1	VRGETno	22,50	12,88	8
	VRGETpm	20,89	10,58	9
	IET	21,89	12,29	9
	Total	21,73	11,45	26
SSR-M: Sess 3	VRGETno	21,13	13,53	8
	VRGETpm	24,78	13,18	9
	IET	20,56	12,27	9
	Total	22,19	12,60	26
SSR-M: Sess 8	VRGETno	21,00	13,29	8
	VRGETpm	22,33	9,26	9
	IET	19,11	12,35	9
	Total	20,81	11,30	26
SSR-CNS: Sess 1	VRGETno	27,13	11,73	8
	VRGETpm	26,78	6,51	9
	IET	26,22	6,67	9
	Total	26,69	8,15	26
SSR-CNS: Sess 3	VRGETno	22,50	15,07	8
	VRGETpm	27,67	8,11	9
	IET	24,56	10,58	9
	Total	25,00	11,19	26
SSR-CNS: Sess 8	VRGETno	20,75	15,23	8
	VRGETpm	27,83	6,23	9
	IET	22,33	12,02	9
	Total	23,75	11,54	26
STAI-S: Sess 1	VRGETno	46,88	20,29	8
	VRGETpm	42,44	15,19	9
	IET	52,78	12,67	9
	Total	47,38	16,12	26
STAI-S: Sess 3	VRGETno	48,38	17,01	8
	VRGETpm	40,33	15,07	9
	IET	42,22	12,29	9
	Total	43,46	14,62	26
STAI-S: Sess 8	VRGETno	42,75	14,65	8
	VRGETpm	35,33	6,71	9
	IET	39,33	11,48	9
	Total	39,00	11,22	26

SSR-M = self-survey of stress responses – motor; SSR-CNS = Self-survey of stress responses; CNSSTAI-S = state-trait anxiety inventory (state); VRGET = Virtual reality graded exposure therapy; IET = Imaginal exposure therapy; Sess 1 = Session 1; Sess 3 = Session 3; Sess 8 = Session 8

Table 14.4 (d) Questionnaire scores at Session 1, 3, and 8.

	Group	Mean	S.D.	N
STAI-T : Sess 1	VRGETno	41,50	17,90	8
	VRGETpm	38,22	8,15	9
	IET	40,44	7,94	9
	Total	40,00	11,53	26
STAI-T : Sess 3	VRGETno	42,25	18,20	8
	VRGETpm	36,67	7,52	9
	IET	38,56	7,50	9
	Total	39,04	11,58	26
STAI-T : Sess 8	VRGETno	40,38	17,71	8
	VRGETpm	36,11	8,13	9
	IET	38,11	7,18	9
	Total	38,12	11,34	26
QAF: Sess 1	VRGETno	204,25	72,77	8
	VRGETpm	200,56	74,35	9
	IET	208,67	57,11	9
	Total	204,50	65,63	26
QAF: Sess 3	VRGETno	195,38	50,29	8
	VRGETpm	190,39	77,80	9
	IET	197,22	52,98	9
	Total	194,29	59,60	26
QAF: Sess 8	VRGETno	140,50	45,83	8
	VRGETpm	156,61	63,46	9
	IET	171,44	59,37	9
	Total	156,79	56,28	26
VR-Low	VRGETno	12,50	10,00	8
	VRGETpm	25,11	24,75	9
Session 1	IET	28,44	21,63	9
	Total	22,38	20,52	26
VR-Low	VRGETno	16,25	16,42	8
	VRGETpm	19,56	18,66	9
Session 3	IET	20,67	23,93	9
	Total	18,92	19,33	26
VR-Low	VRGETno	5,75	6,52	8
	VRGETpm	17,44	24,46	9
Session 8	IET	9,44	13,24	9
	Total	11,08	16,86	26

STAI-T = state-trait anxiety inventory (trait); QAF = Questionnaire on attitudes toward flying; VR-Low = VR scenario sheet low score; VRGET = Virtual reality graded exposure therapy; IET = Imaginal exposure therapy; Sess 1 = Session 1; Sess 3 = Session 3; Sess 8 = Session 8

This decrease in scores has also been found in VRGET [17-19]. We had expected that, since virtual reality environments are a step closer to in vivo exposure, VRGETpm and VRGETno would have resulted in a more significant decrease in scores than would IET. However, this hypothesis was not supported. Of interest was the fact that all three groups showed an increase in some questionnaire scores from pre-treatment levels to the second testing, which followed relaxation sessions. We attribute this to participants confronting their fears instead of avoiding them, and had begun to become more aware of their anxiety.

That both VRGET groups and the IET group showed a decrease in fear as evidenced by the questionnaire scores may mean that all treatments did provide some therapeutic benefit for the individual participants in terms of subjective experience. The scores on the Trait portion of the STAI did not change significantly however. This helps support the fact that answers to self-report questionnaires may not have been influenced by social desirability, since if they had, we might have expected both state and trait scores to have decreased.

Table 14.5 (a) Means and standard deviations for suds scores

Source	Group	Mean	S.D.	N
SUDS AVERAGE FOR SESSION 3	VRGETno	31,56	20,37	8
	VRGETpm	38,75	27,35	8
	IET	22,00	6,44	5
	Total	32,02	21,42	21
SUDS AVERAGE FOR SESSION 4	VRGETno	23,13	13,85	8
	VRGETpm	48,75	30,09	8
	IET	20,15	3,82	5
	Total	32,18	23,79	21
SUDS AVERAGE FOR SESSION 5	VRGETno	19,97	13,61	8
	VRGETpm	55,38	31,84	8
	IET	22,75	12,79	5
	Total	34,12	27,30	21
SUDS AVERAGE FOR SESSION 6	VRGETno	12,47	12,36	8
	VRGETpm	38,13	28,82	8
	IET	26,65	17,83	5
	Total	25,62	23,23	21
SUDS AVERAGE FOR SESSION 7	VRGETno	10,00	10,16	8
	VRGETpm	26,00	15,24	8
	IET	21,55	7,58	5
	Total	18,85	13,51	21
SUDS AVERAGE FOR SESSION 8	VRGETno	7,70	7,82	8
	VRGETpm	15,00	11,88	8
	IET	17,42	5,08	5
	Total	12,79	9,68	21

SUDS = Subjective Units of Discomfort 0 = no anxiety, 100 = maximum anxiety; IET = imaginal exposure therapy without physiological feedback; VRGETno = virtual reality graded exposure therapy without physiological feedback; VRGETpm = virtual reality graded exposure therapy with physiological feedback.

Table 14.5 (b) Two-way ANOVAs for SUDS scores by treatment group.

Source	SS	df	MS	F	p
TIME (MAIN EFFECT)	5.867,19	3,51	1.672,77	7,93	<.001
GROUP (MAIN EFFECT)	9840,59	2	4.920,30	3,69	0,05
TIME * GROUP2 (INTERACTION)	4.529,83	7,02	645,74	3,06	0,08

SUDs self-report scores for VRGET and IET both improved over time, but did not differ significantly by group. Upon examination of the means, the IET group never reported as much anxiety during exposure, nor showed as much decline of anxiety during exposure as either VRGET group. Since we know from previous research that in order to change the fear structure that fear must be activated during exposure, it may be thought that the fear elicited during IET was not as intense as that elicited during VRGET. This could account for the lack of behavioral change in the IET group. A greater percentage of those in both VRGET groups were able to fly without medication at three-months post-treatment follow-up, as compared to the IET group as had been predicted. Only one participant (10%) who received IET reported an ability to fly without medication or alcohol at three-month follow-up. Eight of the ten participants (80%) who received VRGETno reported an ability to fly without medication or alcohol at three-month follow-up, and ten out of the ten participants (100%) who received VRGETpm reported an ability to fly without medication or alcohol at three-month follow-up. However, this difference was not statistically significant, possibly due to sample size.

Although all three groups self-report scores showed a decrease when measured after Session 8, the participants in the imaginal group did not translate this change in attitudes towards flying to a behavioral change, i.e., ninety percent of the group still could not fly without medication or alcohol. Thus, although the IET treatment was effective in reducing subjective anxiety, it was not effective in altering flying behavior.

Even though subjective improvement occurred across all groups, self-efficacy improved much more for the VR groups and this further translated into actual flight behavior. The VRGET groups had an increase in belief that they could fly without drugs or alcohol, whereas the IET had a decrease in their belief that they could fly. In addition, the VRGET groups were more accurate in their assessment of their true ability to fly compared to the IET group.

Table 14.6 Flying behavior at follow-up

GROUP	Flying w/meds	Flying w/o meds	Not flying
VRGETno	1	8	1
VRGETpm	0	10	0
IET	6	1	3
Chi-square (4) = 19.41, p < .001			

GROUP	Change	No Change
VRGETno	8	2
VRGETpm	10	0
IET	2	8
Chi-square (2) = 15.60, p < .001		

14.9 Treatment Maintenance

Of those who called and were accepted for the study, only sixty-three percent (10 out of 16) in the IET group went beyond the 1st intake session when told they would be in the IET group. None of these patients had previously attempted IET prior to the study. And only 38% of imaginals who originally sought treatment (6 out of 16) completed all eight treatment sessions. None of these participants had a positive change in flying behavior after discontinuance of treatment. Two of those six who dropped out after intake chose to pay for virtual reality therapy as patients and the remaining four chose not to seek further treatment at our Center. No one in the virtual reality therapy groups dropped out of the study. Two participants in the VRGETpm group chose to quit treatment after five sessions because they were able to successfully fly without medication and with decreased anxiety.

One participant in the VRGETno group chose to quit treatment after five sessions because of an ability to fly without medication and with decreased anxiety. Based on these experiences, it appears that VRGET is a more "attractive" treatment to the public seeking help with fear of flying. So, from a marketing standpoint, VRGET is much easier to get people to come in for than IET.

14.10   Clinical Implications

It is clear from the present study as well as numerous past studies that imaginal exposure therapy has some limitations in the treatment of persons with fear of flying. Persons may not always be able to hold a clear image in IET or recreate the fear when sitting in the therapist's office. It is also clear from past studies that in vivo exposure suffers from some limitations including cost, uncontrollability, and lack of confidentiality. Given that the results of this preliminary study were quite positive, it would seem that virtual reality graded exposure therapy should be considered a viable option when performing exposure therapy for fear of flying. The fact that virtual reality exposure allows for audio, visual, vestibular, and vibratory stimuli to be presented simultaneously to the participant may account for its success in alleviating fears. These multiple stimuli taken simultaneously constitute a form of "augmented reality" which represents the next step in the evolution of VR systems. It is important to emphasize that VRGET is just a technique-not a therapy. Exposure therapy, formally introduced by Joseph Wolpe in 1958 [53], and the newer technique of VRGET is but a powerful tool to be used as part of a well conceptualized therapeutic intervention.

Although the present study included small sample sizes for the three groups, results were rather dramatic and certainly warrant further investigation. Although the treating therapists were not blinded to the three therapy groups, we feel the explanation given for imaginal therapy provided a positive loading in favor of imaginal therapy and the lack of blinding should therefore not be considered a weakness. The methods used were standardized and reviewed for quality, ant therefore therapist bias if it exists at all should have minimal impact. To determine recidivism, a two year post treatment follow-up is underway.

Obviously as computer hardware and software power advances, more sophisticated VR environments will become available, perhaps with more flexibility and adaptability to individual patients as well as more scenarios. Participants in the current study overall were impressed with the audio and vibratory realness of the simulation, but some commented on the cartoonish nature of the visual environment. This should be solved in the future with advanced computing.

Future studies may help strengthen the case that virtual reality graded exposure therapy may be a more efficient and effective alternative to more traditional techniques of exposure therapy when treating specific phobias.

Notwithstanding the problems with the Denholz 1978 study [6], in which he found an 82% success rate after up to 48 sessions of treatment, it may be that VR is a more efficient treatment but not necessarily a more effective treatment.

14.11 References

[1]   American Psychiatric Association: APA (1994). *Diagnostic and Statistical Manual of Mental Disorders Fourth Edition.* Washington, D.C.: American Psychiatric Association.
[2]   Agras, S.; Sylvester, D. & Oliveau, D. (1969). The epidemiology of common fears and phobias. *Comprehensive Psychiatry, 10,* 151-156.
[3]   Greist, J. H., & Greist, G. L. (1981). *Fearless flying: A Passenger Guide to Modern Airline Travel.* Chicago: Nelson Hall.
[4]   Roberts, R. J. (1989). Passenger fear of flying: Behavioral treatment with extensive in-vivo exposure and group support. *Aviation, Space, and Environmental Medicine,* April, 342-348.
[5]   Solyom, L.; Shugar, R.; Bryntwick, S.; & Solyom, C. (1973). Treatment of fear of flying. *American Journal of Psychiatry, 130(4),* 423-427.
[6]   Denholtz, M. S. & Mann, E. T. (1975). An automated audiovisual treatment of phobias administered by non-professionals. *Journal of Behavior Therapy & Experimental Psychiatry, 6,* 111-115.

[7]   Denholtz, M. S.; Hall, L. A.; & Mann, E. (1978). Automated treatment for flight phobia: A 3 1/2-year follow-up. *American Journal of Psychiatry, 135(11)*, 1340-1343.

[8]   Howard, W. A.; Murphy, S. M.; & Clarke, J. C. (1983). The nature and treatment of fear of flying: A controlled investigation. *Behavior Therapy, 14*, 557-567.

[9]   Beckham, J. C.; Vrana, S. R.; May, J. G.; Gustafson, D. J.; & Smith, G. R. (1990). Emotional processing and fear measurement synchrony as indicators of treatment outcome in fear of flying. *Journal of Behavior Therapy & Experimental Psychiatry, 21(3)*, 153-162.

[10]   Doctor, R. M.; McVarish, C.; & Boone, R. P. (1990). Long-term behavioral treatment effects for the fear of flying. *Phobia Practice and Research Journal, 3(1)*, 33-42.

[11]   Girodo, M. & Roehl, J. (1978). Cognitive preparation and coping self-talk: Anxiety management during the stresof flying. *Journal of Consulting and Clinical Psychology, 46(5)*, 978-989.

[12]   Greco, T. S. (1989). A cognitive-behavioral approach to fear of flying: A practitioner's guide. *Phobia Practice and Research Journal, 2(1)*, 3-15.

[13]   Haug, T.; Brenne, L.; Johnsen, B. H.; Berntzen, D.; Gotestam, K.; & Hugdahl, K. (1987). A three-systems analysis of fear of flying: A comparison of a consonant vs. a non-consonant treatment method. *Behavior Research and Therapy, 25(3)*, 187-194.

[14]   Walder, C. P.; McCracken, J. S.; Herbert, M.; James, P.T.; & Brewitt, N. (1987). Psychological intervention in civilian flying phobia: Evaluation and a three-year follow-up. *British Journal of Psychiatry, 151*, 494-498.

[15]   Wolpe, J.; Brady, J. P.; Serber, M.; Agras, W. S.; & Liberman, R. P. (1973). The current status of systematic desensitization. *American Journal of Psychiatry, 130(9)*, 961-965.

[16]   Borkovec, T. D. & Sides, J. K. (1979). The contribution of relaxation and expectancy to fear reduction via graded, imaginal exposure to feared stimuli. *Behavior Research & Therapy, 17*, 529-540.

[17]   Hodges, L. F.; Rothbaum, B. O.; Watson, B. A.; Kessler, G. D. & Opdyke, D. (1996). Virtually conquering fear of flying. *IEEE Computer Graphics & Applications, 16(6)*, 42-49.

[18]   Rothbaum, B. O.; Hodges, L.; Watson, B. A.; Kessler, G. D.; & Opdyke, D. (1996). Virtual reality exposure therapy in the treatment of fear of flying: a case report. *Behaviour Research and Therapy, 34(5/6)*, 477-481.

[19]   Rothbaum, B. O.; Hodges, L.; & Kooper, R. (1997). Virtual reality exposure therapy. *Journal of Psychotherapy Practice and Research, 6(3)*, 291-296.

[20]   North, M. M.; North, S. M.; & Coble, J. R. (1996). Virtual environments psychotherapy: A case study of fear of flying disorder. *Presence, 5(4)*, 1-5.

[21]   Wiederhold, B.K., Gevirtz, R., & Wiederhold, M.D. (1998). Fear of flying: A case report using virtual reality therapy with physiological monitoring. *CyberPsychology & Behavior: The Impact of the Internet, Multimedia and Virtual Reality on Behavior and Society, 1998, 1*(2), 97-104.

[22]   Wiederhold, B.K., Davis, R. & Wiederhold, M.D. (1998). The effects of immersiveness on physiology. In Riva, G., Wiederhold, B.K., Molinari, E. (Eds.) (1998). *Virtual Environments in Clinical Psychology and Neuroscience: Methods and Techniques in Advanced Patient-Therapist Interaction.* Amsterdam: IOS Press.

[23]   Wiederhold, B.K. & Wiederhold, M.D. (1999). Clinical observations during virtual reality therapy for specific phobias. *CyberPsychology & Behavior: The Impact of the Internet, Multimedia and Virtual Reality on Behavior and Society, 2*(2), 161-168.

[24]   Wiederhold, B.K. & Wiederhold, M.D. (2000). Lessons learned from 600 virtual reality sessions. *CyberPsychology & Behavior: The Impact of the Internet, Multimedia and Virtual Reality on Behavior and Society, 3*(3), 393-400.

[25]   Kosslyn, S.M.; Brunn, J; Cave, K.R.; Wallach, R.W. (1984). Individual differences in mental imagery ability: a computational analysis. *Cognition,*18(1-3):195-243.

[26]   Kalawsky, R. S. (1993). *The Science of Virtual Reality and Virtual Environments.* Rading, MA: Addison-Wesley.

[27]   Regan, E. C. & Price, K. R. (1994). The frequency of occurrence and severity of sideeffects of immersion virtual reality. *Aviation, Space, and Environmental Medicine, June*, 527-530.

[28]   Hodges, L. F.; Rothbaum, B. O.; Kooper, R.; Opdyke, D.; Meyer, T. C.; de Graaff J. J.; Williford, J. S.; & North, M. M. (1995). Virtual environments for treating the fear of eights. *IEEE, July 1995*, 27-34.

[29]   Rothbaum, B. O.; Hodges, L. F.; Kooper, R.; Opdyke, D.; Williford, J. S.; & North, M. (1995). Effectiveness of computer-generated (virtual reality) graded exposure in the treatment of acrophobia. *American Journal of Psychiatry, 152(4)*, 626-628.

[30]   Huang, M.P.; Himle, J.; Beier, K., & Alessi, N.E. (1998). Challenges of recreating reality in virtual environments. *CyberPsychology & Behavior: The Impact of the Internet, Multimedia and Virtual*

Reality on Behavior and Society, 1(2), 163-168.

[31]   Emmelkamp, P.M.G.; Bruynzeel, M.; Drost, L.; Van Der Mast, C. (2001). Virtual reality treatment in acrophobia: A comparison with exposure in vivo. *CyberPsychology & Behavior: The Impact of the Internet, Multimedia and Virtual Reality on Behavior and Society, 4*(3), 335-339.

[32]   Botella, C., Banos, R. M.., Perpina, C., Villa, H., Alcaniz, M. & Rey, A. (1998). Virtual reality treatment of claustrophobia: A case report. *Behaviour Research & Therapy, 36*(2) 239-246.

[33]   Botella, C., Villa, H., Baños, R., Perpiña, C., García-Palacios, A., (1999a). Virtual reality in the treatment of claustrophobia: A controlled multiple baseline design. Proceedings of the Virtual Reality and Mental Health Symposium, *MMVR 7, Medicine Meets Virtual Reality Conference.* January 20-23, 1999, San Francisco, CA.

[34]   Botella, C., Villa, H., Baños, R., Perpiña, C., García-Palacios, A., (1999b). The treatment of claustrophobia with virtual reality: Changes in other phobic behaviors not specifically treated. *CyberPsychology & Behavior: The Impact of the Internet, Multimedia and Virtual Reality on Behavior and Society, 2*(2), 135-141.

[35]   Bullinger, A.H., Roessler, A., & Mueller-Spahn, F. (1998). 3D VR as a tool in cognitive-behavioral therapy of claustrophobic patients. *CyberPsychology & Behavior: The Impact of the Internet, Multimedia and Virtual Reality on Behavior and Society,1* (2), 139-146.

[36]   Carlin, A.S., Hoffman, H.G., Weghorst, S. (1997). Virtual reality and tactile augmentation in the treatment of spider phobia: A case report. *Behavior Research & Therapy, 35*(2), 153-158.

[37]   North, M. M., North, S. M.; Coble, J. R. (1995). An effective treatment for psychological disorders: treating agoraphobia with virtual environment desensitization. *CyberEdge Journal, 5*(3), 12-13.

[38]   North, M. M., North, S. M.; Coble, J. R. (1998). VR therapy: an effective treatment for the fear of public speaking. *International Journal of Virtual Reality, 3* (3), 2-7.

[39]   Botella, C., Banos, R., Guillen, V., Perpina, C., Alcaniz, M. & Pons, A. (2000). Telepsychology: Public speaking fear treatment in internet. *CyberPsychology & Behavior: The Impact of the Internet, Multimedia and Virtual Reality on Behavior and Society, 3*(6), 959-968.

[40]   Jang, D.P.; Ku, J.H., Shin, M.B., Choi, Y.H., & Kim, S.I. (2000). Objective validation of the effectiveness of virtual reality psychotherapy. *CyberPsychology & Behavior: The Impact of the Internet, Multimedia and Virtual Reality on Behavior and Society, 3*(3), 321-326.

[41]   Glantz, K.; Durlach, N. I.; Barnett, R. C.; & Aviles, W. A. (1997). Virtual reality (VR) and psychotherapy: Opportunities and challenges. *Presence, 6(1),* 87-105.

[42]   Rothbaum et al, (2000). Journal of Consulting and Clinical Psychology.

[43]   Foa, E. B., & Kozak, M. J. (1986). Emotional processing of fear: Exposure to corrective information. *Psychological Bulletin, 99,* 20-35.

[44]   Foa, Edna B.; Steketee, G.; & Rothbaum, B. O. (1989). Behavioral/cognitive conceptualizations of post-traumatic stress disorder. *Behavior Therapy, 20,* 155-176.

[45]   Borkovec, T. D. & Nau, S. D. (1972). Credibility of analogue therapy rationales. *Journal of Behavior Therapy and Experimental Psychiatry, 3,* 257-260.

[46]   Howard, W.A.; Mattick, R.P.; & Clarke, J.C. (1982). The nature of fears of flying. Unpublished manuscript, University of New South Wales.

[47]   Scott, W. (1987). A fear of flying inventory. In Kellar, P. & Hayman, S. (Eds), *Innovations of Clinical Practice* (Vol. 7). Florida: Professional Resource Exchange.

[48]   Forgione, A. G. & Bauer, F. M. (1980). *Fearless Flying: The Complete Program for Relaxed Air Travel.* Boston: Houghton Mifflin Company.

[49]   Spielberger, C. D.; Gorsuch, R. L.; & Lushene, R. E. (1970). *Manual for the State-Trait Anxiety Inventory (Self-Evaluation Questionnaire).* Palo Alto, CA: MindGarden, Inc.

[50]   Stevens, James (1996). *Applied Multivariate Statistics for the Social Sciences, Third Edition.* Hillsdale, NJ: Lawrence Erlbaum Associates.

[51]   Keppel, G. (1991). *Design and Analysis: A Researcher's Handbook.* Englewood Cliffs, NJ: Prentice-Hall.

[52]   Schwartz, M. & Associates, editors (1995). *Biofeedback: A Practitioner's Guide.* New York: The Guilford Press.

[53]   Wolpe, J. (1958). *Psychotherapy by Reciprocal Inhibition.* Stanford University Press.

15 Virtual Reality and Telemedicine Based Experiential Cognitive Therapy: Rationale and Clinical Protocol

Giuseppe RIVA, Monica BACCHETTA, Gianluca CESA,
Sara CONTI, Enrico MOLINARI

Abstract. In the past decade medical applications of virtual reality (VR) and telemedicine have been rapidly developing, and the technology has changed from a research curiosity to a commercially and clinically important area of medical informatics technology.
The chapter details the characteristics of the Experiential Cognitive Therapy (ECT), an integrated in-patient/out-patient (4 weeks) and telemedicine approach (24 weeks), that tries to enhance the cognitive-behavioral therapy used in the treatment of eating disorders by means of VR sessions and telemedicine support in the follow-up stage. In particular, using VR and telemedicine, ECT is able to address body experience disturbances, interpersonal relationships, self efficacy and motivation to change, key issues for the development and maintenance of eating disorders that are somehow neglected by actual clinical guidelines. This approach will be highlighted by the presentation of the clinical rationale, its different phases and by systematic analysis of the results obtained in different preliminary studies.

Contents

15.1   Introduction

In the past decade medical applications of virtual reality (VR) technology have been rapidly developing, and the technology has changed from a research curiosity to a commercially and clinically important area of medical informatics technology [1]. As noted by Szekely and Satava [1] "Computer modelling and simulation have become increasingly important in many scientific and technological disciplines owing to the wealth of computational power... Likewise, the development of techniques for acquiring data (for example, medical imaging) has enabled the easy generation of high resolution copies of real world objects from the computer's memory. The development of imaging technologies, such as magnetic resonance imaging, computed tomography, and ultrasound, has made the acquisition of highly detailed anatomical and partially functional models of three dimensional human anatomy a routine component of daily clinical practice" (p. 1305).

This lead to an increasing number of VR applications in medicine [2, 3]. Virtual Environments (VEs) for health care are being developed in the following areas: surgical procedures (remote surgery or telepresence [4, 5], augmented or enhanced surgery [6, 7], and planning and simulation of procedures before surgery) [8, 9]; medical therapy [10-15]; preventive medicine and patient education [16]; medical education and training [17, 18]; visualization of massive medical databases [19]; skill enhancement and rehabilitation [20]; and architectural design for health-care facilities [21].

However, there is a growing recognition that VR can play an important role in clinical psychology, too [22]. One of the main advantages of a virtual environment for clinical psychologists is that it can be used in a medical facility, thus avoiding the need to venture into public situations. Infact, in most of the previous studies, VEs are used to simulate the real world and to assure the researcher full control of all the parameters implied. VR constitutes a highly flexible tool which makes it possible to programme an enormous variety of procedures of intervention on psychological distress. The possibility of structuring a large amount of controlled stimuli and, simultaneously, of monitoring the possible responses generated by the user of the programme offers a considerable increase in the likelihood of therapeutic effectiveness, as compared to traditional procedures [23].

The possibilities offered by VR to clinicians are now improved by the diffusion of the Internet. Since the development of methods of electronic communication, clinicians have been using information and communication technologies for the exchange of health-related information. However, the emergence of new shared media, such as the Internet and virtual reality are changing the ways in which people relate, communicate, and live.

Health care is one of the areas that could be most dramatically reshaped by these new technologies. Distributed communication media could become a significant enabler of consumer health initiatives. In fact, they provide an increasingly accessible communication channel for a growing part of the population. Moreover, in comparison with traditional communication technologies, shared media offer greater interactivity and better tailoring of information to individual needs.

E-health, the integration of and telehealth technologies with the Internet and shared virtual reality is the next logical step. Although e-health is a branch of telehealth, it is differentiated in several important ways. As noted by Allen [24] telehealth to date has been largely non-Internet based and has been characterized by point-to-point (e.g., T1) and dial-up (e.g., telephone, ISDN) information exchange. E-health, on the other hand, is more accessible because of its increasingly affordable ability to communicate through a common set of standards and across operating systems.

This chapter presents a promising combined use of VEs and telemedicine in the assessment and treatment of eating disorders [25-29]. Specifically it describes the characteristics of the

Experiential Cognitive Therapy (ECT) - a VR and telemedicine based treatment to be used in eating disorders' assessment and treatment - by systematic analysis of its rationale and different phases.

15.2 Cognitive Behavioral Therapy in Eating Disorders: some challenges for the future

Cognitive-behavioral therapy (CBT) for eating disorders can be described as "a symptom-oriented approach that focuses on the beliefs, values, and cognitive processes that maintain the eating disordered behavior" [30, p. 436]. This approach is based on the theory that certain cognitive characteristics such as low self-esteem, distorted beliefs about the "meaning" of weight, shape, and appearance, dichotomous logic and perfectionism lead to an over concern about one's body size [31, 32]. This preoccupation leads to the use of compensatory behaviors, such as self-induced vomiting, fasting, excessive exercise and abuse of diuretics or laxatives [33].

The widespread use of CBT derives directly from Fairburn's publication of a detailed treatment manual for the treatment of Bulimia Nervosa [34, 35]. As described by Fairburn and Cooper [36], CBT consists of 19 sessions of individual treatment lasting about 20 weeks. The treatment has three stages. The phase one incorporates the use of psycho-educational principles and behavioral techniques designed to disrupt the cycle of binge eating and purging and help the individual normalize their eating patterns. Self-monitoring, through the use of daily food journals, is firmly established during this phase of treatment.

In phase two, cognitive restructuring and problem solving are used to help the individual identify and challenge distorted thoughts, beliefs, and values that are maintaining the eating disorder. Interpersonal and environmental stressors that trigger bulimic episodes are explored and alternative methods of coping are identified. The final phase of treatment focuses on relapse prevention strategies and the maintenance of progress.

In the cognitive-behavioral approach to the treatment of anorexia nervosa, the therapist focuses on using cognitive restructuring to change distorted beliefs and attitudes [31].

Targets of the treatment are the "meaning" of weight, shape and appearance, which are believed to underlie dieting and fear of weight gain [37]. Recovery from anorexia nervosa is achieved by coupling the use of specific behavioral techniques, which address the normalization of eating patterns and weight restoration (e.g., the use of food diaries, meal plans incremental weight gain), with the use of cognitive techniques (e.g., cognitive restructuring, problem solving, identification and expression of affect), designed to improve self-esteem and develop a sense of personal effectiveness [30].

However, as noted by Mizes [38], some aspects of the actual practice guidelines for CBT "...are based on a combination of research-based recommendations and clinical consensus because of significant gaps in the extant research" (p. 387). In particular there are at least four themes that are somehow neglected by current guidelines for eating disorders: body experience disturbances [39, 40], self efficacy and motivation for change [41], interpersonal relationships [42-44]. and the integration between all the different professional figures involved in the treatment [45].

Even if all these themes are widely discussed in literature, the recommended clinical pratice for them are more based on "expert consensus" than on scientific data. Infact, little empirical work has been done to point out the content of clinical guidelines and to validate their efficacy in treatment.

It is well known that few eating disordered patients are not over concerned with their physical body [46]. It is also known that for most patients, changing the body experience is the hardest part of their recovery [47]. However, standard eating disorder programs provide less therapy and have a smaller treatment effect for body image compared with eating behavior [40, 48].

The same happens when clinicians have to face the lack of motivation for change. The denial of the disorder and resistance to treatment are two of the most vexing clinical problems in these pathologies [41]. Given the importance of managing resistance for succesful treatment, it is surprising that so little research has been done in this area [38].

Moreover, clinical observations of eating disordered patients have described their difficulty engaging in and deriving gratification from non-food-related activities.

Following this point Lehman and Rodin [49] suggest that food can be viewed as a primary source of psychological nurturance by these individuals: they use food to compensate for their inability to get gratification from non-food-related activities. As recently found in a research by Cooley and Toray [50] symptoms of eating pathology were associated with figure dissatisfaction, ineffectiveness, self-efficacy to control eating when experiencing negative feelings, and reward conditions.

It is also well known that the other widespread approaches to the treatment of eating disorders - Interpersonal Therapy, Psychodynamic approach and Family Therapy – have their focus on the patient's interpersonal relationships [42-44]. The stated rationale of Interpersonal Therapy was that the eating disorder occurres as a response to interpersonal disturbances (e.g., social isolation, fears of rejection) and consequent negative moods. So, the treatment aims at encouraging mastery of current social roles and adaptation to interpersonal situations.

Moreover, according to psychodynamic and family systems theorists an eating disorder can be considered a reflection or symptom of a deeper, more pervasive problem in the family's role structure, affective expression, relationship dynamic, and style of interacting [51-53]. As a result, the anorexic or bulimic child has difficulty separating from the family and consolidating an individual identity.

However, standard CBT therapy is more focused on addressing food related cognitions and behaviors than on the development of an empowerment process producing enhanced feelings of self-efficacy, perceived competence and a better approach to interpersonal situations.

Finally, based on current knowledge, a comprehensive program involving different approaches is likely to be needed for obtaining and maintaining results in therapy [54].

15.3 A new VR and Telemedicine based approach: Experiential Cognitive Therapy

For many years, research and practice in eating disorders and weight management have been based largely on an unidimensional, simplistic, weight-loss/weight-gain paradigm because of the common assumption that the major cause of obesity is overeating [55]. In spite of this widespread assumption, however, a review of the literature does not support the notion that fat individuals consume more calories than their lean counterparts. A review of 20 studies by Wooley and colleagues [56] and the findings of two more reviews [57, 58] suggest that, generally, fat people probably do not consume more calories than people who are not overweight. Thus, if fat people do not necessarily eat any more than thinner people, the prescription of a diet may not be warranted or reasonable. This is probably why the long-term success rate for persons using this paradigm has been low [59]. Moreover, more recent follow-up studies after a weight-loss intervention have shown how frequent dieters usually have significantly more weight regain than less frequent dieters [60, 61].

To overcome this unsuccessful approach, our work follows some new thinking in this area of weight and eating disorders treatment [62, 63] that recognizes the dangers of chronic dieting and proposes a focus on body image, motivation for change, self-efficacy, self-acceptance and better nutrition. Specifically our program stresses the following: (a) understanding the origins and reinforcement of negative attitudes toward body image; (b) redefining beauty with regard to fatness and thinnes; (c) examining, treating, and decreasing the restriction in activities and negative feelings many eating disordered patients experience; (d) teaching clients empowerment techniques to support motivation to change and self-efficacy, and (e) developing individualized treatment plans regarding eating behaviors and exercise. We hypothesize that the proposed approach would be effective in increasing the number and variety of clients' daily activities, decreasing their fat phobic attitudes and depression, and increasing their self-esteem.

Experiential-Cognitive Therapy for eating disorders is a relatively short-term, integrated, patient oriented approach that focuses on individual discovery [64]. The treatment lasts about 28 weeks, 4-week inpatient/outpatient treatment and 24-week telemedicine (Internet based) treatment, and it is administered by therapists having a cognitive-behavioral orientation who work in conjunction with a psychiatrist as far as the pharmacological component is concerned. When a multidisciplinary treatment is mandatory (e.g., a suicidal patient), Experiential CT is conducted on an inpatient basis.

However, Experiential CT can be profitably applied also to non hospitalized patients. In this case the treatment has to include nutritional counselling and physical activity to help patients learn to regulate their eating and cope with specific high-risk situations (i.e., increased availability of food or limited control) that cannot be adequately addressed during outpatient therapy.

During the first phase (see Table 15.1), the different therapists carry out one *step* of the psychological process, both with individual and group sessions. The individual work regards assessment by means of psychometric tests, weekly supportive psychological talks, sessions for assessment and therapy carried out using Virtual Reality (VR), and psycho-pharmacological assessment and control. The psychological group therapy is based on weekly group meetings ("closed" group of 5/6 persons) of two hours each. The work group aims both at training for development and acquisition of assertive skills, and at training for assessment and consolidation of motivation. Moreover, during the first phase of the treatment the subjects participate to both bi-weekly psycho-nutritional groups held by nutritionists and to daily group sessions of physical activity. The provided physical activities are:

- Postural gymnastics (in the gymnasium), based on:
- Warm-up
- Abdominal exercises, floor exercises, stretching, agility iter, etc. (60 minutes).
- Aerobic activity through the use of cycloergometers (30 minutes).
- Walks in the open with different levels of difficulty (30 minutes).

During the telemedicine phase (see Table 15.2) the patient has periodical individual contacts - through text, audio or video chat depending on the technologies at patient's disposal - with the therapist who followed him/her during the inpatient/outpatient stage.

These contacts will be fortnightly during the first two months and monthly during the third and fourth months. Six month after dismission, there will be a final individual face-to-face session held in our day-hospital.

Table 15.1 Experiential-Cognitive Treatment: In-Patient/Out-patient Phase

FIRST WEEK	
PSYCHOMETRIC TEST (test)	
PSYCHODIAGNOSTIC INTERVIEW	PRELIMINARY GROUP (motivation to treatment and definition of rehabilitative protocol)
SESSION 1 VR ASSESSMENT + BODY IMAGE (Virtual balance + sitting room)	NUTRITIONAL ASSESSMENT
SECOND WEEK	
SESSION 2 VR EATING CONTROL + INTERPERSONAL REFRAME (Kitchen + bathroom + bedroom)	NUTRITIONAL GROUP (2/3 sessions)
SESSION 3 VR BODY IMAGE (BIVRS)	PSYCHOLOGICAL GROUP (1 session)
SESSION 4 VR EATING CONTROL (Supermarket)	PHYSICAL ACTIVITY
THIRD WEEK	
SESSION 5 VR BODY IMAGE + INTERPERSONAL REFRAME (Gymnasium)	NUTRITIONAL GROUP (2/3sessions)
SESSION 6 VR EATING CONTROL+ INTERPERSONAL REFRAME (Pub)	PSYCHOLOGICAL GROUP (1 session)
SESSION 7 VR BODY IMAGE+ INTERPERSONAL REFRAME (Clothes shop)	PHYSICAL ACTIVITY
FOURTH WEEK	
SESSION 8 VR EATING CONTROL+ INTERPERSONAL REFRAME (Restaurant)	
SESSION 9 VR BODY IMAGE + INTERPERSONAL REFRAME (Swimming pool + beach)	PSYCHOLOGICAL GROUP (1 session)
SESSION 10 VR EATING CONTROL + BODY IMAGE (Kitchen + BIVRS + 9 doors room)	PHYSICAL ACTIVITY
	FINAL GROUP (motivation to out-patient phase)
PSYCHOMETRIC TESTS (Re-test)	

Each patients is also given the possibly of contacting the therapist by e-mail in case of urgencies or emergencies for a maximum of two added contacts each month. The therapist decides, according to the characteristics of the request, the most suitable modality of response among e-mail, chat or telephone. The family of the patient, too, can have a monthly contact by e-mail with the therapist.

During the telemedicine phase are also scheduled six monthly group meetings based on 1-hour text based chat sessions. The groups are composed by the same patients who took part in the group sessions of the inpatient/outpatient phase. In this way the patients already know each other and can discuss with the therapist both on pre-defined subjects concerning assertiveness, self esteem, motivation to change, prevention of relapses, and on other specific individual problems faced during this phase. The patients are also allowed to keep in touch after the group sessions. This reciprocal support (self-help group) can be very useful expecially in the early phases of the outpatient stage: they can feel stronger and less alone in facing the difficulties and the problems of daily life.

Finally, during the telemedicine phase, the patients have to download from Internet at monthly intervals specific text based (booklets) or video based (educational videos) material to be used both for exercises and for the preparation of the individual and group sessions. The topics discussed include assertiveness, self-esteem, body image disturbances, motivation to change and prevention of relapses.

Probably the key novelty of this approach is the use of VR and telemedicine sessions in therapy. [64]. As we have seen in the Introduction, VR is widely used in the treatment of phobias [65-69]. However, it seems likely that VR can be more that a tool to provide exposure and desensitization [70]. As noted by Glantz et al., "VR technology may create enough capabilities to profound influence the shape of therapy" [71, p.92]. In particular, they expect that VR may enhance cognitive therapy. VR can in fact be described as a "cognitive technology", a technology created to influence cognitive operations [72].

Also, the emergence of e-health could have a strong effect on health care. As we have seen, the key characteristic of e-health is the use of shared media. Using the Internet, therapists can present, from a remote site, a wide variety of stimuli and to measure and monitor a wide variety of responses made by the user.

Recently, some researchers have tried to use telehealth in the treatment of eating disorders. Particularly, an American group examined *Student Bodies*, an Internet-delivered computer-assisted health education program designed to improve body satisfaction and reduce weight/shape concerns [73-75]. In a controlled study they evaluated whether a 8-week program offered over the Internet was able to target body image dissatisfaction, disordered eating patterns, and preoccupation with shape/weight among women at high risk for developing an eating disorder. The results suggest that technological interventions may be helpful for reducing disordered eating patterns and cognitions among high-risk women [75].

Moreover, the findings of the next research coming from the same group showed that an Internet intervention with limited face-to-face contact was more effective in improving body image and reducing disordered attitudes and behaviors than a purely face-to-face psychoeducational intervention [73].

As we have just seen, there are different key topics that are neglected by current CBT guidelines: body experience disturbances, motivation for change, empowerment and the integration between all the different professional figures involved in the treatment. We think that VR and telemedicine have enough capabilities to profound influence the shape of therapy by offering new approaches that can match the topics discussed above. In the next paragraphs is detailed the rationale for such assumption.

Table 15.2 Experiential-Cognitive Treatment: Telemedicine Phase

FIRST AND SECOND MONTHS	
Telemedicine based treatment	*Traditional face-to-face treatment*
• 2 E-mail contacts for urgency • 1 E-mail contact between the therapist and the family • 2 individual chats (every 15 days) text, audio or video based according to the hardware owned by the patient • 1 text based group chat on a predefined topic • 1 download of text/video educational material	• self-help meetings between patients (allowed but not scheduled)
THIRD MONTH	
• 2 E-mail contacts for urgency • 1 E-mail contact between the therapist and the family • 1 individual chat (text, audio or video based according to the hardware owned by the patient) • 1 text based group chat on a predefined topic • 1 download of text/video educational material • psychometric tests (follow-up retest)	• self-help meetings between patients (allowed but not scheduled) • Group Session (Day hospital)
FOURTH MONTH	
• 2 E-mail contacts for urgency • 1 E-mail contact between the therapist and the family • 1 individual chat (text, audio or video based according to the hardware owned by the patient) • 1 text based group chat on a predefined topic • 1 download of text/video educational material	• self-help meetings between patients (allowed but not scheduled)
FIFTH MONTH	
• 2 E-mail contacts for urgency • 1 E-mail contact between the therapist and the family • 1 text based group chat on a predefined topic • 1 download of text/video educational material	• self-help meetings between patients (allowed but not scheduled)
SIXTH MONTH	
• 2 E-mail contacts for urgency • 1 E-mail contact between the therapist and the family • 1 text based group chat on a predefined topic • 1 download of text/video educational material • psychometric tests (follow-up retest)	• self-help meetings between patients (allowed but not scheduled) • Virtual reality session and individual psychological session (Day hospital)

15.3.1 VR and body experience

It is no secret that thinness and fitness are in fashion. During the past few decades, Americans have plunged headlong into the pursuit of losing weight to fit an ideal body image [55]. Nevertheless, body-image disturbance and its link with eating behaviors are still two poorly understood and controversial phenomena. Some researchers have asserted that the disturbance should be considered as a key feature of the eating disorders [76].

However, other authors strongly disagree: Hsu and Sobkiewicz [77] have suggested that it may be time for the concept to be abandoned as an etiological determinant of eating disorders.

Probably this current state of controversy is due, in large part, to problems with the way body image has been conceptualised and studied [78]. As underlined by Thompson [79] the construct of body image has been used to describe various phenomena that vary widely in their specific characteristics. Moreover, the frequent study of only one aspect of body image, implicitly assuming that the disturbance is unidimensional, has hindered the advancement of knowledge in this area [80]. Actually, researchers are studying body-image as a multidimensional phenomenon composed by a perceptual and affective dimensions [54, 81], the former referring to apparent perceptual overestimation and the latter referring to the feelings an individual has about his or her body.

Current studies have also underlined the existence of some form of connection between body image and eating behavior. It is well known that few eating disordered patients are not over concerned with their physical body [46]. It is also known that for most of them, changing the body experience is the hardest part of their recovery [47]. Cash [82] recently proposed a general model in which the casual processes in the development of body image and eating disturbances are analyzed. The core features of the model are a separation of historical and proximal influences and the link between body image emotions and adjustive, emotion regulating actions [81]. Such actions include avoiding and concealment behaviors, appearance-correcting rituals, social reassurance seeking, and compensatory actions. Cash's model, has received a recent empirical testing: using a series of different confirmatory factor analysis models (LISREL 7) Riva et al. [83] found a significant causal link between body image dissatisfaction and eating restraint. Specifically, both general and specific body site dissatisfaction appear to have a direct influence on eating restraint.

These results seem to confirm that the desire to improve body image is a significant motivation to embark on weight reduction attempts [76].

Generally, the disturbances of body image associated with the eating disorders can be conceptualised as a type of *cognitive bias* [84-86]. The essence of this cognitive perspective is that the central psychopathological concerns of an individual bias the manner in which information is processed. Usually, it is presumed that this biased information processing happens automatically. Also, it is generally presumed that the process happens more or less outside the person's awareness unless the person consciously reflects upon his or her thought processes (as in cognitive therapy). Mineka and Sutton [87] have identified four common types of cognitive bias in research related to depression and anxiety disorders: attentional bias, memory bias, judgmental bias, and associative bias.

Three of these four types of cognitive bias have been the focus of research related to eating disorders: preoccupation with body size, body dysphoria, and connected problems.

According to Williamson [86], body size overestimation can be considered as a complex judgement bias, strictly linked to attentional and memory biases for body related information: "If information related to body is selectively processed and recalled more easily, it is apparent how the self-schema becomes so highly associated with body-related information... If the memories related to body are also associated with negative emotion, activation of negative emotion should sensitise the person to body-related stimuli causing even greater body size overestimation" (pp.49-50).

In contrast to the great number of publications on body image, only a few papers focus on the treatment of a disturbed body image in eating disorders [54, 79]. Although some general intervention programs for the treatment of anorexia nervosa and bulimia nervosa have included a component that dealt with body image disturbances, in many of these treatments, this aspect of treatment has been virtually ignored. For example, in a review of cognitive-behavioral treatments of bulimia nervosa, Garner, Fairburn, and Davis [88] cataloged 22 treatment components of the 19 available treatment studies. The treatment of body image disturbance was not listed as one of the 22 intervention procedures. Rosen [48] found that the overwhelming majority of studies either did not target body image dysfunction or failed to measure changes following treatment.

There are two different approaches to the treatment of body image disturbances that are actually used from leading researchers and clinicians: cognitive-behavioral and feminist methodologies [81].

Cash and Rosen are the leading figure in the development of cognitive-behavioral strategies for the treatment of body image in eating disorders [48, 76, 89, 90]. Their approach is based on assessment, education, exposure and change of body image. The therapy both identify and challenge appearance assumptions, and modify self-defeating body image behaviors. Moreover, the approach involves the development of body image enhancement activities used to support relapse prevention and maintenance of changes, and the integration with weight reduction programs [76, 89, 90].

The feminist approach tries to help women to accept and celebrate the body they have [91, 92]. However, feminist therapy generally varies from traditional forms of therapy in number of ways. Feminists believe that traditional therapy perpetuates the central role of man in the form of the doctor-patient relationship [93]. So, this approach place the therapist and client in equitable roles. Moreover, feminist therapists usually include more experiential techniques, such as guided imagery, movement exercises, and art and dance therapy [93, 94]. Other experiential techniques include free-associative writing regarding a problematic body part, stage performance, or psychodrama [93, 95].

Even if both methods are actually used by many therapists, the treatment of body image disturbance is moving "in the area of multicomponent intervention methods" [81, p. 322].

A recent model proposed by Thompson and colleagues [81] underlines the complexity behind the development of body image disturbances. In the proposed model, self-esteem and depression mediate between the three formative influences (peers, parents and media) and the frequency of comparison and internalization in the development of the disturbance.

In this sense this model suggests "that individuals low in self esteem and high in depression are more vulnerable to factors that produce an awareness of appearance pressures and thus are more likely to engage in social comparison and internalization, leading to body dissatisfaction" [81, p. 315].

An interesting possibility that ECT tries to address is the integration of the different methods commonly used in the treatment of body experience disturbances within a virtual environment [96]. In particular ECT integrates the cognitive methods of Countering, Alternative Interpretation, Label Shifting and Deactivating, the behavioural method of Temptation Exposure with Response Prevention and the visual motorial approach (see Table 15.3) using the virtual environment in the same way as images in the well-known method of guided imagery [97]. According to this method the therapist, after introducing a selected image, encourages the patient to associate to it in pictures, rather than in word, and to give a detailed description of them.

A choice of this type would not only make it possible to evoke latent feelings, but also to use the psycho-physiological effects provoked by the experience for therapeutic purposes [25, 96]. In practically all VR systems the human operator's normal sensorimotor loops are altered by the presence of distortions, time delays and noise [98]. Such alterations that are introduced unintentionally and usually degrade performance, affect body perceptions, too.

Table 15.3 Therapeutical methods integrated in VREDIM

Methods	Procedures
Socratic style	The therapist uses different questions, usually hypothetical, inverse, and third-person ones to help patients synthesize information and reach conclusions on their own.
Miracle question	The therapist asks the patient to imagine what life would be like without her/his complaint. Answering to this question the patient constructs her/his own solution, which then guides the therapeutical process.
Cognitive	*Countering*: Once a list of distorted perceptions and cognitions is developed, the process of countering these thoughts and beliefs begins. In countering, the patient is taught to recognise the error in thinking, and substitute more appropriate perceptions and interpretations.
	Alternative Interpretation: The patient learns to stop and consider other interpretations of a situation before proceeding to the decision-making stage. The patient develops a list of problem situations, evoked emotions, and interpretative beliefs. The therapist and patient discuss each interpretation and if possible identify the kind of objective data that would confirm one of them as correct.
	Label Shifting: The patient first tries to identify the kinds of negative words she uses to interpret situations in her life, such as bad, terrible, obese, inferior, and hateful. The situations in which these labels are used are then listed. The patient and therapist replace each emotional label with two or more descriptive words.
	Deactivating the Illness Belief: The therapist first helps the client list her beliefs concerning eating disorders. The extent to which the illness model influences each belief is identified. The therapist then teaches the client a cognitive/behavioural approach to interpreting maladaptive behaviors and shows how bingeing, purging, and dieting can be understood from this framework.
Behavioral	*Temptation Exposure with Response Prevention*: The rationale of temptation exposure with response prevention is to expose the individual to the environmental, cognitive, physiological, and affective stimuli that elicit abnormal behaviours and to prevent them from occurring. The TERP protocol is usually divided into three distinct phases: (1) comprehensive assessment of eliciting stimuli, (2) temptation exposure extinction sessions, and (3) temptation exposure sessions with training in alternative responses.
Visual motorial	*Awareness of the distortion*: The patients are instructed to develop an awareness of the distortion. This is approached by a number of techniques including the presentation of feedback regarding the patient's self-image. Videotape feedback is also usually used. Patients are videotaped engaging in a range of activities.
	Modification of the body image: The patients are instructed to imagine themselves as different in several aspects including size, race, and being larger or smaller in particular areas. They also are asked to imagine themselves as younger and older, and to imagine what they look and feel like before and after eating, as well as before and after academic-vocational and social successes and failures.

The somesthetic system has a proprioceptive subsystem that senses the body's internal state, such the position of limbs and joints and the tension of the muscles and tendons.

Mismatches between the signals from the proprioceptive system and the external signals of a virtual environment alter body perceptions and can cause discomfort or simulator sickness [99].

It is also well known that key biases can distort perception of the location and orientation of objects and surfaces in virtual environments. While virtual environment interfaces may be argued to be "natural" in principle, there are many features that can disrupt or distort the natural coupling of actual reaching and walking, to create problems of stability and disorientation, lessons that have been well learned in the flight community [100, 101]. Five critical issues relate to gain, time delay order, travel-view decoupling, and field of view [102].

In a preliminary study, Cioffi [103] analysed these effects and found that, in VR, the self-perception of one's own body undergoes profound changes that are similar to those achieved in the 1960s by many psychologists in their studies of perceptual distortion.

Particularly, about 40% of the subjects felt as if they had "dematerialised" or as if they were without gravity; 44% of the men and 60% of the women claimed not to feel their bodies. Perceptual distortions, leading to a few seconds of instability and a mild sense of confusion, were also observed in the period immediately following the virtual experience.

Such effects, resulting from the reorganisational and reconstructive mechanisms needed to adapt the subjects to the qualitatively distorted world of VR, could be of great help during a therapy aimed at influencing the way the body is experienced [96], because they lead to a greater awareness of the perceptual and sensory/motorial processes associated with them.

As noted by Glantz [71], one of the main reasons it is so difficult to change patients' attitudes towards their body is that change often calls for a prior step - recognizing the distinction between an assumption and a perception: "Until revealed to be fallacious, assumptions constitute the world; they seem like perceptions, and as long as they do, they are resistant to change. We anticipate using VR to help people in distress make the distinction between assumptions and perceptions" (p.96)

This is particulary true for body experience. When a particular event or stimulus violates the information present in the body schema (as happens during a virtual experience), the information itself becomes accessible at a conscious level [104]. This facilitates the process of change and, through the mediation of the self (which tries to integrate and maintain the consistency of the different representations of the body), also makes it possible to influence body image. In previous studies this approach was tested on non-clinical subjects [25, 27, 39]. The results showed that the virtual experience induced in the subjects a significantly more realistic view of their body.

15.3.2   VR in supporting motivation for change and empowerment

Eating disorders are some of the most frustrating and recalcitrant forms of psychopathology. This is mostly due to the strong resistance to change that characterises eating disorders patients, mainly anorectic ones. In fact, it has been hypothesized that treatment recidivism and dropout, commonly observed in this population, may be resulting from programmatic attempts to produce symptom reduction in individuals who are not yet ready to change [105]. In this sense, an effective eating disorders program has to deal with the ambivalent and fluctuating motivation to recovery common in these patients.

A framework for conceptualizing readiness for change in treatment-resistant individuals is provided in the transtheoretical model of change [106-108]. According to Prochaska and DiClemente [109] motivation cannot be considered as a trait or personality: motivation is not something one has but rather what one does. According to this approach, change happens along two interrelated dimensions: stage and process [105, 106]:

- *Stage* refers to an individual's readiness status at a particular moment in time, and
- *Process* refers to what an individual is doing to work on the problem and bring about change.

Based on their research with smokers [109], these authors identified five stages of change that people face in replacing problematic behaviour. These stages can be considered predictable and stable subprocesses within the therapeutic process. The five stages are:

- *precontemplation*: being unaware of or unwilling to change symptoms;

- *contemplation*: seriously thinking about change;
- *preparation*: having the intention of changing soon;
- *action*: actively modifying behavior and experiences to overcome a problem, and
- *maintenance*: working to prevent relapse.

Prochaska and DiClemente [107] hypothesize that dropouts occur when "therapists and clients are too far apart in their expectations on which stage of change they will be working" (p. 287). In fact, the problem behaviour doesn't mean the same thing to the client as it does to the therapist. Moreover, two stages of change are particularly critical for therapy: precontemplation and contemplation.

Patients in the precontemplation stage are not even thinking about modifying their behaviour. In fact, they do not believe their eating or restricting is a problem and, usually, take great pride in their level of self discipline. To move the patient to the next stage of change the therapist works with the client to determine if there is another complaint or goal on which the client wishes to work and for which she can become a customer [110]. VR can support the therapist in identifying possible complaints by immersing the patient in real-life situations not directly connected with the eating behaviours. Using the responses of the patients to the situation proposed; the therapist can help them in identifying a salient goals.

Contemplation is a paradoxical stage of change, since the patient is open to the possibility of change but is stopped by ambivalence. The characteristic style of the contemplator is, "yes, but . . .". Two key techniques are usually in facilitating a shift from the contemplation stage to the determination stage of change [110]. The first technique is the use of the *miracle question*, a typical approach used by the solution-focused brief therapy [110, 111]. The miracle question is used to help the client identify how her life would be different if her eating disorder were miraculously gone. The second technique is the *search for exceptions*: situations in which the patient has been able to manage the problematic eating behaviours more successfully. Using VR to experience the effects of the miracle and the successful situations, the patient is more likely not only to gain an awareness of her need to do something to create change but also to experience a greater sense of personal efficacy.

In general, these techinques are used as triggers for a broader empowerment process. In psychological literature *empowerment* is considered a multi-faceted construct reflecting the different dimensions of being psychologically enabled, and is conceived of as a positive additive function of the following three dimensions [112]:

- *perceived competence*: reflects role-mastery, which besides requiring the skillful accomplishment of one or more assigned tasks, also requires successful coping with non-routine role-related situations;
- *perceived control*: includes beliefs about authority, decision-making latitude, availability of resources, autonomy in the scheduling and performance of work, etc;
- *goal internalization*: this dimension captures the energizing property of a worthy cause or exciting vision provided by the organizational leadership.

Virtual reality can be considered the preferred environment for the empowerment process, since it is a special, sheltered setting where patients can start to explore and act without feeling threatened. In this sense the virtual experience is an "empowering environment" that therapy provides for patients. As noted by Botella [113], nothing the patient fear can "really" happen to them in VR. With such assurance, they can freely explore, experiment, feel, live, experience feelings and/or thoughts. VR thus becomes a very useful intermediate step between the therapist and the real world.

Besides, it is unnecessary to wait for situations to happen in the real world because any situation can be modeled in a virtual environment, thus greatly increasing self-training possibilities. In addition, VR allows the situation to be graded so the patient can start at the easiest level and progress to the most difficult. Gradually, because of the knowledge and control afforded by interaction in the virtual world, the patient will be able to face the real world.

Given to its flexibility, VR is an excellent source of information on self-efficacy. In fact, as underlined by Botella and colleagues [113], "different environments can be designed to practically ensure success in all of the patient's virtual adventures; and occasional difficulties, challenges, and failures can be posed for the patient to overcome.

This means that patients are able to discover that difficulties can be defeated. They also have the experience of a competent, effective, empowered self, and can attribute all this personal competence to internal factors: perseverance and effort." (p. 77).

According to Vitousek et al. [41], another well suited approach to face denial and to support the empowerment process is the *Socratic method*. In this method, the therapist uses different questions to help patients synthesize information and to reach conclusions on their own.

Usually, the therapist poses hypothetical, inverse, and third-person questions [41]: for example, would the significance of body shape change if anorexic patient became stranded on a desert island? Would a patient swallow a magic potion that could remove her fear of normal weight? Would a bulimic client exchange her bingeing and purging for a 5- or 10-pound gain?

VR is well suited to this approach, for its ability of immersing the patient in a real-like situation that she/he is forced to face. Infact, the key characteristic of VR is the high level of control of the interaction with the environment without the constraints usually found in real life. VR is highly flexible and programmable. It enables the therapist to present a wide variety of controlled stimuli and to measure and monitor a wide variety of responses made by the user [114].

Both the synthetic environment itself and the manner in which this environment is modified by the user's responses can be tailored to the needs of each client and/or therapeutic application. Moreover, VR is highly immersive and can cause the participant to feel "present" in the virtual rather than real environment. It is also possible for the psychologist to follow the user into the synthesised world.

The advantages of a VR-based Socratic method are clear. It minimizes distortion in self-report, since there is no script for conforming clients to parrot or oppositional clients to reject; a typical behavior of anorexic individuals.

Moreover, it circumvents power struggles because the therapist can be invisible to the patient and presents no direct arguments to oppose. Finally, evidence is more convincing and conclusions better remembered because they are one's own. As noted by Miller & Rollnick [115] people are "more persuaded by what they hear themselves say than by what other people tell them" (p. 58).

As we have seen before, change often calls for the recognition of the distinction between an assumption and a perception [70]. By using VR, the therapist can actually prove that what looks as a perception doesn't really exist. This gets across the idea that a person can have a false perception. Once this has been understood, individual maladaptive assumptions can then be challenged more easily. In this sense, the use of VR can support the development of a psychologically empowered state [112]: a cognitive state characterized by a sense of perceived control, competence, and goal internalization.

15.4   The design of a VR and telemedicine system for clinical use

Even starting by the above considerations, understanding how to use immersive virtual reality (VR) to support clinical practice presents a substantial challenge for the designers and users of this emerging technology.

15.4.1   The design of a VR system for clinical use

As recently noted by Banos et al. [116] VR has two opposite faces. On one side it can be used by clinicians as a "setting lab where to study anomalous behaviors, emotions and beliefs" (p.284). On the other side, "VR can be also seen as a creator of psychopathology" (p. 288) for its potential of inducing reality judgement and identity problems. Moreover, it is well known that this tool can provoke important side effects such as cybersickness and aftereffects [117], forcing the clinician to a precise planning of his approach to lessen the probabilty of inducing harmful consequences for the patients.

These opposite faces are owed to the peculiar characteristics of VR. This tool is not simply a particular collection of technological hardware, but can be considered as a new *medium* defined in terms of its effect on both basic and major psychological processes [118-120]. According to Bricken [121] the essence of VR is the inclusive relationship between the participant and the virtual environment, where direct experience of the immersive environment constitutes communication. In this sense, VR can be considered as the leading edge of a general evolution of present communication interfaces like television, computer and telephone [122]. Main characteristic of this evolution is the full immersion of the human sensorimotor channels into a vivid and global communication experience [123]. Following this approach, it is also possible to define VR in terms of human experience [124]: "a real or simulated environment in which a perceiver experiences telepresence", where telepresence can be described as the "experience of presence in an environment by means of a communication medium" (pp. 78-80).

As noted by Banos et al. [116], through the experience of telepresence VR can affect cognitive development for "its capability of reducing the distinction between the computer's reality and the conventional reality". Moreover "VR can be used for experiencing different identities and... even other forms of self, as well" (p. 289).

As Mantovani [125] notes, "Virtual reality is a communication environment in which the interlocutor is increasingly convincing in terms of physical appearance, yet increasingly less tangible and plausible in terms of personal identity. This paradox results from juxtaposing a convincing simulation of the physical presence of the other, and the disappearance of the interlocutor's face behind a mask of false identities" (p. 197). It is surely no accident that members of electronic communities very often adopt false 'nickname' identities, and openly accept them in others.

According to Vincelli [23, 126] this situation produces a change with respect to the traditional relationship between client and therapist. The new configuration of this relationship is based on the awareness of being more skilled in the difficult operations of recovery of past experiences, through the memory, and of foreseeing of future experiences, through the imagination. At the same time, the subject undergoing treatment perceives the advantage of being able to re-create and use a real experiential world within the walls of the clinical office of his own therapist. However, this is possible only if the virtual environment is able to support the relationship between the clinician and the patient.

Following the suggestions and feedbacks of the therapist, the patient is not simply an external observer of pictures or one who passively experiences the reality created by the computer, but on the contrary may actively change the three-dimensional world in which he is acting, in a condition of complete sensorial immersion.

This approach shifts the focus of our attention in creating successfully clinical virtual environments. Faithfulness in reproducing the physical characteristics of the "real" environment is not necessarily the only thing to be borne in mind in simulation: the possibility of interaction which virual environments allow is also important. More than the richness of available images [127, 128], the sensation of presence depends on the level of interaction/interactivity which actors have in both "real" and simulated environments [129, 130]. Human action needs a certain amount of freedom of movement to adapt itself smoothly to the needs of a changing environment, which is why a good clinical VR system must grant a certain amount of freedom of movement to the patient who move in it. As noted by Ellis [131] the key questions for a VR designer are: " Can the users accomplish the tasks they accept? Can they acquire the necessary information? Do they have the necessary control authority? Can they correctly sequence their subtasks?" (p. 258). In fact, the successful implementation of virtual environment simulations will directly depend on the answers to these types of questions.

The main consequence of this approach for the design and the development of clinical oriented VR systems is that a patient's presence in an environment exists if and only if that patient can use the VR for cooperating with the therapist and/or other patients, and even for entering into conflict with them. In fact, than the richness of available images [127, 128], the sensation of presence depends on the level of interaction/interactivity which actors have in both "real" and simulated environments [129]. In this sense, emphasis shifts from quality of image to freedom of movement, from the graphic perfection of the system to the actions of actors in the environment.

15.4.2   The design of a telehealth system for clinical use

According to Wootton [132], there are basically two reasons why telehealth is used: "either because there is no alternative, or because it is in some sense better than traditional medicine" (p. 12). In this sense telehealth has been used very successfully for optimising health services delivery to people who are isolated because of social and physical boundaries and limitations [133, 134]. Nevertheless, the benefits of telehealth, because of the variety of its applications and their uneven development, are not self-evident [135, 136]. In a recent study Currel *et al.* [137] assessed all the randomised trials available in scientific literature to verify the effects of telemedicine as an alternative to face-to-face patient care. Although none of the studies showed any detrimental effects from the interventions, neither did they show unequivocal benefits and the findings did not constitute evidence of the safety of telemedicine.

However, the emergence of e-health is supporting the cost-effectiveness of certain applications [138] such as radiology, prisoner health care, psychiatry, and home health care. Its key advantage is the possibility of share different media and different health care tools in a simple to use and easily accessible interface. A recent Australian study showed that the cost-effectiveness of both telehealth and telemedicine improves largely when they are part of an integrated use of telecommunications and information technology [139]. The conclusion of the author, is that it is unwise to promote telehealth in isolation from other uses of technologies in health-care.

Moreover, the research in the area clearly underlines that e-health is not simply a technology but a complex technological and relational process [140]. In this sense, clinicians and health care providers that want to exploit e-health need a significant attention to technology, ergonomics, human factors and organizational changes in the structure of the relevant health service [141].

At this stage, however, there are different shortcomings that limit the potential of this approach. For a detailed description, you can check the conclusions of Chapter 13.

15.5   Virtual Reality for Eating Disorders Modification - VREDIM

Starting from the above rationale the VEPSY UPDATED – Telemedicine and Portable Virtual Environments for Clinical Psychology - European Community funded project (IST-2000-25323) has developed the Virtual Reality for Eating DIsorders Modification - VREDIM – VR system to be used in the Experiential Cognitive Therapy. VREDIM is an enhanced version of the original Virtual Reality for Body Image Modification (VEBIM) immersive virtual environment, previously used in different preliminary studies on non-clinical subjects [25, 27].

15.5.1   VREDIM: Hardware and software

VREDIM is implemented on a Thunder 1300/C virtual reality system by VRHealth, Milan, Italy (http://www.vrhealth.com). The Thunder 1300/C is a Pentium IV based immersive VR system (1300 mhz, 256 mega RAM, graphic engine: Matrox MGA 450 32Mb WRam) including a head mounted display (HMD) subsystem. The HMD used is the Glasstron from Sony Inc. The Glasstron uses LCD technology (two active matrix colour LCD's) displaying 180000 pixels each. Sony has designed its Glasstron so that no optical adjustment at all is needed, aside from tightening a two ratchet knobs to adjust for the size of the wearer's head. There's enough "eye relief" (distance from the eye to the nearest lens) that it's possible to wear glasses under the HMD. The motion tracking is provided by Intersense through its InterTrax 30 gyroscopic tracker (Azimuth: ±180 degrees; Elevation: ±80 degrees, Refresh rate: 256Hz, Latency time: 38ms ± 2).

We used a two-button joystick-type input device to provide an easy way of motion: pressing the upper button the operator moves forward, pressing the lower button the operator moves backwards. The direction of the movement is given by the rotation of operator's head.

VREDIM is composed by different 3D Healing Experiences™ (see Table 15.4) each one individually used by the therapist during ten 45-minute sessions with the patient (see Table 15.1 for the decription of the different 3D Healing Experiences™ used in the sessions).

Each experience was created by using the software Virtools Dev. 2.0 (http://www.virtools.com). Based on a building-block, object-oriented paradigm, Virtools makes interactive environments and characters by importing geometry and animation from several animation packages.

The Virtools toolset consists of Virtools Creation, the production package that constructs interactive content using behavior blocks; Virtools Player, the freely distributable viewer that allows anyone to see the 3D content; Virtools Web Player, a plug-in version of the regular player for Netscape Navigator and Microsoft Internet Explorer; and the Virtools Dev for developers who create custom behaviors or combine Virtools with outside technology. Virtools Dev includes a full-blown software development kit (Virtools SDK) for the C++ developer that comes with code samples and an ActiveX player which can be used to play Virtools content in applications developed with tools such as Frontpage, Visual Basic or Visual C++.

Content created with Virtools can be targeted at the stand-alone Virtools Player, at web pages through the Virtools Web Player, at Macromedia Director, or at any product that supports ActiveX. Alternatively, the Virtools SDK allows the user to turn content into stand-alone executable files. Virtools's rendering engine supports DirectX, OpenGL, Glide and software rendering, although hardware acceleration is recommended.

15.5.2 VREDIM: the ten session

Each session is divided in three phases:

- 15 minutes of psychological individual interview;
- 15 minutes of immersion into Virtual Reality;
- 15 minutes of psychological interview.

During the first interview the therapist investigates the feelings of the subject, the iter of the therapy and will introduce the virtual reality session (see Figure 15.1). In the second interview, the therapist discusses what emerged from the immersion in 3D Healing Experiences™ and analyses emotions, behaviors and cognitions of the patient.

Figure 15.1 The use of VREDIM

The main goal of the first session is to introduce the patient to the procedure and to the instruments needed for exploring the virtual environments (HMD and joystick). The first session is also used to assess any body-related stimula that could elicit abnormal eating behavior. In particular the attention is focused on the patient's concerns about body image, eating, shape and weight. This assessment is normally part of the Temptation Exposure with Response Prevention protocol [46]. At the end of the first 3D Healing Experience™ the therapist uses the *miracle question*, a typical approach used by the solution-focused brief therapy [110, 111]. According to this approach the therapist asks the patient to imagine what life would be like without her/his complaint. Answering to this question in writing the patient constructs her/his own solution, which then guides the therapeutical process [142]. According to deShazer [142] this approach is useful for helping patients establish goals that can be used to verify the results of the therapy.

The next eight sessions are used to assess and modify:

- *the symptoms of anxiety related to food exposure*. This is done by integrating different cognitive-behavioral methods (see Table 15.3): Countering, Alternative Interpretation, Label Shifting, Deactivating the Illness Belief and Temptation Exposure with Response Prevention [39, 46].
- *the body experience of the subject*. To do this the virtual environment integrated the therapeutic methods (see Table 3) used by Butter & Cash [143] and Wooley & Wooley [94]. Particularly in VREDIM we used the virtual environment in the same way as guided imagery [97] is used in the cognitive and visual/motorial approach.
- *the approach to critical interpersonal settings*: using the virtual environments the patient can experience or re-experience critical interpersonal situations and *reframe* them, using different cognitive-behavioral methods (see Table 15.3): Countering, Alternative Interpretation and Label Shifting. Moreover, the therapist presents the patients applicable ways of honestly *communicating their feelings* during the interaction (assertiveness training).

The conclusive session is used for a final analysis of the inpatient/outpatient phase with particular attention to the reached goals, prevention of relapses and maintenance of the therapeutic compliance in the forthcoming outpatient phase.

In all the sessions, the therapists followed the Socratic style: they used a series of questions, related to the contents of the virtual environment, to help clients synthesize information and reach conclusions on their own.

15.5.3   VREDIM: The 3D Healing Experiences™

Each session of Virtual Reality (15 minutes) is divided into four phases reached through successive virtual doors (see Table 15.4):

Table 15.4 Phases included in each VR session

PHASE 1	PSYCHOLOGIST OFFICE
PHASE 2	SPECIFIC 3D HEALING EXPERIENCE
PHASE 3	SAFE PLACE
PHASE 4	PSYCHOLOGIST OFFICE

The *psychologist's office* is the first 3D Healing Experience™. It represents the start and the end of each session, and it has the important function to outline boundaries of the session in virtual reality. It is a neutral and reassuring place which allows continuity in the phases of the individual session: face to face, virtual reality and face to face.

In the psychologist's office there are the following objects: a writing-desk with two comfortable chairs, a bookshelf and complements of furnishings that make the environment more comfortable and hospitable (pictures, carpets, lamps, green plants, etc.)

The *safe place* is 3D Healing Experience™ for the relaxation that is used at the end of each session and, if needed, during the session of virtual reality.

In this environment there is a comfortable armchair that the patients can use for the relaxation. In the room there is a suffused light. On the wall, in front of the armchair, is found a big screen for the projection of the relaxing environment chosen by the patient during the assessment phase. The patients can choose their relaxing environment among four availables:

- Deserted beach;
- Mountain side in autumn;
- Mountain side in winter;
- Country side with flowery fields.

Between the *psychologist's office* and the *safe place* the patient experiences one or more specific 3D Healing Experiences™. The full list of the environment used is reported in Table 15.5. Below is reported a more detailed description of all the 3D Healing Experiences™ used in the ten sessions.

Table 15.5 3D Healing Experiences™ used in VREDIM

1ˢᵗ 3D Healing Experience	Virtual balance
2ⁿᵈ 3D Healing Experience	Sitting room
3ʳᵈ 3D Healing Experience	Kitchen
4ᵗʰ 3D Healing Experience	Bedroom
5ᵗʰ 3D Healing Experience	Bathroom
6ᵗʰ 3D Healing Experience	BIVRS
7ᵗʰ 3D Healing Experience	9 doors room
8ᵗʰ 3D Healing Experience	Shopping centre
9ᵗʰ 3D Healing Experience	Supermarket
10ᵗʰ 3D Healing Experience	Gymnasium
11ᵗʰ 3D Healing Experience	Pub
12ᵗʰ 3D Healing Experience	Clothes shop
13ᵗʰ 3D Healing Experience	Restaurant
14ᵗʰ 3D Healing Experience	Swimming pool + beach

15.5.3.1 Virtual Balance (First session)

The room of the virtual balance is a not very wide environment with windows. The patient can come up to weight herself on the balance in the middle of the room. When the patient comes up on the virtual balance her weight, which has previously been typed in, appears on the display.

This experience is used by the therapist to explore any symptoms of anxiety related to the experience of weighting in the patients and their concerns about eating, shape and weight. The data collected are used to plan the next sessions.

Key questions used for the assessment phase

Reaction to the virtual balance
- What can you see there?
- What are your feelings/sensations?
- Do you have a balance at home?
- Where do you keep it?

Concern about weight
- Do you often weight yourself? How often in a week?
- Now come up to the scales... Touch it *(The therapist "takes" the patient, and the patient's weight, which has earlier been typed in, appears)*. Now tell me how you feel when you see your weight on the display...

Wish to modify one's weight
- Have you tried to do something about your weight in the last few months? How?
- How do you feel when you can't manage to change your weight despite the effort? What do you do to feel better?
- What happens instead when you can manage to change your weight?
- Now imagine that you can change the figures on the display... what figures would you like to appear?
- In your opinion, is it a reasonable weight considering your age, height and actual weight?
- How would you feel if this was your weight?

Influence of one's own weight on the opinions of others
- When you weight yourself, are you alone? Always? *(If so)* Why? Would you feel uneasy if others (relatives, friends) saw your weight?
- If you couldn't be alone, who would you like to be with when weight yourself? What does this other person think about your weight?
- In your opinion, what do you think the signficant others think about your weight? Do you think they give importance to your weight when they judge you?
- *(The therapist expresses his question specifying four groups of people: relatives, friends, acquaintances and strangers)*
- Would you be able to tell me what the signficant others think about you beside your weight? *(Also here the therapist expresses his question specifying four groups of people: relatives, friends, acquaintances and strangers).*

Influence of weight on one's opinion of oneself
- Do you think your life would be different if you had a different weight?
- When you see your weight on the balance and notice a difference *(The therapist supposes both an increase and a decrease of weight)*, what do you think of yourself?
- If in this very moment you had to list the things that are most important to you (work or study, family, friends, etc.) what the rating of weight is?

Influence of other people's weight on one's opinion
- What do you tell to a friend who has the same weight as your?
- When you see somebody who is overweight/underweight *(The therapist chooses the choices that corresponds to the patient's characteristics)*, what do you think about that person?
- Do you think that an overweight/underweight person is happy? *(If So)* Always? *(Through this question the therapist gets the patient to understand the mistake of generalization)*

15.5.3.2 Sitting room (First session)
This 3D Healing Experience™ is used in the first session to allow the patients to familiarize with the virtual reality tools (HMD, joystick) and to learn to move into the virtual environments.

Into the sitting room there are wide windows, a sofa, two comfortable armchairs, a bookshelf, a cocktail cabinet, a table with four chairs and food on it. Complements of furnishings were inserted to make the environment more comfortable (pictures, carpets, lamps, green plants, vases, etc.). Moreover in the room there are some specific objects (TV, HI-FI, phone, newspapers, etc.) that are used to suggest to the patients substitutive behaviors to dysfunctional food intake during the "critical" moments.

The patients can perform some different actions and interact with several objects: to open the cocktail cabinet, to listen music, to watch the television, etc.

This environment is used to identify any symptoms of anxiety related to interpersonal relationships in the patients. These data, too, are collected and used to plan the next sessions.

Key questions used for the assessment phase

Interpersonal relationships
- Do you like staying at home? *(If the patient expresses a preference)* What do you think the reason is?
- *(If the patient dislikes it)* Is there anything that bothers you at home? What are your relations with your relatives *(The therapist expresses his question specifying the different relatives: mother, father, brother/s, sister/s)*.
- *(If the patient likes it)* Is there something that bothers you outside? Other people make you feel uneasy? Why? Is it because of your body?
- Do you think other people look at you because of your body? *(The therapist expresses his question specifying four groups of people: relatives, friends, acquaintances and strangers)*
- What do they think of you?
- Do you think they are right?
- If they noticed your weight has changed *(The therapist supposes both an increase and a decrease of weight)*, what would they think of you? *(The therapist expresses his question specifying four groups of people: relatives, friends, acquaintances and strangers)*

15.5.3.3   Kitchen (Second and Tenth sessions)
The kitchen is the first environment of the second virtual reality session. The virtual room is a quite wide environment with windows, an equipped kitchen (refrigerator, oven, gas-ring, sink, mixer, toaster, etc.), a wide shelf of job, spacious cupboards, a table with four chairs.

Into the kitchen the subject can interact with the presented objects: she can open the cupboards, the refrigerator, the freezer and the oven. Moreover, she can choose and "eat" any of the available food.

As in the previous session, the therapist analyzes the reactions elicited by food. Moreover, any dysfuntional belief and/or feeling is discussed with the patient according to the Label Shifting and Objective Counters methods. The kitchen setting is also used to explore the relationships with other family members (father, mother, brother/s and sister/s).

15.5.3.4   Bathroom (Second session)
In the virtual flat there is also a bathroom that is useful to investigate feelings, sensations and thoughts, of the patients with inappropriate compensatory methods as self-induced vomiting and misuse of laxatives.

In add to the sanitary fittings (shower, bath, wash-basin, WC) in the bathroom there are some towels, a bath-robe, a big mirror, a bath closet, a scales, etc.

The patients can do the following actions: to open the shutters, to enter in the shower, to open the taps of the bath, of the shower and of the wash-basin, etc.

In presence of compensatory behaviors the Temptation Exposure with Response Prevention method is used. Any dysfuntional belief and/or feeling is discussed with the patient according to the Label Shifting and Objective Counters methods.

15.5.3.5 Bedroom (Second session)

The bedroom is used instead with patients having binge episodes in this room or that have difficulties in eating control (night eaters) during the night.

The room is quite large, and the wide windows make it very bright. In the bedroom there is a king bed, two bedside tables with abajour, a big wardrobe, a clothes-hanger, a bookshelf, some shelves, a writing-desk with a computer and a chair. The patients can perform some different actions: to open the wardrobe, to interact with the present food, to eat virtually the food, etc. As in the previous session, the Temptation Exposure with Response Prevention is used in presence of compensatory behaviors. Moreover, the different dysfuntional beliefs and/or feelings are discussed with the patient according to the Label Shifting and Objective Counters methods.

15.5.3.6 BIVRS (Third and Tenth sessions)

This 3D Healing Experience™ - the Body Image Virtual Reality Scale - BIVRS - is a three part virtual world in which the user has to choose between 9 figures of different size which vary from underweight to overweight [114, 144].

Subjects are asked to choose the figures that they think to reflect their current and their ideal body sizes. The discrepancy between these two measures is an indication of their level of dissatisfaction. In the first two zones (one for real body and one for ideal body) the subject chooses between nine 2D images that are shown simultaneously. Opening the central door the patient enters in a third zone where there are two panels showing the ideal body and the real body chosen by the subject in the two preceding zones. The two silhouettes are now presented in 3D and between them is presented the real picture of the patient previously digitised using an EPSON Photo PC camera. The 3D images can be modified using two arrow buttons located around the images. We decided to use both 2D and 3D images to improve the effectiveness of the scale.

Even if existing body image scales use mainly 2D images, using 3D it is easier for the subject to perceive the differences between the silhouettes, especially for specific body areas (breasts, stomach, hips and thighs). Also, here the patients can perform some different actions and interact with several objects: to open the doors, to choose the panels, to turn on the silhouette, etc.

The vision of her own body usually elicits in the user strong feelings that can be matched using the Counterattacking and the Countering cognitive methods. The mirror is also used, as indicated by Wooley and Wooley [94], to develop an awareness of the body image distortion. Finally, the therapist instructs the patient to imagine herself as different on several dimensions including size, race, and being larger or smaller particularly areas.

The subject is also asked to imagine herself as younger, older, what they look and feel like before and after eating and social successes/failures.

15.5.3.7 Nine doors room 9 (Tenth session)

In this room the patient is in front of 9 doors of different sizes varying gradually from the narrowest to the largest. The subject can proceed to the next room only by choosing the door corresponding to her body dimension (earlier inserted in the computer by the therapist). In this room the patients can open only the door corresponding to the size of your hips. When the patient makes a mistake, she is not being able to open the chosen door.

The experience is used as stimuli to support a cognitive approach: the elicited feelings are analysed by the therapist according to the Label Shifting and Objective Counters methods. The feelings and their associated beliefs are identified, broken down into their logical components, replaced with two or more descriptive words, and then critically analysed.

15.5.3.8   Shopping Mall (Fourth, Fifth, Sixth, Seventh and Eight sessions)

This is the more complex environment of our virtual reality system. Into the shopping centre there are several shops and commercial activities - a supermarket, a clothes shop, a gymnasium, a pub, a restaurant - that the patient will explore during different sessions.

The shopping centre is very large and bright. The patient navigating in this environment can observe many people, the shopwindows and the different signs.

15.5.3.8.1   Supermarket (Fourth session)

The supermarket is divided in different departments: fruit and vegetables, cakes and biscuits, cheese and dairy products, pork products, meat and fish, sweets, drinks and alcoholic drinks, deep-frozen food, etc. Into the supermarket there are many people. Near the exit of the supermarket there are two cash-desks, but only one of these is free.

Also in this session the patients can perform some different actions and interact with several objects: to put the food acquired in the shopping bag, to put back the wrong purchases in the shelves, to eat immediately something, to do a list of food, to pay at the cash-desk, etc.

If the patient activates maladaptive behaviors the Temptation Exposure with Response Prevention is used. Moreover, the different dysfuntional beliefs and/or feelings are discussed with the patient according to the Label Shifting and Objective Counters methods.

15.5.3.8.2   Gymnasium (Fifth session)

This virtual environment is divided in four parts:

- Entrance,
- Female dressing room,
- Cyclette and tapie roulant room,
- Fitness room.

Entering in the gymnasium the patient crosses the entrance that has a writing-desk with a computer, chairs, a comfortable sofa, a table with newspapers, a scales, a carpet, some posters, etc. In the female dressing room there are some cabinets, clothes-hangers, platform seats, a big mirror, sports bag, shoes and wears. In the first room of the gymnasium there are some cyclette, a tapie roulant, a side for exercises, mirrors, TV, HI-FI, etc. In the second room there are different fitness machines. In each room of the gymnasium there are many people with sports wear (females and males).

Also in this session the patients can perform some different actions and interact with several objects.

This session is used to reframe the effect of negative appearance related comments from others. Specifically, using the Countering, Alternative Interpretation and Label Shifting methods the patient is instructed to recognize the irrational beliefs (i.e. "I must look good to be liked") that usually underlie the interpretation of the comments. The environment is also used to explore the interpersonal relationships outside the family.

15.5.3.8.3   Pub (Sixth session)

The pub is a very large room arranged in four different areas:

- Counter bar;
- Tables;
- Live music zone;
- Game zone.

The counter bar is well furnished: alcoholic drinks and soft drinks, beer, sweet dispenser, snack dispenser (cheeps, salts, pop corn, etc.), sandwiches, pizza, toast, etc.; near to the counter there is the freezer with ice-creams listed on a sign-board.

In the zone of the tables the patient can find a big screen, some posters, green plants. On the engaged tables there are some drinks (beer, coke, fruit juice, etc.) and some food (salts, sandwiches, toast, ice-cream, slices of cake etc.).

The patients can sit down because there is a free table. They can choose food and/or drinks, listen music, watch the video on the big screen, eat and drink virtually, see the people into the pub, etc.

If the patient activates maladaptive behaviors or binge eating the Temptation Exposure with Response Prevention is used. Moreover, the different dysfuntional beliefs and/or feelings are discussed with the patient according to the Label Shifting and Objective Counters methods. Finally, the environment is used to further explore the interpersonal relationships outside the family.

15.5.3.8.4 Clothes shop (Seventh session)
After to have seen the shop-windows of the clothes shop the patient enters in the little environment subdivided in two parts:

* The inner shop;
* Two dressing room.

Inside the shop the wears are arranged on different shelves and clothes-hangers. Moreover in the shop there are some mirrors, manikins, a counter and two dressing room.

In the two dressing room develops the second part of the seven sessions. In each dressing room can be found a mirror, a chair, a clothes-hanger and with T-shirts (in the first room) and trousers (in the second) of different sizes.

Also in this room the patients can perform some different actions and interact with several objects: to open the doors of the dressing room, to wear T-shirts and trousers, to look herself in the mirror, etc.

Also, this session is used to reframe the effect of negative appearance related comments from others. Specifically, using the Countering, Alternative Interpretation and Label Shifting methods the patient is instructed to recognize the irrational beliefs (i.e. "I must look good to be liked") that usually underlie the interpretation of the comments. The mirror is also used, as shown by Wooley and Wooley [94], to instruct the user to imagine herself as different on several dimensions including size, race, and being larger or smaller in specific areas. The subject is also asked to imagine herself as younger, older, what they look and feel like before and after eating and social successes/failures.

15.5.3.8.5 Restaurant (Eighth session)
The restaurant is a little and hospitable environment. The little hall allows to enter the room with the tables where the patient can sit-down. In the room there are differently engaged tables, comfortable chairs, trolley with cakes and a cocktail cabinet. The patients can perform some different actions and interact with several objects into the restaurant: to sit down at the table, to open and read the menu and to eat and drink virtually.

If the patient activates maladaptive behaviors or binge eating the Temptation Exposure with Response Prevention is used. Moreover, the different dysfuntional beliefs and/or feelings are discussed with the patient according to the Label Shifting and Objective Counters methods.

15.5.3.9 Swimming pool and beach (Nineth session)

The swimming pool and the beach are two different places but inserted in the same virtual environment.

When the patients enter this environment they find themselves in front of a swimming pool surrounded by deck-chairs, towels on the floor, and people sunbathing on the lawn and on the edge of the swimming pool. Some people have a swim.

A path connects the swimming pool with the beach. On the beach there are some people that sunbathe, walk, swim, chat and there are children that play, etc. On the beach there are deck-chairs, beach-umbrellas, dressing room, paddleboat; while in the sea there are some windsurf that move. In this session the patients cannot interact with the objects.

The reframing of the impact of negative appearance related comments from others is the main goal of this session. As before, using the Countering, Alternative Interpretation and Label Shifting methods the patient is instructed to recognize the irrational beliefs that underlie the interpretation of the comments.

Figure 15.2 The swimming pool

15.5.4 VREDIM: Its clinical use

It is possible to outline the possible use of VREDIM in a real clinical setting by analysing the trial therapy [28] of M. a 22-year old female anorectic patient (Weight: 45.5 Kg.; Height: 160 cm; B.M.I.: 17.5). The disturbance was characterized by intense fear of gaining weight, body dissatisfaction, frequent binge eating episodes and self induced vomiting associated with low self esteem.

During her stay, M. experienced five VR sessions. A description of the contents of the sessions is reported below. For the sake of brevity, the dialogue has been shorted and paraphrased in places, but nothing important has been omitted.

Session 1

During the assessment session, when M. went through the virtual environment to the balance, she experienced negative feelings. Her reaction was to move away from display showing her body weight.

M.:   dont't like neither the balance, neither the showed weight.

Therapist: What weight would you like to see?

M: I should arrive to weight 50 Kg at least, also if I am not still ready to accept it.

After getting past the weighing machine, M. enters the sitting room. The sight of the food distributed in the rooms bothers her; faced with the cake, she turns away not to see it.

TH: What do you feel when you see all this food spread around the place?

M: Food creates disorder and represents a temptation. If it were my house, I'd take away everything, especially the cake.

TH: Why the cake in particular?

M: Because the cake could trigger off a crisis in me (a binge) ... I know what I'm like, I wouldn't know how to stop at just one slice.

Emphasizing the uselessness of the binges and of vomiting in countering negative feelings like boredom and loneliness makes it possible to increase in the patient awareness of having to change certain dysfunctional modes of behaviour. This consequently augment her motivation to change.

Identifying M.'s moments of greater vulnerability, with the motives that awake in her the need for binge-eating makes it possible to seek with the patient alternative behaviors to implement in moments of difficulty. The assignment for the next session was in fact, to make her think of behaviors that could represent valid substitutes for her in distracting her from her need for food.

Session 2

The kitchen session opens with a brief feedback on the assessment, with us analyzing with M. the possible alternative behaviours to binge-eating. The patient identifies in loneliness and boredom the elements that trigger her binges. Analyzing with M. the possible modes of behaviour to be adopted for combating the strong desire for food which appears in those moments allows her to increase her self-efficacy and her capacity for self-control.

TH: Have you ever thought about what you could do when you feel lonely and bored, instead of eating?

M: Yes. I must try not to stay at home on my own: I could go out for a walk, look for the company of a friend or ... (looking at the virtual telephone on the table in front of her) telephone somebody.

TH: What qualities are needed to achieve such a behaviour?

M: Serenity, capacity for control, constancy.

Session 3

During navigation in the two rooms of the "ideal body" and the "real body" in BIVRS, the bodily perception results notably distorted. Moving around among the images, M. was uncertain about the "ideal" and "real" figures, and seemed to have considerable difficulty in comparing herself with these images, and in objectivizing her thoughts and her corresponding emotions. M. choose between panels that represent the real body a silhouette of very superior dimensions (you see image) and an ideal body slightly more fat.

M: I see myself in this way, but I don't know whether I am like this!

The therapist invited the patient to enter the central room of BIVRS. The feelings induced by the view of her own digitized image are very strong. M. infact didn't look to the mirror from much time.

M: What a strange to ree me...I am so thin!

The comparison beetween her photo and her chosen image in the room of the real body makes her aware of the great difference existing between the subjective image of her own body and the objective image. Finally, M. managed to realize, and simultaneously verbalize, her misperception of her body image.

TH: *Try to superimpose your photo with the silhouette you have chosen, are they similar?*
M: *No, I notice that I'm thinner than I thought. My illness doesn't make me feel objective and rational... What I see is not the reality. I see myself obese between thin people.*

The following footstep was been to carry her comparing the silhouette representing the real body with the one for the ideal body. The therapist tried to carry her to objectify the inconguity between the awareness to have to incease in weight and the unaware desire of thinness.

The presence in M. of an unconscious desire to be thin is probably objectivized also in a real eating restraint and an increase in physical activity, which has led her to lose 1.3 kg during the last week.

M: *Speaking about this with you has made me understand that my reaction to putting on weight in the first week led me to food restraint. I voluntarily didn't eat everything that was given me. .... Perhaps I'm not ready yet to accept myself with a body that has a few kilos more.*

Session 4

In the fourth session, as M. navigates among the virtual mall, there emerges in her the fear of losing control when faced with sweet things, which for her are still an anxiety-provoking type of food. When she sees some croissants, M. turns and moves away.

M: *I'm not ready yet to eat sweet things! I prefer to put the croissant back in the fridge.*
TH: *Why don't you feel ready yet?*
M: *Because I haven't gotten confidence in myself, I haven't gotten confidence in my capacities.*

The session continues by reinforcing her capacity to control and put into effect modes of behaviour substitute to binge-eating, thus increasing her self-efficacy and self-esteem.

Session 5

In this last session, as she is moving around slowly among the people exercising in the gymnasium, M. is very careful and precise in her descriptions of the models, with the tendency to have a body ideal that is always very thin and not very rounded.

TH: *Try to describe to me your ideal body.*
M: *By ideal body is not plump, well proportioned, without too many muscles, thin, but not bony, not like a skeleton... it mustn't look ill.*
TH: *Would your life be very different if you had an appearance like the one you have just described to me?*
M: *Yes, it would be different, better. I would have more energy, more physical strength, and a mood that is a little less saddened.*

The next step was that of analyzing, with M., the qualities and conditions that allow us to fulfill certain targets. Emphasizing the requisites that M. already owns, the therapist had the aim of increasing her self-efficacy and self-esteem to enable her to see her "healing", which in her opinion is still beyond reach, closer.

TH: *So, what would you have to do and what qualities would you need to succeed in achieving your ideal body?*

M: *First of all, I need regular and proper eating habits; then I should do some sport... I should get some physical activity to keep myself in shape physically, and at the same time relax and wind down,... surely not to consume calories.*

TH: *And what qualities would you need to have?*

M: *... Capacity for control, inner serenity. I'm convinced that physical balance is also matched by psychic balance, and conversely. Who is good inside also looks better outside, and who looks good physically, feels well inside.*

TH: *And do you think you have these characteristics?*

M: *Now I think so, although not always.*

      Also in this session the patient compares herself with her own image reflected in a mirror. This time M.'s reaction is much less strong.

M: *I like myself better than last time.*

TH: *Try describing yourself, describing this image, comparing it with the ones you have just seen when you were navigating.*

M: *I'm not very sure of myself, I should try to appreciate myself more, I should try to feel a bit more at my ease.*

TH: *Why don't you feel at ease?*

M: *Because I haven't got a good appearance, although I surely wouldn't show myself off, like the girls I've just seen were doing; it's not in my nature.*

TH: *So, correct me if I'm wrong, but having a good appearance enables you to feel more secure, to appreciate yourself more and not to feel uneasy in showing yourself to others. Does it also enable you to feel happier?*

M: *Perhaps it does, even though I'm realizing that I'm being a bit less pessimistic than before... Maybe I'm approaching the point where I will feel more serene and happier.*

Entered the Nine Doors room, M. finds herself in difficulty in choosing the door to go through. She walks up to and then away from the different doors several times, finally choosing the middle door, which does not reflect her real body size. This additional test enables the patient to improve her awareness of the distortion of her body image.

TH: *Now you should go through one of these doors to be able to go into the next room.*

M: *(In a not very convinced and uncertain voice) The middle one, I think?*

TH: *Try to go in?*

M: *Isn't it the right one?*

TH: *No, it isn't. In your opinion, why isn't it the right one? (Noting that M. is in some difficulty) Remember what we said in the last session.*

M: *Yes, maybe I've chosen a door that is a little bit too big.*

15.6 Discussion

By clinical reputation, eating disorders are some of the most frustrating and recalcitrant forms of psychopathology. As noted by Vitousek et al. [41]: "Few symptom patterns evoke stronger reactions from professionals and none may require more forbearance and self-questioning to manage... [These] disorders are unpopular with clinicians because of the perception that clients habitually deny, deceive and rationalize to protect their symptomatology" (pp. 391-392). This is mostly owed to the strong resistance to change that characterises eating disorders patients, mainly anorectic and bulimic ones.

Actually, the most used clinical approach in the treatment of these pathologies is the cognitive behavioral therapy. CBT is broadly applicable to, and effective in, the treatment of specific eating disorders: it is recommended as the treatment of choice for Bulimia Nervosa and binge eating in obese patients [35], even if the role of CBT in the overall treatment of Anorexia Nervosa remains surprisingly unexamined [145]. Particularly, CBT has been showed significantly more effective than, or at least as effective as, any form of psychotherapy with which it has been compared [146, 147].

However, as noted by Mizes [38], some aspects of the actual practice guidelines for CBT "...are based on a combination of research-based recommendations and clinical consensus because of significant gaps in the extant research" (p. 387). Specifically there are at least four themes that are somehow neglected by current CBT guidelines for eating disorders: body experience disturbances [39, 40], motivation for change [41], interpersonal relationships [42-44]. and the integration between all the different professional figures involved in the treatment [45].

To overcome these limits, the chapter proposed an integrated therapeutical approach, the Experiential-Cognitive Therapy for eating disorders. The ECT treatment lasts nearly 28 weeks and is divided in two phases:

- 4-week in-patient/out-patient treatment including 10 VR based individual sessions and 5 group sessions;
- 24-week telemedicine (Internet based) treatment including individual and group chat sessions and e-mail support. In this phase text, audio or video chats are used according to the hardware owned by the patient.

The preliminary version of this approach, not including the telemedicine treatment, was tested in different studies on clinical and non clinical samples [25-29, 148-150]. The results show that ECT can be successful in improving the clinical practice in this area. Its multidisciplinary approach, ranging from cognitive-behavioral therapy to motivational group sessions seems to be suitable to the peculiar characteristics of eating disorders. In particular the use of VR was effective in dealing with two key features of these disturbances not always adequately addressed by CBT therapy: body experience disturbances and motivation for change.

The first obtained result is the significant change induced by the treatment on the body image of the patients. In a sample of non-clinical subjects [149], two single cases with anorectic and bulimic patients [28, 148], and in three preliminary clinical trials with 18 obese, 25 binge-eating and EDNOS patients [29, 150], ECT produced a significant change in the body image, usually associated to a reduction in problematic eating and social behaviors. Actual body-image treatment involves a cognitive/behavioural or a visuomotor therapy that needs many sessions. The possibility of inducing a significant change in body image and its associated behaviors using a short-term therapy can be useful to improve the efficacy of the existing approaches. As such, the procedure can be considered as a comprehensive treatment package to break through the "resistance" to treatment in clinical subjects [151].

Second, using ECT, therapists were able to improve the motivation for change in clinical sample. As we have seen before, according to Prochaska and DiClemente [109] it is possible to identify five stages of change that people face in replacing problematic behavior. These stages can be considered predictable and stable subprocesses within the therapeutic process. The five stages are: Precontemplation, Contemplation, Determination, Action and Maintenance/Relapse.

Particularly, a stage of change is critical for therapy of eating disorders: Contemplation. Contemplation is a paradoxical stage of change, since the patient is open to the possibility of change but is stopped by ambivalence. The characteristic style of the contemplator is, "yes, but . . .". Two key techniques are usually in facilitating a shift from the contemplation stage to the determination stage of change [110]. The first technique is the use of the *miracle question*, a typical approach used by the solution-focused brief therapy [110, 111]. The miracle question is used to help the client identify how her life would be different if her eating disorder were miraculously gone. The second technique is the search for exceptions: situations in which the patient has been able to manage the problematic eating behaviours more successfully.

Using the VR sessions to experience the effects of the miracle and the successful situations, the patients gained an awareness of her need to do something to create change but also to experience a greater sense of personal efficacy.

VR also appeared to be well suited to the Socratic approach. In fact, VR immerses the patient in a real-like situation that she/he is forced to face. The advantages of a VR-based Socratic method are clear. It can minimize distortion in self-report, since there is no script for conforming clients to parrot or oppositional clients to reject. Moreover, it circumvents power struggles because the therapist can be invisible to the patient and presents no direct arguments to oppose. Finally, evidence is more convincing and conclusions better remembered because they are one's own.

Change often requires the recognition of the distinction between an assumption and a perception [70]. Until revealed to be fallacious, assumptions constitute the world; they seem like perceptions, and as long as they do, they are resistant to change. By using VR, the therapist can actually prove that what looks like a perception doesn't really exist. Once this has been understood, individual maladaptive assumptions can then be challenged more easily. As underlined by social cognitive theory, performance-based methods are the most effective in producing therapeutic change across behavioral, cognitive, and affective modalities [152]. In fact, the proposed experiential approach could help patients to discover that difficulties can be defeated, so improving their cognitive and behavioral skills for coping with stressful situations.

The final interesting result is the lack of side effects and simulation sickness after the experience in the virtual environment, confirming the possibility of using VREDIM in Experiential CT. This result, confirmed in both studies, is even more interesting given the sample used. Infact, females tend to be more susceptible to motion sickness than males [153].

As such, the use of VR sessions might help as a part of a comprehensive treatment package to break through the "resistance" to treatment in clinical subjects [164, 154]. We assume that the virtual experience might be useful to achieve these goals, not as a magic trick but as a catalyzer in a therapeutic process. Nevertheless, well-designed comparative outcome and follow-up studies that contrast procedurally distinct methods are now needed for verifying these hypotheses.

15.7 Acknowledgments

The present work was supported by the Commission of the European Communities (CEC), in particular by the TELEMATICS programme (Project VEPSY UPDATED – IST- 2000-25323, http://www.psicologia.net; http://www.vepsy.com). Moreover, the authors have benefited from support and contributions coming from many other colleagues. These people include Eugenia Borgomainerio, Margherita Baruffi, Gianluca Castelnuovo, Andrea Gaggioli, Fabrizia Mantovani, Letizia Petroni, Silvia Rinaldi and Francesco Vincelli.

15.8 References

[1]   G. Székely and R. M. Satava, Virtual reality in medicine, *Bmj* 319 (1999) 1305.
[2]   J. Moline, Virtual reality in health care: a survey, in *Virtual reality in neuro-psycho-physiology*, G. Riva, Ed. Amsterdam: IOS Press, 1997, pp. 3-34.
[3]   L. Beolchi and G. Riva, Virtual reality for health care, in *Information Technologies in Medicine*, vol. II - Rehabilitation and treatment, M. Akay and A. Marsh, Eds. Toronto: John Wiley & Sons, 2001.
[4]   R. M. Satava, Virtual reality surgical simulator. The first steps, *Surgery Endoscopy* 7 (1993) 203-5.
[5]   R. M. Satava, Virtual reality and telepresence for military medicine, *Comput Biol Med* 25 (1995) 229-36.
[6]   R. H. Ossoff and L. Reinisch, Computer-assisted surgical techniques: a vision for the future of otolaryngology-head and neck surgery, *J Otolaryngol* 23 (1994) 354-9.
[7]   C. Giorgi, F. Pluchino, M. Luzzara, E. Ongania, and D. S. Casolino, A computer assisted toolholder to guide surgery in stereotactic space, *Acta Neurochir Suppl (Wien)* 61 (1994) 43-5.
[8]   G. L. Dunnington and D. A. DaRosa, Changing surgical education strategies in an environment of changing health care delivery systems, *World J Surg* 18 (1994) 734-7; discussion 733.
[9]   W. K. Muller, R. Ziegler, A. Bauer, and E. H. Soldner, Virtual reality in surgical arthroscopic training, *J Image Guid Surg* 1 (1995) 288-94.
[10]   B. O. Rothbaum, L. F. Hodges, R. Kooper, D. Opdyke, J. S. Williford, and M. North, Effectiveness of computer-generated (virtual reality) graded exposure in the treatment of acrophobia, *Am J Psychiatry* 152 (1995) 626-8.
[11]   B. O. Rothbaum, L. F. Hodges, R. Kooper, D. Opdyke, and et al., Virtual reality graded exposure in the treatment of acrophobia: A case report, *Behavior Therapy* 26 (1995) 547-554.
[12]   B. O. Rothbaum, L. Hodges, and R. Kooper, Virtual reality exposure therapy, *J Psychother Pract Res* 6 (1997) 219-26.
[13]   B. O. Rothbaum, L. Hodges, B. A. Watson, G. D. Kessler, and D. Opdyke, Virtual reality exposure therapy in the treatment of fear of flying: A case report, *Behaviour Research and Therapy* 34 (1996) 477-481.
[14]   B. O. Rothbaum and L. F. Hodges, The use of virtual reality exposure in the treatment of anxiety disorders, *Behav Modif* 23 (1999) 507-25.
[15]   B. O. Rothbaum, L. Hodges, R. Alarcon, D. Ready, F. Shahar, K. Graap, J. Pair, P. Hebert, D. Gotz, B. Wills, and D. Baltzell, Virtual reality exposure therapy for PTSD Vietnam Veterans: a case study, *J Trauma Stress* 12 (1999) 263-71.
[16]   H. Hoffman, A. Irwin, R. Ligon, M. Murray, and C. Tohsaku, Virtual reality-multimedia synthesis: next-generation learning environments for medical education, *J Biocommun* 22 (1995) 2-7.
[17]   J. R. Merril, N. F. Notaroberto, D. M. Laby, A. M. Rabinowitz, and T. E. Piemme, The Ophthalmic Retrobulbar Injection Simulator (ORIS): an application of virtual reality to medical education, *Proc Annu Symp Comput Appl Med Care* 1 (1992) 702-6.
[18]   G. L. Merril and V. L. Barker, Virtual reality debuts in the teaching laboratory in nursing, *J Intraven Nurs* 19 (1996) 182-7.
[19]   J. R. Merril, Using emerging technologies such as virtual reality and the World Wide Web to contribute to a richer understanding of the brain, *Annals of the New York Academy of Sciences* 820 (1997) 229-33.
[20]   W. J. Greenleaf and M. A. Tovar, Augmenting reality in rehabilitation medicine, *Artif Intell Med* 6 (1994) 289-99.
[21]   D. K. Bowman, International survey: Virtual Environment Research, *IEEE Computer* (1995) 56-65.
[22]   F. Vincelli and G. Riva, Virtual reality as a new imaginative tool in psychotherapy, *Studies in Health Technology and Informatics* 70 (2000) 356-358.
[23]   F. Vincelli, From imagination to virtual reality: the future of clinical psychology, *CyberPsychology & Behavior* 2 (1999) 241-248.
[24]   A. Allen, When the ship comes in, *Telemedicine Today* 7 (1999) 7.
[25]   G. Riva, The virtual environment for body-image modification (VEBIM): Development and preliminary evaluation, *Presence, Teleoperators, and Virtual Environments* 6 (1997) 106-117.
[26]   G. Riva, L. Melis, and M. Bolzoni, Treating body image disturbances, *Communications of the ACM* 40 (1997) 69-71.

[27] G. Riva, Modifications of body image induced by virtual reality, *Perceptual and Motor Skills* 86 (1998) 163-170.

[28] G. Riva, M. Bacchetta, M. Baruffi, S. Rinaldi, and E. Molinari, Virtual reality based experiential cognitive treatment of anorexia nervosa, *Journal of Behavioral Therapy and Experimental Psychiatry* 30 (1999) 221-230.

[29] G. Riva, M. Bacchetta, M. Baruffi, G. Cirillo, and E. Molinari, Virtual reality environment for body image modification: A multidimensional therapy for the treatment of body image in obesity and related pathologies, *CyberPsychology & Behavior* 3 (2000) 421-431.

[30] L. A. Robin, M. Gilroy, and A. Baker Dennis, Treatment of eating disorders in children and adolescents, *Clinical Psychological Review* 18 (1998) 421-446.

[31] D. M. Garner and K. M. Bemis, A cognitive-behavioral approach to anorexia nervosa, *Cognitive Therapy and Research* 10 (1982) 403-420.

[32] C. G. Fairburn, Cognitive-behavioral treatment for bulimia, in *Handbook of psychotherapy for anorexia and bulimia*, D. M. Garner and P. E. Garnfinkel, Eds. New York: Guilford Press, 1985, pp. 160-192.

[33] G. T. Wilson, The controversy over dieting, in *Eating disorders and obesity: A comprehensive handbook*, K. D. Brownell and C. G. Fairburn, Eds. New York: Guilford Press, 1995, pp. 87-92.

[34] C. G. Fairburn, A cognitive behavioural approach to the management of bulimia, *Psychological Medicine* 11 (1981) 707-711.

[35] C. G. Fairburn, A cognitive-behavioral treatment of bulimia, in *Handbook of psychotherapy for anorexia nervosa and bulimia*, D. M. Garner and P. E. Garfinkel, Eds. New York: Guilford, 1985, pp. 160-192.

[36] C. G. Fairburn and P. J. Cooper, Eating disorders, in *Cognitive behaviour therapy for psychiatric problems*, K. Hawton, P. M. Salkovskis, J. Kirk, and D. M. Clark, Eds. New York: Oxford University Press, 1989, pp. 277-314.

[37] D. M. Garner and K. M. Bemis, Cognitive therapy for anorexia nervosa, in *Handbook of psychotherapy for anorexia and bulimia*, D. M. Garner and P. E. Garnfinkel, Eds. New York: Guilford Press, 1985, pp. 107-146.

[38] J. S. Mizes, Negleted topics in eating disorders: guidelines for clinicians and researchers, *Clinical Psychology Review* 18 (1998) 387-390.

[39] G. Riva, Virtual Reality vs. Virtual Body: The use of virtual environments in the treatment of body experience disturbances, *CyberPsychology & Behavior* 1 (1998) 129-137.

[40] C. J. Rosen and E. Ramirez, Comparison of eating disorders and body dysmorphic disorders on body image and psychological adjustment, *Journal of Psychosomatic Research* 44 (1998) 441-449.

[41] K. B. Vitousek, S. Watson, and G. T. Wilson, Enhancing motivation for change in treatment-resistant eating disorders, *Clinical Psychology Review* 18 (1998) 391-420.

[42] C. G. Fairburn, P. A. Norman, S. L. Welch, M. E. O'Connor, H. A. Doll, and R. C. Peveler, A prospective study of outcome in bulimia nervosa and the long-term effects of three psychological treatments, *Archives of General Psychiatry* 52 (1995) 304-12.

[43] C. B. Peterson and J. E. Mitchell, Psychosocial and pharmacological treatment of eating disorders: a review of research findings, *Journal of Clinical Psychology* 55 (1999) 685-97.

[44] W. S. Agras, C. F. Telch, B. Arnow, K. Eldredge, M. J. Detzer, J. Henderson, and M. Marnell, Does Interpersonal Therapy help patients with binge eating disorder who fail to respond to cognitive—behavioral therapy?, *Journal of Consulting & Clinical Psychology* 63 (1995) 356-360.

[45] C. M. Grilo, Treatment of obesity: an integrative model, in *Body image, eating disorders and obesity*, J. K. Thompson, Ed. Washington, DC: APA - American Psychological Association, 1996, pp. 389-423.

[46] D. G. Schlundt and W. G. Johnson, *Eating Disorders: assessment and treatment*. Needham Heights, MA: Allyn and Bacon, 1990.

[47] M. Rorty, J. Yager, and E. Rossotto, Why and how do women recover from bulimia nervosa? The subjective appraisal of forty women recovered for a year or more., *International Journal of Eating Disorders* 14 (1993) 249-260.

[48] J. C. Rosen, Body image assessment and treatment in controlled studies of eating disorders, *International Journal of Eating Disorders* 19 (1996) 341-343.

[49] A. K. Lehman and J. Rodin, Styles of Self-Nurturance and Disordered Eating, *Journal of Consulting and Clinical Psychology* 57 (1989) 117-122.

[50] E. Cooley and T. Toray, Disordered eating in college freshman women: A prospective study, *Journal of American College Health* 49 (2001) 229-235.

[51] H. Bruch, *Eating disorders*. New York: Basic Books, 1973.

[52] M. Selvini Palazzoli, *Self-starvation: from individual family therapy to the treatment of anorexia nervosa*. New York: Jason Aronson, 1978.

[53] V. F. Guidano and G. Liotti, *Cognitive processes and emotional disorders*. New York: Guilford, 1983.

[54]   J. K. Thompson, *Body image, eating disorders and obesity*. Washington, DC: APA - American Psychological Association, 1996.

[55]   B. B. E. Robinson and J. G. Bacon, The "If Only I Were Thin..." treatment program: Decreasing the stigmatizing effects of fatness, *Professional Psychology: Research and Practice* 27 (1996) 157-183.

[56]   O. W. Wooley, S. C. Wooley, and S. R. Dyrenforth, Obesity and women—II. A neglected feminist topic., *Woman's Studies International Quarterly* 2 (1979) 81-92.

[57]   K. D. Miller, Body-image therapy, *Nursing Clinics of North America* 26 (1991) 727-736.

[58]   E. D. Rothblum, Women and weight: fad and fiction, *Journal of Psychology* 124 (1990) 5-24.

[59]   F. Grodstein, R. Levine, L. Troy, T. Spencer, G. A. Colditz, and M. J. Stampfer, Three-year follow-up of participants in a commercial weight loss program. Can you keep it off?, *Arch Intern Med* 156 (1996) 1302-6.

[60]   W. J. Pasman, W. H. Saris, and M. S. Westerterp-Plantenga, Predictors of weight maintenance, *Obesity Research* 7 (1999) 43-50.

[61]   E. Stice, R. P. Cameron, J. D. Killen, C. Hayward, and C. B. Taylor, Naturalistic weight-reduction efforts prospectively predict growth in relative weight and onset of obesity among female adolescents, *J Consult Clin Psychol* 67 (1999) 967-74.

[62]   J. D. Allan, New directions for the study of overweight, *West J Nurs Res* 20 (1998) 7-13.

[63]   L. Rapoport, M. Clark, and J. Wardle, Evaluation of a modified cognitive-behavioural programme for weight management, *International Journal of Obesity* 24 (2000) 1726-37.

[64]   G. Riva, M. Bacchetta, M. Baruffi, S. Rinaldi, and E. Molinari, Experiential Cognitive Therapy: a VR based approach for the assessment and treatment of eating disorders, in *Virtual environments in clinical psychology and neuroscience: Methods and techniques in advanced patient-therapist interaction*, G. Riva, B. Wiederhold, and E. Molinari, Eds. Amsterdam: IOS Press, 1998, pp. 120-135.

[65]   L. F. Hodges, J. Bolter, E. Mynatt, W. Ribarsky, and R. Van Teylingen, Virtual environments research at the Georgia Tech GVU Center, *Presence, Teleoperators, and Virtual Environments* (1993) 234-243.

[66]   L. F. Hodges, B. O. Rothbaum, R. Kooper, D. Opdyke, T. Meyer, M. North, J. J. de Graaff, and J. Williford, Virtual environments for treating the fear of heights, *IEEE Computer* 28 (1995) 27-34.

[67]   L. F. Hodges, B. O. Rothbaum, B. Watson, G. D. Kessler, and D. Opdyke, A Virtual Airplane for Fear of Flying Therapy, presented at Virtual Reality Annual International Symposium - VRAIS '96, Los Alamitos, CA, 1996.

[68]   M. M. North, S. M. North, and J. R. Coble, Effectiveness of virtual environment desensitization in the treatment of agoraphobia, *Presence, Teleoperators, and Virtual Environments* 5 (1996) 127-132.

[69]   M. M. North, S. M. North, and J. R. Coble, Virtual reality therapy for fear of flying, *American Journal of Psychiatry* 154 (1997) 130.

[70]   K. Glantz, N. I. Durlach, R. C. Barnett, and W. A. Aviles, Virtual reality (VR) for psychotherapy: From the physical to the social environment, *Psychotherapy* 33 (1996) 464-473.

[71]   K. Glantz, N. I. Durlach, R. C. Barnett, and W. A. Aviles, Virtual reality (VR) and psychotherapy: Opportunities and challenges, *Presence, Teleoperators, and Virtual Environments* 6 (1997) 87-105.

[72]   F. Biocca, Intelligence augmentation: The vision inside virtual reality, in *Cognitive technology: In search of a humane interface. Advances in psychology, Vol. 113*, J. L. M. Barbara Gorayska, Ed.: Elsevier Science Publishing Co, Inc, Amsterdam, Netherlands, 1996, pp. 59-75.

[73]   A. A. Celio, A. J. Winzelberg, D. E. Wilfley, D. Eppstein-Herald, E. A. Springer, P. Dev, and C. B. Taylor, Reducing risk factors for eating disorders: comparison of an Internet- and a classroom-delivered psychoeducational program, *Journal of Consulting & Clinical Psychology* 68 (2000) 650-7.

[74]   M. F. Zabinski, M. A. Pung, D. E. Wilfley, D. L. Eppstein, A. J. Winzelberg, A. Celio, and C. B. Taylor, Reducing risk factors for eating disorders: Targeting at-risk women with a computerized psychoeducational program, *International Journal of Eating Disorders* 29 (2001) 401-8.

[75]   A. J. Winzelberg, D. Eppstein, K. L. Eldredge, D. Wilfley, R. Dasmahapatra, P. Dev, and C. B. Taylor, Effectiveness of an Internet-based program for reducing risk factors for eating disorders, *Journal of Consulting & Clinical Psychology* 68 (2000) 346-50.

[76]   J. C. Rosen, Improving body image in obesity, in *Body image, eating disorders and obesity*, J. K. Thompson, Ed. Washington, DC: APA - American Psychological Association, 1996, pp. 425-440.

[77]   L. K. G. Hsu and T. A. Sobkiewicz, Body image disturbance: Time to abandon the concept for eating disorders, *International Journal of Eating Disorders* 10 (1991) 15-39.

[78]   D. H. Gleaves, D. A. Williamson, K. P. Eberenz, S. B. Sebastian, and S. E. Barker, Clarifying body-image disturbance: analysis of a multidimensional model using structural modeling, *Journal of Personality Assessment* 64 (1995) 478-493.

[79]   J. K. Thompson, *Body image disturbance: Assessment and Treatment*. New York: Pergamon, 1990.

[80]   T. F. Cash and T. A. Brown, Body image in anorexia nervosa and bulimia nervosa: A review of the literature, *Behavior Modification* 11 (1987) 487-521.

[81] J. K. Thompson, L. J. Heinberg, M. Altabe, and S. Tantleff-Dunn, *Exacting beauty: Theory, assessment and treatment of body image disturbance*. Washington DC: American Psychological Association, 1999.

[82] T. F. Cash, The treatment of body image disturbances, in *Body image, eating disorders and obesity*, J. K. Thompson, Ed. Washington, DC: APA - American Psychological Association, 1996, pp. 83-107.

[83] G. Riva, S. Marchi, and E. Molinari, Body image and eating restraint: a structural modeling analysis, *Eating and Weight Disorders* 5 (2000) 38-42.

[84] K. B. Vitousek and S. D. Hollon, The investigation of schematic content and processing in eating disorders, *Cognitive Therapy and Research* 14 (1990) 191-214.

[85] D. A. Williamson, B. A. Cubic, and D. H. Gleaves, Equivalence of body image disturbances in anorexia and bulimia nervosa, *Journal of Abnormal Psychology* 102 (1993) 177-180.

[86] D. A. Williamson, Body image disturbance in eating disorders: A form of cognitive bias, *Eating Disorders* 4 (1996) 47-58.

[87] S. Mineka and S. K. Sutton, Cognitive biases and the emotional disorders, *Psychological Science* 3 (1992) 65-69.

[88] D. M. Garner, C. G. Fairburn, and R. Davis, Cognitive-behavioral treatment of Bulimia Nervosa, *Behavioral Modification* 11 (1987) 383-431.

[89] T. F. Cash, *What do you see when you look in the mirror? Helping yourself to a positive body image.* New York: Bantam Books, 1995.

[90] T. F. Cash, *The body image workbook: an eight-step program for learning to like your looks.* Oakland, CA: New Harbinger, 1997.

[91] M. Bergner, P. Remer, and C. Whetsell, Transforming women's body image: a feminist counseling approach, *Women and Therapy* 4 (1995) 25-38.

[92] M. Dionne, C. Davis, J. Fox, and M. Gurevich, Feminist ideology as a predictor of body dissatisfaction in women, *Sex Roles* 33 (1995) 277-287.

[93] S. C. Wooley, Feminist influences on the treatment of eating disorders, in *Eating disorders and obesity: a comprehensive handbook*, K. D. Brownell and C. G. Fairburn, Eds. New York: Guilford, 1995, pp. 294-298.

[94] S. C. Wooley and O. W. Wooley, Intensive out-patient and residential tratment for bulimia, in *Handbook of psychotherapy for anorexia and bulimia*, D. M. Garner and P. E. Garfinkel, Eds. New York: Guilford Press, 1985, pp. 120-132.

[95] A. Kearney-Cooke and R. Striegel-Moore, Treatment of childhood sexual abuse in anorexia nervosa and bulimia nervosa: A feminist psychodynamic approach, *International Journal of Eating Disorders* 15 (1994) 305-319.

[96] G. Riva and L. Melis, Virtual reality for the treatment of body image disturbances, in *Virtual reality in neuro-psycho-physiology: Cognitive, clinical and methodological issues in assessment and rehabilitation*, G. Riva, Ed. Amsterdam: IOS Press, 1997, pp. 95-111.

[97] H. Leuner, Guided affective imagery: a method of intensive psychotherapy, *American Journal of Psychotherapy* 23 (1969) 4-21.

[98] G. Riva, Virtual reality in neuro-psycho-physiology: Cognitive, clinical and methodological issues in assessment and rehabilitation. Amsterdam: IOS Press, 1997.

[99] J. Sadowsky and R. W. Massof, Sensory engineering: the science of synthetic environments, *John Hopkins APL Technical Digest* 15 (1994) 99-109.

[100] G. E. Riccio, Coordination of postural control and vehicular control: Implications for multimodal perception and simulation of self-motion, in *Local applications of the ecological approach to human machine systems, Vol. 2. Resources for ecological psychology*, P. Hancock, J. M. Flach, J. Caird, and J. K. Vicente, Eds.: Lawrence Erlbaum Associates, Inc, Hillsdale, NJ, US, 1995, pp. 122-181.

[101] R. S. Kennedy and K. M. Stanney, Postural instability induced by virtual reality exposure: Development of a certification protocol, *International Journal of Human Computer Interaction* 8 (1996) 25-47.

[102] C. D. Wickens and P. Baker, Cognitive issues in virtual reality, in *Virtual environments and advanced interface design*, T. A. F. Woodrow Barfield, III, Ed.: Oxford University Press, New York, NY, US, 1995, pp. 514-541.

[103] G. Cioffi, Le variabili psicologiche implicate in un'esperienza virtuale [Psychological variables that influence a virtual experience], in *Del Virtuale [Virtuality]*, G. Belotti, Ed. Milano-Italy: Il Rostro, 1993, pp. 35-43.

[104] B. J. Baars, *A cognitive theory of consciousness.* New York: Cambridge University Press, 1988.

[105] J. Geller, S. J. Cockell, and D. L. Dran, Assessing readiness for change in the eating disorders: The psychometric properties of the Readiness and Motivation Interview, *Psychological Assessment* 13 (2001) 189-198.

[106] J. O. Prochaska, C. C. DiClemente, and J. C. Norcross, In search of how people change, *American Psychologist* 47 (1992) 1102-1114.

[107] J. O. Prochaska and C. C. DiClemente, Transtheoretical therapy: Toward a more integrative model of change, *Psychotherapy Theory, Research and Practice* 19 (1982) 212-216.

[108] J. O. Prochaska, *Systems of psychotherapy: A transtheoretical analysis.* Homewood, IL: Dorsey Press, 1979.

[109] J. O. Prochaska and C. C. DiClemente, Stages and processes of self-change in smoking toward an integrative model of change, *Journal of Consulting Clinical Psychology* 5 (1983) 390-395.

[110] B. McFarland, *Brief therapy and eating disorders.* San Francisco: Jossey-Bass Publishers, 1995.

[111] S. deShazer, *Keys to solutions in brief therapy.* New York: W.W. Norton, 1985.

[112] S. T. Menon, Psychological Empowerment: Definition, Measurement, and Validation, *Canadian Journal of Behavioural Science* 31 (1999) 161-164.

[113] C. Botella, C. Perpiña, R. M. Baños, and A. Garcia-Palacios, Virtual reality: a new clinical setting lab, *Studies in Health Technology and Informatics* 58 (1998) 73-81.

[114] G. Riva, Virtual reality in psychological assessment: The Body Image Virtual Reality Scale, *CyberPsychology & Behavior* 1 (1998) 37-44.

[115] W. R. Miller and S. Rollnick, *Motivational interviewing: Preparing people to change addictive behavior.* New York: Guilford Press, 1991.

[116] R. M. Banos, C. Botella, and P. C., Virtual Reality and Psychopathology, *CyberPsychology & Behavior* 2 (1999) 283-292.

[117] A. Rizzo, M. Wiederhold, and J. G. Buckwalter, Basic issues in the use of virtual environments for mental health applications, in *Virtual environments in clinical psychology and neuroscience: Methods and techniques in advanced patient-therapist interaction*, G. Riva, B. Wiederhold, and E. Molinari, Eds. Amsterdam: IOS Press, 1998, pp. 21-42.

[118] N. I. Durlach and A. S. E. Mavor, *Virtual reality: scientific and technological challenges.* Washington, D.C.: National Academy Press, 1995.

[119] G. Riva, From technology to communication: Psycho-social issues in developing virtual environments, *Journal of Visual Languages and Computing* 10 (1999) 87-97.

[120] G. Riva, Virtual Reality as a communication tool: a socio-cognitive analysis, *Presence, Teleoperators, and Virtual Environments* 8 (1999) 460-466.

[121] W. Bricken, Virtual reality: Directions of growth, University of Washington, Seattle, WA HITL Technical Report R-90-1, 1990.

[122] A. Kay, Computer software, *Scientific American* 251 (1984) 52-59.

[123] F. Biocca and B. Delaney, Immersive virtual reality technology, in *Communication in the age of virtual reality*, F. Biocca and M. R. Levy, Eds. Hillsdale, NJ: Lawrence Erlbaum Associates, 1995, pp. 57-124.

[124] J. S. Steuer, Defining virtual reality: Dimensions determining telepresence, *Journal of Communication* 42 (1992) 73-93.

[125] G. Mantovani, *New communication environments: from everyday to virtual.* London: Taylor & Francis, 1996.

[126] F. Vincelli and E. Molinari, Virtual reality and imaginative techniques in clinical psychology, in *Virtual environments in clinical psychology and neuroscience: Methods and techniques in advanced patient-therapist interaction*, G. Riva, B. Wiederhold, and E. Molinari, Eds. Amsterdam: IOS Press, 1998, pp. 67-72.

[127] T. B. Sheridan, Musing on telepresence and virtual presence, *Presence, Teleoperators, and Virtual Environments* 1 (1992) 120-125.

[128] T. B. Sheridan, Further musing on the psychophysics of presence, *Presence, Teleoperators, and Virtual Environments* 5 (1996) 241-246.

[129] G. J. F. Smets, P. J. Stappers, K. J. Overbeeke, and C. van der Mast, Designing in virtual reality: Perception - action coupling and affordances, in *Simulated and virtual realities*, K. Carr and R. England, Eds. London: Taylor & Francis, 1994, pp. 189-208.

[130] G. Mantovani and G. Riva, "Real" presence: How different ontologies generate different criteria for presence, telepresence, and virtual presence, *Presence, Teleoperators, and Virtual Environments* 8 (1999) 538-548.

[131] N. Ellis, Presence of mind: a reaction to Thomas Sheridan's "Further musings on the psychophysics of presence", *Presence, Teleoperators, and Virtual Environments* 5 (1996) 247-259.

[132] R. Wootton, Telemedicine: an introduction, in *European Telemedicine 1998/99*, R. Wootton, Ed. London: Kensington Publications Ltd, 1999, pp. 10-12.

[133] U. M. O'Sullivan and J. Somers, Southern Health Board--advanced telematic/telemedicine in healthcare services in the south west of Ireland, *Stud Health Technol Inform* 64 (1999) 230-40.

[134] R. Fletcher, Telehealth rescues isolated patients, *Health Manag Technol* 20 (1999) 52-3.

[135] P. Lehoux, R. N. Battista, and J. M. Lance, Telehealth: passing fad or lasting benefits?, *Can J Public Health* 91 (2000) 277-80.

[136] F. S. Mair, A. Haycox, C. May, and T. Williams, A review of telemedicine cost-effectiveness studies, *J Telemed Telecare* 6 (2000) S38-40.

[137] R. Currell, C. Urquhart, P. Wainwright, and R. Lewis, Telemedicine versus face to face patient care: effects on professional practice and health care outcomes, *Cochrane Database Syst Rev* 2 (2000).

[138] B. L. Charles, Telemedicine can lower costs and improve access, *Healthc Financ Manage* 54 (2000) 66-9.
[139] J. Mitchell, Increasing the cost-effectiveness of telemedicine by embracing e-health, *J Telemed Telecare* 6 (2000) S16-9.
[140] L. W. Jerome, P. H. DeLeon, L. C. James, R. Folen, J. Earles, and J. J. Gedney, The coming of age of telecommunications in psychological research and practice, *American Psychologist* 55 (2000) 407-21.
[141] G. Riva and L. Gamberini, Virtual reality as telemedicine tool: technology, ergonomics and actual applications, *Technology and Health Care* 8 (2000) 113-27.
[142] S. deShazer, *Clues: Investigating solutions in brief therapy.* New York: W.W. Norton, 1988.
[143] J. W. Butters and T. F. Cash, Cognitive-behavioral treatment of women's body image satisfaction: A controlled outcome-study, *Journal of Consulting and Clinical Psychology* 55 (1987) 889-897.
[144] G. Riva, Virtual reality as assessment tool in psychology, in *Virtual reality in neuro-psycho-physiology: Cognitive, clinical and methodological issues in assessment and rehabilitation*, G. Riva, Ed. Amsterdam: IOS Press, 1997, pp. 95-112.
[145] C. G. Fairburn and Z. Cooper, The Eating Disorders Examination, in *Binge eating: Nature, assessment, and treatment*, C. G. Fairburn and G. T. Wilson, Eds. New York: The Guilford Press, 1993, pp. 317-360.
[146] G. T. Wilson and C. G. Fairburn, Cognitive Treatments for Eating Disorders, *Journal of Consulting & Clinical Psychology* 61 (1993) 261-269.
[147] G. T. Wilson, K. L. Loeb, T. B. Walsh, E. Labouvie, E. Petkova, X. Liu, and C. Waternaux, Psychological versus pharmacological treatments of Bulimia Nervosa: Predictors and processes of change, *Journal of Consulting and Clinical Psychology* 67 (1999) 451-459.
[148] G. Riva, M. Bacchetta, M. Baruffi, S. Rinaldi, and E. Molinari, Experiential cognitive therapy in anorexia nervosa, *Eating and Weight Disorders* (1998) 141-150.
[149] G. Riva, Virtual environment for body-image modification: Virtual reality system for the treatment of body image disturbances, *Computers in Human Behavior* 14 (1998) 477-490.
[150] G. Riva, M. Bacchetta, M. Baruffi, S. Rinaldi, F. Vincelli, and E. Molinari, Virtual reality based Experiential Cognitive Treatment of obesity and binge-eating disorders, *Clinical Psychology and Psychotherapy* 7 (2000) in press.
[151] W. Vandereycken, The relevance of body-image disturbances for the treatment of bulimia, in *Bulimia nervosa. Basic research, diagnosis and treatment*, M. M. Fichter, Ed. New York: Wiley, 1990, pp. 136-142.
[152] A. Bandura, *Social foundation of thought and action: A social cognitive theory.* Englewood Cliffs, NJ: Prentice-Hall, 1985.
[153] M. J. Griffin, *Handbook of Human Vibration.* London: Academic Press, 1990.
[154] W. Vandereycken, M. Probst, and R. Meermann, An experimental video-confrontation procedure as a therapeutic technique and a research tool in the treatment of eating disorders, in *The psychobiology of bulimia nervosa*, K. M. Pirke, W. Vandereycken, and D. Ploog, Eds. Heidelberg: Springer-Verlag, 1988, pp. 120-126.

Author Index

Printed in the United Kingdom
by Lightning Source UK Ltd.
120861UK00001B/97-105